THE TRAPPER'S BIBLE

THE TRAPPER'S BIBLE

THE MOST COMPLETE GUIDE TO TRAPPING AND HUNTING TIPS EVER

Edited by
Eustace Hazard Livingston

Skyhorse Publishing

Skyhorse Publishing books may be purchased in bulk at special discounts for sales promotion, corporate gifts, fund-raising, or educational purposes. Special editions can also be created to specifications. For details, contact the Special Sales Department, Skyhorse Publishing, 307 West 36th Street, 11th Floor, New York, NY 10018 or info@skyhorsepublishing.com.

Skyhorse® and Skyhorse Publishing® are registered trademarks of Skyhorse Publishing, Inc.®, a Delaware corporation.

Visit our website at www.skyhorsepublishing.com.

20 19 18 17 16 15 14

Library of Congress Cataloging-in-Publication Data is available on file.

ISBN: 978-1-61608-559-9

Printed in the United States of America

TABLE OF CONTENTS

Section III
SKINNING, STRETCHING, CURING, AND TANNING

PREFACE

The book you hold before you is the collective wisdom of some of North America's most prominent trappers, drawn from the heyday of the trade. That is to say, I have collected their writings, collated the information, and boiled down the various and sundry ingredients to render the *Trapper's Bible*. In this mélange you may recognize the acerbic and piquant stylings of Sewell Newhouse, the mellow musings of Stanley Harding, the laconic pragmatism of Elmer Kreps, and several voluminously gassy Andersch Brothers passages. It is therefore in no way my own work, other than the manner in which the contents are selected, arranged, and redacted. With that said, I can safely say from the vantage of standing on the shoulders of those who came before me, that it's crowded around here, because they appear to have all read each others' books and some saw fit to borrow several passages *verbatim*.

Just as the ingredients of the Good Book come from over the centuries and from different authors offering different experiences and advice, which in turn seem to offer conflicting or even contradictory-seeming proscriptions about how best to do something, *The Trapper's Bible* may also sometimes ramble on, repeat itself, and seem to contain similar internal contradictions. In such instances I would advise the reader not to give the treatment a hermeneutic analysis, but to lay it to the diversity of experience, the richness of the text, and as Ecclesiastes put it, that "for everything there is a season." I leave such questions to your better judgment.

You may also note that many of the traps, ingredients, turns of phrase, and attitudes are decidedly antique. Although much of what we call "the good old days" were in no way good, and take for granted the liberties and conveniences of our own time, many of the tools and techniques of yesteryear are just as effective and valid now as they were then—and what's more—tested by time and experience. Drawing from my own experience, I would advise that no nonstick cookware is as durable or effective as my great-grandmother's cast iron skillet, and no shave is as close or economical as my great-grandfather's straight razor. Likewise, several of the old Oneida Community traps that I bought in the year aught-and-nine still work as well as the day they came out of the tempering oven.

One old attitude I do not cotton to is ludicrous and pervasive palaver you come across in old texts about "the dusky races" and "barbarous savages." Inasmuch as an old farmer can tell you how best to plant corn, you can safely ignore his indecent indulgences when he goes into bizarre racial hysterics beginning with "I'm not a racist, but . . ." Dogs is dogs, as the saying goes, for poodles as with mutts. To maintain the utilitarian nature of the book, I've tried to eliminate such irrelevancies, but if there is any I have overlooked, please advise me through the publisher for a subsequent edition.

Herein you will also find information about animals that at this writing are (or in the future, may be) illegal to trap, endangered, or thought to be extinct. Although there are many animals I do not think are fit to trap, if you are in the business of setting out a trap-line, there's no telling what manner of odd creature you may come across. If such is the case and you find an unusual or unexpected creature in one of your traps, the best you can do is to come forewarned. Additionally, just as no ornithological guide to North America would be complete without the Ivory-billed Woodpecker, no trapper's guide could be properly considered of Cecil B. DeMille-variety "Biblical Proportions" without a chapter on the Catamount. Needless to say, you should check your local game laws and keep your nose clean.

Finally, I would be remiss if I didn't mention some words about conduct. *The Trapper's Bible* contains many astute observations about the animals' intrinsic natures, and how to use that knowledge to your advantage. You may come to employ innumerable duplicities, stratagems, and contrivances to lead an animal through its own natural curiosity or sense of self-interest to a place and outcome of your choosing. But there are no surer, more complete, and well-disguised deceptions as the ones we devise for ourselves to justify dubious conduct, even as we plan to conduct it. In the practice of trapping there are many opportunities for a wide latitude of needless waste, of greed, neglect, and of cruelty. If you should find yourself thoughtlessly and cheerfully flaying something you oughtn't, you may do well to consider the steps you took to arrive at that conclusion. Being a fool is simple and easily explained, but I've never known Old Scratch to just snap people up from the ground all of a sudden with nothing more than a mushroom cloud of sulfur as a fare-thee-well. Becoming a *damned* fool is hard work that comes slowly in degrees, by the many screwtwists of self-justified contortion, and is nothing if not banal. Take care that you do not lose your compassion, or injure an animal's dignity, or lay poison or a deadfall where they may be accessible to a child. In some cases, flaying may be too kind, whether through your own conscience, or otherwise.

—Eustace Hazard Livingston
January 31, 2012
New Haven, Conn.

SECTION I
Basic Trapping Skills

CHAPTER 1

Preliminaries

Among the many outdoor occupations, trapping the furbearing animals is perhaps the most pleasant and in many instances is also very profitable.

Trapping and hunting wild animals bring a man face to face with nature. He studies the woods, the running waters, and the growing things. He learns the ways of animals and birds. Even a little experience in woodcraft is valuable. The boy who has started off alone with a few traps on his back, and catches Muskrats, Mink or Skunk, is different from the boy who has never done these things. He has more self-reliance and courage, and these stand him in good stead all his life.

Although trapping was one of the earliest industries of this country, the occupation has not passed away, along with the vanishing wilderness scattered all over North America, in both the thickly settled portions and the more remote districts are thousands of trappers who each season deriving both pleasure and profit from this unique calling.

Trapping in itself is an art. Many of the wild creatures are exceedingly wary and the trapper must match his reason against the instinct, the natural wariness and the acquired knowledge of the animals. This wariness alone has saved some species of animals from extinction, and although man is superior to all brute life, such intelligent animals as the fox and the wolf frequently prove a match for the most expert of trappers.

In order to be successful, one must know the wild animals as a mother knows her child. He must also know and use the most practical methods of trapping, and it is my object to give in this work, the most successful trapping methods known.

These modes of trapping the fur-bearing animals have for the most part been learned from actual experience in various parts of the country.

During past ages many of the wild creatures of the forest and stream were hunted and captured in various ways by the inhabitants of the wilderness,—the flesh of these animals being the principal food of many and the skins being used for clothing; but it was only after furs became a staple article of wearing apparel among civilized nations and the traders had learned of the profits to be made in the fur trade that wholesale and systematic trapping began.

To-day there are thousands of trappers scattered over the United States, Canada, Alaska and Mexico. There is scarcely a farmer, ranchman, or other person whose calling brings him close to nature who is not more or less interested in the fur-bearing animals.

As to the profits to be derived from this occupation, there are professional trappers in the North, South, and West whose catches amount to a full year's income each season, but the number who do as well as that is comparatively small. By far the greater number of trappers are those who follow other occupations and devote only their spare time to the capture of wild animals and they are for the most part farmers and country boys who in this way add to their yearly income.

It is not at all necessary to go into the wilds in order to do successful trapping, and almost any farming section will be found to be a paying trapping ground. Indeed, the country folk will in most cases do far better in their own home district than he would by going into some place with which they are not familiar even though the fur-bearing animals be more plentiful there than at home. In familiar territory they will learn the haunts of each kind of fur-bearing animal, its route of travel, the dens, etc., and this knowledge will be of great value when the actual trapping commences.

Of course all of the various species of animals will not be found in any one section, but where one is missing, there will be some other found in fair numbers. Muskrats are most numerous as a rule in the settled parts of the country and wherever the muskrat is found there the mink is also. Skunks are found almost everywhere and the ease with which they may be captured makes the trapping of them a lucrative business. Foxes are found in most of the hilly sections and while they are not so easily captured, one can make a success of it if he gives the matter careful study and uses sufficient care in setting and attending the traps. In many parts of the South the raccoon is found in abundance as is also the opossum and the otter, the wild cat and other animals are found more sparingly in many parts of the country.

The trapper, no matter where he is located, is certain to meet with many hardships but it is a pleasant calling for all of that and there is a certain amount of pleasure in even the roughest experiences. Once one has followed trapping for a few seasons it is almost impossible to give up the wild, free life. The study of the habits of the wild creatures, which is necessary if one wishes to become a successful trapper brings one into close touch with nature and the work is extremely fascinating.

CHAPTER 2

The Deadfall, Sliding Pole, Clog, Spring Pole, and Balance Pole

In the early days before the steel trap came into general use, the deadfall and the snare were used almost exclusively for the capture of the fur-bearers, but at present when steel traps have reached a high state of perfection, are sold at prices which place them within the reach of all, they are preferred by most trappers and many of the most expert have discarded the wooden traps entirely. However, both the deadfall and the snare are good traps for certain animals and it is well to know how to make and use them for one may sometimes see a good place in which to place a trap but may not have a steel trap along. In such cases the knowledge of how to construct a practical deadfall will be of value. It is true that many of the fur-bearing animals are too cunning to be captured by such a contrivance but some of the most wary fall easy victims to the snare. Some of the most expert fox trappers use the snare in preference to the steel trap but the number is comparatively small.

The deadfall can be made anywhere, with an axe and hard work. It consists of two large poles (or logs when set for bears and other large animals) placed one over the other and kept in place by four stakes, two on each side. The upper pole is raised at one end high enough above the lower to admit the entrance of the animal, and is kept up in that position by the familiar contrivance of the stick and spindle, or "figure four." A tight pen is made with sticks, brush, etc., on one side of this structure at right angles to it, and the spindle projects obliquely into this pen, so that the bait attached to it is about eight inches beyond the side of the pole. The animal, to reach the bait, has to place his body between the poles at right angles to them, and on pulling the spindle, springs the "figure four," and is crushed.

The objections to this contrivance are, first, that it takes a long time to make and set one, thus wasting the trapper's time, and second, the animals caught in this way lie exposed to the voracity of other animals, and are often torn to pieces before the trapper reaches them, which is not the case when animals are caught in steel traps, properly set, as will be shown hereafter. Moreover, the deadfall is uncertain in its operation, and woodsmen who have become accustomed to good steel traps, call it a "miserable toggle," not worth baiting when they find one ready-made in the woods.

POISONING

The objection to this method is that it spoils the skin. Furriers say that the poison spreads through the whole body of the animal, and kills the life of the fur, so that they cannot work it profitably. Poison is used very little by woodsmen at the present time, and dealers dislike to buy or handle skins that have been poisoned.

SHOOTING

This method of killing fur-bearing animals is still quite prevalent in some countries. It is said to be the principal method in Russia, and is not altogether disused in this country. But it is a very wasteful method. Fur dealers and manufacturers consider skins that have been shot, especially by the shot-gun, as hardly worth working. The holes that are made in the skin, whether by shot or bullets, are but a small part of the damage done to it. The shot that enters the body of the animal directly are almost harmless compared with those that strike it obliquely, or graze across it. Every one of these grazing shots, however small, cuts a furrow in the fur, sometimes several inches in length, shaving every hair in its course as with a razor. Slits in the skin have to be cut out to the full extent of these furrows, and closed up, or new pieces fitted in. Hence when the hunter brings his stock of skins to the experienced furrier, he is generally saluted with the question, "Are your furs shot or trapped?" and if he has to answer, "They were shot," he finds the dealer quite indifferent about buying them at any price.

STEEL TRAPS

Many styles of traps have been invented and some of the most promising styles were placed on the market but it is doubtful if any trap will ever be designed which will equal in popularity and general usefulness the old time jaw trap, commonly known as the "steel trap". These traps have been improved in many ways until at present they are almost perfect and are made in sizes and styles to meet all requirements and all conditions of trapping.

The jaw traps possess decided advantages over all other styles of steel or wooden traps. They will capture the most wary animals as well as the most stupid and will work perfectly under all conditions whether set in the water or on dry land, on the snow or on a log or stump or the side of a tree. They may be used with or without bait and if the proper size of trap is used and it is set in the right way it will capture almost any animal that comes that way. What other style of trap possesses all of these advantages?

The experience of modern trappers, after trying all other methods, and all kinds of new fashioned traps, has led them almost unanimously to the conclusion that the old steel trap, when scientifically and faithfully made, is the surest and most economical means of capturing fur-bearing animals. Some of the reasons for this conclusion are these: Steel traps can be easily transported; can be set in all situations on land or under water; can be easily concealed; can be tended in great numbers; can be combined by means of chain and ring with a variety of contrivances (hereafter to be described) for securing the animal caught from destruction by other animals, and from escape by self-amputation; and above all, the steel trap does *no injury to the fur*.

REQUISITES OF A GOOD TRAP

The various sizes of traps adapted to different kinds of animals, of course require different forms and qualities, which will be spoken of in the proper places hereafter. But several of the essentials are the same in all good traps.

1. *The jaws should not be too thin, nor sharp cornered.* Jaws made of sheet iron, or of plates approaching to the thinness of sheet iron, and having sharp edges, will almost cut off an animal's leg by the bare force of the spring, if it is a strong one, and will always materially help the animal to gnaw or twist off his leg. And it should be known, that nearly all the animals that escape, get free in these ways.
2. *The pan should not be too large.* A large pan, filling nearly the whole space of the open jaws may seem to increase the chances of an animal being caught, by giving him more surface to tread upon in springing the trap. But there is a mistake in this. When an animal springs the trap by treading on the outer part of a large pan, his foot is near the jaw, and instead of being caught, is liable to be thrown out by the stroke of the jaw; whereas, when he treads on a small pan, his foot is nearly in the center of the sweep of the jaws, and he is very sure to be seized far enough up the leg to be well secured.
3. *The spring should be strong enough.* This is a matter of good judgment, and cannot well be explained here; but it is safe to say that very many traps, in consequence of false economy on the part of manufacturers, are furnished with springs that are too weak to secure strong and desperate animals.
4. *The spring should be tempered scientifically.* Many springs, in consequence of being badly tempered, "give down" in a little while, *i e.,* lose their elasticity and close together; and others break in cold weather, or when set under water.
5. *The spring should be correctly proportioned and tempered.* Without this, the stronger it is and the better it is tempered, the more liable it is to break.
6. *The form of the jaws must be such as to give the bow of the spring a proper inclined plane to work upon.* In many traps, the angle at the shoulder of the jaws is so great, that even a strong spring will not hold a desperate animal.

7. To make a steel trap lie flat so that it can be hidden nicely, turn the spring around toward the jaw that is fastened, and then pull the loose jaw down.
8. *The jaws must work easily on the posts.* For want of attention to this, many traps will not spring.
9. *The adjustments of all the parts and their actual working should be so inspected and tested that every trap shall be ready for use—"sure to go," and sure to hold.*

German and English traps are almost universally liable to criticism on all points above mentioned and many of the traps made in this country fail in one or more of them.

In addition to the foregoing requisites, every trap should be furnished with a stout chain, with ring and swivel. It is important that the swivel should be well made so that the eyes will turn freely; otherwise, the animal caught may escape by twisting off either his leg or the chain.

As most of those who have never done any trapping know practically nothing regarding the use of traps, I will outline briefly the methods usually employed for the capture of fur-bearing animals before proceeding farther.

Most of the animals which are caught in traps are decoyed by means of bait,—something in the line of food which appeals to its appetite,—so placed that in attempting to reach it the animal places its foot in the trap. The most common way is by setting the trap in the entrance to some natural enclosure, such as a hollow log or stump, a hollow between trees, or a hole in the rocks, or under a stump the bait being placed in the enclosure beyond the trap. Failing to find a natural enclosure, the trapper constructs one, using such material as may be found on the spot. It is advisable as a rule to make as little disturbance as possible and to give the enclosure a natural appearance.

It sometimes happens that an animal can not be induced to approach bait and in such cases the "blind set" is resorted to,—in other words the trap is set without bait in a trail where the animal travels or at the entrance of its den. Failing to find such a place the trapper carefully studies the route of the animal and selects a place where some natural or artificial obstruction will crowd it into a certain spot where he carefully sets his trap in such a way as to catch the animal the next time it comes along. These blind sets are as a rule very successful and many trappers use such methods exclusively.

In setting steel traps, great care is advised for the one who learns to do this most neatly, leaving everything natural is, as a rule, the most successful. One should always be certain to get the trap in the right position for to miss catching an animal not only means its loss for the time being but many of them will become wiser from such experiences and their capture will be more difficult afterwards. The trapper is wise also who gives sufficient attention to the fastening of the trap, thus reducing the animal's chances of escape after it is once caught.

To properly set a steel trap on dry land one should dig a "nest" for the trap, deep enough to allow the covering to be flush with the surroundings and just a little larger than, and of the same shape as the trap when set. This hollow should be lined with dry leaves or moss and the trap placed therein. To make the trap rest solidly so that there is no danger of it being tipped over also to make the jaws set level, the spring should be twisted around towards the jaw which is held down by the trigger or "dog". The trap should then be covered with some light, dry material in

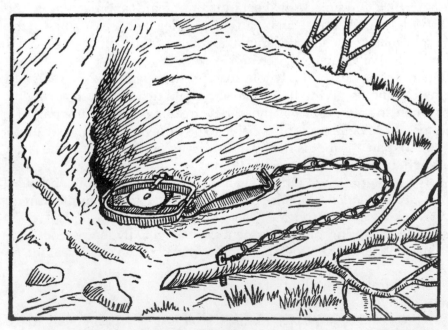

Trap Set in Correct Position at Entrance of Den.

keeping with the surroundings, a few dead leaves or a sheet of paper being used first to prevent the covering from rolling under the pan and in that way prevent the trap from springing. Instead of doing this some trappers place a bunch of cotton or dry moss under the pan but I do not think this advisable.

In all cases when setting traps at dens, on trails or at the entrances of enclosures, the trap should be so placed that the jaws will be lengthwise of the animal's approach so that it will step between the jaws and not over one of them. If the setting is reversed the rising jaw will sometimes throw the animal's foot out of the trap.

THE SLIDING POLE

There are various good methods of fastening and the proper one to use depends on the nature of the surrounding and the species of animal that one is setting for. Water animals should be drowned as quickly as possible after they are caught and in order to secure this result the "sliding pole" is used.

Animals of aquatic habits, when caught in traps, invariably plunge at once into deep water; and it is the object of the trapper, availing himself of this plunge, to drown his captive as soon as possible, in order to stop his violence and keep him out of the reach of other animals. The weight of the trap and chain is usually sufficient for this purpose in the case of the Muskrat. But in taking the larger amphibious animals, such as the Beaver, the trapper uses a contrivance which is called the sliding pole. It is prepared in the following manner: Cut a pole ten or twelve feet long, leaving branches enough on the small end to prevent the ring of the chain from slipping off. Place this pole near where you set your trap, in an inclined position, with its small end reaching into the deepest part of the stream, and its large end secured at the bank by a hook driven into the ground. Slip the ring of your chain on to this pole, and see that it is free to traverse down the whole length. When the animal is taken it plunges desperately into the region toward which the pole leads. The ring slides down to the end of the pole at the bottom of the stream, and, with a short chain, prevents the victim from rising to the surface or returning to the shore.

In order to make this outfit more certain when setting for large animals such as otters and beavers, a stone of six or eight pounds should be tied firmly to the chain but not near enough to the trap to interfere with the action of the swivel.

In trapping for muskrats and mink the usual practice is to simply stake the trap the length of the chain into the deepest water available, the weight of the trap being sufficient to hold the animal under water.

THE CLOG

Some powerful and violent animals, if caught in a trap that is staked fast, will pull their legs off, or beat the trap in pieces; but if allowed to drag the trap about with moderate weight attached, will behave more gently, or at least will not be able to get loose for want of purchase. The weight used in such cases is called a clog.

This is simply a chunk of wood, a pole, brush or stone, the object being to hamper the animal in its movements and prevent it from getting a dead pull on the trap and chain. In fastening to the clog the staple may be used or the chain may be dropped through the ring so as to form a loop which is slipped over the clog, a few snags being left stand to prevent the chain from being drawn over the end. When setting for bears the ring is slipped over the clog,—a pole,—and fastened with a spike or wedge. Some trappers prefer to use a pronged iron drag and this is especially desirable when trapping for the more cunning animals such as the fox, coyote and wolf as the drag may be covered without leaving much sign. A stone may be used in the same manner by securing with wire to the end of the chain.

For the animals mentioned the traps are sometimes staked down solidly, the stake being driven out of sight but this gives the animal a dead pull and they will sometimes escape.

As the object of it is to encumber the animal, but not to hold it fast, the chain should be attached to it near one of its ends, so that it will not be likely to get fast among the rocks and bushes for a considerable time.

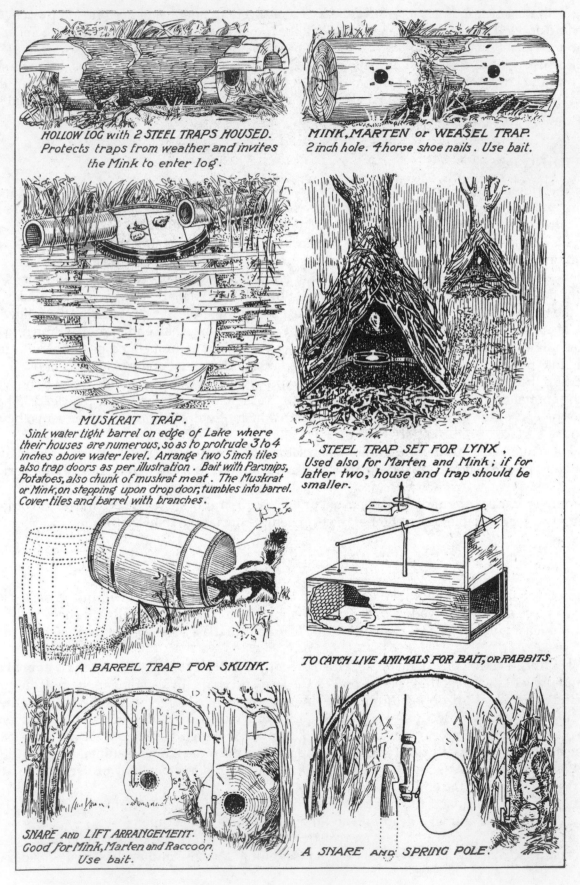

HOLLOW LOG with 2 STEEL TRAPS HOUSED.
Protects traps from weather and invites
the Mink to enter log.

MINK, MARTEN or WEASEL TRAP.
2 inch hole. 4 horse shoe nails. Use bait.

MUSKRAT TRAP.
Sink water tight barrel on edge of Lake where
their houses are numerous, so as to protrude 3 to 4
inches above water level. Arrange two 5 inch tiles
also trap doors as per illustration. Bait with Parsnips,
Potatoes, also chunk of muskrat meat. The Muskrat
or Mink, on stepping upon drop door, tumbles into barrel.
Cover tiles and barrel with branches.

STEEL TRAP SET FOR LYNX,
Used also for Marten and Mink; if for
latter two, house and trap should be
smaller.

A BARREL TRAP FOR SKUNK.

TO CATCH LIVE ANIMALS FOR BAIT, OR RABBITS.

SNARE and LIFT ARRANGEMENT.
Good for Mink, Marten and Raccoon.
Use bait.

A SNARE and SPRING POLE.

THE BUSH CLOG FOR FOXES AND SOME OTHER ANIMALS

Some experienced trappers recommend fastening a fox trap to the butt of a suitable bush cut for the purpose, as a better clog than a pole, intending that the Fox should be able to drag it a short distance. He will not go very far with it, and another trap can then be set in the same place where he was caught. One trapper claims that he caught eight Foxes in one season in a cattle path, and in the same trap-bed, by this method.

THE SPRING POLE

In taking several kinds of land animals, such as the Marten and Fisher, it is necessary to provide against their being devoured by other animals before the trapper reaches them, and also against their gnawing off their own legs, or breaking the chain of the trap by violence. The contrivance used for this purpose is called a *spring pole,* and is prepared in the following manner: If a small tree can be found standing near the place where your trap is set, trim it and use it for a spring as it stands. If not, cut a pole of sufficient size and drive it firmly into the ground; bend down the top; fasten the chain ring to it; and fasten the pole in its bent position by a notch or hook on a small tree or stick driven into the ground. When the animal is caught, his struggles, pulling on the chain, unhook the pole, which, flying up with a jerk, carries him into the air, out of the reach of prowlers, and in a condition that disables his attempts to escape by self-amputation or other violence. The size of the pole must be proportioned to the weight of the game which it is expected to lift.

In theory this device works nicely but in practice it is not found to be perfect as the wood will lose its "spring" if kept beat for some time, especially in freezing weather. The balance pole is more faithful in its action.

THE BALANCE POLE

In some cases where no sapling grows near the place where you wish to set a trap, such as could be used for a spring pole, a balance pole can be rigged. Get a suitable pole and pass it through the fork of a tree or a forked stake driven in the right spot. Fasten a weight to the end opposite the trap, and then elevate this weight by fastening down the trap end of the pole so that it will be released by the struggles of the animal when caught, when the weight will throw both animal and trap in the air.

WEIGHTED CORD

In some situations the same result as the above can be obtained by running a weighted cord or wire over a hook, a nail, or a branch of a tree, fastening the trap to the other end. The main thing is to see that it will work easily and smoothly and the weight not fall off.

The Balance Pole.

RULE FOR BAITING

There is one general principle in regard to baiting animals that may as well be recorded and explained here, as it is applicable to all cases. It is this: Never put bait on the pan of the trap. The old-fashioned traps were always made with holes in the pan for strings to tie on bait; and many if not most novices in trapping, imagine that the true way is to attract the animal's nose straight to the center of action, by piling bait on the pan, as though it were expected to catch him by the head. The truth, however, is that animals are very rarely taken by the head or the body, but almost always by the leg. When an animal pulls at a bait on the pan of the trap, he is not likely even to spring the trap, for he lifts in the wrong direction; and if he does spring it, the position of his head is such, especially if the bait is high on the pan, that he is pretty sure to give the jaws the slip. Besides, bait on the pan calls the attention of the wary animal to the trap; whereas he ought to be wholly diverted from it, and all signs of it obliterated. Bait should always be placed so that the animal in attempting to take it shall put a foot on the pan. This can be done in several ways, all of which will be explained in detail hereafter. But this general direction can be given for all cases that are not otherwise prescribed for: *Place the bait either on a stick above the trap, or in an enclosure so arranged that the animal will have to step in the trap to reach it.*

CHAPTER 3

Trap Maintenance, Traps, and General Methods

In order to keep steel traps in perfect working order they should have a certain amount of attention. Repairs will be necessary at times and before the trapping season commences one should look them all over and see that they are in good condition. The triggers should be so adjusted that the pan will set level. All parts should work freely and the trap should neither spring too easily nor too hard. Rust on traps is not desirable and may be prevented to a great extent by boiling the traps occasionally in a solution of evergreen boughs, maple, willow or oak bark or walnut hulls. This will give the traps a blue-black color and they will not rust for a considerable length of time. New traps will not take the color very well but they should be boiled just the same to remove the oil also the varnish with which some manufacturers coat their traps. Some trappers smoke their traps before setting believing that the odor of the smoke will smother that of the metal. This however is not in my opinion a good idea as clean iron has no odor and the smell of smoke enables the animal to locate the trap, thus having just the opposite of the effect desired.

Others again, grease or oil the traps which is also bad for the same reason and another thing worth considering is the fact that a greased trap does not have as good a grip as one which has not been so treated. For my own part I would rather have my traps red with rust than to have them oiled, and if it is necessary to oil the joints of a stiff working trap, use some oil having practically no odor, never strong smelling substances such as kerosene.

GENERAL METHODS

Beginners will doubtless be glad to get a general idea of the ways or trapping wild animals, before proceeding to consider the various species, and the practice best suited to taking them; for such general knowledge will, from the start, be of the greatest help to everyone in choosing the plan best suited to the particular circumstances met.

As you read, you will notice that certain classes of animals have habits much alike, and that the experienced trapper takes advantage of such habits, and traps those classes on pretty much the same general principles. For example, there is a class to which the Mink and Otter belong, which like to wander along the banks of streams in search of food. Being expert swimmers they are almost equally at home in the water or on land. Their habit is to examine everything they come to, and explore all the little side streams and ditches; so where a rivulet, or little brook empties into the larger stream, there they are sure to go. Having found such a place, if you set a trap there properly, you are pretty sure of a catch if any of those animals are passing that way. To set the trap properly, study the situation. If the water is shallow in the mouth or the rivulet, you can place some obstruction so that the animal will have to pass through a narrow place in which you will set the trap. Sometimes the situation is such that it will be easiest for the animal to walk in the water through the narrow place. In that case you set your trap in the water where he will be most likely to step in it, covering it lightly with mud or wet leaves. This is called a water-set. It requires good judgment, such as must be gained mainly by experience, to tell just where an animal is likely to put down his foot as he walks over a certain spot, and to arrange obstacles, such as sticks stuck in the bank, so that they will lead him to step where you wish him to, and yet so that they look perfectly natural and not excite his suspicion. We can give you a general idea of how to proceed, but there are nice points in the doing of these things which every trapper has to work out for himself.

Sometimes, where the situation is such that a Mink, Otter, or other such animal is likely to walk along the bank of the stream close to the water, an old log, or a large pole may be shoved over the bank so that one end will rest in the water, and so that the animal will have to hug the bank to pass it. Then dig a little pit in this narrow place just large enough to hold the trap. Cover the trap with dead leaves or loose earth, taking care that no lumps get under the pan to prevent the trap from springing. Make everything look perfectly natural and your chances will be good. When a trap is set on land in such a situation it is called a land-set or dry-set.

In all cases where the trapper plans to catch an animal by fixing obstructions so that it will go through a narrow place, he should set his trap so that the bottom piece and jaws are in the line of the path the animal will take, and not across it, because if set straight in line the jaws are less likely to throw the animal out when the trap springs.

Culverts under railroads are often used by wild animals of wandering habits, like the Muskrat, Mink and Otter, as they will never cross over a track when there is a way under. If water is running through the culvert such animals will be following the stream, and their signs may be found.

If the bank of the main stream is rather high and steep, an animal of this class is likely to swim for quite a distance until good footing can be found on the lower part of the bank again. But he will always swim close to the bank and be ready to climb out of the water at the first good chance. So if you shove an old, half rotten log over the bank at such a place and set a trap on the lower end of it, just under water, covering and hiding it skillfully, the animal is very likely to climb up and put his foot in it. If there is no old log handy, perhaps you can dig out a little pocket in the bank, making the floor of it under water, and set the trap there, putting a bit of moss on the trap. This, if well done, would look natural to such an animal, and he would not hesitate to climb out there.

These methods are all good but there are others which will occur to you as you study the art.

Then there is another class of animals, like the Muskrat and Beaver, which is most easily trapped at the entrance to their houses, or their holes in the bank. For these the trap is usually set under water at the mouth of the entrance, the depth varying from two or three to eight inches, according to the size of the animal. Where bait is used in trapping Muskrats, for example, there is quite an art in placing it so that the animal will have to step in the trap to get it. Old trappers claim they can usually catch a Muskrat by either foot desired, simply by the way they place the bait. This requires study and practice.

Still another class of animals, like Foxes and Wolves, which roam about without caring to keep by water, follow their sense of smell in searching for food. The trapper takes advantage of this fact by attracting them with things they like best, after putting out a supply to be eaten before a trap is set, to get them in the way of coming to that place for more. These animals will travel miles when they smell something they like. Then the trapper carefully places his traps, concealing all signs, and so does a profitable business.

In regard to the use of scents and odors in attracting animals, there is much difference of opinion; but all are agreed in this, that wild animals like the scent or smell of their own kind and are attracted by it. Many animals like the strong odor of the Skunk and Muskrat. Foxes and Wolves, like Dogs, will urinate where others of their kind have done so. A few drops of the musk of any animal will attract others of his species. This is a general fact to be borne in mind while trapping.

In setting traps in any situation there are some points the beginner must constantly bear in mind, such as these:

1. To see that the trap sets level and on a firm bed. Dig a little place for the bottom and cross piece to rest in, if necessary.

2. To see that no dirt, stone or stick has got under the pan of the trap in a way to prevent it's springing. In trapping for large animals, where there is danger that smaller animals might spring the trap, put a bunch of sheep's wool or a little twig under the pan; giving it just enough support to avoid this danger.

3. To never allow carelessness in setting or concealing the trap. The beginner must take all the care he knows how to do. Even then the animals will often *laugh at his unskillful ways as they pass by the traps.*

4. When possible conceal the trap by lightly covering it with dried grass, dead leaves, powdered rotten wood, or other such material, choosing whichever will look most natural in the location.

5. Where the trap is set in shallow water and a bit of moss is put on the pan to make it took like a dry, safe stepping place, never use all dry moss, because it will swell when wet and the animal would not get caught high enough on the leg to hold.

If a youth wishes to learn to trap and can arrange to accompany some experienced trapper who is visiting his traps, it will be of great advantage, for he would learn more in a week than he could from his own first experience in months. But such a youth must bear in mind, although it will be well not to speak of it, that no one trapper knows it all. They have different ideas and ways, and disagree on many points. So the boy must observe quietly, saying but little, and study the art for him or herself.

These remarks will give you a general idea of what you have to do. Now read carefully what is said in the following pages about trapping each variety of animals, and you will have about all the knowledge of the subject possible to get from books. The rest must be worked out in the woods.

As most of our states have made laws regulating the times and seasons when animals may be trapped or hunted, it will be well for everyone to inform himself in regard to this before starting out on his campaign.

CHAPTER 4

The Number of Traps and the Season for Them

As to the number of traps that one can handle, this depends on conditions. The kind of animals that one intends to trap for, the nature of the country, the method of setting and tending traps, the amount of fur to be found, etc., must all be considered. The muskrat trapper who is in a good location where traps may be set from a boat or in the marshes where muskrat houses are plentiful as on some parts of the Atlantic Coast, can easily handle from seventy-five to a hundred or more traps, looking at them once a day. The marten trappers of the Northwest sometimes use five or six hundred traps, but the traps are not set far apart and the trapper spends a number of days in going over the line. In the thickly settled districts there are comparatively few who use more than five or six dozen traps for they must be seen each day, and for beginners from two to three dozen traps will be sufficient.

In some localities there are not many dens and trappers make use of about all when trapping that section, but in other parts of the country dens are so numerous that to place a trap at each is impossible. In states where groundhogs (woodchucks), are numerous there are often a hundred or more dens along a single bluff or rocky bank. To have enough steel traps to set one at each is something few trappers do, yet two or three deadfalls in connection with a line of steel traps is all that is necessary and the trapper can move on to the next bluff where dens are numerous and set another trap or two. As a rule it is where there are many dens, close together, that deadfalls make the best catches, yet when you find a good den anywhere, set or construct a deadfall.

All trappers have noticed when tracking animals in the snow that they visit nearly every den along their route, not always going in but just sticking their head in. When thus investigating, the animal smells the bait and is hungry (as nine times out of ten the animal is hunting something to eat), and if your trap is set properly you are reasonably sure to make a catch.

In the North, Canada, Alaska and some of the states on the Canadian border where trapping is made a business, it is no uncommon thing for one man to have as many as one hundred and fifty traps and some have out twice that many, or three hundred. Marten trappers in the trackless forests often blaze out a route fifty or more miles in length, building shelters along the line where nights are spent.

The trapper who only spends a few hours each day at trapping and lives in thickly settled districts will find that it is hard for him to locate suitable places perhaps for more than thirty to fifty traps, yet if these will be looked at properly during the season the catch will justify the time and labor in building.

The number of deadfalls and snares that each trapper should construct in his section must largely be determined by him, depending upon how large a territory he has to trap over without running into other trappers grounds. It will be little use to build traps where there are other trappers as trouble will occur, traps may be torn to pieces, etc. Yet there are many good places to build traps in your immediate locality no doubt. If there are any creeks near and woods along the banks you will find good places at both creek and in the woods. If in sections where there is no forest; like some western states, deadfalls trapping may be difficult from the fact that there is nothing to build them with.

In such cases the portable traps, can probably be used to advantage, but best of all in such places is steel traps.

The number of deadfalls and snares that a trapper can attend to is large, from the fact that the game is killed and as the weather is usually cold, the traps need not be looked at only about twice each week.

In the North, many trappers have such long lines that they do not get over them only once a week. The trouble where deadfalls are only looked at once in seven days is that other animals are apt to find the game and may injure the fur, or even destroy the pelt.

Where snares with spring pole attachment are used, and the weather is cold, the trapper need not make the rounds only once a week, as all animals will be suspended in the air and out of the reach of flesh eaters.

South of 40 degrees where the weather is not severe, it is policy to look at traps at least twice a week, and in the extreme South the trapper should make his rounds every day.

It will thus be seen that a trapper in the North can attend more deadfalls and snares than one in the South or even in the Central States. No trapper should have more traps or longer lines than he can properly attend to. The fur bearing animals are none too numerous without having them caught and their pelts and fur spoiled before the arrival of the trapper.

SEASON FOR TRAPPING

Furs are in their best condition when they are taken in cold weather. In winter the flesh side of the skin is of a creamy white color, and such skins are rated as prime by the buyers. The fur is then thick, glossy, and of the richest color; and the tails of such animals as the Mink, Marten and Fisher are then full and heavy. The texture of the skin itself is firm and strong.

With the advent of warm weather, the skins become softer and more spongy, and the animals begin to shed their coats. The inside of the pelts turn dark, two dark strips along the back usually appearing first; the hairs loosen, the furs are no longer prime, but are comparatively valueless.

Because of these changes, the length of the trapping season in any locality depends on the coming and going of cold, frosty weather and the further north one traps the longer the season will be, at least in the Northern Hemisphere.

But there is a difference in animals in regard to their furs being prime, even in the same locality and with the same weather. Skunks are about the first to get in good condition in the fall. They may sometimes be trapped in October in the north, but November is safer. They begin to shed their coats in February, when most fur-bearing animals are at their best. By November the Raccoon is prime, and the Otter, Badger, and Wild Cat may also be trapped in our Northern States. By December most animal are prime, although Muskrats and Beaver are at their best from January to May. It will be seen that those which become prime early in the fall go out of condition early in the spring, and vice versa. For trapping Muskrats in particular, the best time is spring, while Mink, Marten, Fisher, Bear, Foxes and Wolves are at their best in mid-Winter. It does not pay to trap after warm weather begins.

The proper season to begin trapping is when cold weather comes. The old saying that fur is good any month that has an "r" in does not hold good except in the North. Even there September is too early to begin, yet muskrat and skunk are worth something as well as other furs. In the spring April is the last month with an "r." In most sections muskrat, bear, beaver, badger and otter are good all thru April, but other animals began shedding weeks before.

The rule for trappers to follow is to put off trapping in the fall until nights are frostily and the ground freezes.

Generally speaking in Canada and the more Northern States trappers can begin about November 1 and should cease March 1, with the exception of water animals, bear and badger, which may be trapped a month later. In the Central and Southern States trappers should not begin so early and should leave off in the spring from one to four weeks sooner—depending upon how far South they are located.

At the interior Hudson Bay posts, where their word is law, October 25 is appointed to begin and May 25th to quit hunting and trapping with the exception of bear, which are considered prime up to June 10. Remember that the above dates are for the interior or Northern H. B. Posts, which are located hundreds of miles north of the boundary between the United States and Canada.

The skunk is the first animal to become prime, then the coon, marten, fisher, mink and fox, but the latter does not become strictly prime until after a few days of snow, says an old Maine trapper. Rats and beaver are late in priming up as well as otter and mink, and tho the mink is not strictly a land animal, it becomes prime about with the later land animals. The bear, which is strictly a land animal, is not in good fur until snow comes and not strictly prime until February or March.

With the first frosts and cool days many trappers begin setting and baiting their traps. That it is easier to catch certain kinds of fur-bearing animals early in the season is known to most trappers and for this reason trapping in most localities is done too early in the season.

Some years ago when trapping was done even earlier than now, we examined mink skins that were classed as No. 4 and worth 10 or 15 cents, that, had they been allowed to live a few weeks longer, their hides would have been No. 1 and worth, according to locality, from $1.50 to $3.50 each. This early trapping is a loss to the trapper if they will only pause and think. There are only so many animals in a locality to be caught each winter and why catch them before their fur is prime?

In the latitude of Southern Ohio, Indiana, Illinois, etc., skunk caught in the month of October are graded back from one to three grades (and even sometimes into trash), where if they were not caught until November 15th how different would be the classification. The same is true of opossum, mink, muskrat, coon, fox, etc.

Skunk are one of the animals that become prime first each fall. The date that they become prime depends much on the weather. Fifteen years ago, when trapping in Southern Ohio, the writer has sold skunk at winter prices caught as early as October 16, while other seasons those caught the 7th of November, or three weeks later, blued and were graded back. Am glad to say that years ago I learned not to put out traps until November.

That the weather has much to do with the priming of furs and pelts there is no question. If the fall is colder than usual the furs will become prime sooner, while if the freezing weather is later the pelts will be later in "priming up."

In the sections where weasel turn white (then called ermine by many), trappers have a good guide. When they become white they are prime and so are most other land animals. In fact, some are fairly good a week or two before.

When a pelt is put on the stretcher and becomes blue in a few days it is far from prime and will grade no better than No. 2. If the pelt turns black the chances are that the pelt will grade No. 3 or 4. In the case of mink, when dark spots only appear on the pelt, it is not quite prime.

Trappers and hunters should remember that no pelt is prime or No. 1 when it turns the least blue. Opossum skins seldom turn blue even if caught early—most other skins do.

SEASON'S CATCH

The reason that many trappers make small catches, each season, is from the fact that they spend only an hour or so each day at trapping, while at most other business the party devotes the entire day. The trapper who looks out his grounds some weeks in advance of the trapping season is not idling his time away. He should also have a line of traps constructed in advance of the trapping season.

There is a fascination connected with trapping that fills one with a strange feeling when all alone constructing deadfalls and snares or on the rounds to see what success has been yours. I have often visited traps of old trappers, where from two to five carcasses were hanging from a nearby sapling.

There are several instances on record where two animals have been caught in one deadfall at the same time. A well-known trapper of Ohio claims to have caught three skunk in one deadfall at one time a few years since. Whether such is an actual fact or not we are unable to say.

The cases on record where two animals have been caught are so well substantiated that there is little room left to doubt the truth of same.

The catching of two animals at the same time is not such an extraordinary occurrence as many, at first, think. If two animals should come along at the same time and, smelling the bait, begin a meal, the result is easily seen.

While trapping with deadfalls is a humane way of catching fur-bearing animals, another thing in their favor is that skunk are usually killed without "perfuming" themselves, trap and trapper as well. Then, again, if once caught, there is no getting away.

Trappers in the forest always have the necessary tools, axe or heavy hatchet and knife, with which to build a deadfall, while their steel traps may all be exhausted and none set within miles. A deadfall is built and perhaps on the trapper's return an animal is lying dead between the poles.

During extreme cold weather there is but little use to look at traps set for skunk, raccoon, etc., as they do not travel. Before a thaw or warm spell the entire line should be gone over and all old bait removed and replaced with fresh bait.

Like many another trapper you will visit your traps time after time without catching much if any fur, yet if your traps are properly constructed and are spread over a large area, you will catch considerable fur during the season.

Deadfalls and snares can be strung out for miles and while they should be looked at every other day, in good trapping weather, they can be neglected, if the trapper cannot get around more than twice a week, without game escaping. If you visit your traps frequently there will be no loss from injury to fur. While it is true, should a small animal be caught in a heavy trap, one built for much larger game, it will be considerably flattened out, yet the skin or fur is not damaged. There is nothing to damage your catch, in most sections, unless yon do not visit your traps often enough in warm weather, when they may be faintly tainted. Most trapping is done, however, in cool weather, but occasionaly there may come a warm spell when skins become tainted. If found in such condition skin as soon as possible and place upon boards or stretchers.

Another thing greatly to the advantage of the deadfall and snare trapper is the fact that a trapper never knows just when he will be able to visit his traps again; the unexpected often happens, and should it be a day or so longer than expected the deadfall or snare still securely holds the game.

As all experienced trappers know, the first night of a cold spell is a splendid one for animals to travel (they seem forewarned about the weather) and a good catch is the result. If the trapper is a "weather prophet" his traps are all freshly baited and in order, for this is the time that game is on the move—often looking up new and warm dens and generally hungry. Should the next days be cold and stormy the trapper should get over the line as promptly as possible. After once getting over the line after the "cold spell," it is not so important that traps be looked at for some days again.

The successful trapper will always be on the watch of the weather. Some animals, it is true, travel during the coldest weather, but there are many that do not, so that the trapper who sees that his deadfalls are freshly baited when the signs point to warmer weather. After days and nights of severe weather most animals are hungry and when the weather moderates they are on the move.

"I have more than one hundred deadfalls and catch large numbers of skunk," writes a Connecticut trapper. "A few years ago a trapper within two miles of here caught more than 60 coon in deadfalls. Since then coon have been rather scarce, but I am going to try them this coming fall. I prefer red squirrel for skunk bait to anything else, and extract of valerian for scent. Try it, trapper—it can't be beat. I have used it for twenty years and can catch my share every time."

The trapper that makes the largest catches usually is the one that has deadfalls and snares in addition to steel traps. Recently two trappers wrote of their season's catch and added that a good proportion was caught in deadfalls and snares. These trappers were located in Western Canada; marten 54, lynx 12, mink 19, ermine 71, wild cat 11, foxes 18.

While these trappers did not say, it is presumed that the foxes were caught in snares or steel traps, for it is seldom that one is caught in a deadfall. In Canada and the New England States, where foxes are plentiful, the snare is used to a considerable extent.

Skunk, mink, ermine, weasel and opossum are easily caught in deadfalls. One trapper in a southern state is said to have caught 94 mink, besides 38 coon and 57 opossum, in 28 deadfalls, from November 25th to February 25th, or three months.

There is no doubt but that a trapper who expects to remain months at the same place should have a few deadfalls. These traps, like steel traps, to make catches, do not depend upon numbers so much as correct and careful construction and setting. A half dozen deadfalls located at the right places, carefully built and properly set, are worth probably as much as fifty carelessly constructed and located at haphazard.

Some object to deadfalls because fox are seldom caught in them. It is true that few fox are taken in deadfalls, although in the far North some are, and especially Arctic and White fox.

The deadfall trapper, however, who gives care and attention to his traps finds them fur takers. They can be built small for weasel or a little larger for mink, marten and civet cat; or larger for opossum and skunk; still heavier for coon and wild cat and even to a size that kills bear.

Some trappers find the mink hard to catch. At some seasons they are easy to take in deadfalls. In the 1880's in five winters eight mink were caught in one deadfall. The first winter one was caught; second, two; third, three; fourth and fifth, each one.

If our memory serves us right, the trap was first built in the fall of 1887, and was located on the bank about ten feet to the left of a sycamore, which at that time was standing. There was a den under the tree entering near the water, with an outlet on the bank only a few feet from the trap, and near where the pen and bait were located.

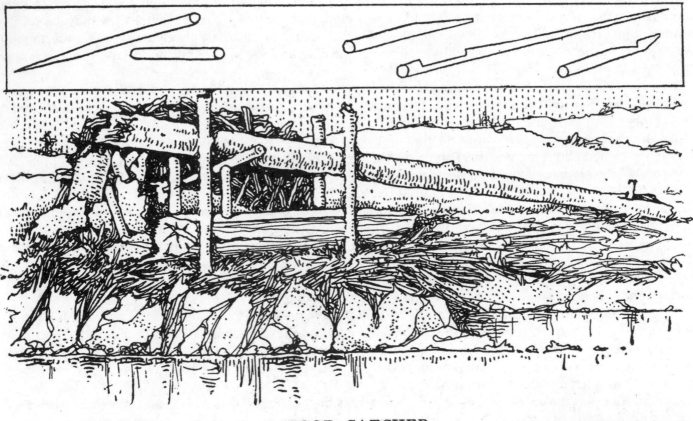

A GOOD CATCHER.

This deadfall was built much like the illustration shown here. While the fall was of hickory, not a vestige remained when looking at the place in September, 1906.

The pen should be built strong and tight so that the animal will not tear it to pieces and get at the bait from the rear. The "fall" or top pole can be of any kind of wood, but hickory, oak, beech, maple, and other heavy wood are all good. The pole should be heavy enough to kill the animal without placing any weights on it. When building it is a good idea to let the top pole extend about a couple of feet beyond the pen. This will give more weight on the animal when the trap falls.

The two piece triggers may work hard, especially if the log used for the fall has rough bark on. In this case it might be well to smooth with your axe or hatchet. In setting with the two piece trigger make them out of as hard wood as can be found. The long piece can be slightly flattened on the under side, or the side on which the upper end of the upright or prop sets. The prop should be cut square on the lower end while the upper end might be a little rounding, as this will tend to make the top or bait trigger slip off easier.

In setting raise up the top pole and hold in position with the knee. This gives both hands free to adjust the triggers. When you think you have them right, gradually let the weight off your knee and then try the trigger. You will soon learn about how they are to be set.

The bait should be tied on or the bait trigger may have a prong on to hold the bait. If you find the bait gone and the trap still up the chances are that it was set too hard and the animal stole the bait.

Of late years in some sections, mice have been very troublesome, eating the bait. In other places birds are bait stealers, and for this reason it is best to set traps rather hard to throw.

The location of a deadfall has much to do with the catch. Old trappers know if they were to set a steel trap in a place not frequented by fur bearers that their catch would be next to nothing. The same applies to all sets, whether steel traps, snares or deadfalls.

In the illustration it will be noticed that the opening or the side which the animal enters for bait is facing the creek. When building these traps it will be found best to leave the open side toward the water if trapping for mink or coon, as they generally leave the edge of the water going directly to dens along and near the bank.

The under log in the deadfall shown does not extend but a few inches beyond the two end stakes. It should extend eight or ten inches beyond. The four stakes at pen must be of sufficient length that when the trap is set they extend above the top or fall pole. If they did not, the trap in falling, might catch on the end of one of the stakes and not go down.

Along streams these traps need not be close. A couple to the mile is plenty. Of course, if there are places where dens are numerous more can be built to advantage, while along other stretches of water it may be useless to build them at all. It all depends upon whether animals travel there. You cannot catch them in any kind of trap if they are not there.

For opossum, skunk; mink, civet cat, coon, ermine, etc., find where the animals live or where they go frequently searching for food. If building where there are dens, either locate within a few feet of the one that appears bent or just off the path that the animal takes in going from one to the other. Have the open part next to path and say only three feet off.

Marten trappers, while placing traps on high ground, do not par so much attention to dens and paths, for these animals spend much time in trees looking for squirrels, birds, etc., but go through the forest "spotting a line" and locate a deadfall in likely ground about every 200 yards, or about 8 to the mile.

CHAPTER 5

Tracks and Signs

Old and experienced trappers can read the signs of the forest and stream with a degree of accuracy that to the amateur is surprising. In this way he can make a fair estimate of the number and kinds of fur-bearing animals found in a locality, while the novice would see nothing, or if he did see the tracks and signs he would not be able to distinguish them, one from another.

To be able to read the signs accurately is essential for successful hunting and trapping. The expert trapper will know instantly, on seeing a track, just what animal it was that passed that way, and by knowing its habits will know about when it is likely to return, and how to place a trap for its capture. He can also tell with fair accuracy at what time the animal passed that way, and frequently, will know whether it was a male or female; whether it was looking for food or a place of rest, whether it was on its regular route of travel and where it was going. To the novice all of these signs are unintelligible.

The art of sign reading can be learned only from experience. While the writer can distinguish the signs and tracks of the fur-bearing animals, to put this knowledge in print is exceedingly difficult. However, I will endeavor here, to describe the tracks of the fur-bearing and game animals, and believe that the description will be of value to the amateur.

Before the coming of the tell-tale snow, and the myriads of tracks which then appear, the stream with its muddy or sandy shores is perhaps the most promising place in which to look for signs. In the mud alongside of a pool of water, the tracks of that busy little animal the muskrat, can be seen.

The trail of this animal is accurately shown in the drawing. When seen at the water's edge, and only a few tracks are visible, the trail appears irregular, but if one can see where it has walked for some distance, it will be noted that the animal has a regular step, some five or six inches in length, and there is also the trail of the dragging tail, most plainly seen in the soft muddy bottom of the still, shallow water. In the snow the track will appear the same. Only the prints of the hind feet are visible, the front feet being very much smaller, and the print being obliterated by those of the hind feet. When the animal is running the prints of all four feet are readily discernible. The print of the hind foot will measure about two and a fourth inches in length if the full impression of the foot is to be seen.

In addition to the tracks other signs may be seen. Where the animals are found in fair numbers they will have well defined trails leading from the water. Where the bank is steep the trails are sometimes worn an inch or more in depth, owing to the muskrat's habit of sliding down the bank, which habit is not practiced in play, but for convenience. Other signs are the droppings on the logs which extend into the water; the dens with an accumulation of grass at the entrance; also the scratch signs on the bank, the feed beds, houses, etc.

All signs are plentiful in early fall, and at such times the novice is likely to overestimate the number of animals, as the muskrat is very active at that season.

The signs of the beaver are very similar to those of the muskrat, but the tracks are much larger, and owing to the fact that the level of the water in the vicinity of a beaver lodge, is raised far above the muddy shores, by the dam the tracks are seldom seen. However, the house and dam with the fresh cut wood, and well used trails are all of the signs that are needed. Old houses and dams are found frequently, but if there is no fresh cutting about, one may be certain that the house is uninhabited.

One of the most puzzling things to the novice is to know the number of inmates, that is, whether or not it is a full family, but methods of determining this are given in the chapter dealing with this animal. In the North the beavers are ice bound during the winter months, but occasionally one may find them emerging from the water at some springhole near the lodge or dam, and at such times the tracks may be seen in the snow.

The trail of the otter is unmistakable, owing to its peculiar, floundering, sliding mode of travel. It is seldom seen except in the near vicinity of the water. In the snow, the track is well defined and resembles the trail made by dragging a small log, the footprints in the bottom of the trail being very distinct. The length of jump is from four to eight feet, depending on the condition of the snow, and the footprints will measure about two inches in diameter.

They travel under the ice whenever possible and one may see frequently where the otter has bored into a snow bank at the water's edge, trying to locate a weak spot in the ice. When they have been working under the ice for some time one may find where they have been entering at, and emerging from the spring holes near the shore. At such places the snow will be packed down solidly and remains of fish may be found.

When there is no snow, one may learn of the most frequented localities by the number of slides and landing places. At the landing places the droppings will be found, and they may be distinguished from those of other animals from the large proportions of fish bones and scales.

Another animal which will be found frequenting the waterways is the mink. The track of this little animal may be found along the muddy shore, where the steep bank crowds it down to the water's edge. At other times it will travel several rods from the water, and after the ice forms, will run on the ice, seldom going far from the shore. Its method of travel is an easy lope, and the footprints are nearly always in pairs about three inches apart one somewhat in advance of the other, and separated by a distance of from one to two feet. The footprints measure from one to one and three-fourths inches in length. They are sometimes found entering the water at spring holes in the ice, and at open places in the rapids.

About the outlets or inlets of lakes and ponds, and at the log-jams or drifts on the stream one may sometimes find small, slender pointed droppings on the stones or logs. These sign will show unmistakably that the route is regularly used by at least one mink.

The track of the weasel is similar to that of the mink, but is smaller, but as the weasel is not a water animal, its tracks are more likely to be seen along the fences and where logs and rocks are plentiful. Here the trail will be found leading here and there in an aimless sort of way, and entering every nook and corner, where the persistent little hunter thinks it may find a sleepy "bunny" or some other animal or bird. The length of jump is from sixteen to twenty inches and the footprints measure about one or one and a fourth inches in length.

The marten has a similar method of travel and makes a track like those of the mink and weasel, being a little larger than the track of the mink and the footprint is broader and more rounded; the foot being heavily furred the toes do not show so distinctly. The trail will be found leading through the gullies and depressions of the heavily timbered places, and occasionally they also travel on the ridges.

Few signs are seen when the ground is bare but in the dark, sheltered ravines, the droppings may sometimes be seen on the logs, resembling those of the mink, but somewhat larger. Sometimes one may also find where they have killed a bird or rabbit.

There is practically no difference between the track of the fisher and that of the marten except in size. The footprints of the fisher are perhaps a trifle more distinct, and will measure from two to two and a half inches in length, the distance between each set of tracks being from two and a half to four feet. The tracks of both the marten and the fisher are found in the same kind of places, but the fisher is more of a rambler and more given to rambling in the open country. When the ground is bare one may see occasionally where they have killed and eaten rabbits, in which case very little will remain except the fur and toes of the victim.

Although the skunk is a member of the great weasel family, its method of travel is decidedly different from that of the weasel, for it seldom lopes, but has a slow, measured walk. The length of step is about five or six inches, and the footprints are from one to one and three-fourths inches in length. The trail is rather broad, and if the snow is deep and soft the animal sinks deeply, so as to make a trail with its body; however, the skunk seldom travels when the snow is in that condition.

Signs of the skunk may be noted also in summer and early fall. Occasionally one will find in the field, small excavations varying from an inch and a half to four or five inches in depth, nicely rounded and funnel shaped. This is the work of the skunk, and it was hunting for insects or grubs.

The most conspicuous signs, however, are the dens, which may be found along the steep, gravelly hill-sides. Although the woodchuck makes a similar den, one may be able to distinguish them, as a rule. If the den is inhabited by skunks one will usually find black and white hairs clinging to the mouth of the den, also will be likely to find a pile of droppings somewhere near, and to one side of the entrance.

The walk of the opossum is similar to that of the skunk, but the trail is broader, the footprints more spreading and the toes turned outward. The feet being naked, the toes show very plainly. Their tracks are only seen after a warm night, when the snow is melting, and the dens are seldom found unless one can follow the trail. The footprints will measure from one and a fourth to two and a half inches in diameter.

The tracks made by the animals of the dog family, the fox, coyote and wolf, are all similar, practically the only difference being in size. The foxes make the smallest tracks, that of the red fox being about two or two and a fourth inches in length and the length of step is about fourteen inches. The female makes a narrower track than the male, the same being true of many animals. There is no difference in the tracks of the silver, cross and red foxes, they being all of the same variety, but the gray fox makes a shorter and rounder track, easily distinguished from that of the red fox.

In early fall one may see the droppings of the fox along the old wood roads and stock paths, and they may be distinguished from those of the dog by the remains of apples and other fruits which are found there. Occasionally one may see the tracks in the mud or dust of the old roads in the woods, and sometimes the dens are to be found.

As before mentioned the track of the coyote is identical with that of the red fox, except that it is larger. The length of step is about sixteen inches and the track will measure about two and one-half inches in length by two inches in width.

The track of the timber wolf is larger, that of a full grown specimen measuring about three inches in width by four in length, the length of step being about eighteen or twenty inches.

As the tracks of the dogs are similar so also are those of the cats, the wild cat, lynx and cougar, or mountain lion, the only difference being in size. The two first named are plainly shown in the drawings, and as will be noted, that of the wild cat is the smallest, and will measure about two inches in diameter with a step of about fourteen inches.

The lynx makes a step of about the same length and the footprint of a large one will be from three to three and a half inches in width.

The cougar makes a larger track than the lynx, otherwise there is no difference.

Occasionally one may find where these animals have killed game; the lynx will eat all but the feet of a rabbit. The droppings may also be seen at times. They resemble somewhat those of the fox, but are slightly larger, and never show remains of fruit, as the lynx never eats vegetable food.

Along the streams arid shores of the lakes and ponds one may see in summer and early fall the tracks of the raccoon, where the animal has traveled the strip of mud at the water's edge, looking for frogs and fish. One may trace the animal along the stream and will find that at times it has waded in the shallow water, and then again has gone the lope along the water's edge, or, perhaps has made a side journey to some cornfield. At such places if coons are plentiful, one may find a trail leading through the fence into a field. In parts of the South where these animals are abundant, trails may also be found along the ponds and swamps.

The coon, like the bear, steps on nearly the entire bottom of the foot, instead of the toes only, as do the cats and some other animals, therefore, the footprint is usually long and narrow, and the foot being bare on the bottom, the long, slender toes show up distinctively. The animal has the loping method of travel, like the mink and weasel, but shows the print of a hind foot beside that of the front foot, the right and left alternating. The prints of the hind foot will measure from three to four inches in length, when the entire track is visible.

One is not likely to mistake the track of the bear, as it is the largest of the furbearing animals. As far north as Pennsylvania, its tracks will occasionally be seen in the snow, but north of that tier of states, the bears seldom move about after the coming of snow. The tracks may sometimes be seen in the mud and wet moss of the northern swamps, also on the shores of the lakes and along the streams.

The bear has a shuffling mode of walking and turns its toes outward. It is fond of walking on logs and will do so frequently, where fallen timber is plentiful. The track of a large black bear will sometimes measure eight inches in length, and that of the grizzly bear will be much larger.

Although the tracks are not often seen, other signs are to be found, such as logs and stumps, torn open by the bear in its search for ants, etc., small poplars broken down in order to secure the young leaves, claw marks on chestnut and black gum trees, overturned rocks, and those most noticeable signs, the marked trails, which are mentioned in the chapter describing this animal.

While the deer are not classed among the fur-bearing animals, they are interesting to all trappers, and I have shown drawings of the footprints of the common deer, the moose, the caribou, and the three most common species of rabbits, namely; the common cottontail, the snow-shoe rabbit, or varying hare, and the jack rabbit. The tracks shown in one-fifth size are of the cottontail.

As will be noted in the drawings of the deer tracks, that of the hind foot is narrower and more pointed than that of the front. The doe also makes a smaller and more slender track. The average track will measure about two and a fourth inches in length. The moose makes a similar track, but it is much larger and will measure about four and a half to five and a half inches. The track of the caribou will average somewhat smaller than that of the moose and is of decidedly different shape. It is not so pointed, and the hoof being split much higher, it spreads out more, also the prints of the two small toes on the back of the foot are to be seen in nearly all cases, while the moose does not always show them.

Almost everybody is familiar with the track of the rabbit, but I have shown those of the three species mentioned, mainly to show the difference in size. The feet being furred heavily, the prints of the toes seldom show, except on hard snow.

Some of these tracks were drawn from memory, but others were sketched from the actual trails. On the whole, I think they will be found to be accurate, at least near enough to enable anybody to distinguish the trails of the various animals, and I think that the descriptions and illustrations will be of value to the amateur trapper when looking over his territory and locating the runways of the animals that he proposes to catch.

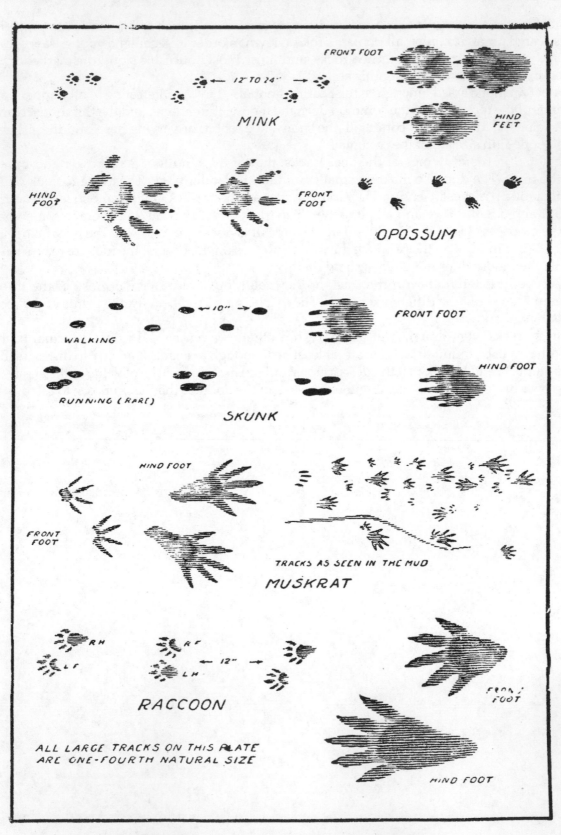

Tracks of Furbearing Animals.

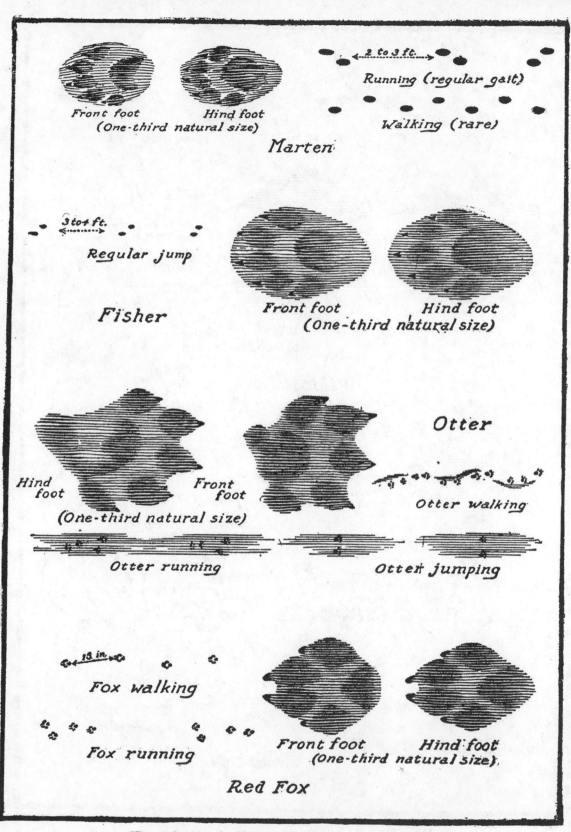

Front foot   Hind foot
(One-third natural size)

2 to 3 ft.
Running (regular gait)

Walking (rare)

Marten

3 to 4 ft.
Regular jump

Fisher

Front foot   Hind foot
(One-third natural size)

Otter

Hind foot   Front foot

(One-third natural size)

Otter walking

Otter running   Otter jumping

13 in

Fox walking

Fox running

Front foot   Hind foot
(One-third natural size)

Red Fox

Tracks of Furbearing Animals.

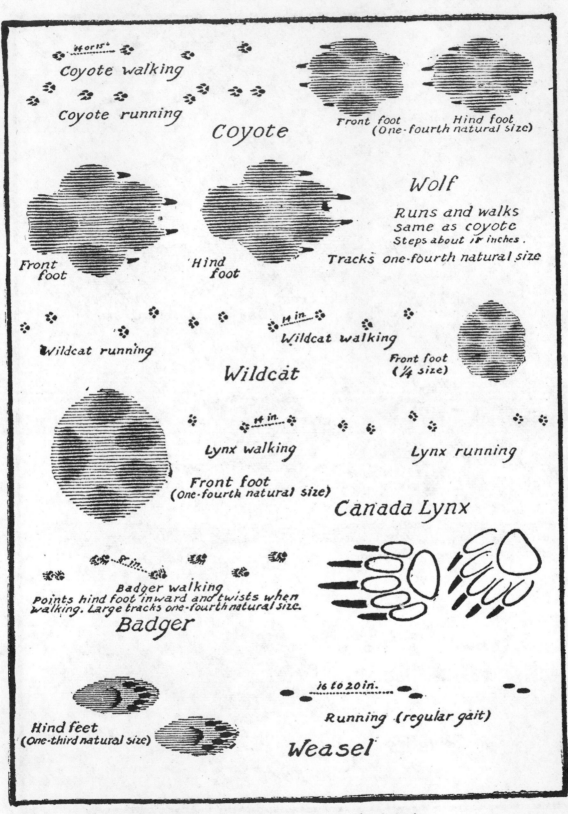

Tracks of Furbearing Animals.

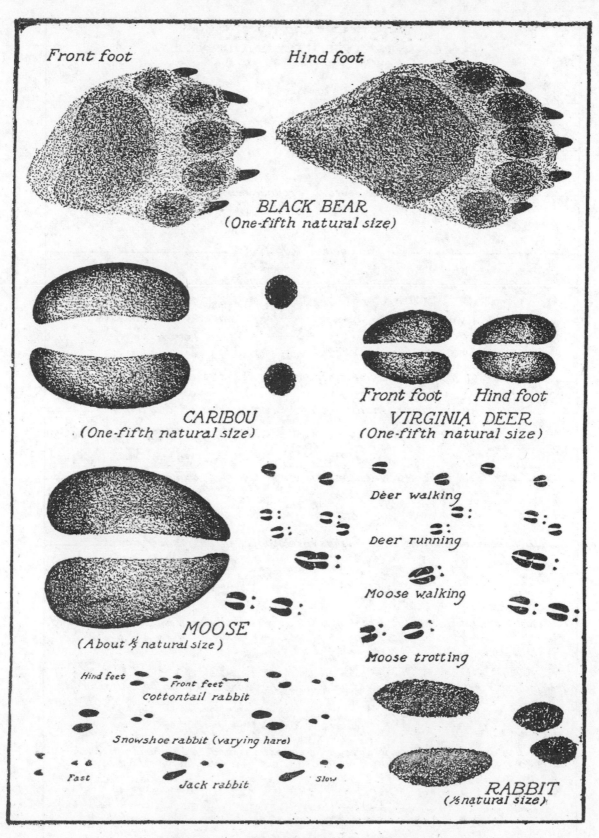

Front foot   Hind foot

BLACK BEAR
(One-fifth natural size)

CARIBOU
(One-fifth natural size)

Front foot   Hind foot
VIRGINIA DEER
(One-fifth natural size)

Deer walking

Deer running

Moose walking

MOOSE
(About ⅕ natural size)

Moose trotting

Hind feet   Front feet
Cottontail rabbit

Snowshoe rabbit (varying hare)

Fast   Jack rabbit   Slow

RABBIT
(⅕ natural size)

Tracks of Game Animals.

DEER TRACKS
AND WHAT THEY INDICATE.
By J. W. SHATTUCK, Hague, N.Y.

Natural walk, even register, no hops or jumps, every step registered 18 to 20 inches.

Track of a Buck, normal walk, even register, rather slow progress, 15 to 18 inches apart.

Easy lope 10 to 12 feet,   ground fairly level.

A good gait 10 to 16 feet.

Going at his best, badly frightened, or slightly wounded.

Walk of a wounded deer, uneven register, wounded in hip or shoulder.

Wounded in hip or shoulder but not broken, leaps average 8 feet.

Trail of deer, tracks indicate slight drag in snow of 6 to 8 inches.

Trail indicates deer has his right hind leg broken.

Trail indicates that the deer has his foreleg broken rather low down.

Trail indicates that deer is shot just back of shoulder, will soon lie down if not too closely followed.

Trail indicates that deer is shot low down in shoulder, bone broken or badly fractured.

Trail indicates that animal is shot through the intestines and liver, bullet probably entered side slantingly, passing through body, out near shoulder. Short lived.

Badly wounded internally, will soon be found lying down. ~

CHAPTER 6

Various Steel Traps

In the preceding pages I have made frequent mention of the Newhouse and other brands of traps and the work would hardly be complete without a description of these traps.

The Newhouse traps were designed by Sewell Newhouse, a resident of Oneida Co., New York, sometime prior to the year 1840 and the first of these famous traps were manufactured by the inventor in a little blacksmith shop, all of the work being done by hand.

These traps were traded to the neighboring Indians and gradually became famous throughout the country. Early in the 1850s, Mr. Newhouse moved to Kenwood, in Madison County and established a larger shop. It was at this time that he joined the Oneida Community and as the demand for the goods soon exceeded the output, the firm decided that the business must be enlarged and accordingly a small factory was erected.

The business proved prosperous and it was found necessary to enlarge the plant from time to time in order to increase the output and supply the demand which was increasing rapidly as the traps became the largest manufacturers of steel traps in the world.

Great care is used in the tempering of the springs and it is a fact well known to the users of this goods that the Newhouse-type spring is more reliable and more durable than any other.

The nearly perfect state of the Newhouse trap as it is made at present, has only been reached after years of study and experiment and many of the improvements have been brought about by the trappers themselves, with whom this firm has a large correspondence. They are always pleased to receive any suggestions for the improvement of their traps.

Although the Newhouse is a cheap trap, quality considered, it was soon found necessary to manufacture a line of cheaper traps and several styles were placed on the market. These were remodeled and changed in various ways to meet the demands of the consumer, and the names were changed with the style.

Those made at present are known as the "Hawley & Norton," the "Oneida Jump" and the "Victor". The Hawley & Norton is made in the same style as the Newhouse, but is lighter. The Victor is also made in this style and it is safe to say that it is the most popular trap on the market. More of them are used than of any other brand and being so cheap they are especially liked by the beginner and by those who do not make trapping their leading occupation. In thickly settled districts where traps are often taken by thieves, many trappers prefer to use these cheaper grades of traps.

The Oneida Jump trap is a distinct departure from the Newhouse pattern. It is a high grade trap but very light and its shape allows it to be placed where an ordinary trap could be set only with difficulty. Instead of having the long bow spring as in the other styles it has a short spring located inside of the jaws and under the pan, and it is attached to one end of the bed plate of the trap. This makes the trap very compact and it takes up very little room either when set or sprung. The traps have been on the market a comparatively short time but they have already become quite popular.

All of these traps are made in sizes from No. 0 to No. 4 and the Newhouse is made in additional sizes and in special styles as described in the following pages.

NO. 0 NEWHOUSE TRAP

Spread of Jaws, 3½ inches

This, the smallest Trap we make, is used mostly for catching the gopher, a little animal which is very trouble-some to western farmers, and also rats and other vermine. It has a sharp grip and will hold larger game, but should not be overtaxed.

NO. 1 NEWHOUSE TRAP

Spread of Jaws, 4 inches

This Trap is used for catching muskrats and other small animals and is sold in greater numbers than any other size. Its use is well understood by professional trappers and it is the most serviceable size for catching skunks, weasels, rats and such other animals as visit poultry houses and barns.

NO. 81 AND 81½ NEWHOUSE TRAP

Spread of Jaws, No. 81, 4 inches; No 81½, 4⅞ inches.

Occasionally animals free themselves from traps by gnawing their legs off just below the trap jaws where the flesh is numb from pressure. Various forms of traps have been experimented with to obviate this difficulty. The Webbed Jaws shown above have proved very successful in this respect.

Noting the cross-section of the jaws, as illustrated at the left, it is plain the animal can only gnaw off its leg at a point quite a distance below the meeting edges. The flesh above the point of amputation and below the jaws will swell and make it impossible to pull the leg stump out of the trap.

No. 81 Trap corresponds in size with the regular No. 1 Newhouse and the 81½ to the regular No. 1½.

NO. 91 AND 91½ NEWHOUSE TRAP

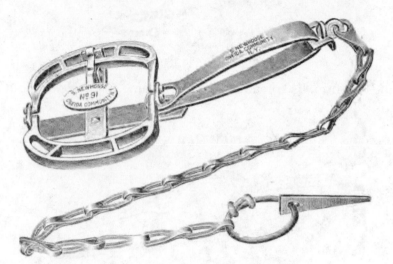

Spread of Jaws—91, 5¼ inches; 91½, 6¼ inches

The double jaws take an easy and firm grip so high up on the muskrat that he cannot twist out. A skunk cannot gnaw out either.

These traps are especially good for Muskrat, Mink, Skunk and Raccoon.

All parts of the No. 91, except the jaws, are the same size as the regular No. 1 Newhouse, while the 91½ corresponds to the regular No. 1½.

NO. 1½ NEWHOUSE TRAP

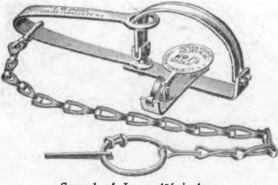

Spread of Jaws, 4⅞ inches

This size is called the Mink Trap. It is, however, suitable for catching the Woodchuck, Skunk, etc. Professional trappers often use it for catching Foxes. It is very convenient in form and is strong and reliable.

NO. 2 NEWHOUSE TRAP

Spread of Jaws, 4⅞ inches

The No. 2 Trap is called the Fox Trap. Its spread of jaws is the same as the No. 1½, but having two springs it is, of course, much stronger.

NO. 3 NEWHOUSE TRAP

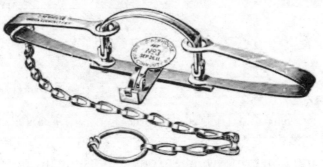

Spread of Jaws, 5½ inches

This, the Otter Trap, is very powerful. It will hold almost any game smaller than a bear.

NO. 4 NEWHOUSE TRAP

Spread of Jaws, 6½ inches

This is the regular form of Beaver Trap. It is longer than the No. 3 Trap, and has one inch greater spread of jaws. It is a favorite with those who trap and hunt for a living in the Northwest and Canada. It is also extensively used for trapping the smaller Wolves and Coyotes in the western stock raising regions.

NO. 2½ NEWHOUSE TRAP

The No. 2½ Newhouse Trap is a Single Spring Otter Trap. It is used more especially for catching Otter on their slides. For this purpose a thin, raised plate of steel is adjusted to the pan so that when the trap is set the plate will be a trifle higher than the teeth on the jaws. The spring is very powerful, being the same as used on the No. 4 Newhouse Trap. The raised plate can be readily detached if desired, making the trap one of general utility.

NO. 3½ NEWHOUSE TRAP

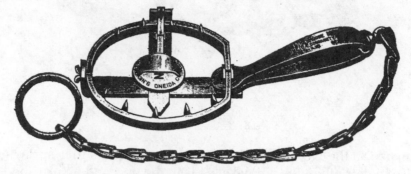

Spread of Jaws, 6½ inches

In some localities the Otter grows to an unusual size, with great proportionate strength, so that we have been led to produce an especially large and strong pattern. All the parts are heavier than the No. 2½, the spread jaws greater and the spring stiffer.

NO. 21½ NEWHOUSE TRAP

Single Spring. Same as a No. 2½, but without Teeth or Raised Plate

NO. 31½ NEWHOUSE TRAP

Single Spring. Same as No. 3½ but without Teeth or Raised Plate

Spread of Jaws—No. 21½, 5¼ inches; No. 31½, 6½ inches

This trap is the largest smooth jaw, single spring size that we make. Professional trappers will find them especially valuable when on a long trapping line as they are more compact and easier to secrete than the large double spring traps. The springs are made extra heavy.

✍ **NOTE**

The 21½ is practically a single spring No. 3, and the 31½ a single spring No. 4.

NO. 14 NEWHOUSE TRAP

Spread of Jaws, 6½ inches

This trap is the same in size as the No. 4 Beaver, but has heavier and stiffer springs and offset jaws which allow the springs to raise higher when the animal's leg is in the trap and is furnished with teeth sufficiently close to prevent the animal from pulling its foot out.

NO. 4½ NEWHOUSE TRAP

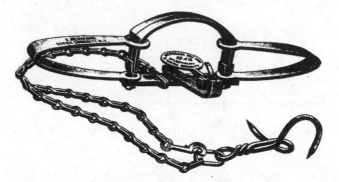

In response to a demand for a new model of the Newhouse Trap especially adapted to catching Wolves, we have perfected a trap which is numbered 4½ and will be called the "Newhouse Wolf Trap."

This trap has eight inches spread of jaw, with other parts in proportion and is provided with a pronged "drag," a heavy snap and an extra heavy steel swivel and chain, five feet long, warranted to hold 2,000 pounds. The trap complete with chain and "drag" weighs about nine pounds.

For a full description of the latest and best methods for using these Wolf Traps, send a two-cent stamp for our illustrated circular on "How to Catch Wolves with the Newhouse Wolf Trap" by Ernest Thompson-Seton, the well known artist, author and trapper of Toronto, Ontario.

NO. 50 NEWHOUSE TRAP

Spread of Jaws, 9 inches

This trap is intended for catching small size Bears. In design it is exactly like the Standard No. 5 Bear Trap, only that the parts are all somewhat smaller. Weight, 11¼ pounds each.

NO. 150 NEWHOUSE TRAP

Spread of Jaws, 9 inches

This Trap is identical with No. 50 excepting that the jaws are offset, making a space five-eighths between them. This allows the springs to come up higher when the Bear's foot is in the trap and thus secure a better grip. Also there is less chance of breaking the bones of the foot. Weight, 11¼ pounds each.

NO. 5 NEWHOUSE TRAP

Spread of Jaws, 11¾ inches.

This trap weighs nineteen pounds. It is used for taking the common Black Bear and is furnished with a very strong chain.

NO. 15 NEWHOUSE TRAP

Spread of Jaws, 11¾ inches.

To meet the views of certain hunters whose judgment we respect, we designed a style of jaw for the No. 5 trap, making an offset of three-fourths of an inch, so as to allow the springs to come up higher when the Bear's leg is in the trap. This gives the spring a better grip. Customers wishing this style will please specify "No. 15."

NO. 6 NEWHOUSE GRIZZLY BEAR TRAP

Spread of Jaws, 16 inches. Weight, complete, 42 pounds

This is the strongest trap made. We have never heard of anything getting out of it when once caught. It is used to catch Lions and Tigers as well as the Great Grizzly Bear of the Rocky Mountains.

NEWHOUSE GOPHER TRAPS

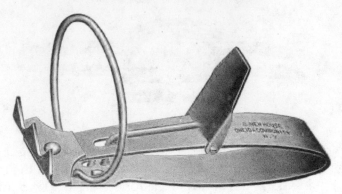

In making this trap we have adapted the Newhouse Steel Spring to the service of catching Gophers. This very important part of the trap is made exactly as are our regular Newhouse Game Trap Springs. It is lively and powerful, for it is carefully tempered. It is thoroughly tested and stamped with our name and is fully warranted.

The method of setting the Newhouse Gopher Trap is very simple and convenient, as will be seen from the illustration and adds materially to the satisfaction of the user. Packed in pasteboard boxes holding one dozen each.

THE NEWHOUSE CLAMPS

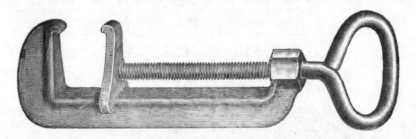

Every trapper knows how difficult it is to set a large trap alone in the woods, especially in cold weather, when the fingers are stiff, and the difficulty is greatly increased when one has to work in a boat. One of these clamps applied to each spring will, by a few turns of the thumbscrews, bend the springs to their places, so that the pan may be adjusted without difficulty. No. 4 Clamp can be used on any trap smaller than No. 4½. No. 5 and 6 are strong clamps, carefully made and especially adapted to setting the large traps, Nos. 4½ to 6. They dispense with the inconvenient and dangerous use of levers. With them one can easily set these powerful traps. These clamps are also useful about camp for other purposes.

Spread of Jaws, 3½ inches. This, the smallest trap made, is used mostly for catching the gopher, a little animal which is very troublesome to western farmers, and also rats and other vermin. It has a sharp grip and will hold larger same, but should not be overtaxed.

Spread of Jaws, 4 inches. This Trap is used for catching muskrats and other small animals, and sold in greater numbers than any other size. Its use is well understood by professional trappers and it is the most serviceable size for catch-ink skunks, weasels, rats and such other animals as visit poultry houses and barns.

Spread of Jaws, 4 inches. Occasionally animals free themselves from traps by gnawing their legs off just below the trap jaws, where the flesh is numb from pressure. Various forms of traps have been experimented with to obviate this difficulty. The Webbed Jaws shown above lave proved very successful in this respect.

Noting the cross-section of the jaws, as illustrated at the left, it is plain the animal can only gnaw off its leg at a point quite a distance below the meeting edges. The flesh above the point of amputation and below the jaws will swell and make it impossible to pull the leg stump out of the trap.

The No. 81 Trap corresponds in size with the regular No. 1 Newhouse.

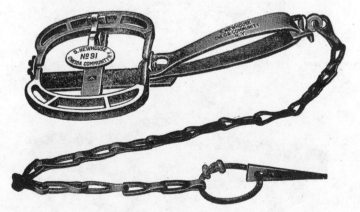

Spread of Jaws—91, 5¼ inches; 91½, 6¼ inches. The double jaws take an easy and firm grip so high up on the muskrat that he can not twist out. A skunk cannot gnaw out either.

These traps are especially good for muskrat, mink, skunk and raccoon.

All parts of the No. 91 except the jaws are the same size as the regular No. 1 Newhouse, while the 91½ corresponds to the regular No. 1½.

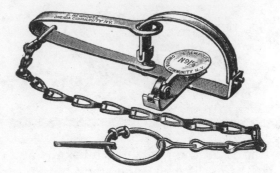

Spread of Jaws, 4⅞ inches. This size is called the Mink Trap. It is, however, suitable for catching the wood-chuck, skunk, etc. Professional trappers often use it for catching foxes. It is very convenient in form and is strong and reliable.

Spread of Jaws, 4⅞ inches. The No. 2 Trap is called the Fox Trap. Its spread of jaws is the same as the No. 1½ but having two springs it is, of course, much stronger.

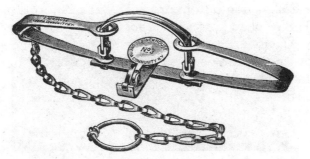

Spread of Jaws, 5½ inches. This, the Otter Trap, is very powerful. It will hold almost any game smaller than a bear.

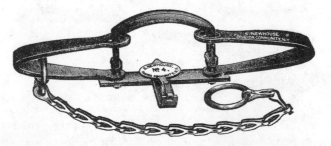

Spread of Jaws 6½ inches. This is the regular form of Beaver Trap. It is longer than the No. 3 Trap, and has one inch greater spread of jaws. It is a favorite with those who trap and hunt for a living in the Northwest and Canada. It is also extensively used for trapping the smaller wolves and coyotes in the western stock raising regions.

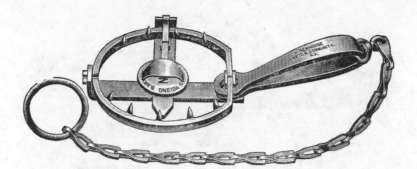

Spread of Jaws, 6½ inches. In some localities the otter grows to an unusual size, with great proportionate strength, so that the manufacturers have been led to produce an especially large and strong pattern. All the parts are heavier than the No. 2½, the spread of jaws greater and the spring stiffer.

Spread of Jaws, 5 inches. The above cut represents a Single Spring Otter Trap. It is used more especially for catching otter on their "slides." For this purpose a thin, raised plate of steel is adjusted to the pan so that when the trap is set the plate will be a trifle higher than the teeth on the jaws. The spring is very powerful, being the same as used on the No. 4 Newhouse Trap. The raised plate can be readily detached if desired, making the trap one of general utility.

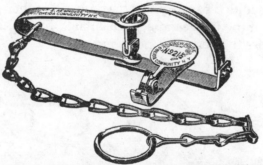

Single Spring.   Same as No. 2½ but without Teeth or Raised Plate.

Single Spring. Same as No. 2½ but without Teeth or Raised Plate.

NO. 31½ NEWHOUSE TRAP

Single Spring. Same as No. 3½ but without teeth or Raised Plate.

Spread of Jaws—No. 21½, 5¼ inches; No. 31½, 6½ inches. These traps are the largest smooth jaw, single spring sizes that are made. Professional trappers will find these especially valuable when on a long trapping line, as they are more compact and easier to secrete than the large double spring traps. The springs are made extra heavy.

✍ **NOTE**

The 21½ is practically a single spring No. 3, and the 31½ a single spring No. 4.

Spread of Jaws, 6½ inches. This trap is the same in size as the No. 4 Beaver, but has heavier and stiffer springs and offset jaws, which allow the springs to raise higher when the animal's leg is in the trap, and is furnished with teeth sufficiently close to prevent the animal from pulling its foot out.

Clutch Detachable—Trap can be used with or without it.

Spread of Jaws, No. 23, 5½ inches; No. 24, 6¼ inches. The inventor of this attachment claims to have had wonderful success with it in taking beaver. The trap should be set with the clutch end farthest from shore. The beaver swims with his fore legs folded back against his body, and when he feels his breast touch the bank he puts them down. The position of the trap can be so calculated that he will put his fore legs in the trap, when the clutch will seize him across the body and hold him securely.

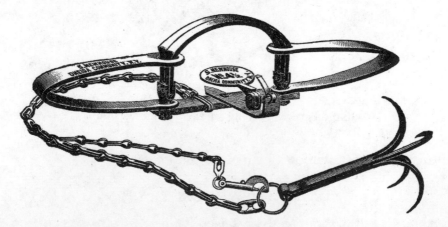

In response to a demand for a new model of the Newhouse Trap especially adapted to catching wolves, the manufacturers have perfected a trap which is numbered 4½ and is called the "Newhouse Wolf Trap."

This trap has eight inches spread of jaw, with other parts in proportion, and is provided with a pronged "drag," a heavy snap and an extra heavy steel swivel and chain, five feet long, warranted to hold 2,000 pounds. The trap complete with chain and "drag" weighs about nine pounds.

Spread of Jaws, 9 inches. This trap is intended for catching small sized bears. In design it is exactly like the standard No. 5 Bear Trap, only that the parts are all somewhat smaller. Weight, 11¼ pounds each.

Spread of Jaws, 9 inches. This trap is identical with No. 5 excepting that the jaws are offset, making a space five-eighths inch between them. This allows the springs to come up higher when the bear's foot is in the trap, and thus secure a better grip. Also there is less chance of breaking the bones of the foot. Weight, 11¼ pounds each.

Spread of Jaws, 11¾ inches. This trap weighs nineteen pounds. It is used for taking the common black bear and is furnished with a very strong chain.

Spread of Jaws, 11¾ inches. To meet the views of certain hunters whose judgment is respected, the manufacturers designed a style of jaw for the No. 5 trap, making an offset of ¾ of an inch, so as to allow the springs to come up higher when the bear's leg is in the trap. This gives the spring a better grip. Those wishing this style should specify "No. 15."

Spread of Jaws, 16 inches. Weight, complete, 42 pounds. This is the strongest trap made. We have never heard of anything getting out of it when once caught. It is used to catch lions and tigers, as well as the great Grizzly Bears of the Rocky Mountains.

This cut illustrates Bear Chain Clevis and Bolt, intended as a substitute for the ring on the end of the trap chain, when desired.

With this clevis a loop can be made around any small log or tree without the trouble of cutting to fit the ring. The chain is made five feet long, suitable for any clog, and the prices of bear traps fitted with it are the same as with the regular short chain, and ring.

Every trapper knows how difficult it is to set a large trap alone in the woods, especially in cold weather, when the fingers are stiff, and the difficulty is greatly increased when one has to work in a boat. One of these clamps applied to each spring will by a few turns of the thumb-screws, bend the springs to their places, so that the pan may be adjusted without difficulty. No· 4 Clamp can be used on any trap smaller than No. 4½. No. 5 and 6 are strong clamps, carefully made and especially adapted to setting the large traps Nos. 4½ to 6. They dispense with the inconvenient and dangerous use of levers. With them one can easily set these powerful traps. These clamps are also useful about camp for other purposes.

CHAPTER 7

Building Deadfalls

During the centuries that trapping has been carried on, not only in America but throughout the entire world, various kinds of traps and snares have been in use and taken by all classes of trappers and in all sections the home-made traps are of great numbers. The number of furs caught each year is large.

The above was said by a trapper some years ago who has spent upwards of forty years in the forests and is well acquainted with traps, trappers and fur-bearing animals. Whether the statement is true or not, matters but little, although one thing is certain and that is that many of the men who have spent years in trapping and have been successful use the deadfalls and snares as well as steel traps.

Another trapper says : "In my opinion trapping is an art and any trapper that is not able to make and set a deadfall, when occasion demands, does not belong to the profession. I will give a few of the many reasons why deadfalls are good.

1. There is no weight to carry.
2. Many of the best trappers use them.
3. It requires no capital to set a line or deadfalls.
4. There is no loss of traps by trap thieves but the fur is in as much danger.
5. Deadfalls do not mangle animals or injure their fur.

THE POLE DEADFALL.

6. It is a humane way of killing animals.
7. There is no loss by animals twisting off a foot or leg and getting away.
8. Animals are killed outright, having no chance to warn others of their kind by their cries from being caught.
9. Trappers always have the necessary out fit (axe and knife) with them to make and set a deadfall that will kill the largest animals.
10. The largest deadfalls can be made to spring easy and catch small game if required.
11. Deadfalls will kill skunk without leaving any scent.
12. Deadfalls are cheap and trappers should be familiar with them.

It is a safe proposition, however, that not one-half of the trappers of today can build a deadfall properly or know how to make snare and many of them have not so much as seen one.

First a little pen about a foot square is built of stones, chunks, or by driving stakes close together, leaving one side open. The stakes should be cut about thirty inches long and driven into the ground some fourteen inches, leasing sixteen or thereabout above the ground. Of course if the earth is very solid, stakes need not be so long, but should be so driven that only about sixteen inches remain above ground. A sapling say four inches in diameter and four feet long is laid across the end that is open. A sapling that is four, five or six inches in diameter, owing to what you are trapping for, and about twelve feet long, is now cut for the "fall." Stakes are set so that this pole or fall will play over the short pole on the ground. These stakes should be driven in pairs; two about eighteen inches from the end; two about fourteen farther back. (See illustration.)

The small end of the pole should be split and a small but stout stake driven firmly thru it so there will be no danger of the pole turning and "going off" of its own accord. The trap is set by placing the prop (which is only seven inches in length and half an inch thru) between the top log and the short one on the ground, to which is attached the long trigger, which is only a stick about the size of the prop, but about twice as long, the baited end of which extends back into the little pen.

The bait may consist of a piece of chicken, rabbit or any tough bit of meat so long as it is fresh and the bloodier the better. An animal on scenting the bait will reach into the trap—the top of the pen having been carefully covered over—between the logs. When the animal seizes the bait the long trigger is pulled off of the upright prop and down comes the fall, killing the animal by its weight. Skunk, coon, opossum, mink and in fact nearly all kinds of animals are easily caught in this trap. The fox is an exception, as it is rather hard to catch them in deadfalls.

The more care that you take to build the pen tight and strong, the less liable is some animal to tear it down and get bait from the outside; also if you will cover the pen with leaves, grass, sticks, etc., animals will not be so shy of the trap. The triggers are very simple, the long one being placed on top of the upright, or short one. The long triggers should have a short prong left or a nail driven in it to prevent the game from getting the bait off too easy. If you find it hard to get saplings the right size for a fall, and are too light, they can be weighted with a pole laid on the "fall."

I will try and give directions and drawing of deadfalls which I have used to some extent for years, writes

SMALL ANIMAL FALL.

a Maine trapper, and can say that most all animals can be captured in them as shown in illustration. You will see the deadfall is constructed of stakes and rocks and is made as follows: Select a place where there is game; you need an axe, some nails, also strong string, a pole four inches or more in diameter. Notice the cut No. 1 being the drop pole which should be about six to seven feet long. No. 2 is the trip stick. No. 3 is string tied to pole and trip stick. No. 4 is the stakes for holding up the weight. No. 5 is the small stakes driven around in the shape of letter U, should be one foot wide and two feet long. No. 6 is the rocks. No. 7 is the bait.

Now this is a great trap for taking skunk and is soon built where there are small saplings and rocks. This trap is also used for mink and coon.

The trapper's success depends entirely upon his skill and no once can expect the best returns unless his work is skillfully done. Do not attempt to make that deadfall unless you are certain that you can make it right and do not leave it till you are certain that it could not be any better made. I have seen deadfalls so poorly made and improperly set that they would make angels weep, neither were they located where game was apt to travel. The deadfall if made right and located where game frequents is quite successful.

Another thing, boys, think out every little plan before you attempt it. If so and so sets his traps one way, see if you can't improve on his plan and make it a little better. Do not rush blindly into any new scheme, but looks at it on all sides and make yourself well acquainted with the merits and drawbacks of it. Make good use of your brains, for the animal instinct is its only protection and it is only by making good use of your reasoning powers that you can fool him. Experience may cost money sometimes and loss of patience and temper, but in my estimation it is the trapper's best capital. An old trapper who has a couple of traps and lots of experience will catch more fur than the greenhorn with a complete outfit. Knowledge is power in trapping as in all other trades.

This is the old reliable "pinch head." The picture does not show the cover, so I will describe it. Get some short pieces of board or short poles and lay them on the stones in the back part of the pen and on the raised stick in front. Lay them close together so the animal cannot crawl in at the top. Then get some heavy stones and lay them on the cover to weight down and throw some dead weeds and grass over the pen and triggers and your trap is complete. When the animal tries to enter and sets off the trap by pressing against the long trigger in front, he brings the weighted pole down in the middle of his back, which soon stops his earthly career.

This deadfall can also be used at runways without bait. No pen or bait is required. The game will be caught coming from either direction. The trap is "thrown" by the trigger or pushing against it when passing thru. During snowstorms the trap requires considerable attention to keep in perfect working order, but at other times is always in order when placed at runways where it is used without bait.

The trap can also be used at dens without bait with success. If used with bait it should be placed a few feet from the den or near any place frequented by the animal or animals you expect to catch.

THE PINCH HEAD.

Of course we all admit the steel trap is more convenient and up-to-date, says a New Hampshire trapper. You can make your sets faster and can change the steel trap from place to place; of course, the deadfall you cannot. But all this does not signify the deadfall is no good; they are good and when mink trapping the deadfall is good. To the trapper who traps in the same locality every year, when his deadfalls are once built it is only a few minutes' work to put them in shape, then he has got a trap for the season.

I enclose a diagram of a deadfall (called here Log Trap) which, when properly made and baited, there is no such a mink catcher in the trap line yet been devised. This trap requires about an hour to make and for tools a camp hatchet and a good strong jackknife, also a piece of strong string, which all trappers carry.

BOARD OR POLE TRAP.

This trap should be about fifteen inches wide with a pen built with sticks or pieces of boards driven in the ground. (See diagram.) The jaws of this trap consist of two pieces of board three inches wide and about three and a half feet long, resting edgeways one on the other, held firmly by four posts driven in the ground. The top board or drop should move easily up and down before weights are put on. The treddle should be set three inches inside level with the top of bottom board. This is a round stick about three-fourths inch thru, resting against two pegs driven in the ground. (See diagram.) The lever should be the same in size. Now put your stout string around top board. Then set, pass lever thru the string over the cross piece and latch it in front of the treddle. Then put on weights and adjust to spring, heavy or light as desired. This trap should be set around old dams or log jams by the brook, baited with fish, muskrat, rabbit or chicken.

I herewith enclose a drawing of a deadfall that I use for everything up to bear, writes a Rocky Mountain trapper. I hate to acknowledge that I have used it to get "lope" meat with, because I sometimes believe in firing as few shots as I can in some parts of the Mountains.

Drawing No. 1 shows it used for bait; a snare can be used on it al the same time by putting the drop or weight where it isn't liable to fall on the animal. Put the weight on the other side of tree or make it fall with the animal to one side. In this case a pole must be strictly used. A good sized rock is all right for small animals. The closer spikes 1 and 2 are together and the longer the tugger end on bottom, the easier it will pull off.

Fig. 1.—Spike driven in tree one-half inch deeper than spike No. 2 (Fig. No. 2) to allow for notch.

3—Bait on end of trigger.

4—Heavy rock or log.

5—Wire, fine soft steel.

6—Trigger with notch cut in it.

7—Notch cut in trigger Fig. 6. Spike No. 2 must have head cut off and pounded flat on end.

In setting it across a trail a peg must be driven in the ground. In this peg the spikes are driven instead of tree as in drawing No. 1. The end of brush stick in between peg and trigger end and when an animal comes either way it will knock the brush and it knocks out the trigger. Good, soft steel wire should be used. In setting this deadfall along river bank a stout stick can be driven in bank and hang out over water. This stick will take the place of a limb on tree. One end of a pole held in a slanting position by weighing one end down with a rock will do the same as limb on tree. If a tree is handy and no limb, lean a stout pole up against the tree and cut notches in it for wire to work on.

BAIT SET DEADFALL.

1—T-rail.

2—Log.

3—Trigger same as for bait on top deadfall drawing.

4—Stake driven in ground with spikes driven in it same as above in tree.

5—Spikes same as above.

6—Wire.

7—Tree.

8—Brush put in trail with one end between trigger and peg to knock off trigger when touched.

This deadfall has never failed me and when trapping in parts of the country where lynx, coyote or wolverine are liable to eat marten in traps, use a snare and it will hang 'em high and out of reach. Snare to be fastened to trigger.

Of course a little pen has to be built when setting this deadfall with bait. In setting in trail it beats any deadfall I have ever used for such animals as have a nature to follow a trail. A fine wire can also be tied to the trigger and stretched across trail instead of a brush and tied on the opposite side of trail. I like it, as the weight can be put high enough from the ground to kill an elk when it drops.

TRAIL SET DEADFALL.

CHAPTER 8

Bear and Coon Deadfall

I will explain how to make the best bear deadfall, also the best one for coon that ever was made, writes an old and successful deadfall trapper. First get a pole six or eight feet long for bed piece, get another sixteen or eighteen feet long and lay it on top of bed piece. Now drive two stakes, one on each side of bed piece and pole and near one end of bed piece. About 18 or 20 inches from first two stakes drive two more stakes, one on each side of bed piece and fall pole. Now drive two more stakes directly in front of your two back stakes and about two inches in front.

Next cut a stick long enough to come just to the outside of last two stakes driven. Then whittle the ends off square so it will work easy between the treadle stakes and the two inside stakes that your fall works in; next raise your fall pole about three feet high. Get a stick about one inch thru, cut if so that it will be long enough to rest against your treadle and that short stick is your treadle when it is raised above the bed a piece, cut the end off slanting so it will fit against the treadle good.

Slant the other end so the fall pole will fit good. Now five or six inches front the top of the slanted stick cut a notch in your slanted stick. Go to the back side, lift your pole up, set the post on the bed piece. Place the top of the slanted stick against the fall

BEAR OR COON DEADFALL.

pole. Then place the pole off post in the notch in slant stick. Press back on bottom of slanted stick and place your treadle against the stick. Your trap is set. Make V shape on inside of treadle by driving stakes in the ground, cedar or pine, and hedge it in tight all around. If such there is not, make it as tight as you can. Cover the top tight, the cubby should be 3 feet long, 3 feet high and wide as your treadle stakes.

Stake the bait near the back end of cubby. Be sure the treadle is just above the bed piece. Take the pole off the cubby to set the trap as you have set it from this side. You can set it heavy or light by regulating the treadle. I sometimes drive spikes in the bed piece and file them off sharp as it will hold better. You can weight the fall poles as much as you like after it is set. Don't you see, boys, that the old fellow comes along and to go in he surely will step on the treadle. Bang, it was lowered and you have got him.

This is the best coon deadfall I ever saw. The fall pole for coon should be about 14 inches high when set. Set it under trees or along brooks where you can see coon signs. Bait with frogs, crabs or fish, a piece of muskrat or duck for coon. Build it much the same as for bear, only much smaller. You will find this a successful trap.

I will describe a deadfall for bear which I use, and which works the host of any I have tried, says a Montana trapper. I have two small trees about 80 inches apart, cut a pole 10 feet long for a bed piece and place in front of trees then cut a notch in each tree about 27 inches above the bed piece, and nail a good, strong piece across from one tree to the other in the notches. Cut a long pole five or six inches through for the deadfall, place the larger end on top of bed log, letting end stick by the tree far enough to place on poles for weights.

Then cut two stakes and drive on outside of both poles, and fasten top of stakes to the trees one foot above the cross piece. Then on the inside, 30 inches from the trees, drive two more solid stakes about 2 feet apart and nail a piece across them 6 inches lower than the cross piece between the trees. Then cut a lever about three feet long and flatten one end, and a bait stick about two feet long. Cut two notches 6 inches apart, one square on the top and the other on the bottom, and both close to the top end of bait stick.

Fasten bait on the other end and then raise up the deadfall, place the lever stick across the stick nailed between the two trees, letting the end run six inches under the deadfall. Take the bait stick and hook lower notch on the piece nailed on the two stakes and place end of lever in the top notch, then cut weights and place on each side until you think you have enough to hold any bear. Then put on as many more and it will be about right. Stand up old chunks around the sides and back and lots of green brush on the outside. Get it so he can't see the bait.

It doesn't require a very solid pen. I drive about three short stakes in front and leave them one foot high, so when he pulls back they will come against him, and the set is complete. You can weight it with a ton of poles and still it will spring easy. The closer together the two notches the easier it will spring.

This trap can be built lighter and is good for coon. In fact, will catch other fur bearers, but is not especially recommended for small animals, such as ermine and mink.

CHAPTER 9

Otter Deadfalls

At the present day when steel traps are so cheap and abundant it may sound very primitive and an uncertain way of trapping these animals for one to advocate the use of the deadfall, especially as every hunter knows the animal is much more at home in the water than on land. But on land they go and it was by deadfalls the way-back Indians killed a many that were in their packs at the end of the hunting season.

Of course these wooden traps were not set at haphazard thru the brush as marten traps, but were set up at the otter slide places, and where they crossed points in river bends, or it might be where a narrow strip of land connected two lakes. These places were known from one generation to another and the old traps were freshened up spring and fall by some member of the family hunting those grounds.

These special deadfalls were called otter traps; but really when once set were open for most any animal of a medium size passing that path. The writer has known beaver, lynx, fox and in one instance a cub bear to be caught in one of these deadfalls. There was a simplicity and usefulness about these traps that commended them to the trapper and even now some hunters might use them with advantage.

When once set, they remain so until some animal comes along and is caught. I say "caught" because if properly erected they rarely miss. They require no bait and therefore are never out of order by the depredations of mice, squirrels or moose birds. I knew a man who caught two otters together. This may sound fishy, but when once a present generation trapper sees one of these traps set he will readily believe this apparently impossible result is quite likely to happen.

The trap is made thus: Cut four forked young birch about five feet long, pointing the lower ends and leaving the forks uppermost. Plant two of these firmly in the ground at each side of the otter path, three inches

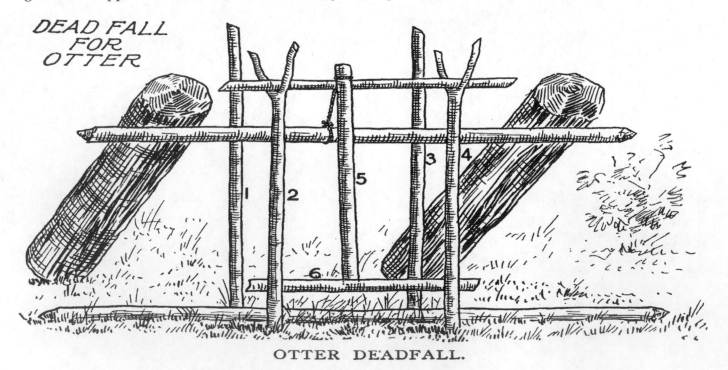

DEAD FALL FOR OTTER

OTTER DEADFALL.

apart between them and about twenty inches across the path. These must be driven very hard in the ground and a throat piece put in level between the uprights across the path from side to side. As a choker and to support the weight of logs to kill the otter, cut a pole (tamarae preferable) long enough to pass three feet each side of your picket or uprights, see that this falls easy and clear.

Now cut two short poles for the forks to lay in from side to side of the path, being in the same direction as the choker. At the middle of one of these short poles tie a good stout cord or rope (the Indians used split young roots), making a loop of same long enough to lay over the pole in front and down to the height the choke pole is going to be. When set, next conies the trigger which must be of hard wood and about a foot long, round at one end and flat at the other. A groove is hacked out all around the stick at the round end. This is to tie the cord to.

The choke stick is now brought up to say twenty inches from the ground and rested on top of the trigger. A stick about an inch in diameter is placed outside the pickets and the flat end of the trigger is laid in against this. The tied stick to be about eight inches from the ground. The tying at the end of the trigger being at one side will create a kind of leverage sufficiently strong to press hard against the tied stick. Care must be taken, however, to have this pressure strong enough but not too strong for the animal to set off.

Now load each end of the choke stick with small laps of wood to insure holding whatever may catch. A little loose moss or grass is placed fluffy under tread stick when set to insure the otter going over and not under. When he clambers over the tread stick his weight depresses it, the trigger flies up, letting the loaded bar fall on his body, which holds him till death.

While my description of the making of a deadfall for otters is plain enough to me; yet the novice may not succeed in constructing one the first time. Still if he is a trapper he will very soon perceive where any mistake may be and correct it. I have used both steel traps and deadfalls and although I do not wish to start a controversy yet I must say that a deadfall well set is a good trap. For marten on a stump they are never covered unless with snow, nor is the marten when caught destroyed by mice.

Of course, to set a deadfall for otter it must be done in the fall before the ground is frozen. Once made, however, it can be set up either spring or fall and will, with a little repairs, last for years. I am aware the tendency of the age is to progress and not to use obsolete methods, still even some old things have their advantages. Good points are not to be sneered at and one of these I maintain for spring and fall trapping in a district where otter move about from lake to lake or river to river is the old time Indian deadfall.

CHAPTER 10

Marten Deadfalls

Having seen a good many descriptions of deadfalls in the H-T-T lately, writes a Colorado trapper, I thought I would try to show the kind that is used around here for marten. It is easily made, and can always be kept above the snow.

First, cut a pole (z) five or six inches through and twelve feet long, lay it in the crotch of a tree five feet from the ground. Then cut two sticks two inches through and fifteen inches long, cut a notch in each three inches from the top and have the notch in one slant downwards (B), the other upwards (A). The sticks should be nailed on each side of the pole (z), the top of which should be flattened a little. Have the notches about six inches above the top of the pole.

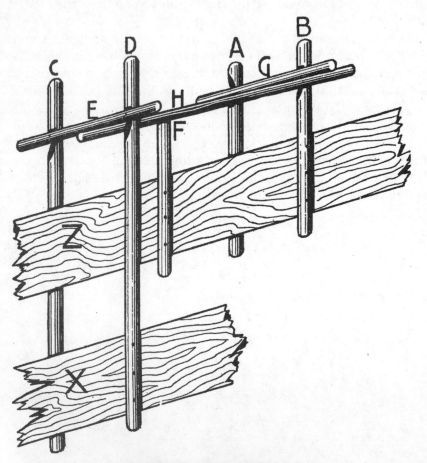

MARTEN DEADFALL.

Cut another stick 10 inches long (F), cut the top off square and nail it six inches farther down the polo on the same side as (B), have the top five inches above the top of pole (Z). Now cut two more sticks two and one-half, feet long (C-D), cut a notch in each two inches from the top and nail a stick (E) across them in the notches, so they will be about seven inches apart. Set a straddle of the pole (Z); they should be two inches farther down the pole than (F). Then cut another pole (X) ten feet long, lay it under (Z), lift up one end of it and nail the stick C and D to each side of it. See that when the sticks C, D, and E are lifted up they will fall clear and easily.

Now cut a bait stick (G) one half inch through and seven inches long, sharpened at one end. Cut another stick (II) an inch through and fifteen inches long; flatten a little on one side. To set the trap lift up C, D, E and X, and put the end of II under E and rest it on the top of F, hold down the other end while you put the bait stick (G) in the notches A and B, then let the end of H come up on the outside of B against the end of G. Put the bait on the other end of G; when the end is pulled out of the notch the trap will spring and spring easily if made properly. Lay a block of wood at the back end and some small sticks on top, so the animal will have to crawl under E to get the bait. Muskrat makes the best bait for marten.

52

When you find a tall straight spruce or something that is pretty straight (not a balsam) cut it about a foot over your head, says a Northwestern trapper, or as high as you can. When you have cut it, split the stump down the center two feet. Be careful doing this, for you are striking a dangerous blow as I have good cause to know and remember. Trim out the tree clean and taper off the butt end to make it enter into split. Drive down into split about fourteen inches. Cut a crotch into ground or snow solid.

Now cut the mate of this piece already in, split and put into split and into crotch on top of other. Have the piece heavy enough to hold wolverine. See cuts for the rest. Cover bait as shown in cut. I do not make my trip sticks the same as others, but I am afraid that I cannot explain it to you. See cuts for this also. Use your own judgment. Of course you will sometimes find it is not necessary to go to all this bother. For instance, sometimes you will find a natural hanger for your trap. Then you don't have to have the long peg or pole to hold it stiff.

This trap is used heavy enough by some "long line" trappers for wolverine. They blacken bait and cover as shown in No. 4. In the two small illustrations the triggers are shown in No. 1 separate and in No. 2 set. A is the bait and trip stick, B the lever, C is the upright. B in No. 1 is where the bait should be.

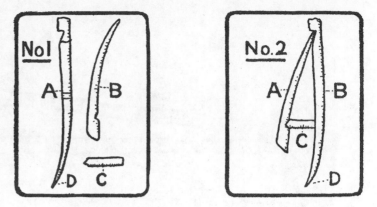

MARTEN TRAP TRIGGERS.

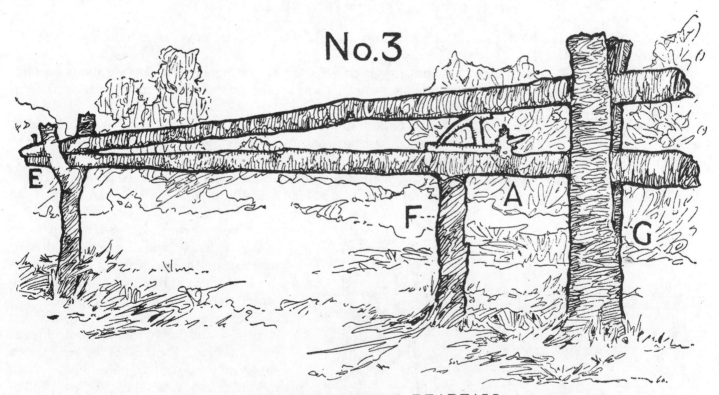

ANOTHER MARTEN DEADFALL.

In No. 3 A is bait, E is pin which fastens deadfall to under pole and prevents deadfall from turning to one side. F is post to keep under pole from bending.

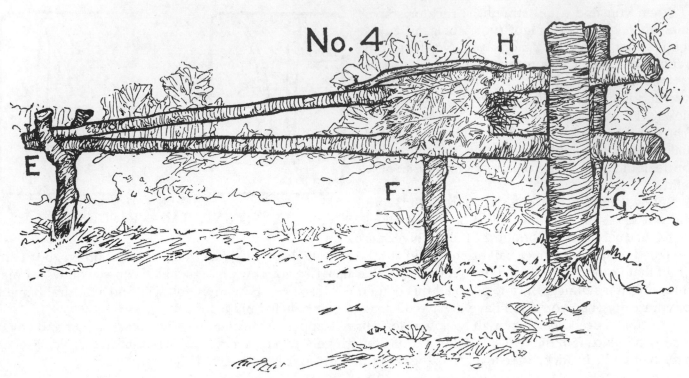

HIGH BUILT MARTEN DEADFALL.

In No. 4 HH are nails which fasten down a springy piece of wood to keep cover over bait. Cover with fir or spruce boughs.

Another deadfall much used by marten trappers is constructed by cutting a notch in a tree about a foot in diameter, altho the size of the tree makes little difference. The notch should be four inches deep and a foot up and down and as high up as the trapper can cut—four or five feet.

Only one pole is needed for this trap as the bottom of the notch cut answers for the bed or bottom piece. (See illustration.) The pole for the fall should be four inches or more in diameter and anywhere from six to ten feet in length, depending upon the place selected to set.

The end fartherest from the bait or notched tree must be as high as the notch. This can be done by driving a forked stake into the ground or by tying that end of the pole to a small tree if there is one growing at the right place.

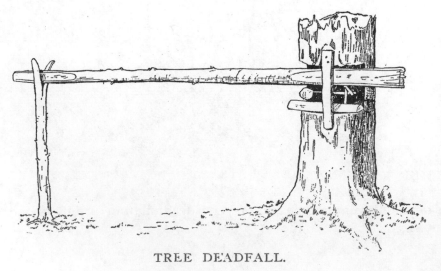

TREE DEADFALL.

If the pole for the fall is larger than the notch is deep, the end must be flattened so that it will work easy in the notch, as a piece of wood has been nailed over the notch to hold the fall pole in place.

The triggers used are generally the figure 4 and set with bait pointing as shown. There is no place for the marten to stand while eating bait, only in shelf, and of course when the spindle is pulled, down comes the pole killing the animal.

This shelf protects the bait and bed piece and the snow does not fill in between and require so much attention as the one first described.

This deadfall may also be built on a stump with a small enclosure or pen and the two-piece trigger used. Most trappers place the bait or long trigger on bottom pole, when trapping for marten. It will be readily seen that a marten, to get the bait, will stand between the "fall" and bed or under pole and of course is caught while trying to get the bait.

The height that deadfalls for marten should be built depends upon how deep the snow gets. In the fall and early winter they can be built on the ground or logs and other fur-bearers are taken as well.

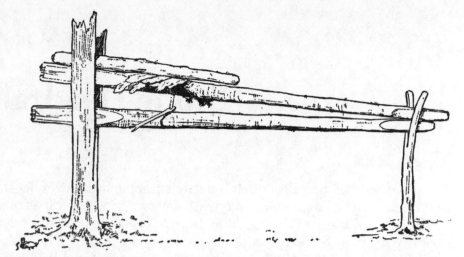

MORE MARTEN TRAP TRIGGERS.

A few inches of snow will not interfere with the workings of deadfalls on the ground, but deep snows will. To make catches the trapper must clean out under the fall pole each round. This is no small task. The trapper is always on the lookout for suitable places to construct marten deadfalls.

When the snows get several feet deep, and the trapper makes his rounds on snowshoes, the deadfalls constructed several feet above the ground are the ones that make the catches.

CHAPTER 11

Stone Deadfalls

The stone deadfall here described is used by trappers wherever flat stones can be found and is a good trap to catch skunk, opossum, mink and other small game in. The trap is made as follows:

The figure 4 trigger is best for this trap and is made after this manner: standard (1) is made by cutting a stick five or six inches long out of hard wood and whittling it to a flat point, but blunt at one end; (2) is about five inches long with a notch cut within about one and one-half inches of the end with the other end made square so that it will fit in (3) which is the bait stick. This is only a straight stick sixteen or eighteen inches long, while the other end of the stick should have a small prong on it, a tack driven in, or something to hold the bait in position. The best way will be to tie the bait on also.

After you have found a flat stone weighing from 50 to 100 pounds, depending upon what, game you expect to trap, select the place for the trap, first place a small flat stone underneath so that your game will be killed quicker and also so that the upright trigger will not sink into the ground. Lift up the large, or upper stone, kneeling on one knee before the stone resting the weight of the stone on the other. This leaves both hands free to set the trap. This is done by placing the triggers in the position shown in illustration and then letting the stone down very easily on the triggers. You should keep your knee under the stone all the time until you see that it comes down easily and does not "go off" of its own weight. The bait should always be put on before the trap is set. This trap will go off easy and you must be careful that the bait you put on is not too heavy and will cause the trap to fall of its own accord.

This trap can be made to catch rabbits which will come in handy to bait other traps for larger game. In trapping for rabbits bait with apples, cabbage, etc.

This trap does not take long to make, as no pen need be built, the top stone is large enough to strike the animal, making no difference in what position it gets when after the bait. A stone two or three inches thick and say thirty inches across and the same length or a little longer is about the proper size for skunk, opossum, etc., but of course larger or smaller stones can be used—whatever you find convenient.

FLAT STONE TRAP.

This trap consists of a flat piece of stone supported by three fits of wood, the whole trouble being in making these three fits right, and this can be done by carefully comparing the description here given with illustrations, whenever they are referred to. The parts are all made of wood about three-eighths of an inch thick. Fig. 1 is thirteen inches long, with notches about one-sixteenth of an inch deep cut in its upper side, two of the notches near together and at one end, and another four and a half inches from the first two. The latter notch should be cut a little sloping across the stick.

Figure 1 represents a top view and the piece next below it is a side view of the piece of wood as it should be made, and end fartherest from the notches being trimmed to a point to hold the bait. This constitutes the trigger.

The lever is shown in Fig. 2, the cut above giving a side view and that below it a bottom view of this part of the trap. The piece of wood needed for it is six and one-half inches long, one inch wide at one end, and tapering down to three-sixteenths of an inch at the other; a notch is cut across the under side one and a half inches from the wide end. Level off the upper side of the narrow end to about one-half the original thickness. If the flat stone to be used is a heavy one, the notch must not be more than 1 inch from the end; otherwise the leverage on the notches would he greater than is desirable, tending to hold the parts together too rigidly.

The upright post, Fig. 3, is seven inches long, slightly forked at the bottom (to make it stand firm and prevent twisting round when in use), the upper end beveled from the front backwards at an angle of about 45 degrees. The front of the upright is the side that would face a person standing exactly opposite the trap when set.

On the right side cut a long notch, half the width of the wood in depth, commencing the hollow slope of the notch one inch from the lower end and making the square shoulder just three inches from the bottom of the post; level the shoulder off from the front so as to leave only a narrow edge. Place the post upright, (see Fig. 4) it's forked end standing on a small piece of wood or flat stone, to prevent it from sinking into the ground; bait the pointed end of the trigger and hold it up horizontally with its middle notch, catching behind the shoulder of the notch in the upright post; then place the beveled end of the lever in the notch at the end of trigger, the notch in the lever laying on the edge of the top of the upright post.

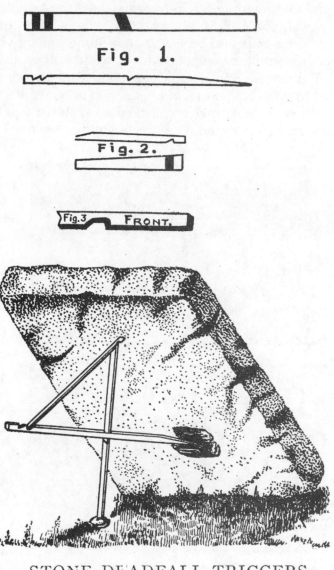

STONE DEADFALL TRIGGERS.

Lastly, make the stone rest on the top of the lever, arranging the stone so that the bait will be near the lower end of the stone.

It is a good plan to hollow out the ground somewhat under where the stone falls, to allow a space for the pieces of the Fig. 4 to lay without danger of being broken. The bait, also, should be something that will flatten easily and not hard enough to tilt the stone up after it has fallen.

The trouble with most deadfalls usually set, is in the weight of stone. When you get one heavy enough it will not trip easy when game takes hold, and oftentimes break head piece where the head takes hold of standard. The head piece from stone down to where standard sets in notch should be fully 2¼ inches, so when stone starts to fall it throws triggers out from under; otherwise, stone will catch and break them.

Young trappers when you are making triggers preparatory for your sets, tie each pair together separately as they are finished, then when you are ready to set there are no misfits. Now we are up to the bait stick. It should under no condition, be more than 9 inches long, and oftentimes shorter will answer better. A slotted notch on one end the width of triggers, and sharpened at the other, is all that is necessary. Then the bait will lay on the foundation of trap within 5 or 6 inches of front of the trap. Don't put bait away back under stone. You loose all the force when it falls.

In building foundations for traps the utmost caution should exercised in getting them good and solid. (See how well you can do it instead of how quick.) Begin in the fall before the trapping season is on, locate and build your trap, and be sure the top stone is plenty heavy, raise it up and let it fall several times. If it comes together with the bang of a wolf trap and will pinch a hair, so much the better.

To illustrate: While squirrel shooting one morning in the fall of 1905, I was standing on a ledge where I used to trap for coons, and I happened to remember of a trap underneath me. I just thought I would see if it was there. I went down and kicked away the drifted leaves and found it intact and ready for business. When I lifted it up the foundation was as solid as the day I put it there, and that was in the fall of 1890, and I want to say right here that it took all the strength I had to set it.

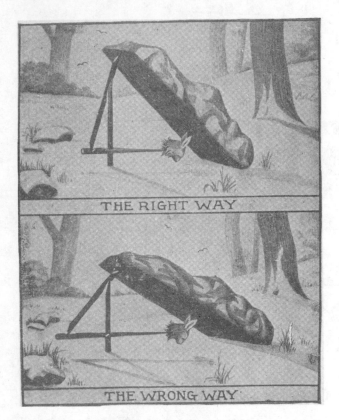

RIGHT AND WRONG WAY.

Trappers, if you will try one or more of the above described deadfalls for those skunk. I think you can tie their pelts about your neck for protection cold mornings, and none will wiser as far as smell goes, provided, however, you put some obstruction to the right and left of the trap so it will compel his skunk ship to enter direct in front, and then carefully adjust the length of bait stick so stone will crush him about the heart. I have taken quite a lot of skunk and very few ever scented where the head and heart were under stone, writes an Ohio trapper.

I always had a preference for above described traps for many reasons, yet if you live where there is no stone, you are not in it.

Deadfalls come in handy sometimes and with no cost whatever—unless the cost is building them. Will send two illustrations of the stone deadfalls writes a successful deadfall trapper. Will say that there is a right and a wrong way to set the deadfall. If you want to make sure of your catch never set your deadfall flat with short triggers shaped like figure 4, but make long triggers instead and have the weight or choker sit almost upright and draw the top trigger close to the one that it rests on at the bottom. In this way you have a trap that will be very easy to touch off.

The way that some set their deadfalls the animal can remove bait without being caught, simply because they draw the bait out from under the trap and stand far enough away to be out of danger of being caught. I can take a two hundred pound weight and set a deadfall that will catch a small field mouse but it would not do to have them knock that easy for you will get game that is too small to handle.

CHAPTER 12

The Bear Pen

I will give a description of a bear pen, writes a Canadian trapper. The bottom of the floor is made first of two logs about (1-1) nine feet long and nine or ten inches thick. They are placed side by side as shown in cut and two other logs (2-2) nine feet long and eighteen inches in thickness are placed one on each side of the bottom logs. Then cut two short logs about twelve or fourteen inches thick and long enough to reach across the pen and extend about six inches over each side. Notch these down, as shown in cut (3-3) so that the top of the logs are about three or four inches higher than the sides.

Cut notches in the top of these logs so that when logs 4-4 will lay solid on top of the other side logs. If they don't lie solid enough bore holes in the ends of the short logs and drive wooden pins in the holes. The top of the short logs and the inside of the 1ong logs should be flattened and a short block (5) fitted loosely in one end, and the other end should be closed by a block driven down in notches cut in the sides of 4-4, as shown in small cut. The top of the block (6) should be about five inches lower than the top of the side logs. Notches are next cut in the side logs, directly over this block, so that when the roller (7) is in place, it will fit down snugly on this block. The roller is about five inches thick and should turn easily in the notches.

Rear end view of Trap.

BEAR PEN TRAP.

The next step is to make the lid. It should be made of two logs of such a size that they will entirely close the top of the trap. They are notches down and pinned onto the roller and block 5. These logs should project over rear end of pen about four or five feet. Before pinning these logs in places, a hole should be made for the bait stick, half of it being cut in each log. Pins should be driven in the side logs, over the roller, so that the bear cannot raise the lid. Two crotches are then cut and set up at the sides of the trap and spiked solid to the sides. A short pole is then placed in the crotches and a long pole, running lengthwise of the trap, is fastened to the lid at one end with wire and the other ends fits into a notch in the bait stick when the trap is set. The bait stick has a spike driven thru it on the inside of the trap to keep it from pulling through.

To set the trap, pile stones on the end of the lid until it will tip easily, then put a pole thru under lid and go inside and fasten the bait on the bait stick. Then pull the long pole down and hook it into the notch in the bait stick. Remove the stones from lid and take the pole from under it and the trap is set and ready for the first bear that comes along. If the lid does not seem heavy enough, pile stone on it. A trap of this kind may be made by two men in half a day and will be good for a number of years.

The log trap is one of the very best methods of taking the bear, it beats the deadfall all to nothing, says an old and experienced Ohio bear trapper. It is a sure shot every time; I have never known it to fail except where the pen had stood for a number of years and become rotten. In a ease of that kind the bear would have no difficulty in gnawing his way out. This trap or pen, as I shall call it, has been time tried and bear tested. My father used to make these traps and many is the time when a boy I have ridden on horseback upon a narrow path, cut for the purpose of letting a horse pass along and on nearing the pen heard the growling and tearing around of the bear in the pen and the hair on my head would almost crowd my hat off.

Go about building it this way: First select the spot where you have reason to believe that bear inhabit; now having made your selection, get a level place and on this spot lay a course of logs with the top flattened off; this may be eight by three feet. This being done, commence to lay up the house of logs six to eight inches in diameter. Three sides of each log should be flattened; these will be the top, bottom and the inside. It is necessary this be done, for they must fit closely together in order that the bear cannot get a starting place to gnaw. This is why I suggest that the inside of the log be flattened. It is a well-known fact that you can put any gnawing animal into a square box and he cannot gnaw out for he cannot get the starting point.

Lay a short log first, then a long one, notching each corner as you go so the logs will fit closely together. Now for the front corners; drive a flattened stake into the ground, letting the flattened side come against the logs. Now as you proceed to lay on a course of logs pin thru the stake into each log. Now go on up until you get a height of about four feet, then lay on, for the top, a course of short logs commencing at the back end.

BEAR ENTERING PEN.

Between the second and third logs cut out a little notch and flatten the under side of this log around the notch; this is to receive the trigger, which is made of a small pole about three inches thick. Put this into the hole and let it come down within ten inches of the floor. Then cut a notch in the side facing the front of the pen and so it will fit up against the under side of the leg with the notch in; now you may make a notch in the trigger about six inches above the top of the pen and on the same side of the trigger that the first notch was made. Now the trigger is ready except adjusting the bait.

Next lay a hinder on top of the pen and upon either end of the short course of logs; pin the binders at either end so the bear cannot raise the top off the pen. You may also lay on three or four logs to weight it down and make it doubly sure. You may pin the first short top log in front to the side logs to keep the front of the pen from spreading. Now we have the body of the pen complete.

The door is the next thing in order. The first or bottom log ought to be twelve feet long, but it is not necessary for the balance of them to be that length; flatten the top and bottom of each log so they will lie tight together, also flatten off the inside of the door so it will work smoothly against the end of the pen. Lay the logs of the door onto the first or long log, putting a pin in each end of the logs as you lay them on. Go on this way until you have enough to reach the height of the pen and fully cover the opening.

Another way of fastening the door together is to get the logs all ready, then lay them upon the ground and pin two pieces across the door. Either way will do. Now the door being in readiness, put it in its place and drive two stakes in the ground to keep the animal from showing the door away. If these do not appear to be solid enough to support the door against an onslaught, you may cut a notch in the outside of the stake near the top; get a pole eight feet in length, sharpen the ends, letting one end come in the notch of the stake and the other into the ground; this will hold the door perfectly solid. Cut a slight notch in the top log of the door for the end of the spindle and the next move is to raise the door to the proper height. Set a stud under the door to keep it from falling. Get your spindle ready, flatten the top of either end a little, then cut a stanchion just the right length to set under the spindle on the first top log.

Tie your bait onto the lower end of the trigger, one man going inside to put the trigger in the proper place. To facilitate the springing of the trap, lay a small round stick in the upper notch of the trigger, letting the end of the spindle come up under the stick and as the bear gets hold of the meat on the bottom of the trigger the least pull will roll the trigger from the end of the spindle. However, it will spring very easily as the stanchion under the end of the spindle is so near the end.

This kind of trap can be made by two men in one day or less, and it often happens that the hunter and trapper wants to set a trap for bear a long way from any settlement or road. The carrying of a fifty pound bear trap a distance of twenty or thirty miles is no little task. Then again, this trap costs nothing but a little time and the trapper's whole life is given over to time. One man can make this trap alone and set it, but it is better for two to work together in this work, for in case the door should spring upon him while he was inside he would be forever lost. I have caught two wildcats at once in this pen, but it is not to be expected that you will get more than one bear or other large animal at a time.

CHAPTER 13

Portable Traps

In describing a portable deadfall, an Indiana trapper writes as follows: We took a piece of sawed stuff 2 × 4, say 5 feet long, then another the same size and length. For upright pieces to hold the main pieces so one would fall square on the other, we used sawed stuff 1 × 3, two pieces set straight up and down at each end, or about far enough to leave the back end stick out three inches, and front end or end where the triggers set, 6 inches.

Nail these 1 × 3 two on each end as directed above, nail to lower piece 2 × 4 only, then at back end bore a hole through the two uprights and also upper 2 × 4, or the piece that falls, put a bolt through, or a wood pin if the hole in the 2 × 4 is larger than those through the uprights; then you are ready to raise it up and let it "drop" to see whether it works smoothly or not.

DEN SET DEADFALL.

Better nail a block 2 × 4 between the tops of the uprights to keep them from spreading apart, then it is ready all except the triggers and string for them to run against. It is portable, yon can pick it up and move it anywhere, only a stake or two needed driven down on each side. Where string is shown as tied to little bush should be a small stake.

"SHEAR TRAP"

I send a drawing of a trap called the "Shear Trap," writes an Eastern trapper. This is not a new trap, neither is it my own invention. I have used this style and can recommend it to be O. K., cheap, easy made, light to move, will last and will catch most any small animal.

This trap is made as follows: Take 4 strips of board 4 feet 4 inches long, by 3 inches wide. Bore one inch hole two inches from end of all four of them. Now make two rounds about 13 inches long and put two of the boards on each side of the round. At the other end put the two middle boards on the other round (see illustration). Make one other round fifteen inches long, same size as the others. Put the two outside boards on it, forming two separate frames at the other end—so the two inside boards can turn on the round to which they are coupled.

Take two strips three inches wide, two feet and six inches long. Bore one inch hole two inches from the top end and put round broom stick thru it seventeen inches long. Fasten all the rounds by wedges or small wooden pins.

Stand the two strips last mentioned on the outside of the frame at the end they separate and make them fast so as to stand perpendicular. For bait stick take lathe or one-half inch board one inch wide. Bore hole as shown in cut (figure 6) cut notch (figure 2). For trigger any stick 18 inches long, ⅝ inch thick will do: tie string 2 inches from end and tie other end at figure 1, pass the short end under round from the outside (figure 3) and catch in notch in bait lath (figure 2), the other end bait at figure 4. Put weight at figure 5. Cover trap at figure 6 to keep animal from going in from back up to figure 7. For bait I use fresh fish, muskrat, bird, etc., and scent with honey or blood.

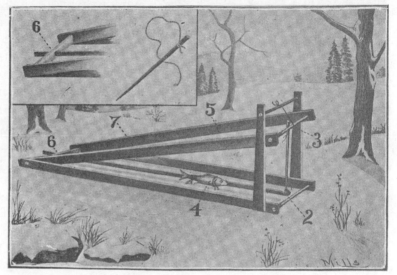

PORTABLE WOODEN TRAP.

THE BARREL TRAP

I promised in my last letter to describe the barrel trap, says a Northwestern trapper, which I use for capturing rats. Other trappers may have used this trap for years, but I only mean this for the young trappers who know nothing about this trap.

Take any kind of an old barrel made of hard wood (a salt barrel makes a good one), and fix a board on one side of the top with a hinge. Let one end of the barrel project out directly over the barrel to within about 5 or 6 inches of the other side. Arrange it so that the end of the board not over the barrel is a little the heaviest so when the rat tilts down the end in the barrel it will come back to place again·

Place a bit of parsnip apple, or celery near the end of the board over the barrel so when the rat reaches his front feet over on the board it will tilt down and let him in the barrel to stay. Bury the barrel near a river or creek to within about 2 or 3 inches of top of barrel, so there will be from 6 inches to 1 foot of water in the barrel. If there is much water in the barrel the most of the rats will be dead when von visit your traps. Several may be captured in one night in this kind of a trap.

BLOCK TRAP

Saw a small log in blocks from 4 to 6 inches long. Bore an inch hole through the center. Take nails and drive them so that they form a "muzzle" in one end and have the nails very sharp. Fasten your blocks with a piece of wire and put it in the runway or on a log or anywhere that a coon will see it, and nine out of ten will put his foot into it. I bait with honey. I caught 75 or 80 coons this season with "block" snares.

I put stoppers or false bottoms in one end of the block, piece of corn cob or anything will do. Cut the foot off to get the animal out of this snare.

The illustration shows a square block with the hole bored in the side. This is done to better show how it should be done, although when set the hole should be up. Bait with a piece of fresh rabbit, frog, or anything that coon are fond of.

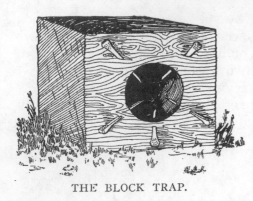

THE BLOCK TRAP.

Instead of the blocks the auger hole can be bored in a log or root of a tree if a suitable one can be found where coon frequent.

THE "NOXEMALL" DEADFALL

The best material is spruce, but if spruce is not to be had, hard wood is better than soft. Follow directions closely; never use old, dozy wood; good, sound, straight-grained material is the cheapest to use. A good way to get your material is to go to the saw-mill, select good straight-grained 2 × 4 studding, have them ripped lengthwise again, making four strips out of the original 2 × 4, each strip being two inches wide by one inch thick; then have them cut in the lengths—two standards (A), 14 inches long; (B) two side pieces, 2½ feet long; (C) two drop bars, 2½ feet. Bore a hole in each piece with a one inch bit, two inches from the end of the piece to the center of the hole. (D) A piece of lath about 8 inches long, with one end beveled off to fit in slot of E; tie a piece of small rope, about a foot long, two inches from the other end. (E) A piece of lath, 2½ feet long, with a slot cut crosswise two inches from one end and a piece of rope tied two inch from the other end, about a foot long.

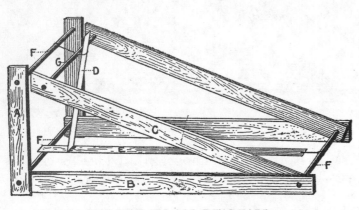

THE NOX-EM-ALL DEADFALL.

If you get your material at the mill have four rounds (F) turned out of oak or maple (must be hard wood), three of them being 12 inches long, one being 8 inches long, ⅞ inch in diameter. They must be some smaller than the hole, as they swell when wet.

Your trap is now ready to put together. Take one 12 inch round slip on the side pieces B first, then the two standards A; next place a 12 inch round in the holes in the top of the standards. The front end of the trap is done, except fastening the standards to the round and the setting apparatus to the top round of standards. Next take the remaining 12 inch round slip on the drop bars C first, then the side pieces B outside; next place the short round G in the front end of drop bar C.

You can drive nails thru the outside pieces and the round. Where there are two pieces on a side on one round, fasten thru the outside piece, always leaving the inside piece loose so that it will turn on the round. A much better way, altho it is more work, is to bore a hole thru the side piece and round and drive in a hard wood plug. This is the best way, because if any part of the trap breaks you can knock out the plug much easier than to pull out a nail. The holes should be bored with a ¼ inch bit.

Tie the rope attached to E to the rear round, leaving two inches play, between E and the round. Tie the rope attached to D to the top round of standards, leaving two inches play at top and two inches between lower end of D and bottom round.

First place a stone on the drop bar, weighing 20 pounds. Then raise the drop bar high enough so that you can place the short lath under the round of drop so that the weight rests on the rope. These is the secret of setting. The pressure on top forces the lower end to fly up. Now place the beveled end of the short lath in the slot of the long lath and the trap is set.

Hang your bait from the drop bars, under the weight, about eight inches from the front. The game will then come to the side of the trap. Never tie bait on the lath.

Set the trap in front of the hole, block up by setting up two stones V shape on the upper side of hole, forcing game thru the trap to enter or come out.

CHAPTER 14

Some Triggers

During my trapping experiences I remember of visiting an old trapper's deadfalls and at that time I had never seen or used any trigger other than the figure 4, but this trapper used the prop and spindle. I looked at several of his traps; in fact, went considerably out of my way to look at some eight or ten of them. Two of these contained game—a skunk and opossum. I had often heard of these triggers, but was skeptical about them being much good. I now saw that these triggers were all right and on visiting my traps again set a few of them with these triggers. Since that time I have never used the figure 4.

The prop and spindle I know will look to many too hard to "go off," but they can be set so that they will go off fairly easy. It is not necessary that the trap be set so that the least touch will make it go off. It is best to have the trap set so that mice nibbling at bait will not throw it.

Trappers who have never used the deadfall will, no doubt, find that after they use them a short time and become better acquainted with their construction and operation that they will catch more game than at first. This is only natural as all must learn from experience largely, whether at trapping or anything else.

The prop is a straight piece about seven inches long and about one-half inch in diameter. The spindle, or long trigger, is about the size of the prop, but should be sixteen or eighteen inches long with a prong cut off within two inches of the end to help hold the bait on more securely. See cut elsewhere showing these triggers and of the figure likewise. These illustrations will give a better idea of how the triggers are made to those who have never seen or used them.

I saw some time ago where a brother wanted to know how to make a deadfall, writes an Illinois trapper. I send a picture of one that I think is far ahead of any that I have seen in the H-T-T yet, that is, the triggers. I have seen deadfall triggers that would catch and not fall when the bait was pulled at, but there is no catch to these.

Trigger No. 1 is stub driven in the ground with, a notch cut in the upper end for end of bait. Stick No. 5 to fit in No. 3 is another stub driven in ground for bait stick No. 5 to rest on top. No. 3 is a slick, one end laid on top of bait stick outside of stub No. 2, the other end on top of lower pole. No. 4 is the prop stick. One end is set on stick No. 3 about one inch inside the lower pole the other end underneath the upper pole. The × represents the bait. When the bait stick is pulled out of notch in stub No. 1, the upper pole comes down and has got your animal.

If you find your bait is caught between the poles you may know the bait is not back in the box far enough If you find the trap down and bait and bait stick gone, you may know that the bait is too far back. The animal took his whole body in before he pulled the bait.

I have tried to describe this trap for the ones that don't know how to make a deadfall.

Somebody wants to know how to make a good deadfall. Well the plans published in back numbers of H-T-T are all right except the figure four sticks and bait. Make your sticks like this, and you will be pleased with the way they work, says an experienced trapper.

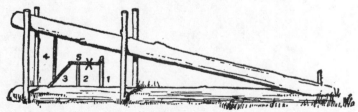

ILLINOIS TRAPPER'S TRIGGERS.

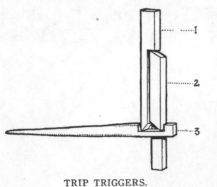

TRIP TRIGGERS.

No. 2 flat view. The trigger sets in the slanting cut in side of No. 2. Don't put bait on trigger. Put it in back end of pen and pin it to the ground. Turn trigger across opening slanted slightly in, then yon get them by neck or shoulders. The longer the slot in the trigger, the harder they will trip. Set as straight up as possible.

Make 1 and 2 of hard wood. Saw a block 3½ inches long and split into ¾ inch squares. Make cuts square with a saw and split out the part you don't want. Bevel ends with a hatchet. Make trigger of green hard wood stick with bark on.

I cut a tree from 8 to 10 inches in diameter and cut off 7 feet long. Split the piece open and bury one piece on a level with the earth—split side up— and place the other half on top. I hew off any bumps and make a perfect fit. Then I cut out bushes the size of my arm, and drive them down on each side of my fall and leave them an inch or two higher than I expect my top log to be when set. Be sure to begin far enough at the back to force the animals to go in at the front. I use the figure four triggers and tie the bait to the long trigger.

Another trigger is made as follows: Cut two forks and lay pole across just in front of the log on top of the forks. Take another piece of timber about four feet long, tie a string to each end and let one end have a trigger and the other be tied on your top log. I drive a nail in the top log and tie the string to it, and I call this my Fly trigger. It acts as a lever, for when the fly comes up over the piece on the forks and the trigger goes over half way back by the side of the log, and the trigger about a foot long—straight and thin, and sticks under the log—have a short trigger tied to the fly pole and a forked sapling the size of your finger and long enough to stick in the ground to hold the trigger. Put the bait on long trigger and catch the short trigger through the fork and let it catch the long trigger. This trigger leaves the fall open in front and is the one I prefer.

Take two small logs about 10 or 12 feet long, large enough to break a coon's back, and make a pen about midway, or one-third from front end, to put the bait in, and the trigger. Two foot boards, or saplings will do, and make the pen so that the animal will have to step across the bottom log and take the bait, and be sure to set so that the top log will fall across the mink, coon, skunk, or opossum, as tiny are the animals I kill with the fall. Use fly pole triggers as above, for this deadfall.

I make these falls near the runways of the animals I wish to catch. When I am sure to stay at a place, I build my falls in the summer and by the trapping time they look old and natural.

CHAPTER 15

Trip Triggers

The deadfall shown here can be used at dens or in paths where animals travel frequently. When set across the entrance of dens it will catch an animal going in without bait. That is, it will catch an animal going in without bait. That is, it will catch an animal going in, as the triggers are so constructed that they can only be pushed towards the bait as shown in illustration. If the trap is to be used at dens without bait the regular figure 4 triggers had best be used; but set extending along the log instead of back into the pen. An animal in entering will strike the trigger and down comes the fall.

The trap shown here and the triggers are made as follows: Cut two logs and lay one on the ground. This log should be at least·four feed long. Place it firmly on the ground with flat side up. This log need not be as flat as shown in illustration, but should be flattened slightly. Drive two stakes three feet long within a foot or so of one end (8) and (9).

Now come to the other end and drive two more (10) and (11). Stake ten which is directly opposite from (11) you want to be careful not to split, as one of the triggers rests on it. The fall is now placed in position, that is the upper log. The end of this is split and a stake driven in the ground so that the fall will not turn between the stakes but is held firmly. See that the fall will work easily up and down; that the stakes are not so close together that the fall binds, yet it wants to fit snugly.

ANIMAL ENTERING TRIP DEADFALL.

Cut trip stick (4) and trigger (3), lifting the fall up with one knee and place end of (3) onto (4) slightly, so that a small pressure on (4) will spring the trap. After you have the trap set spring it to see that it works all right. If the trap works all right and you are setting across the entrance of a den the pen of course is not wanted. If you are setting in paths or near dens, drive stakes in a semi-circle as shown in illustration, but the stakes should stick above the ground some eighteen inches or about as high as the "fall" pole when set. It is a good plan to throw leaves or grass on the stakes.

A small notch (5) should be cut in upright post (8) for trip stick to fit in to hold it up to that end. Be careful, however, that this notch is not cut too deep. The bait (6) is placed back in the pen and fastened with wire or a stake driven thru it into the ground. The open space over bait is now covered over and the entire trap can be made to not look so suspicious by cutting brush and throwing over it excepting in front of the bait. An animal in going in for bait steps on or pushes the long stick (marked 4 at one end and 5 at the other) off of (3) and is usually caught.

This is another good trip trigger deadfall. A short log should be laid on the ground and the two stakes driven opposite each other as in the trap just described. These stakes are not shown, as a better view of the triggers and workings of the trap can be had by omitting these.

In the illustration the "fall" pole is weighted, but it is best to have the pole heavy enough and not weighted. The stakes on which the upper or cross piece is nailed should be from twelve to eighteen inches apart. The cross piece need not be heavy, yet should be strong so that the weight of the fall will not bend it.

TRIP TRIGGER FALL.

The pens or enclosures used cannot be covered, as this would interfere with the workings of the triggers. If the pen is sixteen inches or higher very few animals will climb over to get bait, but will go in where the trapper wants and if properly made and set are apt to catch the game.

Along in the late seventies or beginning of the eighties, when a good sized muskrat would bring about as much as a common prime mink, and a steel trap was quite a prize to be in possession of. I had perhaps two dozen traps, some old fashioned, that would quite a curiosity at present, besides a few Newhouse No. 0 and 1.

That was in Ontario, Canada. Skunk, mink, coon, muskrat and fox were the furs in that part, Waterloo, Brant and Oxford Counties. Later I used this deadfall with success in Iowa and other sections, so that there is no doubt but that it will be found a good fur catcher in most localities.

I used to catch a great deal with deadfalls,— picture of which I here enclose. I have seen nearly all the different makes of deadfalls and have tried some of them, but the one I here send you the picture of, which can be easily understood, is the one I have had the most success with. I believe they are the best, and an animal can't get at the bait without striking it off, besides some animals will examine a bait without touching it. This deadfall, if they are curious enough just to enter inside and put their foot on the trigger stick, they are yours if the trap is set properly.

CANADIAN TRIP FALL.

This style of deadfall can be successfully used over skunk holes, game runways and there you do away with the bait yard. This style of trap is much easier made, as it requires very little skill. Just a few straight sticks about the size round of a came, a little twine. You can catch most any animal from a weasel to a raccoon. The illustration shows the "fall" or upper pole weighted. In our experience we have found it more satisfactory to have the "fall" heavy enough to kill the animal without the weight. It is often hard for the trapper to find a pole of the right size and weight for the "fall"' and the next best way is to place additional weight as shown.

First make a pen in the form of a wigwam, driving stakes well into the ground to keep the animal away from the rear of the trap. It should be open on one side. Place a short log in front of the opening and at both ends of this drive stakes to hold it in place and for the long log to work up and down in. The top log should be six or eight feet long, according to size of animal you aim to use trap for, and about the same size as the bottom log. Cut a forked stick about 12 inches long for the bait stick, notching one end and tapering the other as shown in Fig. No. 2. A stick 24 inches long should then be cut and flattened at both ends.

To set the trap, raise one end of the upper log and stick one end of the flattened stick under it, resting it upon the top of the stake on the outside of the log. Place the bait stick, point downward, inside the pen upon a chip of wood or rock to keep it from sinking into the ground and set flat stick in the notch. When the animal pulls at the bait it turns the bait stake and throws the cross piece out of the notch of the bait stick and let the top log fall.

THE TURN TRIGGER.

CHAPTER 16

How to Set

In explaining size pen some make them 2 feet long, writes a New York trapper, while one 12 inches long (as used on this trail), is sufficient; not only that, but it is superior for the following reasons: A 2 foot pen would let the animal pass inside and beyond the drop when sprung, unless the animal stepped on the treadle.

The Indians' trap is made by cutting a sapling 3 or 4 inches in diameter off the butt end cut a piece 2 foot and place on the ground for a bed piece; drive four stakes, two on either side of bed piece, leaving a space between of 12 inches, using the balance of pole for the drop to play between the stakes. For balance of pen a few stakes, bark or slabs cut from a tree.

For a spindle, cut from a hemlock, spruce or other dry limb a piece eight or ten inches long, sharpen one end to a point, the other end flatten a trifle for an inch or two on the underside, so that when placed on the bed piece it will lay steady. Now with a sharp knife, commence ½ inch back, and round off top side of spindle on which to place a standard four inches in length, cut from same material as spindle.

In setting, place the bait on the spindle so as to leave a space of only six inches from bait to the standard; now take spindle in left hand, standard in right hand, kneel down, raise the drop placing one knee under it to hold it up the right height. Lay spindle onto center of bed piece and place the standard on top of spindle, letting drop rest on top of standard so as to keep the pieces in position. Now by moving the standard out or in on the spindle, the spring of the trap can be so ganged that it will set safely for weeks or months, sprung easily, and hold anything from a weasel to a raccoon.

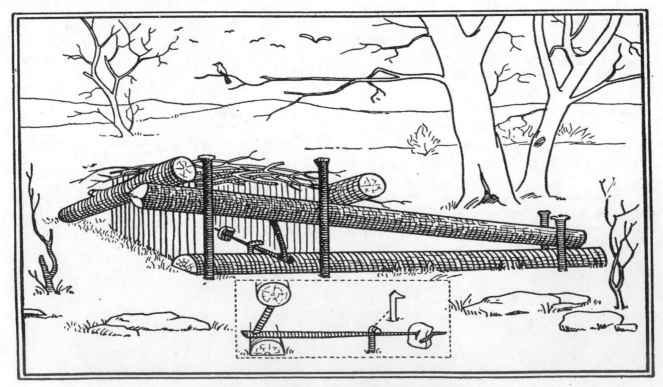

TWO PIECE TRIGGER TRAP.

It is sure, as it kills immediately, giving them no chance to escape by twisting or gnawing off their legs. It is not so quickly made and set as a steel trap, and never gives "Sneakums" inducements to approach it for future use. After the trap is set, place bark or something suitable between the stakes above the drop and cover top of pen so as to compel the animal to enter in front, and at the same time ward off snow and sleet from interfering with its workings. Weight the drop pole on either side of pen by placing on chunks of wood or stone.

There are several ways to set deadfalls, as different triggers are used. The manner in constructing these traps is varied somewhat in the different sections. The illustration shown here is of a trap that is used to a considerable extent in all parts of America. The trapper for marten in the far North, the opossum trapper of West Virginia, Kentucky and Missouri, the skunk trapper of the New England States and the mink trapper of the West have all used this trap with success. It is for the hundreds of young and inexperienced trappers that the deadfall is shown here.

The trigger as shown, that is the one extending back into the pen, is all one piece. This trigger is usually cut from a bush and often requires some time to find one suited. If you intend to build a few traps of this kind it is well to be on the lookout in advance for suitable triggers. This trap is set with only two triggers, the one with the straight part extending back into the pen and the prong on which the "fall" is resting and the other trigger is driven into the ground so that it is only a little higher than the under log of the trap.

This trap can be set with the triggers known as figure 4 if preferred. Coon, mink, opossum, skunk and marten are usually not hard to catch in deadfalls, although now and then an animal for some reason is extremely hard to catch.

In building deadfalls it is best to split the end of the pole fartherest from the pen or bait and drive the stake there. This will hold the upper or "fall" pole solid, so that there will be no danger of its turning of its own weight and falling.

STRING AND TRIGGER TRAP.

I enclose plan and description of a deadfall I have used with success on skunk and other fur animals, writes a trapper from New York State. Never having seen anything like it described I thought it might be a help to those using these traps. During November and December, 1897, I caught 11 skunk in one deadfall like this one.

Stakes are driven in the ground to form the pen same as on figure 4 or other deadfall, but no brush or sticks should be laid on top of pen as it would prevent the vertical stick from lifting up. A small log or board with stones on may be laid on pole for more weight. The pole may be from ten to fifteen feet long and about three inches in diameter. XX 18 inches or more out of the ground and one-half inch in diameter; B 20 inches, × one-half inch; C about 16 × ¾ inches; D 20 × ¾ inches; E same as AA only not crotch; F ¼ inch. Rope long enough to go around pole and over B and tie around C. D should be from 1 to 3 inches above ground according, to what is being trapped. Bait should be laid on ground or fastened to stake near middle of pen.

CHAPTER 17

When to Build

If you have determined upon your trapping ground it is best to build your traps in advance of the trapping season, so that they will become old and weather beaten. This, of course, is not necessary as traps are often built, baited and on the return of the trapper the following morning game securely caught. While the above is often true, deadfalls can and should be built in advance of the trapping season. There are at least two reasons for this: first, it allows the traps to become weather beaten and game is not so suspicious; second, all the trapper has to do when the trapping season arrives is to visit and set his traps.

Some object to deadfalls on the ground that they require lots of work to build and that a trapper's time is valuable at this season of the year. Such may be true of the amateur, but the professional trapper usually has much idle time in August, September and early October, when he is glad to look out for trapping grounds for the coming winter. It is a day's work for one man to build from eight to twelve deadfalls, depending of course upon how convenient he finds the pole to make the fall. The other material is usually not hard to find or make. That is stakes, chunks and rocks. If you only build six or eight traps and construct them right they are worth twice as many poorly built. When properly built they will last for years, requiring but little mending each fall at the opening of the trapping season. Taken all in all we do not know that a certain number of deadfalls take up any more time than an equal number of steel traps. In fact more deadfalls can be set in a day, after they are built, than steel traps.

When it is stated that you will perhaps do as well at home as elsewhere, this, of course, depends upon where you are located, how many trappers there are in your section, etc. If there is but little to be caught then you had best go elsewhere, but trappers have been known in thickly settled sections to catch from $50 to $300 worth of fur in a season, lasting from November 1 to March 15. Of course in the far north, where trapping can be carried on from October 15 to June 15, or eight months, the catch is much larger, and as the animals caught are more valuable, the catch of a single trapper is sometimes as high as $600 to $1,000.

The trapper who stays near home has the advantage of knowing the territory. If he was to visit a strange section, although a good trapping locality, he would not do so well as if he were acquainted with the locality and knew the locations of the best dens. Then again his expenses are heavier if he goes into a strange section, yet if there is but little game near your home, and you are going to make a business of trapping, go and look up a good trapping section. Under these conditions it best for two or three to go together. There is no necessity of carrying but little baggage other than your gun, for at the season of the year that prospecting is done there is but little difficulty in killing enough game to live on.

After you have once found a good trapping section, and built your cabin, deadfalls and snares, you can go there fall after fall with your line of steel traps, resetting your deadfalls with but little repairs for years. You will also become better acquainted with the territory each season and will make larger catches. Do not think that you have caught all the game the first season, for generally upon your return the next fall you will find signs of game as numerous as ever.

In locating new trapping grounds, if two or three are together and it is a busy time in September, let one of the party go in advance prospecting. This will save much valuable, time when you make the start for the fall and winter trapping campaign. It will pay you to know where you are going before you make the final start.

CHAPTER 18

Where to Build

In determining where to set deadfalls or locate snares if you will keep in mind the dens where each winter you have caught fur-bearing animals, or their tracks have often been seen in the snow or mud, and build your traps and construct snares at or near such places you are pretty sure to not go astray.

The location, of course, depends largely upon what kind of game you are trying to catch. If mink or coon, there is no better place than along streams where there are dens. If there should be a small branch leading off from the main stream, at the mouth of this is often an excellent place to locate a trap. It should not be too near the water as a rise would damage or perhaps float off at least part of your trap. Sometimes farther up this small stream there are bluffs and rocks; at such places, if there are dens, is just the place to build deadfalls. If there are several dens, and the bluff extends along several hundred feet, it perhaps will pay to build two or three traps here.

In cleared fields, woods or thickets skunk are found anywhere that there are dens you can construct a trap. While, as a rule, the thinly settled districts are the best trapping sections, yet skunk, muskrat and red fox are found in greatest numbers in settled sections, while opossum, raccoon and mink are found in fairly well settled districts. It is therefore not necessary that you should go to the wilderness to make fairly good catches. While the trapper in the wilderness has the advantage of no one disturbing his deadfalls, yet he has disadvantages. The trapper who means business need not go hundreds of miles away, but if he will build a line of traps along some stream where there are mink, or in the thickets and along rocky buffs for skunk, raccoon, opossum, etc., he will be surprised at results.

In some sections land owners may not allow trapping, but usually they will, especially if you take the pains to ask before you commence building or setting your traps.

The fact that you have your traps scattered over a large territory gives you better chances of making good catches, for most animals travel quite a distance from night to night. You may have traps at some stream that is eight or ten miles from your home and a mink may come along that does most of its seeking for food miles farther up or down this stream, nearer, perhaps, where it was raised, and you get him. Thus you see by going only ten miles away you may catch animals that really live twenty. Just how far a mink may travel up or down a creek or river I do not know, but it is certain that they go many miles and traps may make a catch of a mink that lives many, many miles away. Of course along small streams they may not go so far. Often, however, they continue their travels from one stream to another.

If you are an expert trapper you can very easily detect, if you are in a good, locality, especially if in the fall—September and October. These are the two months when the most prospecting is done. Going along streams at this season tracks are plainly seen and in the forests at dens signs, such as hair, bones and dung. Often you will come upon signs where some bird has been devoured and you know that some animal has been in the locality. Old trappers readily detect all these signs and new ones can learn by experience.

It is not absolutely necessary to build traps at or near dens. Some years ago, I remember when doing considerable trapping in Southern Ohio, I came upon a deadfall built near a small stream that ran thru a woods. I looked around for dens, but saw none. Why this trap had been built there was a puzzle to me. One day I happened upon the owner of the trap and asked him what he expected to catch in that trap.

In reply he pointed to a bush some rods distant in which hung the carcasses of two opossum and one coon—caught in the trap. While there were no dens near, it was a favorite place for animals to cross or else they came there for water. This same trap was the means of this old trapper taking two or three animals each winter, while other traps at dens near caught less. There is much in knowing where to set traps, but keep your eyes open for signs and you will learn where to build traps and set snares sooner or later.

Yes, boys, the deadfall is a splendid trap if made right, says an Arkansas trapper. I will tell you how to make one that will catch every mink and coon that runs the creek. Take a pole four feet long and four inches through, next get a log six inches through and eight feet long. Use eight stakes and two switches. Use the figure four trigger, but the notches are cut different. Both of the notches are cut on the top side of the long trigger and a notch cut in the upright trigger and down the long trigger. The paddle part is sixteen inches long. When the trap is set the paddle wants to be level and one-half inch higher than small logs, then your two switches comes in this to keep the paddle from hitting the bark on side logs.

TRAIL OR DEN TRAP.

Next is where to set. If along a creek, find a place where the water is within three feet of the bank, set your trap up and down the creek at edge of water, dam up from back end of paddle to bank with brush or briars, then from front end into water three or four feet. You will find the upright trigger has to be a good deal longer than the notch trigger. You can use round triggers if you want to by nailing a shingle five inches wide on the long trigger stick. Be sure and have your paddle muddy if setting along creeks. You want to put a little stone back beyond paddle, so when the trap falls it will not burst paddle. Now you have a trap easy made and sure to catch airy animal that steps on paddle, which is five inches wide and sixteen long. You don't need any bait, but you can use bait by throwing it under paddle. This trap is hard to beat for small game.

I make a deadfall that sets without bait, writes an Illinois trapper. It is made like any other only different triggers. Set it across path, over or in front of den or remove a rail and set it in the corner of a fence where game goes thru. Use thread in dry weather, fine wire for wet. Two logs for bottom is bettor than one, make triggers high enough to suit the animal you wish to catch; if he hits the string or wire he is yours.

CHAPTER 19

The Proper Bait

Bait is sometimes difficult to get, but usually the trapper will get enough with his gun and steel traps to keep his line of deadfalls well baited, without difficulty. In trapping, all animals caught after the pelt is taken off should be hung up so that other animals cannot reach them, but will visit your traps.

There are two objects in hanging up bait: First, other animals coming along are apt to eat them and not visit your deadfall; second, should you run out of bait you can cut a piece from the animal hanging up, bait your trap and go to the next. While bait of this kind is not recommended, sometimes it comes to this or nothing. Fresh bait is what is wanted at all times, yet the trapper cannot always get what he knows is best and consequently must do the next best. Perhaps by his next visit he has bait in abundance.

The writer has known trappers to use a piece of skunk, opossum, muskrat, coon, etc., that, had been caught some weeks before and hung up in a sapling where it froze and on the next visit the trap baited with skunk contained a skunk. This shows that when an animal is very hungry it is not very particular what it eats.

In the early fall while food of all kinds is easy to find, any animal is harder to entice to bait and at this season bait should be fresh if the trapper expects to make profitable catches. The trapper should always carry a gun, pistol or good revolver with which to help kill game to supply bait for his traps. Steel traps set along the line will also help to keep the supply of bait up at all times. If yon are successful in securing a great deal of bait, more than will be used on that round, you will find it an excellent idea to leave some at certain places where it can be secured on the next round should it be needed.

Bait may consist of any tough bit of meat; but rabbit is an excellent bait. Quail or almost any bird is good. Chicken also makes good bait. Squirrel is all right. For mink, fish is excellent. Mice, frogs and muskrat can all be used. Remember that the fresher and bloodier the bait the better—animals will scent it much quicker. They are also fonder of fresh bait than that which has been killed for days or weeks as the case may be.

In baiting it is important to see that the bait is on secure. It is a good idea to tie it on with strong thread or small cord. The amount of bait to put on a single trap is not so important. Most trappers use a rabbit in baiting ten traps or less; the head makes bait for one trap, each foreleg another, the back about three and each hind leg one, although each hind leg can be cut to make bait for two traps.

The spindle or trigger is run thru the bait and should be fastened on trigger near the end as shown in illustration elsewhere. The securing of bait on the trigger is an important thing. If it is not on securely and the trap is hard to get off, the animal may devour bait and the trap not fall. If the trigger is only sticking loosely in the bait, it is easy for an animal to steal the bait. Usually the observing trapper knows these things and are on their guard, but for those who are using deadfalls this season for the first time, more explicit explanation is necessary.

The bait should extend back into the pen about a foot and the pen should be so constructed that the bait touches nowhere only on the trigger. The animal in eating the bait usually stands with its fore feet upon the under pole, or just over it. In this condition it can readily be seen, that if its gnawing at the bait twists the trigger off the upright prop what the consequences will be—the animal will be caught across the back. An animal standing in the position just described will naturally pull down somewhat on the bait and in its eagerness to get the bait pulls and twists the spindle, or trigger, off the upright prop.

It is a good idea to try the trigger. That is, place the triggers under the fall just the same as you would if they were baited and you were going to set the trap. By doing this you will find out about how you want to set the triggers so that they will work properly. There is much in being acquainted with the working of traps. Study them carefully and you will soon learn to be a successful trapper.

CHAPTER 20

Traps Knocked Off

If you find that your traps are "down" each time you visit them and the bait gone, the pen is perhaps too large and the animal, if a small one like a mink, is going inside to devour bait. Animals usually stand with fore feet upon lower log and reach into pen after bait, but at times they have been known to go inside. In this case the animal is not in danger as when the "fall" comes down the animal is not under it. If such is the case, that is, the animal entirely inside the pen, the trigger will be caught under the fall and the trapper knows that whatever is molesting his trap is doing so from the inside. All that the trapper has to do is lessen the size of the pen. This can be done by placing small stones or chunks on the inside of the pen or by driving stakes on the inside. By doing this the outside appearance is not changed.

If, on the other hand, the trigger, that is the long one or spindle, not the short prop, is pulled out each time and often carried several feet, the trap is set too hard to "fall" and should be set easier. If the prop, or upright piece, is cut square across the top, take your knife and round off the edges so that the trigger will slip off easier. Again the pen may be torn down and the animal takes bait from the rear. Here is where it pays to build traps substantial. In such cases rebuild the pen, making it stronger. Should it be torn down on subsequent visits, the game is perhaps a fox. Of course if the pen has been torn down by some trapper or passing hunter, you can readily detect same by the manner in which it has been done. If the trapper is satisfied that it is an animal that is doing the mischief, he wants to plan carefully, and if he is an expert trapper, a steel trap or two will come into good play and the animal will be caught in the steel trap. The pen will not be torn down again.

When traps are down note carefully the condition that they are in; see that the "fair" fits on the lower pole closely, and by the way, when building this is an important thing to notice—that the fall fits snugly on the lower or under pole.

If a snare or spring pole is up but nothing caught, simply reset. Should many snares be up "thrown" and no catches, the trouble should be located at once. The noose is probably too large or small or made of limber or too stiff string or wire, or maybe it is too securely fastened. When resetting, note all these carefully and experience will sooner or later enable you to set .just right to make a catch. If a certain snare is bothered continually, it will do no harm to set a steel trap where you think chances best of taking the animal. It matters but little to the trapper how the animal is caught, as it is his pelt that is wanted.

In using the trip triggers with or without bait, the trapper should fasten the bait by either driving a peg through it and into the ground or tieing.

In most instances the animal will throw the trap before getting to the bait, but it is well to take this precaution in case, for any reason, the animal should not step on the trip trigger at first.

Sometimes a small animal may jump over the trip trigger in order to get the bait and in its endeavor to get bait will strike the trigger. The animal does not know that the trigger is dangerous, but now and then either steps or jumps over. Generally they step on the trigger, for if the trapper is "onto his job" the bait and trigger are so placed that the animal thinks the trip trigger is the place to put his foot.

In using without bait the trigger is so arranged that the animal rubs or steps on the trigger when entering or leaving the pen or if at a trail or runway when passing along.

CHAPTER 21

Other Traps

TREADLE TRAP FOR SMALL ANIMALS

This will be found a most excellent trap. It should be made of the commonest outside boards of pine, and be stained, not painted, so that it may not be at all conspicuous. Fig. 1 is the floor of the trap, twenty-two inches long, fourteen inches wide, and three-quarters inch thick. It must be made in two pieces, so as to admit of the treadle or trigger being screwed onto the edge of one of the boards, which must then be nailed together with two battens two inches wide, and half an inch thick. A strip is cut out six inches long and half an inch wide at a, and the heel of the trigger works in the opening, and is screwed through the hole at *f* (*see Fig*. 4,) onto the edge at *a* (*see Fig*. 1). Fig. 2 is the lid, which should be made solid or in two pieces like Fig. 1, but two inches shorter; *b* is a staple to receive the end of the lever; *c* is a hole to allow the iron stanchion (*Fig.* 3) to pass through without grazing; *d* is a hole three inches in diameter, with its centre four and a half inches from the hinge end of the lid. An oblong

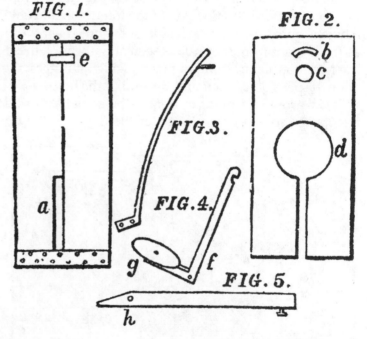

piece is cut out from this hole to the hinge end half an inch wide, so as to allow the neck of the trigger to work freely. The hinges may be made of pieces of old stirrup leather.

Fig. 3 is an iron stanchion made of half-inch round iron, flattened at the foot, and having two holes for screws. It must be bent to a radius of fifteen inches. Half an inch from the other end it must have a pin riveted in, about the thickness of a quill, standing out at right angles, and about three-quarters of an inch long. The stanchion is screwed onto the floor at *e*.

Fig. 4 is the trigger and plate. From notch to *f* is four and half inches; from *f* to *g*, three inches. The plate is a piece of round sheet iron, three and a half inches in diameter, with a hole in it, to be riveted to the trigger.

Fig. 5 is a wooden, lever three-quarters of an inch wide and half an inch thick, to reach from the top of the trigger, when set, to the staple, *b* in Fig. 2. Two inches from the end, as at *h*, is a hole to receive the pin in the top of the stanchion, and at the other end a lath-nail to catch the notch in Fig. 4.

Fig. 6 is the trap when set.

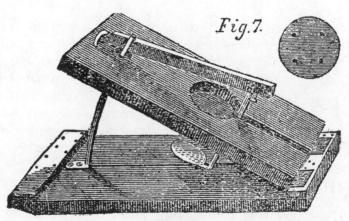

FIG. 6.

Fig. 7 is a round piece of sheet iron four inches in diameter, with four holes punched in to tie the hait on. To set the trap, put the lever on to the iron stanchion, raise the lid till the end of the lever catches under the staple, press the other end down, and let the nail catch the notch in the top of the trigger, and weight the lid with stories. Having tied the bait on Fig. 7, merely place it on the hole *d*, with the bait downwards, but not too low. The animal reaching up to smell at it, lets the trap off by setting its feet on the trigger plate, and is crushed by the falling lid.

THE HARROW TRAP

A trap, useful for its catch-and-hold-fast qualities, combined with simplicity of action, furnishes the subject for the accompanying illustration; a description of the latter will be the best guide for the construction of the trap.

The exterior portion consists of an oblong box without lid, from which one end has been taken out, and rather deeper than it is wide. The box shown in the engraving has been temporarily deprived of one of its sides in order to afford a plain view of the interior arrangements. A false bottom, A, is made to fit loosely in the box; a hole is bored through each side of the box, near the end and as far above the inside level of the true bottom as it is distant from the end, as seen at *E*; through these holes pieces of stout wire are driven into the edges of the false bottom, forming pivots on which it hinges, the false bottom having first been so adjusted as to leave an inch space between it and the end of the box.

Next provide a piece of board, the same width as the inside of the box, and long enough to reach, in a sloping direction, two-thirds of the depth of the box; through the board drive nails or pointed wires to project like the teeth of a harrow. Lift the bottom up till the end touched the lid; in this position use the upper side of the bottom as ruler to mark a line on the inside of each side of the box; fasten the harrow permanently, in a position parallel to and about an inch distant from the ruled lines. One end of a strong spiral spring, *D.* is attached to the side of the box, the other end being secured to the upper side of the movable bottom. This spring must be arranged so as not to interfere with the harrow when the bottom is raised up. In its present state the bottom would always remain elevated; to keep it down in its place a catch, *B* is fastened by a staple to the inside of the box. The catch consists of a piece of wire, stout, enough to remain in shape when in use., and bent in the manner shown in Fig. 2, the upper branch being employed for holding the bait: the lower end being bent at right angles to catch underneath the end of the movable bottom and sustain it in a horizontal position. It will be seen that a very slight pull on the bait, will set the catch free, but have a very opposite effect on any animal that may be on the platform, which is instantly drawn up by the spring against the spikes above, helplessly impaling the rash but unfortunate intruder.

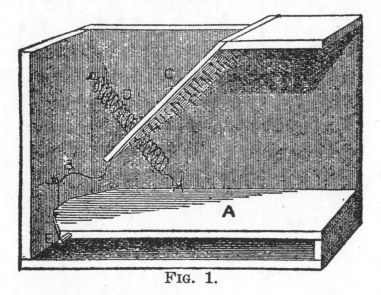

FIG. 1.

The size of the trap and the strength on the materials should be adapted to the purpose for which it is intended. This is a very effective trap, and lias only one objection, common to all traps which catch and hold fast—that of cruelty to the animal caught

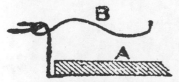

THE BOX PIT-FALL

The advantages of this trap consist in its simplicity of construction, its never missing, and the fact of its always keeping itself set for use.

It consists of a box without any lid, a foot square, and eighteen inches deep, or the deeper the better. Procure a sheet of tin just large enough to fit easily inside the box; scratch a straight line, *a*, Fig. 1. exactly across the centre, and terminating in the middle points of two opposite sides; at each end of the line solder a loop of tin as seen at *b*, Fig. 2; over the middle of the line, and at right angles across it, solder or rivet a strip of tin in the form of a loop, extending an inch and a half on each side of the line, and bagging or arching out about two inches. In the centre of the loop, bore a hole, through which pass a string with a weight attached, to hang down three or four inches, as seen at *a*, in Fig. 2. The weight must be just enough to serve as a counterpoise to keep the tin in a horizontal position. The tin is then fastened inside the box, so as to form a platform about three inches below the top edge of the box. This is done by driving two pieces of stout wire, one through each side of the box, so as to pass through the small loops which were soldered onto the edges of the tin: these pivots form the only support of the tin platform, which swings freely on them, the weight of a small mouse jumping onto it being sufficient to tilt the platform, and let the mouse drop down into the box.

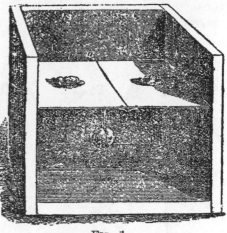

FIG. 1.

As soon as the tin is relieved of the weight of the mouse, the counterpoise brings it again to a level position. The bait is placed on each side of the tin, and fastened by a string passing through holes in the tin made for that purpose. Without this precaution the bait would fall off the first time it was disturbed. The box should be sunk into the ground with its tipper edges level with the surface, in a favorable location, and may be made a permanent

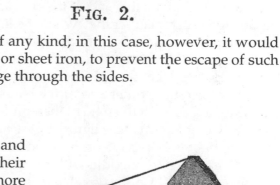

FIG. 2.

institution in barns or other places infested with small vermin of any kind; in this case, however, it would perhaps be advisable to line the lower portion of the box with tin or sheet iron, to prevent the escape of such animals as have enterprise and teeth enough to work their passage through the sides.

THE RABBIT TRAP

There is one -great disadvantage in some of the most ingenious and successful traps, which is that they are frequently so intricate in their details, that they are by no means easy to construct, and still more difficult to describe with any degree of accuracy or precision. The old fashioned rabbit trap is very free from any drawback of this nature, and the rabbit who mistakes its interior for a private dining-room, will also find that there is no draw-back at all in it worth mentioning.

Although this trap derives its name form being the one usually employed of rabbits, there are very few animals that this trap will not catch, provided they are not very small. The construction of the box which forms the trap is the first thing to be explained; the material had better be tolerably hard wood, about three-quarters inch in thickness, and properly seasoned to prevent shrinking. The two side-pieces of the box should each be twenty-on inches long and nine inches wide;

FIG. 1.

the bottom is the same length as the side-pieces, and seven inches wide; the end-piece for the back of the trap is eighteen inches high and seven inches wide, the upper part beveled almost to a point; this form is not absolutely necessary but gives a neater appearance to the trap. Nail the side-pieces against the edges of the bottom; set the back-piece upright in the end, and nail it fast through the sides and bottom. The movable lid consists of two parts; the lid itself twenty inches long and seven inches wide, and the end-piece eight and a quarter inches long and seven wide; nail the end of the lid onto the top edge of the end-piece, and plane off the edges of the lid and flap, to allow the whole to work freely inside the box.

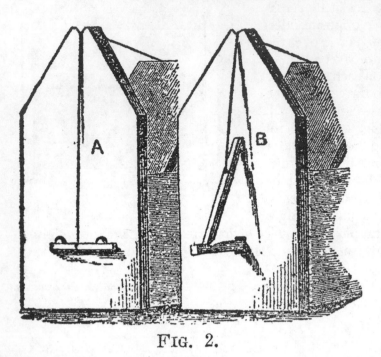

FIG. 2.

Bore a hole through each of the side-pieces, four inches from the tall end, and three-eighths of an inch from the upper edge. Through each of these holes drive a piece of stout wire (two inches long., pointed at one end), one into each edge on the lid; these serve for hinges on which the lid works. This completes the box part of the trap. To make it effective, first bore a hole through the tall end- piece., four inches above the bottom, and two and a half inches from the right side of the box, making the hole just large enough to admit freely a round stick of wood, about the thickness of an ordinary lead pencil, this last to be four inches long, to be used as a bait-stick: provide another strip of wood for a string-piece, six inches long, and somewhat thicker than the bait-stick; next fasten the end of a piece of strong cord (whip-cord, for instance), to the middle point of the extreme edge of the lid; cut a nick in the top point of the tail end-piece, pass the string over the nick, and down the back of the end-piece (as seen at *A*, Fig. 2); tie this end of the cord to the string-piece, two inches from its end, adjusting the length of the string in such manner that, when the lid of the box is down, the string-piece to which the cord is attached will hang down on the back of the end-piece ten inches above the bottom of the box.

At a point on the back, two inches distant from the left side and four inches above the bottom, drive in a nail or screw, so that the head will project, say half and inch. To set the trap, put the bait on the end of the bait-stick, insert the other end of the bait-stick from inside the box, into the hole, allowing it to project outside the back about half an inch; then pull the string-piece down, slip the shorter end under the nail, and let the other longer end catch slightly but securely underneath the projecting end of the bait-stick. The lid of the trap will be found to have been raised six inches, affording free ingress to any animals passing by; the first one that ventures to meddle with the bait will set the string-piece free, down comes the lid, enclosing the prisoner effectually in the box. There is another plan for setting the trap, as shown at *B, Fig.* 2: in this case the bait-stick needs to be eight inches long, with a notch cut near the near the end, and made to project four inches outside the ends, is secured, the long end in the notch on the bait-stick, the other short end in nick cut in the side of the box, directly above. This last mentioned method is inferior to the plan first described; as, from the nature of the arrangements, the bait-stick is held too firmly, and is apt to allow of considerable interference with the bait before the parts become set free. As an additional improvement, a stout piece of glass might be inserted in a corresponding aperture cut in the middle of the lid; not for the benefit of the captured animal, but to allow of the animal being seen before opening the trap. As the comfort of the animal has been alluded to, a few small auger holes bored in the sides of the box, high up, will afford a supply of fresh air, and make its captivity less harassing.

THE COOP TRAP

A trap, capable of catching any bird that feels itself growing thinner for want of a dinner, can be made with the exercise of a little ingenuity and an ordinary coop.

There is at least one great advantage in the use of this kind of trap: it is very effective in catching the bird, and also furnishes it, when caught, with a safe and airy enclosure, in which it can enjoy a fair meal without fear of intrusion or interruption, and where it can chuckle at the disappointment of the other poor birds shut out from like privileges.

Supposing a coop to be ready at hand, procure a thin strip of rattan, or a flexible piece of willow; its length should be such that, when bent into a semi-circular arch, the height of the arch will be a little more than half the diameter of the coop. Through each end of the rattan, burn a hole with a piece of hot wire; nail the ends onto the inner edge of one side of the coop in such position that all parts of the curved rattan are well inside the opening of the coop; also using nails that fit loosely through the holes, and allow the rattan some freedom of motion; next get a straight stick, B, with a fork at one end, and long enough, exclusive of the fork, to support one side of the coop when tilted up at an angle of about thirty degrees; another one end, as shown at C.

The straight part of this stick should be one inch less than the straight part of the forked stick, B. To set the trap, raise up one side of the coop to the height of the fork of the stick, B; insert the crook of C through the fork and underneath the edge of the coop, forming a catch on which the side of the coop rests; press the lower end of C back, inside the rattan hoop, and lift the latter from the ground just high enough to catch and hold the end of the stick, C. Lastly, strew some appropriate bait on the ground inside the hoop. An examination of the engraving will show plainly that when a bird hops onto the rattan, the suspended Hoop will fall to the ground, releasing the end of the stick C the coop, thus deprived of its only support, will immediately fall and enclose the bird.

In case it should be desired to make a coop trap, and there is no coop readily to be obtained, a good substitute can be arranged without much trouble. The engraving here given represents a coop trap made with one of these substitutes, and this is the way to set about it: Nail four pieces of wood together to form a square frame; at each corner fasten firmly a piece of strong cord about three feet long, lay the frame on the ground with the cords gathered inside it. Next collect a sufficient number of sticks or twigs, as nearly the same thickness as possible, and as long as the side of the frame; commence by laying two sticks, one along each of two opposite sides of the frame, across their ends lay two more sticks, forming a square with the first two; across the ends of the last two place two more parallel with the first two, but not quite so far asunder; continue alternate layers of two sticks each, laid gradually closer together, causing the enclosed space to assume the shape of a square pyramid. When near the top, reach inside with the arm, and draw the cords up carefully so that one of the cords will lay along each inside corner of the pyramid. Holding the four ends together loosely over the top opening, continue the building of the sides until the opening is only four or five inches square. Then get a square piece of inch board a trifle larger than the aperture; bore a hole in the middle, large enough to hold the four cords easily; draw the ends of the cords through the hole, lay the board with its cross-grain ends across the top pair of sticks; draw the cords and tie them possible over a peg of hard wood four inches long. By means of the peg, the cords can be further tightened by twisting them, If they should at any time become slackened, the peg being secured behind a nail driven in the board, to prevent untwisting. Lastly, trim off the projecting ends of the sticks, and the result will be a firmly constructed that can be used as a trap or for any other purposes to which a regular coop may be applied.

THE SIEVE TRAP

This is one of the traps that involves more patience in its use than ingenuity in its construction. It consists of a sieve tilted up on its edge, and kept in that position by a thin stick or rod of the length requisite for

the purpose, depending entirely on the size of the sieve. Strew bread-crumbs, seed, or any appropriate bait underneath the sieve; tie a thin twine to the middle of the stick; and retire to a convenient place out of sight with the other end of the twine.

This is the time when patience comes into requisition; a bird is sure to get under the sieve some time or other, when by a pull on the string the sieve falls down, covering up the bird, and patience is rewarded—more or less, according to the kind of bird caught.

THE BRICK TRAP

The trap just described is undoubtedly a very old one, but there are no means of finding out the exact era in which it was first employed.

There is another device for catching birds, that has probably existed ever since the invention of bricks; and as there is ample evidence that some of the Egyptians, who lived no end of years B. C., were wholesale manufacturers of bricks, it is fair to conclude that it may, possibly at least, be of Egyptian origin.

This view is further corroborated by the frequent recurrence of a three-pronged sign, very similar in appearance to the trigger of the Brick-Trap, in the Egyptian inscriptions, still extant, written in the "hiero-glyphics of the period." Be this as it may, there is no doubt of its excellence for trapping small birds, as it has stood the test more than long enough to establish the fact.

The necessary articles for its construction are first, three bricks; next a fiat slab of stone, wood, or other material obtainable; in default of all these, another brick will answer the purpose almost as well, except that, on account of its weight, the trap is perhaps less easily sprung.

Drive into the ground a peg standing three inches high, its top being trimmed so as to leave a very small flat surface; procure a small twig with two forks branching out, one on each side; cut the twig and forks equally about three inches long, leaving a short butt half an inch long at the junc-tion of the forks, and cut the sides of the butt flat above and below The front brick is laid on its edge one inch in front of the peg; the two other bricks are then placed, also on edge, parallel to one another, so as to enclose a space behind the front brick, the width of the space being just the width of the flat stone or lid. Then lay one end of the flat stone on the ground, between the side bricks, the front end just resting on the inner edge of the front brick. To set the trap, lift up the front end of the lid; lay the flat butt end of the twig on the top of the peg, the prongs point-ing backwards over the enclosure; on the top of the butt, place upright another straight piece of twig, just long enough to support the lid in such a position as to admit a bird easily into the interior of the trap. The adjustment of the parts is given in an illustration, *a*, showing the peg, &c., without the bricks. Strew some breadcrumbs or seeds inside the trap, and as soon as a bird, attracted by the bait, hops onto the edge of the trap, and thence onto the forked branches of the trigger, its weight will throw the upright twig off the top of the peg, and the lid falls down, enclosing the bird in the trap.

THE CROW TRAP

The contrivance used for this purpose has about the same claim to be termed a trap, as the addition of a French roof would have to be called building a house. It is, fact, a method of ornamenting a bird, and by its own voluntary act, with a roof which completely covers its head, and sticks to it closer than a mutual friend. It is peculiarly adapted for young crows just beginning to forage on their own account. These birds are, from their extreme youth upwards, exceedingly shy, if not cunning, and are rarely induced to "step into the parlor" of a regular trap; but, as they are very partial to the bugs and worms brought to the surface of earth just newly ploughed, they can be met on their own ground in the following manner:—Construct a number of small cones of stiff paper, large enough to receive the head of a young crow, smear the inside of the larger end with bird-lime (*see page* 40), place them point downwards in the newly turned earth, just firmly enough to prevent the wind from disturbing them; drop a grub worm or bit of meat into each, and retire out of sight. The crow, always on the alert for just such food, in attempting to pick up the bait with its beak, also picks up the cone, which adheres firmly to its head, shutting out all power of vision and frequently of respiration; the bird becomes, in a moment, so thoroughly bewildered that it can be approached and caught easily in the hand.

The utility of catching crows early in the season may be open to some question, as they tend to rid the ground of not only destructive worms, but the grubs which, later in the season, develop into prolific insect egg-producers. Allowing all this to be greatly to their credit, if they would only confine themselves strictly to that line of feeding, it would be very short-sighted to destroy them; but the havoc they make with newly planted seeds is generally quite, if not more than enough to overbalance their efforts in the right direction.

THE BARBEL TRAP FOR RATS

A serious objection to many of the different traps usually employed for catching rats is that each trap will catch only one rat at a time; a great improvement in this respect may be made without much trouble, and at very small outlay, and furnishes the means of catching them by wholesale. Procure a barrel which is water-tight, at least at the lower part; place a lump of stone or rock in the bottom, and pour in sufficient water to nearly cover the rock, leaving only enough of it bare to allow of a resting-place for a single rat. Instead of the head, stretch a piece of very thick paper over the top of the barrel, and fasten it securely by means of a cord passed around the outside of the barrel, just below the upper hoops; damp the paper slightly with a moist sponge, and it will become tight when dry. On the paper strew cheese parings, etc., several days in succession, so as to get the rats accustomed to come there for their regular rations without fear or suspicion. As soon as the rats appear to have got sufficient confidence to come regularly to supper, cut a cross in the middle of the paper, and spread the feast as before.

The first rat that comes will drop through into the water, and soon establish his headquarters on the limited dry spot of rock prepared for his accommodation. The next candidate for a free lunch also gets a drop too much; and, obeying the natural law of self-preservation, tries to win a footing on the dry part of the rock; the fact of its being of limited size, and, moreover, already occupied, does not deter him in the least; he sees only room for one, and in his estimation that means "number one." Unfortunately for the new comer, the first rat labors under the same opinion, and the two proceed to argue the point with such determination that all the rats in the immediate neighborhood hasten to see and judge for themselves of the cause for the disturbance, it is scarcely necessary to add that they all find out very conclusively what was the matter, and to the entire satisfaction of the owner of the barrel.

The use of paper as a cover for the barrel, though thoroughly effective, will only answer for temporary purposes, as the middle corners of the paper will soon become permanently depressed; if, however, greater durability is desired, the paper may be replaced by more substantial material.

A sectional plan is here given of an arrangement for this purpose, which is easily made, and will last for a long time in good working order. The illustration represents a barrel, cut in half longways, in order to show the manner in which the lid is constructed.

The lid consists of a circular piece of thin wood, a little less in diameter than the open end of the barrel, so that, when it is fixed in its place, there will be about half an inch free space all round it to ensure perfect freedom in its action.

A bar of wood, an inch and- a half or two inches square, is made just long enough to fit exactly across the middle of the open end of the barrel.

Now, take the lid the bar across its center, and mark off the width of the bar across the exact middle of the lid; saw this strip out, and the lid will then consist of two leaves or flaps, which, when hinged onto the under side of the bar, will be just the size of the original lid. On the upper side, and aboiu the middle point of each flap, a cord is fastened, either to an eyelet placed there for the purpose, or by passing the end of the cord through a hole in the lid, and secured underneath by a knot. The cords are passed over the bar, and hang down into the barrel, a notch being cut in the back edge of each flap, to allow the cords to work freely. A weight is then fastened to the loose end of each cord, sufficiently heavy to keep the fiap to which it is attached in a horizontal position, but not heavy enough to percent a very light pressure on the flap from depressing it easily.

The bar is lastly nailed in its place in the barrel, which should be so that the lid is about four or five inches down below the top edge of the barrel, and the lid is ready for action. The hinges and cords must work very freely; thin catgut suggests itself as a desirable material to ensure smooth and durable cords: and strips of bright tin tacked on the bar under the cords would probably add to their freedom of action.

As this trap sets itself, the bait must be fastened on the top of the flaps, to prevent it from falling off; much bait is not needed, as the rat has rarely time for more than a hurried smell of it, before his attention is taken up by other and more pressing business.

Another method, perhaps still simpler, of constructing a self-adjusting lid, is as follows: Provide a circular lid, a little smaller than the open end oï the barrel; exactly in the center insert a small stick perpendicularly, say six or eight inches long; at the end of the stick fix a weight, just sufficient to act as a counterpoise to keep the lid level; a potato stuck on the end of the stick will probably be sufficient for the purpose. Then bore a hole on each side of the barrel, about four inches from the top, the two holes exactly opposite

Fig. 1.

one another; through drive a short wire into the edge of the lid, and the swing-lid is complete and ready to receive the bait, and also all the rats that are enterprising enough to try and carry away the attractive morsel.

THE GARROTE TRAP

The illustration given in Fig. 1 gives a very correct view of this trap when set and ready for use. Provide two stout switches about thirty inches long, sharpen them at both ends, bend one of them into the form of an arch and plant it firmly in the ground; bend the other one into the same form and plant it by the side of the first one, leaving about an inch clear between them. Cut a number of stakes, plant them in the ground so as to make a circular fence, of which the second arch forms a part, enclosing a space about a foot in diameter, to which the only entrance is through the arches. Drive a notched peg into the ground at the back of the enclosure, opposite the center of the arch; cut a piece of twig a little longer than the height of the arch; this twig should have a short, natural fork sloping away from its side, to which the bait is fastened; at the lower end of the twig on the side opposite to the fork, cut a notch to fit into the notch in the peg that has been driven in the ground; hold the twig upright, and on the forked side, at a level with the top of the arch, cut another notch. Next get a hooked stick, shaped like *a* in Fig. 2, just long enough to reach from the outer arch hack to the upright twig.

On a line with the arches, and three feet distant from them, drive into the ground a crotched stick, in such manner that the crotch is level with the top of the arches. Get a stiff pole some six feet long, weighted at one end with a heavy stone firmly tied to it; at the other end of the pole fasten a loop of cord or fine wire in the shape of a U, the same width and height as the entrance under the arch.

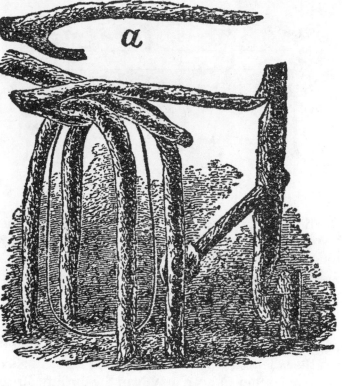

FIG. 2.

To set this trap, lay the pole across the crotch, adjusting it so that the loop hangs *exactly between the arches*; place the hook of the stick, a, under the front arch (see Fig. 2), the remainder of the stick extending over the pole and back into the exposure; catch the end of it in the upper notch of the upright twig and secure this last by its lower notch to the notch in the peg which has been driven in the ground; let the fork which holds the bale point a little sideways from, rather than towards the entrance of the arch, as it will make the springing of the trap more certain. Any animal that goes for the bait must first pass partly through the arches; as soon as it seizes the bait the upright twig becomes displaced, the hooked stick is thus set free, and the loop hoists the animal up by its hind-quarters, and holds it firmly caught against the top of the arches.

This is an excellent snare for rabbits, raccoons, and other animals of like size.

DOUBLE-BOX GARROTE TRAP

The accompanying illustration represents a useful and easily constructed trap for catching minks, muskrats and any other small animals. It consists of a box about a foot long (see Fig. 1) open at both ends, and large enough to allow any of the above mentioned animals to pass through easily. About two inches from each end, saw a groove across and right through the thickness of the top of the box; this forms a slit at each end through which the loops hang. These loops are made of stout wire, bent to conform somewhat to the inside shape and size of

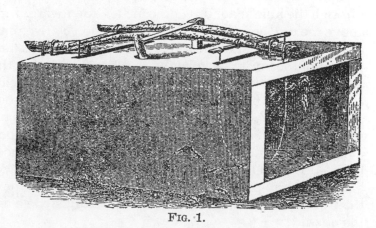

FIG. 1.

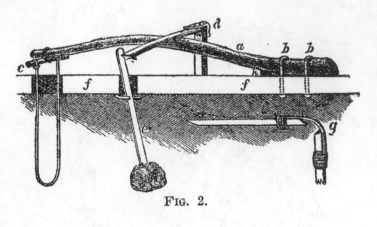

FIG. 2.

the box, the ends of each loop projecting upwards through the slit, and fastened firmly into the ends of a cross-bar of hard wood, such as a strip of hickory, which we will call the loop-piece.

The springs, which are required to draw up the loops, are made of hickory, tapering, and as strong as compatible with the necessary flexibility; the construction and arrangement of these springs are seen in Fig. 2. The butt end of the hickory spring is fastened down near the end of the top of the box, f, by wires, b b passing through holes bored in the box; the thinner end being considerably elevated by a block, h, placed as seen in the diagram.

This diagram represents the arrangements for one loop only, in order to make it plainer; it must, therefore, be remembered that the spring of the other loop will have, its butt underneath the loop-piece of this one, and the two springs lay side by side, ends reversed.

The spring having been fastened at the butt end, the other thinner end is firmly fastened to the loop-piece to which it belongs, at c. Midway between the grooves, and about an inch from the side of the spring, bore a hole in the top of the box, f f, through which a piece of wood, e, passes; this is long enough to hang about three inches down in the box, to hold the bait, and project upwards two inches; a strong peg is passed through it just at the inside line of the top of the box; this is to hold it down when in use. On the side of the projecting part cut a notch. Next take two strips of wood; hinge them together with a strap of leather, as seen at n. Nail the upright strip to the side of the box, as shown at d: trim the top strip or lever just to reach the notch in the stick, beveling the end of it, to make it catch slightly but firmly in the notch.

The other spring is made and fixed in the same manner, and connected with the loop-piece to which it belongs.

To set the trap, the springs are pressed down, and kept so by bringing the hinged lever over them, securing the end of the lever in the notch of the bait-stick, the whole arrangement being clearly shown in Fig. 1. Now any animal entering the box, by either end, will have to place his body in the loop in order to get the bait; a very slight nibbling at the bait will set the lever free from its notch, and both loops spring upwards with a snap, the animal being held firmly against the top of the box by the loop in which it was standing.

SINGLE-BOX GARROTE TRAP

This trap consists of a box a foot in height and width, and eighteen inches long, open at one end. Cut a hole through the top of the box five inches from the closed end; a stick of wood is made to hang loosely through the hole, extending nine inches downwards into the interior of the box, and projecting three inches above the top; being secured in this position by two pins or pegs driven through the stick, one underneath, and the other outside the top on the box; a small distance should be left between the upper cross peg and the top of the box, so as to allow the stick free play in the hole. In the upper part of the upright stick, about an inch above the box, cut a notch. Now bore two clean gimlet holes in the top of the box, four inches apart, and, say, five inches from the front edge of the box, as shown in the illustration; through these holes pass the ends binding wire, leaving as wide a loop as possible inside the box; tie each end of the wire once round a piece of stick held horizontally across of the box, and make the ends of the wire about a foot long; join the ends and twist them into a firm loop; the position, direction, and arrangement of the wire, are plainly given in the illustration. Lastly, cut a piece of wood for a lever, ten inches long; fasten one end with a piece of wire passed through two holes bored in the top of the box, near together and four inches from the front of the box. The wire should be adjusted so as to hold that end of the lever about an inch above the box-lid.

The trap is now ready to be set; this is done as follows: Select a position for the trap near a young tree or flexible sapling some six feet high; strip it or its branches, bend the top down and fasten the top loop of the wire firmly to it; place the bait on the lower end of the upright bait-stick; draw the cross-stick (which holds the wire loop) down onto the top of the box; adjust the lever over it so as to hold and keep the loop down, and secure the other end of the lever very lightly in the notch of the bait-stick. The whole arrangement is so clearly sketched by "our artist" that any detailed description of the trap really seems superfluous. It will be seen that no animal can get at the bait without having his body completely encircled by the loop; and the slightest pull on the bait will loosen the lever from the notch, allowing the loop to spring upwards with a jerk, and holding the animal firmly in such a position that its legs have nothing to take hold of.

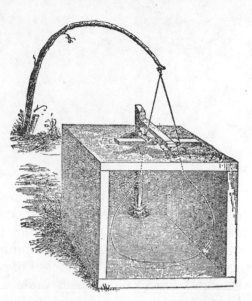

CHAPTER 22

Snares

Traps which depend on a wire loop set in a box, for their catching principle, are usually very effective, especially where they can be set in the near neighborhood; but when they have to be carried any considerable distance, box-traps of any kind are not only cumbersome, but also preclude the possibility of using more than a very few at a time. Something less bulky, and therefore more portable, is required for more extended use; and this leads to the subject of snares, some of which will be described hereafter. They will be found to be, for all practical purposes, quite as successful and reliable as any of the regularly built traps; and, indeed, in some points decidedly preferable.

THE GROUND SNARE

One of the best snares in existence is here represented.

The mechanical portion consists of only three pieces of wood: a bait-stick, ten inches long, pointed at one end, and a notch cut one inch from the other end; an upright post to drive firmly into the ground and stand eight inches high, with a wide shoulder cut in its side four inches from the top, also a deep notch on the back of it, one inch from the top; lastly, a piece of wood three and a half inches long, beveled at each end to a flat edge, to serve as a holder to unite the parts when in use. In order to make the foregoing parts available for use, select a spot conveniently near a flexible young tree about five or six feet high, from which the branches should be stripped; about four feet distant from it drive the upright post into the ground with its upper notch or back facing the tree; using the post as a starting-point, drive small stakes into the ground pretty close together, and three inches high, so as to enclose a circular space in front of the post, a foot in diameter, taking care that the tops of the stakes all incline somewhat inwards, to ensure free action to the wire noose.

The next thing is to set the snare: First, attach the end of a piece of fine brass binding wire about two feet long firmly to the top of the tree; the other end of the wire being fastened to the middle of the short holding-piece, keeping the flat side of the latter upwards. Make a wide loop at the end of another piece of fine wire, cut off enough of the wire to allow of a noose loosely surrounding the staked enclosure, pass the end through the loop, and secure this end to the wire that has already been attached to the tree, and at a point a few inches above the holding- piece. To set the snare, place the bait on the pointed end of the bait-stick; lay the bait-stick, notch upwards, under the shoulder that is on the side of the post, allowing it to project four inches behind the post; next, draw the holding-piece down, insert one end of it securely in the notch on the back of the post, the other end firmly but slightly in the notch on the end of the bait-stick; arrange the noose carefully around the outside of the enclosure, and the snare is ready for all comers. When an animal attempts to get at the bait, the stakes around the enclosure compel it to place its fore-feet within it. The moment the bait is disturbed, the tree springs up to its former position, drawing the noose tight around the animal's body just behind the shoulders.

The construction and application of the wooden parts of this snare are somewhat similar in principle to the support used for a figure-four trap (see page 17) with the difference, however, that the mutual arrangement of the parts, which in the trap are required to sustain a downward pressure, has to be modified in the snare in order to resist an upward strain. This style of snare recommends itself for its entire simplicity, and its portability; a sufficient number of each of the parts to make fifty traps amount to only a trifling burden to carry, as the stakes for the enclosures can be cut on the spot in the woods; and, for all purposes where animals are to be caught on the ground, it is almost infallible in its operation.

THE PORTABLE SNARE

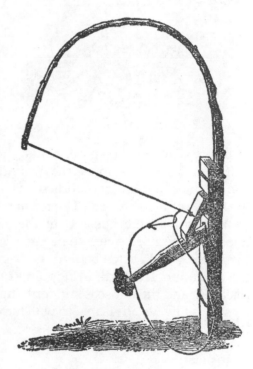

This is an ingenious modification of the snare just described, which requires no staked enclosure, and catches the intruder by the neck instead of around the body. It can therefore be applied to catching animals or birds up a tree or in any place where an upright bough can be found to serve for a spring; it can, moreover, be carried in the pocket complete, and be set in working order in less than five minutes.

The parts required in its construction are three; first, a piece of wood ten inches long, for the upright, having an oblong mortise cut through the middle of it, and a notch on its side two inches from the upper end; next, the bait-stick, five inches long, and flat, one end fitting easily into the mortise, where it is secured by a piece of stout wire driven through the upright, the other end of the stick being sharpened to hold the bait; a notch is cut on the upper side of the bait-stick, an inch and a half from the mortise; and, lastly, the holder, a piece of wood four inches long, beveled to a flat edge at each end; to the middle of this, with its flat side downwards, attach a piece of fine brass binding wire, two feet long, terminating at the other end in a firm loop; about two inches from the holder fasten another piece of the wire long enough to make a noose some seven inches in diameter, as shown in the illustration. This completes the arrangements. The snare is set by fastening the upright piece with wire in the stem of a flexible sapling five or six feet in height, stripped of its branches and twigs; attach the looped end of the wire (which is fastened to the holder) to the top of the sapling; draw the holder down, and insert one end of it firmly in the notch of the upright, the other end being made to catch lightly, but securely, in the notch on the bait-stick. The noose should be carefully adjusted so as to form a circle, of which the bait is the center, exactly The moment the bait is interfered with, the effect is instantaneous, the noose catching the animal or bird round the neck, and suspending it aloft in the air.

This snare is substantially the one used by poachers in those countries of Europe where catching birds or animals by means of snares is forbidden by law, and punished as a crime. In this country there is nothing to prevent their use. The only parties who are likely to be injured by catching small birds are the farmers, who are thus deprived of their only defense against their worst enemies, the worms, grubs and grasshoppers.

The few birds caught in snares, however, bear no comparison to the slaughter of birds by powder and shot, in some localities amounting almost to extermination—their untimely death serving no other practical purpose than the amusement supposed to be afforded to the gunner.

THE BIRD SNARE

For catching small birds there are few contrivances better or simpler than the snare shown in the engraving here given. To construct one of them, first cut a piece of bramble, willow, or other flexible twig, about eighteen inches long; bend the ends together into the shape of a horse-collar, and tie them fast, leaving the thicker and pro-

jecting two inches beyond the point of union; lay this *spreader* down flat, and on the upper side of the projecting end cut a clean notch. Next, select a flexible switch, some four feet long; plant the thicker end firmly in the ground, and tie a piece of whipcord, about eighteen inches long, to the thin end; tie the other end of the cord around the middle of a small bit of wood for a *catch*, two inches long, one end of which is beveled to a flat edge. On the cord, three inches from the catch, fasten a strong horse-hair, or very fine catgut (such as is used for trimming fish-hooks), full two feet long; the end being made into a firm loop, so as to form a running noose of the whole. Cut another twig, sixteen or eighteen inches long, pointed at both ends; drive the ends into the ground so as to form an arch about twenty inches distant from the upright switch, and at right angles to it; bring the notch of the spreader exactly under the inside of the arch; and, at the point where the wide end of the spreader touches the ground, drive a peg firmly, leaving the peg projecting two inches above the ground.

In order to set the snare, adjust the inside of the wide end of the spreader against the peg, one and a half inches elevated above the ground; draw the catch down behind and underneath the arch, making one end of the catch lay perpendicularly against the outside of the arch, and secure the other flattened end in the notch of the spreader. The tension of the whipcord will keep the spreader suspended above the ground. Lastly, arrange the noose over the arch and loosely on the ground around the spreader, the bite of the noose being raised over the peg and laid across the wide end of the spreader; without this latter precaution, the noose would catch behind the peg when the snare was sprung. The bait is strewed on the ground inside the spreader. The bird, in hopping on the spreader, causes it to drop down from the catch, the switch is released, and the noose is suddenly tightened, sweeping the top of the spreader, and catching the bird by the legs. It is always advisable to watch the snare, as a bird, when caught, will soon flutter to death.

CHAPTER 23

Net Traps

THE CLAP-NET

The clap-net is a favorite trap with bird-fanciers. It is set in motion by a person watching it, who thus has the opportunity of leaving alone any birds that come within its range, and are not suited for his purpose. It consists of two pieces of close netting, made of fine, strong thread, each fifteen feet long and five feet wide. Next, provide four rods, each five feet long and about an inch thick, of any light wood that will not split easily; bore a hole through each of the rods, about an inch from one end (a red-hot wire is the best instrument for this purpose, as it makes a clean hole without danger of splitting) ; into the other end of each rod screw a strong brass ring. Procure also four pieces of wood, eight

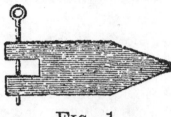

FIG. 1.

inches long (or long enough to hold firmly when driven into the ground), and about three inches wide; sharpen one end of each to a point: at the other end of each cut a slot two inches deep, and bore a hole straight through both of the shoulders of the slot, to receive a stout wire pin, as shown in Fig. 1.

Take one of the nets and two of the rods; fasten each *narrow* end of the net to one of the rods, whipping it securely from end to end, taking care that the ring ends of both rods lay on the same side of the net. Next, take the other, and fasten it to the two remaining rods in exactly the same manner as the first.

Select a level piece of ground, free from stones, high tufts of grass, etc.; lay one of the nets extended flat on the ground, and 2t C C (*see Fig. 2, right-hand net*) drive one of the slotted pieces firmly into the into the ground, one at that end of each rod which has a hole bored in it; the flat side of the slat laying in the direction of the long side of the net. Insert the end of each rod into the slot ready to receive it, and hinge it securely by drawing the wire through. Five feet away from each of the points, marked C and exactly on a line with C C, drive a strong peg, D, sloping away from the net; pass a strong cord through the rings on the rods, knotting it to each ring, and leaving the cord between them just long enough to stretch the net square; fasten each end of the cord to the pegs, drawing it tight, and keeping the net in true square. Proceed with the other net in the same manner, locating its slot-pieces, C C (*see left-hand net*), each six feet distant from and opposite to the corresponding points, C C, of the first net. Lastly, take a cord twenty feet long, fasten its ends to the brass rings of the two rods, B B, forming a slack loop. Another cord, E, is attached to and a little to one side of the middle of the loop. By drawing the cord, E, in a direction away from the nets and slantingly upwards, the nets will flap over and secure any bird on the open space between them. The draw-cord is placed somewhat away from the middle of the loop, in order to make one of the nets move a little faster than the other, and cause them to overlap one another without fouling.

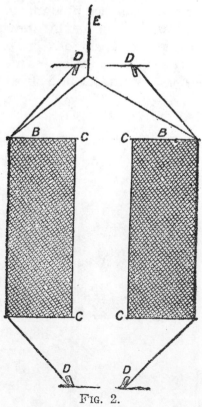

FIG. 2.

NET TRAP FOR BIRDS

The solid part of this neat little trap consists of two pieces of board, sixteen or eighteen inches square; these are nailed together at the edge, as shown in the illustration. Bend a piece of stout wire into the shape of an arch, the same height as the upright board, leaving the ends of the wire long enough to twist into an eyelet at each end; fasten each eyelet with a small staple to the joint of the board, so as to form free-acting hinges at the bottom of the arch. Lay the wire arch flat on the lower board and whip the edge of a piece of netting firmly on the whole wire from hinge to hinge; leaving the wire in the same position, fasten the other edge of the net to the upright board, using only sufficient net to enclose the space needed. Now raise up the wire flat against the upright board; on each side of it, a short distance from the hinges, fasten an elastic (*b*), stretch it tightly and fasten the other end to the side of the lower board, as seen in the engraving; these will draw the wire and netting down, and keep them so, when the trap is sprung.

Provide a strip of wood about three-eighths of an inch square; to one end of strip of leather to form a hinge, and nail the leather on the middle point of the upper edge of the upright board; the hinged strip or spindle should be long enough to reach, hanging down, to within about three inches of board. The platform, of which a diagram is given (*a*), consists, of three parts; the foot-board of thin wood (cigar-box is just the thing), about four inches square; the upright, three-quarters of an inch square, and long enough to reach the lower end of the spindle; and the hinge-piece, a piece of thin wood (similar to that used for the foot-board). The three parts of the platform are arranged as follows: one end of the upright post is nailed to the hinge-piece, near the edge, the opposite edge of the hinge-piece is fastened by a strip of leather to the bottom of the upright board; and the foot-board fastened against the post (*see diagram*) so as to be horizontal when the trap is set. This is done by first lifting the spindle up out of the way; next drawing the wire arch up flat against the upright board; the spindle is then brought straight down so as to keep the wire from falling down; lastly, the lower end of the spindle is secured by drawing up the upright of the platform just high enough for the extreme end of the spindle to rest behind it. The bait is placed on the foot-board, and the weight of a bird hopping on it to feed will be sufficient to depress the platform, set free the spindle, and allow the wire and net to come down with a snap, catching the bird alive and unharmed.

BAT FOWLING NET

This is a contrivance for catching birds at night, and is constructed as follows: Two light poles of ash or other light flexible wood some eight feet long are bent at one end, as shown in the. illustration, each being kept

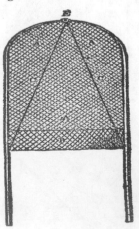

in a bent position by a cord, *C*, one end of which is tied to the top of the pole, the other end secured about half way down. The two bent ends are hinged together by a strip of leather, at *E*. A fine net, *A A A* seven feet long and four feet wide, is fastened between poles, the bottom end of it being turned up about eight inches, forming a bag or pocket, *B*.

The method of using this net is as follows: There must be three persons engaged—one to hold the net, another to carry a lantern, and a third to beat the bushes, &c. The darkest nights should be chosen, and if a stiff breeze is blowing so much the better, for the birds then roost low and are not able to hear so well. The net should be held about a foot from the bush, &c., and the lantern so held that the light be thrown evenly all over the back of the net. The bush should then be slightly beaten, and the birds, on being disturbed, will fly against the net, which should be instantly closed and brought to the ground, and the birds secured.

This mode of bird-catching cannot be too quietly performed, and the lantern should be covered in walking from one place to another, and, indeed, at all times when not actually in use provided it be not too dark to see one's way. Thick bushes are the favorite resort of small birds, as also the sides and eaves of corn and hay-stacks. In sheds thatched with straw, sparrows are easily taken by throwing the light, from the lantern up the corners of them, and then beating the thatch. The birds will fly to the light and gradually flutter down the wall, when they may be taken with the hand.

CHAPTER 24

Spring Pole Snare

While the deadfall is good for most animals, there is no one trap that fills all requirements and in all places. Some animals may be shy of deadfalls that can be taken in spring poles, snares and steel traps. This trap is easily and cheaply constructed. It should be made near dens or where animals travel frequently.

If a small bush is not growing handy, cut one. Drive a stake deeply in the ground, pull it out, stick the larger end of the bush cut into it. The explanation of this trap is as follows: 1, bait stick; 2, trigger; 3, noose made of wire or stout cord; 4, stay wire made of wire or cord; 5, bait; 6, spring pole.

SPRING POLE AND SNARE.

By noting carefully the illustration this trap can be built easily. The size of the bush or spring pole, of course, depends upon what sized animals you are trapping. This trap will take small game such as mink, opossum, skunk, etc., or can be made large and strong enough to catch mountain lion or black bear.

The snare is made have building a round fence in a place where there is plenty of small trees. Select two about four inches apart for noose and snare entrance, and another long springy one for spring pole 6 or 7 feet long, bend this down and trim it. Have a noose made of limber wire or strong string and a cross piece. Having cut notches in the sides of the trees for the same to fit, have it to spring easy. For snaring rabbits have the fence quite high.

Observe the above description and you can readily make. No. 1 is the noose, No. 2 is spring pole, No. 3 fence, No. 4 bait. This snare already explained can be made any time in the year while the dead fall can only be constructed when the ground isn't frozen.

The snares can be either made of twine or wire. Many fox and lynx snare trappers in the North use small brass wire.

Snares work well in cold weather and if properly constructed are prettysure catchers.

A—Spring pole.

B—Staple.

C—Two small nails driven in tree. (Three inch nail head, end down, with snare looped at each end with a foot of slack between. As soon as the D—three inch nail is pulled down, it will slip past the nail at top end, when spring pole will instantly take up the slack, also the fox, to staple and does its work.)

E—Slack line or wire.

F—Loop should be 7 inches in diameter and bottom of loop ten inches from the ground.

Remarks—The nails should be driven above staple so it will pull straight down to release the snare fastening.

A great many foxes hove been caught in this country by the plan of the drawing: outlined, writes J. C. Hunter, of Canada. A—the snare, should he made of rabbit wire four or live strand twisted together. Should be long enough to make a loop about seven inches in diameter when set. Bottom side of snare should be, about six inches from the ground. E—is a little stick, sharp at one end and split at the, oilier, to stick in the ground and slip bottom of snare in split end, to hold snare steady.

B—is catch to hold down spring pole. C—is stake. D—is spring pole. Some bend down a sapling for a spring pole, but we think the best way is to cut and trim up a small pole about ten feet long; fasten the big end under a root and bend it down over a crotch, stake or small tree. Snare should be set on a summer sheep path, where it goes through the bushes.

Stake might be driven down a foot or more back from the path, where a branch of an ever-green bush would hang over it so as to hide it and a string long enough from stake or trigger to snare to rest over path.

The setting of a snare is done thus: A good sound tamarac or other pole fifteen or twenty feet long is used for the tossing. The butt end of this must be five or six inches in diameter and the small end about three inches. A tree with a crotch in it is then selected to balance the pole upon. Failing to find such a tree in the proper place, an artificial fork is made by crossing two stout young birch or tamarac, firmly planted in the ground, and the two upper points tied together six or ten inches from the top. The balancing or tossing pole is lodged in this fork so that the part towards the butt would out-weigh a bear of two or three hundred pounds suspended from the small end.

Next a stout little birch or spruce is selected and a section of three or four cut off. From this all the branches are removed, except one, the small end is pointed and driven deep into the ground a few inches at one side of the bear road. The snare is made of three twisted strands of eighteen thread cod line and is firmly tied to the tossing pole. A few dried branches are stuck in the ground each side of the path, the pole is depressed so the very end is caught under the twig on the stick driven in the ground for that purpose and the noose is stiffened by rubbing balsam branches which leave, enough gum to make it hold its shape.

SMALL GAME SNARE.

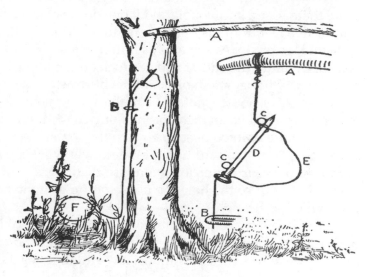

WIRE AND TWINE SNARE.

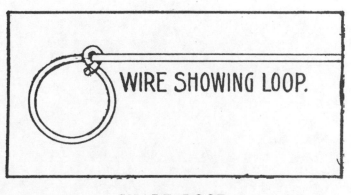

SNARE LOOP.

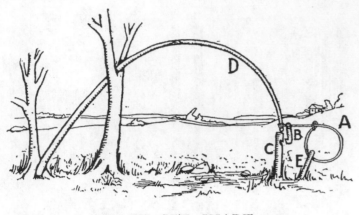

PATH SET SNARE.

The noose is kept in the proper position (the bottom being about sixteen inches above the road and the diameter being about eleven inches by blades of dry grass looped to it and the ends let into a gash on sticks at each side, put there for that purpose. No green branches are used in the hedge about the road because this would make the bear suspicious. The snare is now complete and the hunter stands back and examines it critically. His last act is to rub some beaver castor on the trunk of some tree standing near the road, ten or twelve feet from the snare. This is done on another tree at the same distance on the opposite side of the snare.

Bears are attracted by the smell of the castor and rub themselves against the tree in the same way as a dog rubs on carrion. When finished rubbing on one tree lie scents the other and in going to get at the fresh one tries to pass thru the snare. He feels the noose tighten about his neck and struggles; this pulls the end of the tossing pole from under the branch trigger, up goes the pole and old Bruin with it.

My way, according to a Massachusetts trapper, to trap skunk without scenting, and it is successful, is to snare them. Use a spring pole and if one does not grow handy, cut one and set it up as firmly as possible about four or five feet from the burrow and to one side. Probably the ground is frozen and you will have to brace it up with logs or stones or perhaps lash it to a stump or root. When the top of the pole is bent down it should be caught under the end of a log or rock on the opposite side of the hole so that it can easily be dislodged by an animal, either going in or out of the burrow.

The snare or noose is attached to the spring pole directly over the center of the burrows an the bottom of the noose should be an inch and half or two inches from the ground to allow the animal's feet to pass under it and his little pointed nose to go thru the center. Set the noose as closely over the entrance of the hole a possible and one or two carefully arranged twig will keep it in place.

Strong twine is better for the noose than large cord as the skunk is less liable to notice. When a skunk passes in or out of the hole the noose becomes tightened about his neck and slight pull releases the spring pole which so strangles him.

While this may seem an elaborate description of so simple a trap, still, like any other trap, set in a careless, half-hearted manner it will meet with indifferent success and, the simple the snare with a little thought and ingenuity can be applied in almost any situation for the capture of small game.

CHAPTER 25

Trail Set Snare

Many of the boys, writes an Indiana trapper, have come forth with their particular snares and methods of making same, all of which I believe are good but most of them require to be baited, which is one bad feature as applied to certain districts, for such has been experience that in many localities it is utterly impossible to get animals to take bait. This snare may be used as a blind or set with bait as your trapping grounds, or rather the animals, may require.

It is very inexpensive and so simple any boy can make it. First get a strip of iron one-eighth inch thick, three-eighths or one-half wide. Cut it in nine inch lengths and bend in the shape of Fig. 2, having drilled a one-fourth inch hole in either end. Next secure some light sheet iron, or heavy tin, cut in pieces 2¾ inches by 5¾ inches for the pan, and drill a one-fourth inch hole in center of same as shown in Fig. 3. It is now a very easy matter to: rivet the pan or Fig. 3 to Fig. 2. This done, take some 20 penny spikes and cut off the heads as per Fig. 1.

Now brass, or preferably copper wire, can be had on spools at most any hardware store, which is used for the loops, as it is so pliable yet sufficiently strong to hold any of the small fur bearers, as it is made in many sizes. Use the brass or copper wire only for the loops, as ordinary stove pipe wire is just the article for the finishing of the snare.

For a blind set to be placed in the run of the animals, make a double loop, that is, two loops for each snare. Now, take a bunch of these with you and find the runs

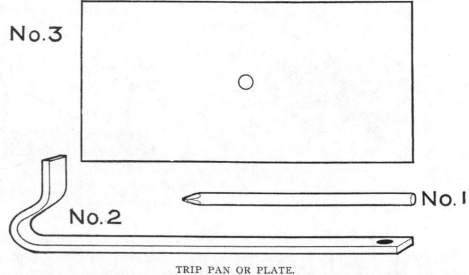

TRIP PAN OR PLATE.

or follow the ravines and creeks where they feed. If you can find a tree in a favorable spot on their runs, take one of your heartless spikes and drive in the base of the tree a few inches from the ground.

Now take No. 2 with the pan riveted thereon and hook bent and over spike, driving spike into tree until pan is level and until there is just room enough to hook loop, of wire over head of spike. (See illustration.) Dig out under pan so same can fall when stepped upon. Then secure a rock or chunk of sufficient weight and fasten to other end of wire. Throw this over limb of tree and hook loop year-head of a spike, having first put No. 2 in place.

Put one loop on one side of the pan and the other loop on the other side, so that an animal coming either way will step upon the pan to his sorrow. This done, drive a staple in tree over wire running from spike to limb, which will prevent the animal being pulled over the limb and escaping.

Having covered everything up with the natural surroundings and left no signs, you may claim the first furrier that happens that way and he will be waiting for you. This snare may also be used s with the ordinary spring pole by driving spike in a stake, then the stake in the ground, in which case it is best to make the usual V-shaped

DOUBLE TRAIL SET.

pen with stakes or stones, covering same over at top and setting so the pan will be right in the mouth of the pen and the single loop just between pan and bait. In this way they tread upon the pan just before they reach the bait.

You find this snare easily thrown. They will not cost you over three cents a piece, and any man can easily carry one hundred of them and not be half loaded.

In many ways the snare is splendid for lynx. Here in Western Ontario, says a well known trapper, where the lynx seldom take bait, they may be taken quite easily in snares set on snow-shoe trails. Fig. 1 shows a wire snare set on such a trail. I go about it in the following manner: Having found a suitable place along the edge of some swamp or alder thicket, I cut a spruce or balsam tree, about ten or twelve feet long, and throw it across the trail. I press the tree down until the stem of the tree is about twenty inches above the trail, and make an opening in the trail by cutting a few of the limbs away on the under side of the trail. Then I set a couple of dead stakes on each side so as to leave the opening about ten inches wide and hang my snare between these stakes and directly under the stem of the tree.

Fig. 1.   Fig. 2.   Fig. 3.

TRAIL SET SNARES.

The snare should be about nine inches in diameter and should be fastened securely to the tree. It should also be fastened lightly to the stakes on either side, so it will not spring out of shape. The best way is to make a little split in the side of each stake, and fasten the snare with a very small twig stuck in the split stake.

I make the snares of rabbit wire, about four or five plies thick, twisted. Some trappers prefer to use a cord. The dark colored codfish line is best, and it is best to use a spring pole snare, and Fig. 3 shows the method of tieing and fastening to the stakes. It will be seen that when the lynx passes his head through the snare he only needs to give a slight pull to open the slip knot and release the spring pole.

To prevent the rabbits from biting a cord snare, rub it well with the dropping of the lynx or fox and also, never use any green wood other than spruce or balsam, as any fresh green wood is sure to attract the rabbits. You may also put a small piece of beaver castor along the trail on each side of the snare, and you will be more sure of the lynx, as beaver castor is very attractive to these big cats.

We will now proceed to make another spring pole snare, altho the one described before is more practical, says a Colorado trapper. It is made like the preceding one except the trigger, etc. This one is to be used on a runway without any bait whatever. The illustration shows the trigger as it appears in the runway. No. 1 is the trip stick; No. 2, the stay crotch; No. 3, the trigger; No. 4, the loop; No. 5, the pathway, and No. 6, the stay wire.

PATH SNARE.

The animal in coming on down the path (5) passes its body or neck through the loop made of stout soft insulated wire (4); in passing it steps on the trip stick (1) which settles with the animal's weight, releasing the trigger (3) which in turn releases the stay wire (6) and jerks the loop (4) around the animal; the spring pole onto which the stay-wire it attached lifts your game up into to the air, choking it to death and placing it out of reach of other animals that would otherwise destroy your fur. A small notch cut in the stay crotch where the end of the trip stick rests will insure the trigger to he released. This will hold the trip stick firm at the end, making it move only at the end where the animal steps.

CHAPTER 26

Bait Set Snare

This snare I consider good for such animals as will take bait.

No. 1 and 2, headless wire nails driven horizontally into tree about ten inches from ground.

No. 3, a No. 10 or 12 wire nail with head used to catch under No. 1 and 2.

No. 4, bait stick or trigger. No. 3 passes through No. 4.

No. 5, bait, frog tied to bottom of No. 4.

No. 6's snare, fastened to No. 3 by two half hitches, then fastened to No. 3 by two half hitches, then fastened to seven or spring pole.

No. 7, spring pole.

Nos. 8, 8, small stakes driven in ground to form a pen.

RAT RUNWAY SNARE.

UNDERGROUND RAT RUNWAY.

No. 3

RUNWAY AND CUBBY SET.

LOG SET SNARE.

COW PATH SNARE.

Nos. 9, 9, two small twigs split at top to hold snare loop in place.

Nos. 1 and 2 should he about 4 inches apart

No. 3 goes through a gimlet hole in No. 4. About three inches from the top use any small round stick from ½ to 1 inch in thickness, not necessary to flatten No. 4 as in illustration. Use it natural bark on. From hole in No. 4 to bottom end should be about 7 inches.

Snare loop about 6 inches in front of bait, held in place by 9, 9, slightly leaning against 8, 8.

It can be plainly seen that if an animal takes No. 5 in its jaws and tries to remove it, it moves out the bottom of No. 4, moving forward No. 3, until, flip! up she goes. The top of No. 4 must be tight against the tree when set.

LIFTING POLE SNARE.

No. 3 should just catch under No. 1 and 2, then it takes but ½ inch to pull on bait to spring it. Bait with frogs, fish, tainted meat for skunk, and pieces of rabbit, or bird, for mink.

The lynx, like the wolverine, is not afraid of a snowshoe track, and will follow a line of rabbit snare for long distances, and when lie sees a bunny hanging up, he, without the least compunction, appropriates it to himself, by right of discovery.

When he does this once he will come again and the Indian hunter, knowing this, at once sets a snare for "Mister Cat." Sometimes when the thief has left a portion of the rabbit, a branch house is built up against the trunk of some tree, the remains of the rabbit placed at the back and the snare set at the doorway.

A stout birch stick is cut about three or four feet long and lodged on a forked stick at each side of the door and about two and a half feet high. To the middle of this crossbar the end of the twine is tied; No. 9 Holland is generally used, or No. 6 thread codline. This is gummed by rubbing balsam branches up and down the twine in the same way as the bear snare. The noose is held in shape in one or two places at each side by a light strand of wood or blade of grass and a couple of small dry sticks are placed upright under the snare to prevent the cat from passing beneath.

The loop is almost as large as for a bear and as high from the ground, if not higher. The lynx has long legs and carries his head straight in front of him and takes a snare by pushing thru it, or by a rush, never crouching and then springing.

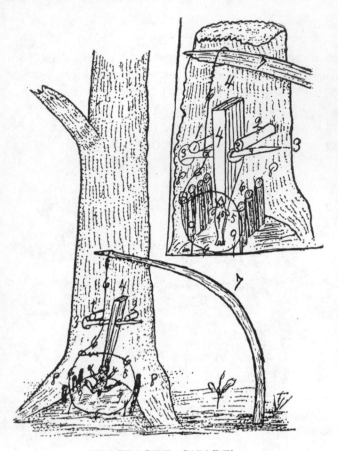

BAIT SET SNARE.

As the resort of rabbits is a young growth of country, there are also lynx in the greatest numbers. Rabbits and partridges are their principal food. When the Indian enters a new piece of country to set rabbit snares to support his wife and family and sees signs of lynx, he combines the two kinds of hunting and as he goes along, once in a while, lie bars his snowshoe track by placing a lynx snare in the way. The lynx are fond of the smell of castor, as indeed are most animals, so the hunter rubs a little on a tree at each side of Ins snare for the cat to rub against when he comes that way.

The snare is never tied to anything immovable, as they are very powerful and would break the twine. As soon as the noose tightens the cross piece comes readily away from the supports and the cat springs to one side. The stick, however, either knocks him a blow or gets tangled in his legs. This he tries several times, but with the same result, that bothersome stick is always hanging to his neck. About the last effort he makes to free himself is to ascend a tree. This, however, is nearly always fatal, for after he gets up a certain distance this troublesome stick is sure to get fast back of some limb. The lynx by this time, having become a pretty cross cat, makes matters worse and the hunter finds him hanging dead, at times twenty or thirty feet from the earth.

CHAPTER 27

The Box Trap

This trap is put to various uses. The beginner usually has one or two with winch he traps for rabbits. In fact they are great for that for the animal is not injured, which is often the case when shot or caught by dogs. Rabbits caught in box traps are therefore the best for eating.

The trapper who wants to secure fur-bearers alive to sell to parks, menageries or to start a "fur ranch" usually uses the box trap.

The size for rabbits is about 30 inches long by 5 wide and 0 high. The boards can be of any kind but pine, poplar, etc., being light is much used. The boards need only be a half inch thick. To make a trap you will need four pieces 30 inches long; two of these for the sides should be six inches wide; the other two for top and bottom should be 5 inches. These pieces should be nailed on the top and bottom of the sides. This will make the inside of the trap six inches high by four wide. It is best to have your trap narrow so that the animal you are trapping cannot turn in the trap.

In one end of the trap wires or small iron rods should he placed (see illustration). These should be about an inch apart. In the other end the door is constructed. This can be made out of wire also. The bottom of door should strike about eight inches inside. It will be seen that an animal pushing against the door, from the outside, raises it, but once on the inside the more they push against it the tighter it becomes.

The trap can be set at holes where game is known to be, or can be placed where game frequents and baited. If bait is used place a little prop under the door and place bait back in trap a foot or more. Bait to use of course depending upon what you are trapping.

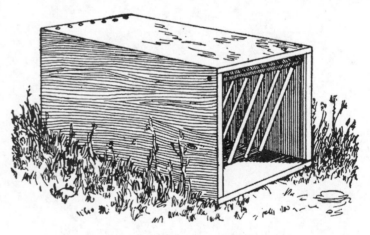

THE BOX TRAP.

The trap described is about right size for the common rabbit and mink. For skunk and opossum a trap a little larger will be required.

For mink and other animals that are gnawers the traps should be visited daily for they may gnaw and escape. If impossible to visit traps daily they should be lined with tin.

In many places these traps, with a door at each end, are used for catching muskrat. They are set in their dens under water and either tied or weighted down. The rats are caught either going in or leaving.

In making these traps the beginner is apt to make them too wide—so the animal can turn within. This is a mistake for it gives tie game more freedom and room to gnaw to liberty.

The animal simply goes in and is there until the trapper conies along and removes the game. Skunk can be drowned when caught in this trap without scenting if the trapper knows how to go about it.

The trap should be handled carefully. Take to water sufficiently deep to cover the trap and slowly sink then either weight the trap or hold down until the animal is drowned.

The box trap is a humane trap if visited daily. They are rather unhandy to carry about and few trappers want many, yet under certain conditions they are very useful. They can be made during idle time. For mink and other shy animals they should be handled as little as possible. They should be made of old boards or at least avoid all appearances of newness.

Some sections saplings to make deadfalls cannot be had and for the benefit of such, a wooden trap, three feet long and six inches wide and deep, is a good manner to take muskrat, writes a Western trapper. The boards can be cut out of any old lumber. In each end is a wire door, hung on hinges at the top. These doors rise at the slightest push on the outside, but will not open from the inside. The trap is sunk in the water at the entrance to the den and is fastened there. A muskrat in entering or leaving the den is sure to enter the trap.

The animal, of course, could gnaw out, but will drown before it has time to accomplish this. Several rats are often taken, where they are numerous, in a night. Traps of this kind can be used to best advantage in lakes and ponds or where the height of the stream does not vary much. If they are set along creeks and rivers you want to fasten them securely or take them up before heavy rains, as they are almost sure to be washed away.

I see in a recent number where George Walker wanted some one to tell through H-T-T how to make box trap to catch muskrat. Here is a good way:

First take four boards 36 inches long, nail together leaving both ends open. Next a small gate, consisting of a square piece of wood supplied with a few stiff wires is then pivoted inside of each opening so as to work freely and fall easily when raised. The bait is fastened inside the center of the box. The animal in quest of the bait finds an easy entrance, as the wires lift at slight pressure, but the exit after the gate has closed is so difficult that escape is almost beyond question. To insure further strength it is advisable to. connect the lower ends of the wires by a cross piece of tine wire twisted about each. If you have good luck you can catch two and three in this trap each night. Set in two or three inches of water where muskrat frequents, or set in skunk dens.

CHAPTER 28

The Coop Trap

This trap is used with great success for catching wild turkey, pheasants, quail and other feathered game. In some states the law forbids the use of this and similar traps.

The trap is built like an ordinary rail pen. In fact some use small rails when constructing this trap for wild turkey, while others build of small straight poles. The pen is usually six feet or more square and about three high. The "coop" is stronger if drawn in from bottom to top (see illustration). The top must be covered and weighted.

A ditch is now dug about a foot wide. This ditch should begin about three feet from coop and lead within. Corn or other grain is scattered on the outside and in the trench leading into the coop. On the inside considerable should be scattered in the leaves and small but short twigs.

The turkeys once on the inside will eat the grain and scratch among the leaves which generally partly fill the trench and as the birds are usually looking up, when not eating, they do not think of the trench thru which they entered.

The same trap will catch quail, but of course is built much smaller. About three feet square being large enough and a foot high is sufficient. Some have built quail coops out of cornstalks and report catches.

The quail coop should have the ditch leading to the inside the same as described for turkey. Of course the ditch should be much smaller—only large enough for one bird to enter at a time. On the inside of coop it is a good idea to lay a board six inches or wider over the ditch. The bait should be wheat or other small grain or seeds that the birds like. Scatter thinly on the outside and in the trench, but on the inside place more liberally. Chaff or leaves should be placed on the inside so that the birds in scratching for the grain will partly fill up the hole thru which they came.

Quail, turkey and other feathered game once on the inside and after eating the bait never think of going down into the ditch and out, but walk round and round the coop looking thru the chinks and trying to escape.

THE COOP TRAP.

The largest catches are made by baiting where the birds frequent for some days or even weeks before trying to make a catch. It is well to make the coops long in advance so that the birds will be accustomed to them, especially wild turkey.

These traps are some times used with the figure 4 trigger, but when thus set seldom more than one or two birds are caught at a time.

CHAPTER 29

The Pit Trap

This method of catching game and for hearing animals is not much used, as the labor in connection with making a pit trap is considerable. The method, however, is an excellent one for taking some of the larger animals, especially when they are wanted for parks, menageries, etc., uninjured.

The pit should be several feet deep and bait placed as shown. Another way is to cover the top with rotten limbs, leaves, etc., and place the bait on this. The animal in trying to secure the bait breaks thru.

The dirt from the pit should be removed in baskets. Catches are made by digging a pit across animal runways or trails. When the ground is not frozen or during rainy weather it is well to place a board several inches wide at top. The animal in going over its usual trail steps upon the frail covering and falls thru.

While the pit trap is mostly used for capturing large game, it can be used to advantage for taking many of the smaller fur bearers.

THE PIT TRAP.

Where muskrat are numerous, instead of digging a pit, secure a box about three feet deep. The width and length make no difference. Place a few liat rocks in the bottom and place in the water where rats frequent. Make the box solid. The box must be water tight. The weight should bring the top of box to within a few inches of water. A couple of boards or chunks should be so placed that the rats will climb up them and to the box along the edge of which the bait is placed.

The pit trap can be used where, skunk and other animals frequent. Bait the place for some days before the pit is dug.

If the pit is to be used without bait, then find the runways of the animal and dig the pit. While some animals may not be shy, if a little fresh dirt is lying around, yet it is best to be very careful and carry all earth taken out of pit a few rods to one side. Pits of this kind should be several feet deep.

The success the hunter or trapper has in using this method will depend largely upon his knowledge of the game he is after. Unless the animal or animals are wanted alive, the work to make a pit is too great and the chances of a catch never certain. This way is not practicable under ordinary circumstances, yet where the game is wanted alive and sound, is worth trying.

CHAPTER 30

Trappers' Secrets: Oils, Unguents, and Other Stinky Stuff

SOME RULES AND REGULATIONS ON TRAPPING

- Prepare traps, decoys, stretchers, and pick out trapping grounds one to three months in advance.
- Start to trap when the weather is real cold—never before November—better wait until December.
- Stop trapping in the spring as soon as the skins begin to get red, and the fur thin, pale and shedding. The skin is generally thick when the fur is thin.
- Remove the skin promptly from the animal unless the car-cases is found in a frozen state.
- If time permits educate fur-bearing animals to visit places where you intend to place your traps.
- Post yourself thoroughly in manner of skinning, and how skins should be prepared to bring best prices.
- Don't try to fool buyers by overstretching a skin. They know their business and are not blind, beside overstretching hurts the skin.
- Keep furs away form artificial heat and from the sun. Rapid drying by the stove or sun in not desirable, and tends to curl tips. Hang furs in a cool and shady place.
- Do not cut off ears, nose, or mutilate the skin, and if accidentally cut, sew portions together before drying in Indian style.
- Skunk, opossum, raccoon, mink, and similar animals can be smoked out of their abode by the use of sculpture or brimstone.
- Never dry skins by the fire or close to artificial heat, neither expose them to the sun.
- Never make a practice of handling traps with the bare hands, especially when about to set them.
- Scrape all fat and meat off the skin before drying. Skins should be stretched shortly after being scraped and while yet very green. Give the skins as much as possible their natural size and do to overstretch any particular part.

DECOYS: TRAPPERS' SECRETS

The list below gives names of various oils—natural and artificial—used by hunters and trappers. Elsewhere in this book will be found how the oil is used, when and where applied.

ARTIFICIAL OILS

Oil of Fenugreek.
Oil of Amber.
Oil of Asafetifa.
Oil of Lavender.
Oil of valerian.
Oil of Rhodium.
Oil of Anise.
Oil of Cumin.

NATURAL MUSK

Oil of Beaver from Beaver.
Oil of Mink from Mink.
Oil of Otter from Otter.
Oil of Musk from Muskrats.

FISH OIL

This preparation is made by cutting up various sixes and kinds of fish into small pieces, placing into a bottle and exposing same to the sun, loosely corked. In about 3 to 4 weeks of continued exposure the contents should be pressed through a sieve, separating the oil, which should be run into a bottle having a small neck. The smaller the fishes the better the oil.

If fish oil is unobtainable and the trapper should run out of this preparation, pooches sardines and use them a s bait, or make oil therefore. A small ten cent box will go quite a ways. Salmon is also very good.

MATRIX AND URINE FROM ANIMALS

Matrix and urine form the female fox, wolf and dog during period of coition makes and excellent bait for wild animals of the dog family. This preparation in order to retain the odor should be tightly corked up and used similarly to other artificial and natural oils.

Matrix from the female mink or marten taken from the animal during the cumulative period is probably the best attraction for the male species. Capture one or more females, dip or hold rear parts into sweet oil or alcohol, later kill the animal, cut out the sexual parts, place all into a bottle which cork tightly. Smear beyond or about the traps.

DECOY

Dung of any species, also their urine will attract like kind.

Place urine and dung in a bottle, cork tightly and use small quantity at each setting. This decoy is especially good during the rutting season.

FOX AND WOLF DECOY

3 oz. Urine of a dog, fox or wolf (female preferred).
1 oz. Oil of valerian.

Mix well, use 5 to 10 drops on stake, stump of tree or protruding rock. Fox, wolf, in fact all animals of the dog kind, are attracted by this decoy and will urinate. Set traps 12 to 14 inches from trunk of tree. Bury and cover traps in the usual way.

MINK DECOY

¼ Musk of Mink.
¼ Musk of Muskrat.
¼ Matrix of Mink.
¼ Oil of Cumin.

Mix well. If too thick add urine of the female mink or alcohol. Keep corked. Use few drops.

COYOTE OR FOX BAIT

1 oz. oil of cumin;
1 oz. oil of rhodium;
½ oz. asafetida (grated);

Wart of horse, size of hickory nut (grated).

Alcohol to cut and make compound to consistency of dough. Place in wide necked bottle, 6 oz larger; keep corked. Use in two or three weeks. Smear small quantity close to traps oil some stick or bush.

TO OVERCOME SMELL OF IRON

To overcome the smell of iron as well as human scent, nothing is better than a mixture of compound made out of catnip. Mink, fox and nearly all other animals are familiar with the peculiar catnip odor; and if this compound is smeared over the traps and hands, all strange odors are overcome. The animals, familiar with the odor are not suspicious.

Procure a quantity of catnip and mash it between stones or in some old mill and add enough liquid to make a thick paste. Place this into a screw top can or bottle, use when you want it.

MINK SCENT

½ oz. essence of peppermint.
2 oz. fish oil.
2 oz. honey.

MINK BAIT

¼ part musk of muskrat, ¼ part musk of mink, ½ part alcohol. Keep corked up in warm place ten days before using.

FOX MUSK

Musk taken from the glandal sac of the fox is excellent for attracting like species. Use this musk as you would the musk of beaver, muskrat and other natural decoys. It is an undisputed secret held sacred by old trappers that natural musk will attract its own kin of animals quicker and from a greater distance than any other preparation. It is also necessary to use the utmost care in trapping for sly Mr. Fox.

OIL OF OTTER (MUSK)

This is obtained from the animal by extracting the substance from the two small glands on the belly of both sexes, often called oil stones. This natural oil is used by experienced trappers with splendid results in attracting these species.

MANURE OR DUNG BAIT

Obtain manure or urine of the animal that you seek to capture and if this is unobtainable, procure the droppings of the domestic dog, but what is still better, from tame foxes or wolves. Droppings from the sheep are also handy and of good avail.

MUSK OF BEAVER OR BEAVER MEDICINE

(The following four formulas are natural baits and will fool the oldest beaver and other animals.) Make cold and preserve in a large-neck bottle.

(1)   Castors of one beaver,
      20 drops oil of cinnamon,
      10 drops oil of anise,
      Urine of beaver sufficient to make the consistency of mush.

(2) Castros of one beaver,
      7 drops oil of sassafras,
      7 drops oil of anise,
      10 drops oil from the oil stone.
(3) Castros of one beaver,
      10 drops Jamaica rum,
      5 drops oil of anise,
      5 drops of cloves,
      5 drops oil of sassafras,
      5 drops of rhodium,
(4) Castros of one beaver,
      to drops oil from oil stone,
      Urine of beaver sufficient to make all the consistency of mush.

MINK SCENT

A Pennsylvania trapper writes as follows: Take two or three scent bags found at the root of the mink's tail and place them in a 3 or 4 ounce large-necked bottle, over which pour 1½ oz. of oil of anise; fill remainder with water. Now take sharp knife or chisel and cut bag into as many pieces as possible. Cork up and leave stand in warm place. Do not permit it to freeze. This is a good scent for capturing mink and similar animals. Have had best of luck and can recommend it to any trapper, and I feel confident that he will be successful in attracting mink.

MINK DECOY

This bait is especially adapted for the mink during their running season. It is prepared as follows:

"During the fall months, or in fact any time that I have occasion to capture a mink, I remove the animal's scent bags, which are placed within a 2 oz. bottle into which I pour 1 oz. of alcohol and 10 drops of oil of anise. Cork and let stand in a warm place. Two scent bags to 1 oz. alcohol and to drops of anise is correct; larger quantities in same proportion can be made."

SECRET METHOD

My method and secret of success is to warm the jaws, springs, pan and every portion of the steel trap except the trigger, with withes (hemlock preferred). Even the wire traps are wound around with these withes by me. On the ends and edges to hold withes from coming off. I tie with waxed thread. This method removes the smell of iron land I do not have to cover up sets so heavily with earth, as the traps already resemble the surroundings very much. Of course, I remove the newness of my work with damp dirt which is rubbed or smeared into the covering. Probably if smeared with wax tallow and a little consortium, the setting would require no bait or other decoy, but I have never tried it.

JESS MCARTHUR.

NATURAL MINK SCENT OR LURE

If one is successful in capturing a female mink when the animal is in hear, do not injure or kill her, especially if the animal's scent to attract the male to the trap is desired. Obtain a pint of pure sweet oil and dip her hind parts into the oil and hold her therein for 10 or 15 minutes. Immediately thereafter place the oil in a bottle which cork tightly. A few droops sprinkled on the twigs or in the vicinity of traps, or place four or five drops on a leaf and place it in abode beyond the trap or in hollow log.

The trapper who favored us with the above claims to have success, and gives good reason for believing that this natural scent is much stronger than that obtained from the dead mink. No alcohol is to be added and if the preparation is to be kept over the summer months, it should be placed in an ice house and kept there, otherwise in the lowest possible temperature.

Perhaps after obtaining the natural scent from the animal in the above method, it would be advisable to kill the mink and by removing that portion of the animal and placing it in a bottle in connection with alcohol, one would be able to ascertain more positively, especially if used in connection with the first named preparation as to which is the best. If the latter preparation is to be made place parts into a wide-necked bottle, holding three to four ounces, and fill with alcohol.

FRED O'FLYNN

MY FAVORITE FOX SCENT AND BAIT

"I prefer skunk, woodchuck or muskrat for bait. Theses I cut into small pieces about as large as an egg. This preparation is made during the summer months, placed in a clean screw-top can and exposed to the sun so as to become tainted. The scent that I use is made out of pure skunk glands, pure strained honey (not sugar-fed honey, but clover and flower honey.) This scent is especially good for the fall months. During the winter months I obtain the matrix from a female fox taken during the animal's running season, and in addition to this I take the musk of two or three muskrats and a small quantity of pure strained honey. Mix these well together and I assure you that same will attract the male fox and is probably the strongest scent in existence. I have also had good success in trapping foxes with scent made out of frog eggs; mix with the musk of muskrats and glands of the skunk. I wish my brother trappers best success."

G. W. O

HOW TO MAKE DECOY TO CAPTURE FOXES, WILD CATS AND OTHER ANIMALS

Mr. J. H. Van Ness, a Michigan trapper, gives us the following secret and claims to have been very successful when ever the bait or decoy a stated below is used:

Remove from the legs of horses a piece of cork. A piece the size of an ordinary hickory-nut is sufficient to make one pint. Cut or shave this piece of cork into small shavings and put same into a pint of lard, also place a piece of asafetida as large as a bean therein, and cook these three articles together. Let them boil for several hours over a slow fire. Stir continually and keep shavings from settling. A peculiar, strong odor will arise just as soon as boiling begins; the women folks will leave the room and the dog and cat will begin to sniff and smell. After it has boiled for two or three hours remove from the stove and permit to cool.

Smear this preparation above or about the traps, but never upon them. The fox, wild cat, and even the domestic dog as well as cat, is likely to enter the trap. This bait will attract these animals from long distances. It is very powerful, and, as aforesaid, had always been very successful.

"I usually wear gloves in handling traps preparatory to setting them, also boil my traps or bury them for a few days in order to remove the smell of iron."

We are indebted to Mr. C. A. Beech, an Iowa trapper, for the following decoy that he claims to have used and continues to use for trapping mink, wolf, fox, skunk and other carnivorous animals. The following formula is based on a pint of preparation.

Take a pint frit jar and fill one-third full with blood. Blood from domestic animals will do, especially from calf, dog or hog. Add the following: 2 teaspoonfuls or 2 fluid drams oil of cinnamon; 2 teaspoonfuls of powdered asafetida; 2 teaspoonfuls oil of cloves; grind a nutmeg or pound it between rocks so that it is very fine, and place in the mixture; mix thoroughly. Boiling is unnecessary. Keep bottle corked up for at least 5 to 10 days and then run through a cloth or thin sieve. After it is strained, return the liquid in any kind of bottle and throw away the thick stuff. Before throwing away the thick stuff be sure and squeeze all the liquid therefore.

"This preparation should be used in similar manner to other good preparations by smearing above or about the traps. Being very powerful, it will attract animals for a great distance."

HONEY-BAIT

This bait is commonly used for bears. Save Mr. Bear the trouble of climbing trees and give him his heart's delight. Place this bait near the steel trap, snare or deadfall, or within and about the dugout. Take a quantity of honey, place in a vessel, add one-tenth part of beeswax and a few drops oil of anise. Place pan upon a stove and allow to come to a boil. Stir frequently to prevent burning or becoming settled. This preparation, after it is cold, can be used in various ways. Some trappers cut up a dried sponge, attaching each small piece to a wire or string and permitting the sponge to become soaked with the preparation. The object of attaching the wire or string is that the sponge may be conveniently tied to trap or thereabouts. Never smear traps with this preparation, unless you want to catch the bear by the head, and that certainly is not desired. If traps are set close to brush, smear that bait on latter, about four to five feet above the ground.

DECOY FOR WOLVES

If you have tried everything and cannot get the wolf to the trap, try the following: Obtain the bladder from a dog or wolf (either sex) which empty in a jug or bottle. If your traps are already prepared in the form of a cluster, take a piece or porous wood and the contents of the jug over it, saturating same thoroughly. A Montana trapper assured us that he has succeeded in capturing hundreds of wolves in his times. After he caught the first wolf he always saved the water from the animal and used it in his next set. This same party caught enough wolves to help him pay off the mortgage on the ranch. The bounty and the skin, not only in Montana, but in other states, amount to considerable money. This method is certainly worth trying.

FOX BAIT

A mixture made of the following has been successfully used by various trappers. Take all or part of a muskrat carcass and place within a screw-top jar, one holding two quarts preferred. Then take the fat of the skunk, also the scent bags. Procure three field mice and place entrails of same within the can. Screw lid on can, not too tight , and place in a pile of heated manure and leave for two or three weeks. This mixture should be well stirred before it is placed in the pile, but thereafter the can should be kept closed as much as possible. When one has occasion to use this preparation, take a stick and smear this within the abode or at other convenient places to which the fox or wolf is to be attracted.

MINK BAIT

Mr. O. G. Wells states that he ties a live crawfish with thread to the pan of trap. Tie thread to each arm. Close to the body, but not in the joints. Then the both threads together and fasten body to pan so that the fish will be able to move but not off the pan. The trap should be set in shallow water close to the shore, and the bait should almost reach the level of the water. As the mink travels along the shore in search of food he will see the bait, and in endeavoring to remove it with his food will spring the trap and become a victim.

SECTION II
The Animals

CHAPTER 1

The Weasel

(Ger. Wiesel, Sw. Vessla, Lat. Putorius Vulgaris.)

This little carnivorous animal, the smallest of the marten or weasel family, is found in nearly every state and territory in the Union, Audubon says, "also in Alaska." What Dr. Coupes says of the Putorius ermine, with slight modifications, is also true of the weasel: "A creature of thoroughly and conspicuous circumpolar distribution, extending probably as near the pole as any land animal, it is modified, when changed at all, by latitude as expressed in the climate to which it is subjected, state of its food supply, etc."

WHITE WEASEL

The American weasel resembles the European, but a difference of length in the vertebrae and color of fur on the tip of tail, is noticeable, and climatic condition so Europe, like that of this hemisphere are responsible for the variation in body, size, color, etc.

On this continent we can divide this little courageous animal into separate groups, so as to give a closer and more definite description of their size, color, habits and respective value of their skins from the manufacture's point of view.

The smallest weasel on this continent is chiefly found in the southern and middle states, often seen and known to inhabit western as well as Atlantic states. It is sometimes confused with yond northern species during the summer months, which it closely resembles, and perhaps occasionally, at least it is so claimed by naturalists, seen in northern states as far as New York, Minnesota and Washington. This species is easily distinguished from the larger variety by its short tail, smallness of body and continued brown, chestnut or chocolate dress, winter and summer. The belly portion however, is covered with a strip of light colored fur, beginning with extreme end of upper lip, continuing along its neck, belly, and ending at the anus, though somewhat dividing and terminating systematically at the inner portion of the knee.

The body measures six to seven and one-half inches, rarely eight inches, to which a tail varying from two, two and one-half or three inches, must be added. The black furred tip of tail is less conspicuous. The animal is equally ferocious, and its small size enables it to enter openings apparently not exceeding one inch in diameter.

Probably the best known amongst the weasel is the large, brown, chocolate, chestnut colored animal that inhabits the middle, northern, eastern and western states. Is found sparingly in the southern states and Canada.

The body of this species measures ten to fourteen inches from nose to root of tail, the latter attaining a length of from four to eight and one-half inches, depending upon the maturity of the animal. The body is more cylindrical and plump, as compared with the first described species. Has as unusually long neck, and its tail (of variable length), attains a greater length as compared with either of the other two species. The cars are large, high, and orbicular. The legs are much stouter and its toes fairly covered with long, coarse hair over-lapping the claws. The habits of this species, like all others, is terrestrial, arboreal and not aquatic.

During the late spring, summer and fall months, the body is covered with rather a thin pelage of brown, chocolate or chestnut color with a somewhat lighter colored undergrowth of fur fibers. The belly portion, beginning with center lip is of a yellowish cast, and this color extends to the inner portion of the legs. Quite often a white strip of fur is noticed extending from the lip, net and chest, and terminating near the anus. At other times the under lip is covered with clear white pelage and the belly with the aforesaid yellow or whitish fur. The above described change in the animal's pelage is especially true of those inhabiting the extreme northern pars of the United States. The clear white pelage covers the entire body, head, limps and tail, with the exception of the extreme pencil-like tip. It should be noted that not all the animals change their outer garment from the brown to the white color, especially in the middle section of this country where the climatic conditions are not as favorable as compared with the animals inhabiting the more northern part of the United States.

I have seen and examined as many as three thousand skins in one season that more or less indicated the change from the white to the brown and the brown to the white fur, and at intervals examined hundreds of skins taken from animals during the winter months that failed to realize for the owner any remuneration, due to the predominating brown color, occasionally partly colored with intermingled white and brown guard hairs, and semi-brown undergrowth of fur fibers. Only such skins having a clear white coat of fur, have any commercial value. These are sold as ermine skins, at a lower range of prices, thought objections are plentiful. This species is easily distinguished by the furrier, due to its long tail and smallness of body as compared with the Siberian ermine.

Our approach of cold weather, (October, November), the outer garment gradually changes from brown to the white ermine coat of fur, and by December or latter part of November the animal's outward appearance resembles that of the ermine.

The last species, often called the "American Ermine" is found in the northern part of the United States, Canada, and Alaska. It resembles the Siberian ermine more closely than the other two species above described. (See article under Ermine.)

I know of no animal that is more courageous when size and ferocity is considered, than the weasel. It openly wages war upon many of the large quadrupeds, and by its quickness, ferocity and deadly attack, causes dreadful ravages amongst them.

The body is extremely elongated and appears longer on account of its neck amend head being of same circumference, and its ability to stretch its body, especially when seeking to enter small crevices of rocks, knot-holes, as well as other openings made by such animals as the mouse, rat or squirrel. The legs are very short and thin, and the paws extremely tender, being covered with a hairy growth and its toes are the possessors of sharp claws which are used to great advantage by the animal in climbing. It inhabits plains as well as mountains, and is known to roam in the forests where it seeks its principal food supply. Even the large muskrat falls prey to the little weasel, also moles and rabbits; is known to enter the chicken coop, killing as many as twenty-five birds in one night. It is extremely fond of killing small animals and birds, not only for food purposes, but more so for pleasure. It possesses unusual courage and seemingly with unlimited daring and boldness, affronts large animals; is known to pounce upon sheet, calves and other domestic animals, who rid same off their backs with difficulty. No small animal possesses immunity from the weasel, but in its turn is also hunted and destroyed by the larger species of its tribe, such as the mink, marten and other carnivore.

Its favorite hold or bite is on the victim's neck, head or throat. Notably will the weasel or ermine lay in wait for a possible victim, but stealthily follow the tracks and pounce upon the victim's back, which unaware of the danger, succumbs in a rather one-sided combat. It pursues birds of all kinds and it is common for hunters to disturb the animal while so occupied.

A certain European writer relates and instance where a large bird of prey captured a weasel, and with it in its talons, rose in the air. In a few minutes, however, the bird began to show signs of uneasiness, rising rapidly in the air, or as quickly falling and wheeling irregularly around, whilst it was evidently endeavoring to force some obnoxious thing from it with its feet. After a short, but sharp contest, the bird fell suddenly to the earth, not far form the observer who intently witnessed the interesting maneuver, and saw the weasel, apparently unhurt, scamper away. Upon examination he found that the wease had severed a large blood vessel, also ate a big hole under the bird's wing.

The animal frequently visits nests located in the loftiest trees, in clefts and rocks, in search of eggs young and old birds. Many a mother bird has lost her life in protecting her young, and often in such battle the weasel, in misjudgment of distance, weakness of branch or limb, and at other times due to the savage attack of the mother, is hurled to the earth.

The mother brings forth a litter of four to eight young at a time, which are born blind, and generally in a hollow tree or log under a pile of rocks or in some burrow, softly padded with hay, dry leaves and similar vegetation. If the young are in danger, the mother will carry them off in cat fashion to a place of safety and protects them with unusual courage and if necessary, with her life. The mother loves her young dearly, who like kittens are amusing and playful. An instance is recited where the mother sacrificed her life in protecting her young in a desperate encounter against a dog, who upon the close of the combat was bleeding furiously about the lip, head, cars and neck. At the age of twelve months the young have generally attained their maturity and the life of the animal I from six to ten years.

One must accede to this animal a wider and more extended range of activity against a greater variety of objects; possessing persevering and enduring powers of chase, with a natural lover of destructiveness, taking more life than is necessary for its actual wants. The great cats, who procure their food supply by particular

mode of attack, their hunger being satisfied, quietly wait until again prompted by hunger. This is not so with the weasel or ermine. No animal or bird with insufficient strength or other powers of self defense, is beyond their ruthless and relentless pursuit. This enemy assails them not only on the ground, but under it, on trees, and some claim, in the water. Swift and sure of foot, keen of scent, he is able to track, run down his prey, and make the fatal spring upon them unawares; owing to litheness and slenderness or body he is able to follow the smaller animals through the intricacies of their hidden abodes and kill them in their homes. It is evident that if he does not kill simply in gratification of supreme bloodthirstiness, he at any rate deliberately kills more than is necessary for his requirements. His parallels cannot be found among the larger Carnivora. Yet which one of the larger animals will defend itself or its young at such hazardous risks? The physiognomy of the weasel will suffice to betray its character. The teeth are almost of the highest known raptorial character; the jaws are worked by enormous masses of muscles covering all the side of the skull. The forehead is low, the nose shape, the eyes small, penetrating, cunning and glitter with an angry, green light. There is something peculiar, moreover, in the way that this fierce face surmounts a body extraordinarily wiry, lithe, and muscular. When the creature is glancing around, with the neck stretched up, and flat triangular head bent forward, swaying from one side to the other, we catch the likeness in a moment—the image of a serpent.

Long, slender body, short legs, small feet. The Fur is short and pure white in winter, except a black tip to the tail. In the summer the color changes, varying from a light, dull brown to a rich, dark brown; tip of tail remains black.

Alaska, Newfoundland, Canada and Northern States as far south as Colorado, Iowa, Central Illinois and Pennsylvania.

The White Weasel is a great wanderer, traveling miles in a single night. It likes to follow old tumble-down stone walls overgrown with weeds, or along old fences, and will squeeze into every crevice or hole it can find.

They make their dens under stumps or in the hollow roots of old trees. They also take possession of the burrows of ground-squirrels or rabbits, the occupants of which they kill.

The food of the White Weasel consists of mice, moles, shrews, rabbits, poultry and young birds and their eggs.

They are very prolific, having two or three litters a year and from four to eight in a litter.

For a White Weasel set build a small enclosure of sticks or stones. Set a trap in the entrance. Place a rabbit head or some other bait on a stick beyond the trap so that the animal will have to go over the trap to reach the bait. Fasten the trap to a clog, as a larger animal may be caught.

Under old roots, crevices in rocks, or any small, natural cavities are good places for White Weasel sets.

When the Fur of the White Weasel changes to brown, it becomes of little or no value, at the most not worth over five to ten cents. Some Weasel are caught just when the Fur is turning white, and have a few grey hairs on the back. These are called Greybacks and are worth considerably less than the pure white skins.

Often White Weasel are caught that have yellow "stains" on the back. These are known as "stained" Weasel, and are not worth as much as the pure white skins. There is no way of removing the "stain."

White Weasel should be skinned "cased" and shipper flesh out.

The Weasel proper, *(Pulorius Vulgaris)* is the smallest member of a large family which includes such animals as the Mink, Marten, Ermine and Fisher. It inhabits nearly all parts of the United States and Canada, its characteristics of size, color, etc., varying with the latitude.

Of white Weasels, or American Ermine, the best furred skins come from Alaska, and the region across to Nova Scotia and Newfoundland. An unusually large breed or strain of them is found in the mountain regions of Maine.

Weasels are best caught in steel traps, set in the mouths of old muskrat holes, openings under barns or hen houses, or similar places. Eresh Muskrat meat or a bit of fish or fowl can be used for bait to advantage.

The weasel is the smallest of all carnivorous animals and the various species and varieties are distributed over the greater portion of northern Asia, Europe and North America. In this country alone naturalists recognize some twenty species and sub-species, most of which are found in Canada and Alaska, also the northern and western states. Of these it is only the northern varieties, those which become white in winter that are of importance to the trapper.

On one occasion I knew a farmer who had turned a drove of fair-sized pigs into a pasture, and one day, hearing a wild squealing over along the pasture fence, went to investigate. He found the entire drove of porkers running along the fence and squealing from terror and following them was a little brown weasel.

Curiosity is highly developed in the weasel. Many times I have seen them in my camp at night and if I remained perfectly quiet they would approach to within a few feet and stand upright on their hind legs to get a good view. At the least movement, however, they would disappear only to return a minute later.

As before mentioned the weasel is a bloodthirsty creature, and when it finds some food that is to its liking it can scarcely be driven away. On various occasions I have found them attempting to remove the bait from my traps and such times I would adjust the trap so as to be very easily sprung, and then step aside and wait for the animal to be caught.

The White Weasel.

The weasel has a sharp eye and a keen nose. While trapping in the North I would always keep on hand a supply of snared rabbits for use as bait, and often weasels would come into the camp at night, attracted by the bait, and it is interesting to note how quickly they could scent out the freshest rabbit in the pile and by biting into its ears would attempt to drag it away. Quite often they were able to move a fair sized rabbit. I usually kept a trap setting in my camp and in this way in one season caught fifteen weasels in one camp.

I have never learned anything regarding the breeding habits of the weasel, but judging from the large numbers of these animals found in favorable localities I would say that they are very prolific.

For trapping this animal I recommend the No. 1½ trap and prefer a trap that is loosely hinged and springs easily, such as the Victor. Any trap will hold a weasel but when caught in the smaller sizes they quite often double up about the jaws and when they die and freeze in that position it is difficult to remove them from the trap. With the 1½ they are always caught over the body and there is little trouble from that source. As the animal is so very light in weight it is necessary that the trap springs very easily. There are various styles of rat traps on the market which make excellent weasel traps, but as one never knows what animal may happen along, I prefer to use the steel trap.

My method of setting is to place the trap inside of a small enclosure of chunks of wood, bark, sticks or whatever is most convenient. No covering is needed but when setting on the snow I make a bed of evergreen boughs for the trap to rest oil. Rotten wood will answer just as well. I fasten the bait with a stick just back of the trap so that the weasel will be obliged to stand on the trap when attempting to remove the bait, for it should be remembered that they will never eat any food where they find it if able to move it away. Fasten the trap securely for some larger animal is likely to be caught. I do not place the traps far apart, where tracks are seen in fair numbers, and I drag a fresh killed rabbit from set to set, splitting it open with a knife so as to leave a bloody trail. Any weasel that strikes the trail is sure to follow it.

For bait I prefer rabbit to anything else as it contains more blood than other baits and fresh blood is the only scent that I know of which will attract the weasel.

In order to obtain good prices it is necessary that the fur be kept clean and I use a small cloth bag in which to carry my catch.

The tracks of the weasel resemble those of the mink but are considerably smaller. The average length of jump is perhaps about eighteen inches.

TRAPPING THE WEASEL

As soon as the snow is on the ground and the weather sufficiently cold, take at may 'O' traps ass you have or can carry, and having a hatchet, go to the woods and locate the runways or some abode that the weasel frequents. If you find such abode, set one or more traps in the immediate vicinity or therein. Place cotton or wool underneath the pan and see that the pan works very easily. Cover trap with rotten wood, etc. If you are unable to find a hole, endeavor to kill a rabbit. If you are successful, take a knife and strike the animal in the neck so as to bleed slowly. Now walk along dragging the animal behind; when you come to a convenient locality, set your trap, permitting the rabbit's blood to drop in the vicinity, if advisable hand a small piece of the rabbit above the trap. Proceed until all the traps are used up.

N.C.A

TRAPPING THE WEASEL

A few years ago I never bothered to skin a white weasel, because the skin was usually worth only five or ten cents, but of late years. I have devoted as much time to weasel trapping as to mink and skunk, I use No.1 traps which I set close to the inches from the ground so that the weasel will be able to reach it when standing on his hind legs. The meat is securely fastened to the tree, which forces the weasel to jump around.

One funny experience I had last winter: I saw a weasel run into a hollow tree. The opening was no more than a good sized knot hole. I thought to myself "Ah, ha, Mr. Weasel, I've got you." I immediately went to work, took my hatchet and made a large excavation and stapled the trap with the pan facing the knot hole to the tree. I was careful so as to give plenty of room for the jaws to close. The next morning when I came the trap had a firm hold of Mr. Weasel's head; in fact the bones were considerably bruised after I had taken off the skin.

F. C. MARSH.

TRAPPING THE ERMINE OR WEASEL

The Weasel and ermine kill indiscriminately for food and pleasure such birds and animals as it can master; chief amongst them are mice, rats, rabbits, ground and chirping squirrels and nearly all birds and fowls, both wild and domestic. Both of these diminutive monsters in their

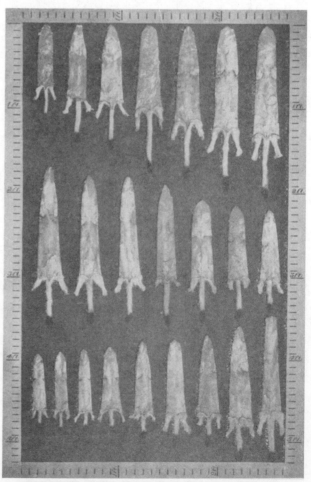

WEASEL AND ERMINE SKINS "Raw"
All Sizes. Scale Shows Inches and Feet.

ceaseless quest for food and to satisfy their individual irresistible craving for blood, dart from one opening into another, whether that be a hollow log, burrow, stone pile or crevice of a rock. Upon exploration, should the abode be unoccupied, the animal's stay is a momentary one, and it will immediately decamp, taking the shortest rote to the next opening: if inhabited, a general tumult follows. The weasel and ermine are more beneficial than detrimental in farming communities and should only be killed when continued losses of poultry occur. The animal's favorite hold is upon the neck, and it quenches its insatiable vampire-like thirst by lapping the blood from its victim.

If the animal's capture is desired it can be accomplished by steel traps placed in their run-ways, holes, crevices, burrows, etc. In most cases, the animal is taken in traps originally set for mink and marten. The same methods as are applied to mink and marten should be followed in the capture of these two animals. A good place to set the steel trap is in a hollow tree, hollow log, abandoned hole or abode of other animals, and in the front or rear of small openings through which the animals enters. Wire traps can be used advantageously, so can tree traps; the latter can be utilized in various places. Bait is unnecessary when the traps are set in their habitual run-ways; at other places a piece of meat hung over the trap, or head of a chicken or rabbit, placed within the abode, will answer admirably.

The skins should be handled similarly to mink or marten skins; the fur part can be on the out or inside. A three-piece stretches in recommended; the skin is very tender, and great care must be exercised in stretching and removing the skin from the stretcher not to tear or burst it. Only white-furred skins should be marketed as the brown skins have no commercial value, but should one of the latter species be capture, it is a useless waste of time to skin the animal and stretch the skin.

Traps can be baited with bits of meat, hung over the trap. A good place to set the trap is in a hollow tree, hollow log, abandoned holed or abodes of other animals. Bait should be used.

CHAPTER 2

Ermine

*(White Weasel. Ger. Hermelin, Sw. Hermelin, Eng. Stoat &
Ermine, Lat. Putorius Erminea.)*

As Stated elsewhere, this animal resembles the Siberian Ermine very closely and there is no apparent good reason why the change in name from White Weasel to Ermine is improper from a commercial and scientific standpoint. Dr. Coupes, after a thorough examination, heralds the change, and in his view we fully concur. The only difference noticeable is that the body is slightly smaller, the fur not as long, neither quiet as silky. The peculiar subpart-like yellow color is noticeable in all species of the erminen, also the pencil-like formation on tip of tail.

Summer and Winter Dress.   **THE WEASEL AND ERMINE.**   From Original Painting. Property of Andersch Bros.

The animal does change its outer garment periodically but the change is not so sudden as certain authors relate. Bell states: "The winter change of color which this species so universally assumes in the northern climates is affected not by loss of the summer coat, and the substitution of the new one for the winter, but by the actual change of the color of the existing fur." Another prominent author states his views in the following words: "The transition from the summer to the winter colors, is primarily occasioned by actual change of temperature, and not by the mere advance of the season." Mr. Blyth, commenting upon the above two assertions, has the following to say: "Authors are wrong in what they have advanced respecting the made in which this animal changes it color, at least in autumn; for in a specimen which I lately examined, which was killed during the autumnal change, it was clearly perceivable that the white hairs were all new not the brown changed in color."

Close observation of the animal and more so in the handling of thousands of skins from animals killed at different period of the year, give one the opinion that animal changes, rather sheds, its coat twice a year. In autumn, September and November, varying somewhat in the different latitudes, the summer hair, gradually, almost imperceptibly, drops out, and is immediately succeeded by a fresh coat, which in the course of ten to twenty days becomes white. In the spring months the change in color is just the opposite. The change is natural, not only from the outward appearance, but also from the flesh part of the skin. The inner part of the skin, after all flesh and fat is removed and becomes dry, has the natural white and prime color. The skin is thin and clear, not so when the skin is removed from the animal during its shedding period in the spring, at which period the outer portion of the skin is black and unprimed. At this period the new fur fibers are still perceptible and the old guard or outer hairs are loose in their respective cells. Subsequently the change in color of this animal's fur comes in periods when other animals shed their outer garment to a greater or less extent.

The male is invariably larger than the female. Both are provided with glands from which the animal when under the influence of fear, anger or sexual passion, emits a peculiar fluid of a highly penetrating, offensive and horrible odor. In color the fluid is yellow, and it is believed that this fluid is responsible for the yellowish, sulphur-like color of the pelt. Others again state positively that this peculiar color on the fur is the result of the animal's unclean habits, abode, and continued contact with their own or the mate's water. The fluid containers or glands are situated one on each side of the anus just upon the verge of the opening. On the animal slightly averting the anus, these papillae may be readily perceived. Slight pressure will cause them to stand erect, and at the animal's pleasure may squirt and distribute its fluid in a firm spray at a variable distance not exceeding two feet. At other times the fluid trickles in drops or in a stream about its parts.

The average measurement of skins received from Canada and northern part of United Stated indicate that the body of the largest animal is 15 inches in length and the yearlings about 8 to 9 inches. Many skins are received indicating that they were taken off from kittens measuring 5 to 6 inches in length and ¾ to 1 inch in width. The large skins usually measure 13 to 15 inches long, 2½ to 3½ wide. The length of tail, varying some what, is usually 2 to 4 inches. Once in a great while a clear white skin with a longer tail, is received, but presumably this is an exception, and possibly the animal emigrated from a more southern latitude. A large number of brown skins (summer) from the same region received during the late spring and summer months, are practically of the same size and dimensions. See illustrations of skins elsewhere in this volume, also article "Trapping and preparing Skins."

This animal as well as the weasel, shows no sign of becoming exterminated. Higher prices for their pelts has a tendency to increase the activity on the part of the hunter and trapper in pursuing same, as will be seen in the table of number of skins marketed in this country and London. In former years the ermine fur was controlled by royalty, and certain penalties by law were attached to outside persons wearing garments made from these skins, but of late years, owing to the large number marketed, and from other causes, the skins are used for various purposes and by all classes of people, not only in Europe, but also in the United States and Canada.

The price of the skins varies considerably, depending upon the demand and supply. The skins of the European ermine ranges from 500 to $2.50 while that of the American species including the white northern weasel, very seldom exceeds $1.00 and in most cases 25 to 75 cents being paid the trapper. The last two years however, are an exception, and the ruling price for good skins ranged from 75 cents to $1.25 one American concern alone marketing in London 60,000 skins.

The skins are used for various purposes, principally for ladies wearing apparel, on royal clothes and garments, at other times in connection with other furs, principally with krimmer. Persian lamb, seal, etc. The yellowish, sulphur-like parts are used in conjunction with the black pencil-like tip of the tail. Manufacturers dislike the sulphur-like color on the skins; such skins are commercially called "stained" and bring a less price than those that are clear white.

The Ermine belongs to the Weasel family, has the general Weasel shape and appearance, and inhabits the northern parts of Europe and Asia. It is a small animal, measuring only fourteen inches in total length, of which the tail occupies four inches. There is, however, considerable variation in the size of individuals. The Ermine is carnivorous and a most determined hunter. It preys on hares, rabbits and all kinds of small quadrupeds, birds and reptiles. It is very fond of rabbits, of which, especially the young, it destroys great numbers. The pheasant arid partridge also suffer greatly from its predicate. It pursues its game with courage and pertinacity and rarely suffers it to escape. It is also a great plunderer of birds nests of all kinds. Its favorite mode of attack is by fastening on the neck and sucking the blood of its victim.

The color of the Ermine in summer is a light reddish brown on the tipper parts of the body, and lighter tinted or nearly white underneath In winter, in high northern latitudes, its fur changes to a delicate cream-colored white, on all parts of the body except the tip of the tail, which retains its black color and forms a fine contrast to the rest of the body. It is only in the coldest portions of Norway, Sweden, Russia and Siberia that the Ermine becomes sufficiently blanched in winter be of any commercial value. Russian Asia furnishes the greater portion of those caught. In England the Ermine, when in its summer coat, is commonly called the Stoat, and, on account of its predaceons habits, is thoroughly detested.

Ermine fur was formerly monopolized by the royal families and nobility of Europe, but now finds its way into the general markets, and among European furs is next in importance to the Sable.

The same general methods should be pursued in trapping the Ermine as in the case of the Mink and Marten.

CHAPTER 3

Mink

(Ger. Nertz, Lat. Putorius (Lutrcola) vison.)

It is not commonly known that think and skunk are now the greatest producers of revenue to the American hunter and trapper; the reader can judge for himself, especially after perusing the table on a subsequent page, which gives the number of skins marketed in a given period.

The mink belongs to the weasel family and is found in North America, Europe and Asia. Naturalists divide the North American mink into two, sometimes into three, separate species, but I believe that there is no good occasion to make such division. If same is desirable from a descriptive and scientific point of view there can easily be made as many as two or three divisions of animals in a single state, and probably twenty or thirty in the entire northern hemisphere. The fur trade has its own division, for instance: Southern, Southwestern, Central, Eastern, Northern, Fish, Prairie, Cotton and the fine Northeastern and Canadian.

MINK

This animal differs notably from the weasel or ermine in its larger size, much stouter form, and lasting color of its pelage. It resembles the marten, also the wild ferret. The ears are short, well rounded, furred both side, and the adjacent fur covers members in certain altitudes. The head is small, rather low and flat, sub-triangular, with a rather well rounded otter like mouth. The lower portion of its mouth is small. The extremity of the Snout is protuberant and definitely naked.

Its legs are stout, short, and well proportioned. The front legs measure 1¾ to 2¼ inches in length, the rear ones always exceeding the front by ½ to ¾ inches. Each of the four feet have five rather long toes, which are armed with short, crooked claws. The claws are retractable at will by the animal. The body is long, slender, and with its slender neck has a general vermiform appearance, and measures from nose to root of tail 12 to 26 inches in length, to which a tail of 6 to 9 inches is to be added. The above variation in size is further explained elsewhere. The male always exceeds the female by ¼ to 1-3 its size.

Its pelage varies extensively in color, length, quality, and density, according to the section the animal inhabits, but the fundamental color is brown. The further south one goes, the coat of the animal becomes paler, while just the opposite is true in the northern latitudes. The tail is always a few shades darker that the fur on the body and invariably is this also true of the animal's back as compared with the fur on its belly. A white spot is common on the animal's breast, other times this spot appears only on the lower lip. Once in a while a mink will have a few white hairs on the extreme tip of its tail, otherwise the color of its pelage is fairly uniform.

The outer garment consists of two distinct sets of fibers, the inner or undergrowth of fur fibers proper, and the outer or guard hairs. The former are soft, silky, downy, adhering very closely together, and in color are usually lighter that the predominating guar hairs. While the former are $\frac{3}{8}$ to $\frac{1}{2}$ inch long, the latter always protrude $\frac{1}{4}$ to $\frac{3}{8}$ of an inch above the undergrowth, consequently $\frac{3}{4}$ to $1\frac{1}{4}$ inches long. The guard hairs are coarse, smooth, glossy, rather pointed and well distributed all over the body, becoming shorter about the head and feet and longer at the tail; on the latter the hairs are inclined to stand out horizontally, giving it a bushy appearance.

Southern Mink are found in all parts of the southern states. The animal attains a size of 16 to 18 inches with a tail 6 to 8 inches in length. Its fur is rather coarse, especially is this true of the lower growth. The guard hairs are also coarse and comparatively pale and void of luster.

From Original Painting.   Property of Andersch Bros.   **THE NORTHERN MINK**   Northern Michigan.

Southwestern Mink found in these states along rivers, creeks and lakes. Are about the same in size as the more southern species, but are better furred, more robust, and their skins always command a better price from the dealer and furrier. The fur is more dense and of better color and larger individual specimens are also noticeable.

The Northeastern Mink that inhabits Maine, New Brunswick, parts of Quebec and that particular section, is comparatively small. The body is 10 to 14 inches, with a tail 5 to 6 inches long. The fur during the latter part of December and January is extremely beautiful. The rarest, best and highest priced skins come from that section, especially when its small size is considered. The fur is soft, silky, not so deep 'or long, but very dark, rather of the wavy and changeable color type.

As the name indicated, the Prairie Mink is found chiefly in prairie sections, about streams or in light growth of timber. He becomes very large in northern states, notably so in Dakota and Manitoba. While the ordinary size of the prairie mink, especially those inhabiting the open sections of the middle west, and west, is from 22 to 30 inches, the writer has seen minks and their skins measuring 32 to 36 inches from nose to root of tail, and with the latter a total of 43 inches over all. The animal and skin, while extraordinarily long, were other wise well proportioned. The former in a natural position at middle of body measured 12 to 12½ inches in circumference and 3½ to 4 inches in diameter, the skin averaging in width from shoulder to rear portion, 4½ to 5 inches. The pelage of this species is somewhat coarse, but of fair color and very suitable for coat collars, cuffs, etc. Under no circumstances must the pelage of the prairie mink be compared with southern coarse mink, as these northern skins are worth twice to three times as much. The female is much smaller than the male, and has a more valued coat being finer in texture and darker in color.

Fish Mink attain an average size, are more aquatic, live in and about water more than other species and their food consists chiefly of fish. The fur is more evenly distributed, the outer guard hairs protrude less over the fur fibers or lower growth, as is the case with the other species. In general the fur is more sleek, top hairs shorter and all are of more uniform color, in this respect resembling a lot of dark, brown, glazed coffee beans. The odor of the animal is constantly that of fish and seemingly this odor remains in the skin for a long time.

It is claimed that the white underground Cotton Mink is rather more of a freak of nature that a distinct species, and that this growth is quite unnatural, sometimes caused by sickness, other times by confinement. Some naturalists seem to think that this peculiar color crops out at intervals, and for explanation go back generations when it was claimed that there were no mink, but ermine, and that in the ages of evolution as explained by Darwin, such are the reminders of the changes that were brought about in the natural course of evolution. Such minks are found sparingly in the central, western and middle states. Apparently the theory that this species is more of a freak, must give room for additional thought, as hundreds and thousands of skins are annually marketed showing these particular characteristics. The general construction of its body, size, habits, etc., resembles the other minks. It does not breed separately, but in connection with the regular species, thus indicating harmony amongst them. The outer garment is practically the same as on other species, and the only difference noticeable is that instead of having brown or dark colored fur fibers, its undergrowth of fur resembles cotton, being clear white. Occasionally this white cotton like growth is noticeable only on section of the skin, particularly on the top of the animal extending 4 to 6 inches from the root of its tail, other parts having the normal color. On account of the animal resembling the other very closely, hundreds of trappers are annually disappointed, being obliged to accept a lesser price for such skins; many inexperienced buyers purchase these skins without knowing the difference until they come to sell them. The easiest way to detect these cotton or white underground mink, is by blowing into the fur at various places, especially just beyond the tail. Such skins cannot be used advantageously in their natural condition and are either dyed or blended.

The mink is very active, light of foot, carnivorous, and its essential aquatic nature leads it to seek in general well-watered sections; will scarcely ever be found far away from water except it be caught during the journey it makes from one stream or lake to another. Its amphibious mode of like is well known to all hunters, trappers and those that come in contact with this carnivore. His movement on land lacks something of the extraordinary agility displayed by the more slender bodied weasel. It habitually prowls about stone piles, frequents underground retreats, and is altogether a more openly aggressive marauder, not less persistent or courageous in its attack. In its coming and going is almost imperceptible. Its ability to climb trees is unquestioned; it scarcely frequents them but will take to the tree if it thins its capture can be averted.

Its keen sense of smell enables it to track and trace other animals, consequently is less concerned for a fresh supply of food than most other animals. Its principal food is fish, frogs, reptiles, muskrats, mice, and rats; birds and fowls of all kinds are relished. Much to the detriment of the farmer, it frequents the hen roost, but in this respect it is not as much and unnecessary slayer as the weasel or ermine, though instances are recorded where as many as forty chickens were killed by a single mink 1½ to 2 inches m diameter, is well noted and in the event that the opening is too small, it can increase it in a remarkably short time. The male and the female can at their pleasure, emit from their respective glands a horrible smelling odor.

The rutting season usually begins in latter part of February or first part of March. At this time the male wanders carelessly along the shore of streams and lakes, having in mind only the search for the female. Apparently the male is on foot day and night and during this period is more easily trapped. The female is scarcely seen at this time being in some adore, obviously to keep away form the male as much as possible.

During the month of April or early part of May, the mother brings forth a litter of four to six young, which are carefully hidden in some hollow log, burrow or cave. The mother continues with her young until they are about half-grown, and pays particular attention to keeping them away from the male, who if opportunity presents, will kill its offspring. The animal attains its maturity in one year, the female arriving at age of puberry at the end of this period. The young are born blind and remain so for four or five weeks.

Mink can be tamed if taken young, especially before they have their sight. It is unwise to attempt to tame the animal after the age of three to six months, and especially if he or she is of a vicious disposition. If taken young, by continued petting and handling, they become like domesticated ratters and have all the playfulness of young kittens. At a later period they become extremely mischievous as their keen sent leads them to pantries, hen houses, dovecotes, and a canary bird in a room is very annoying to them. The animal's extensive power with the mouth can hardly be estimated unless one has seen the animal in a trap, cage, box or other place of captivity. When wild minks are confined with tame ones, the latter always prove stronger and come off victorious in the contest that ensues.

The Mink in neither nocturnal nor diurnal. It travels alike at night and during the day. It is perfectly indifferent to the time—it may be a dark, stormy night or a bright, sunshiny morning.

There are various methods of trapping the Mink, both on land and in the water. When the trap is set on land, cover it lightly with material in keeping with the surroundings, and fasten to a clog, "spring pole" or "balance pole." When the trap is set in or near the water, fasten to a "sliding pole" or stake it out into the water the entire length of the chain.

The following is a good water set: Find a sleep bank where the water is not deep. Make a hole in the bank eight or ten inches deep and about three or four inches in diameter. Put a piece of bait in the hole. Set the trap in the water at the mouth of the hole and cover with mud or wet leaves.

If you can find little sandbars, along a stream projecting into the water, set a trap on one of these bars under water about an inch or two deep. Fix a small fish on the point of a stick out in the water, about a foot from the trap, and push the stick down until the fish is partly under water.

Another method is to find a Mink trail along a stream, then get some old dry slicks and stick them in the ground across the trail and about six inches out in the water, leaving a narrow passage in the trail between the sticks. Set a trap in this passage and cover lightly.

Where Mink travel along a lake, find the outlet and lay a hollow log across the stream. Set a trap in the log, covering it with fine rotten wood. The Mink will try to run through the log and will be caught.

When streams are frozen up, find a jam or drift extending across the stream. Set a trap in an opening in the drift near the bank. Cover with wet leaves and fine drift dirt. If you cannot find a good opening, make one.

Mink should be skinned "cased" and shipped flesh side out.

Mink are ramblers in their habits, except in the breeding season. They feed on fish, frogs, snakes, birds, mice, and muskrats; and the hen-roost frequently suffers from their depredations. They are very-fond of specked trout and pretty sure to find out the streams where these fish abound. Their breeding season commences about the last of April, and the females bring forth from four to six at a litter. The young are hid by the mother till they attain nearly half their growth, as the males of this species, as well as of the Marten, Fisher, Weasel, Panther, and most carnivorous destroy their young when they can find them.

Mink can be taken either on land or in the water. Experts generally prefer to take them on land. The trap should be set near the bank of a stream. If one of their holes cannot be found, make a hole by the side of a root or a stump, or anywhere in the ground. Three suies of the cavity should be barricaded with stones, bark, or rotten wood, and the trap set at the entrance. The bait may be full, birds, or the flesh of the muskrat, cut in small pieces; and it should be put into the cavity beyond the trap, so that the animal will have to step on the trap in taking the bait. The trap should be concealed by a covering of leaves, rotten vegetation, or, what is better, the feathers of some bird. In very cold weather the bait should be smoked to give it a stronger smell·

Mink can be attracted long distances by a scent that is prepared from the decomposition of eels, trout, or even minnows. These fishes are cut in small pieces, and put in a loosely-corked bottle, which is allowed to hang in the sunshine for two or three weeks in summer, when a sort of oil is formed which emits a very strong odor. A few drops of this oil on the bait, or even a stick without bait, will draw Mink effectually.

The chain of the trap should be fastened to a spring-pole strong enough to lift the animal, when caught, out to the reach of the Fisher, Fox, and other depredators; or, if the trap is set near deep water, it may be attached to a sliding-pole, which will secure the game by drowning it. Both of these methods are fully described on preceding pages.

One successful trapper uses codfish for bait and considers it the very best thing. Others make a strong point of preparing their traps by boiling them in ashes and water, or in water with hemlock boughs, or coating them with beeswax, or fir balsam or some animal or fish oil, to cover all odors which the animals would distrust. Canned sardines make good mink bait. Skunk scent and feathers attract all bird-eating animals, and allay their suspicions. Each trapper thinks the method by which he has succeeded is the best, but whatever the method, the cunning of the animal, and his suspicious nature and keen nose, have to be reckoned with.

As we have said on previous pages, the Mink as much given to wandering along the banks of streams and ponds. On such rambles lie explores all the holes in the bank, all the little brooks and ditches emptying into the larger stream, and guided by this knowledge the experienced trapper has little difficulty in catching him, either in water-set or land-set.

When the streams are open Mink may often be caught by putting several small live fish on a string and leaving them in shallow water inside a V shaped enclosure, setting the trap at the large or open end. Both the Mink and Raccoon like to catch and eat such little fishes and they are not suspicious of such an arrangement.

Sometimes when they are wandering up a stream and have to pass around an old dam, a very good place may be found to set a trap down near the water where they have passed before. Study the signs,

PRACTICAL SUGGESTIONS BY TRAPPERS

—When the ditches and creeks are frozen over, set one or more traps in the warm water that comes out of running drain tiles, or in the mouth of a tile which happens to be dry during the winter, as Mink sometimes make these their homes.

—Where there is a small air-hole in the ice place a trap directly under this hole. For this set the water should not be over four inches deep.

—If a Mink makes a hole through a snowdrift he will use it again and a trap set in it will catch.

—If you catch a female Mink, reset the trap, as the chances are good to catch the male soon and erhaps several males in the running season. Find where an old Muskrat hole leads down to the edge of the water from the top of the bank. A trap set in the lower end of this hole will catch Mink, as they seldom miss a chance to explore such a hole.

—The entrails of Muskrat, Rabbit, chicken or duck make better bait than the whole animal or bird. Dig up the ground to set the trap in fresh earth, unless it is a water-set or swamp-set on some log.

—In winter notice where Mink travel, scrape away the snow, chop On dig up the ground, set a trap on the loose dirt and scatter some egg shells or feathers around.

—Mink go out on mud flats at now tides to catch crabs and other food. When they have eaten enough they will collect a supply and store in some hollow log above tide water for future use. This is a good place to set a trap.

—If you find a hollow log open at both ends close up one end after putting some bait inside that end Set your trap about a foot inside the log at the other end, making the entrance free and clear. The Mink will smell the bait and run into the log and trap. Trailing the liait along the ground up to the log helps.

—In setting where the bank guides a Mink into the water, thrust a dead stick into the bank horizontally about three inches above the trap, so he will crawl under it and be obliged to step in the trap.

—Where a log rests with one end in the water and the other end on the bank, fasten your bait on the under side of the bank end, about ten inches from the ground, and set your trap under the bait.

—For Mink scent, use the matrix of a female Mink preserved in the oil of the wild duck.

—If there is snow, set your trap in his well-used path, covering with a little dry snow. Damp snow will freeze into a crust so the trap will not spring.

—Find their path close to water. Follow this path to a steep place where they are forced to enter the water. Set your trap an inch and a half or two inches under water exactly where the path enters, and cover it with a few soaked leaves.

—If earth worms are put in a bottle loosely corked and hung in the sun until the oil tries out of them, you will have one of the strongest stinks known. Some use it as a trapping scent.

—Even an old and trap-shy Mink will walk into one set m a bed of dry hen manure. A peck of this will make a good bed. Proceed the same as with a bed of chaff, only place a light wad of cotton under the pan of the trap.

—Another plan which requires some labor is to find a small brook which is frozen over, cut a channel in the ice right across the brook from bank to bank, then drive down stakes not more than one inch apart, leaving one space in the stakes where the water is not more than one or two inches deep. Set a No.1½ Newhouse trap in this space, fastened to a wire or sliding pole so that when caught the Mink can get to deep water and drown. No bait is necessary, as the Mink has to pass through the line of stakes where the trap is. Put a Bolivia on the ice over the trap and stakes, and throw snow or brush on top so the water will not freeze where the trap is.

—Bait your trap with a live duck or chicken. No Mink will pass without stopping to kill the bird.

—Punch a hole through the bank which overhangs shallow water, having it slope so the Mink can climb up or slide down. Place trap under water if possible, covering it with a few water-soaked leaves.

—Try setting traps in the holes you will find in the banks of streams, patting bait outside the hole about six feet from trap, and cover the bait with a flat stone, so he will have a hard time to get it. The Mink will eat a little, then dive into one of the holes, and yon have him.

—Good sets for Mink may often be found where steep rocks, or the stone of a bridge extend into water, where the bridges span streams, in runways back of the sleepers.

—After cold whether sets in, when setting in shallow water for Mink, choose a place where the current runs swiftly and is not likely to freeze up.

—Lay a hollow log along a Mink path, between steep banks and the water. Use brush to block any passageway except through the log, and set a trap in each end of the log.

—Take a crab, tie a string to one paw, and put it under some stump where Mink run on dry land, not in water. Set trap so crab cannot spring it. The crab will live a week.

—Live mice make good Mink bait.

—Where there is a saw-mill on a stream use the saw dust to cover your trap. Make it look as if the saw dust had just floated down from the mill. Put a bit of loose cotton under the pan of trap.

—Find a place where Mink have a hole in a snow drift. Dig a narrow cut or ditch sideways into the drift where you will be sure to strike the hole. Set a trap in the runway, and cover up your ditch so it will be dark. Once in his hole the Mink is not so suspicious, and very likely will walk into your trap.

—Red squirrel is excellent Mink bait; Beaver musk is fairly good.

—Chaff that mice have run over and thoroughly scented, when sprinkled around a trap, is good.

—Cut your bait in several small pieces, so that the Mink has to make several trips to your set.

—Nearly always there are springs around lakes and swamps which Mink will be sure to visit when traveling that way. What is called a "bait house" may be made at such a place. Drive sticks in the mud where the water is two inches deep, so that the tops lean together to form a roof which you will afterwards cover with moss, sods or small twigs. Drive these sticks so as to make a pen about a foot wide in the form of a horse-sloe, and leave an opening three inches wide in which to set the trap. Put some good bait, like fresh Muskrat meat, in the back of this pen and fasten the trap properly.

—If you find a log lying with one end in the water and the other on the low bank with sandy beach between, stick chunks of wood or stones under the log so that the Mink will have to go around them in the water under the log. Set a No. 1 trap right under the log in an inch of water and stake out in deeper water. Scatter a little bait by the sides of the log.

—In setting traps for Mink, the Indian would take a Muskrat and drag it around in the vicinity of the trap. He said, "When Mink strike trail he no leave till he find meat" The meat was always placed so that he got into the trap before he got to the meat. E. K. Lent.

—A good way to trap Mink in winter is to find a hole in the ice where the Mink passes and reposes. Set a No. 1½ trap in the hole and bait it with a bird or chicken's head. Fasten a pole six or eight feet long and have a long chain attached to it, so the Mink will slide into the water and drown.

—When Mink tracks are seen along the stream and the ground favors, this is a good plan : Drag some bait or scent on a short route from the water and back to it. A piece of meat or an old fowl which has been killed, split open and scented with fish oil, oyster juice or oil and asafetida, loosely sewed up, makes a good drag. Set several traps exactly in the path of the drag. The Mink will run along the trail, there being nothing to arouse his suspicion, and get caught.

—When there is no snow on the ground Mink often follow Muskrat trails. If a piece of fowl or other good bait be placed two or three feet from the trail the Mink will follow his nose and turn aside to get it, unless he is closely pursuing a Muskrat.

—Where two brooks unite and there is a little sand-bar on the point, pit a piece of Muskrat meat on a stick which leans out over your trap, which should be in two inches of water.

—An old half-breed Indian set two traps on top of a newly finished Muskrat house, put a few drops of scent on a leaf at the very top of the house, and spitted a small piece of Muskrat meat near the traps.

—For Mink I use a No. 1 or No. 1½ trap. The latter is preferable. For scent that obtained from the scent bags of the Mink or Weasel, mixed with anise oil, is the best decoy I ever used. This scent is found near the root of the tail in round bags about the size of a pea, and is a yellow liquid smelling very strong.

—After setting the trap, I scatter feathers around and over it The Mink seeing the feathers and scenting what he supposes to be a Weasel, will dig up the whole works looking for something a Weasel has overlooked, and he is mighty lucky if he don't get into the trap. Canned sardines make good Mink bait, and the sardine oil is good to mix with the scent in the scent bottle. Skunk scent and feathers attract and allay the suspicion of all bird eating animals.

HORACE R. LITTLE.

—A good set for Mink is to kill a Rabbit and set him in the position you are accustomed to see him in the woods, where a Mink is likely to travel. Dig a little hole on each side of the Rabbit large enough for your trap. Set a trap in the hole, one on each side of the Rabbit, and cover with small leaves; for they are not so likely to clog the jaws of the trap as large ones. If you use care enough you will most likely get the first Mink that sees the Rabbit, even if he is not hungry, for a Mink will kill for the sake of killing.

—Another way is to dig a hole about a foot deep and six inches wide and straight into the bank, having about two inches of water in it; cut a forked stick and run it through your bait; stick it into the back end of the hole and set your trap at the entrance under water. This is also an excellent set for Coon and Muskrat, but of course must be used in open weather.

T. J. FOREMEN, Ohio.

—In regard to catching Mink, I think a good way is to take the scent bag. especially in tie running time, and hang it up above the traps. If a passing Mink gets the scent, he is pretty sure to go there.

—In the stream at the outlet of a small lake, an old trapper built a "mink-house" of flat stones, placing them about eight inches away from the steep-rocky bank, so as to form a chamber about eight inches wide by eighteen long, and fourteen high, with a three or four inch depth of water in and about the front. Putting large pieces of fresh fish in the back end of this stone house, and setting a No. 1½ steel trap just inside the entrance, he found this to be his most profitable set, catching many dollars worth of Mink in a few weeks.

—I get the best results from water-sets when I can find the creek at the right stage, where there is a small raceway or narrow running stream between two deep holes of water. I place my traps in this stream under the water about two inches and I catch nearly every Mink that passes up or down the creek.

—A Mink will keep on the bank at the edge of the water when lie strikes a deep hole, but when he comes to a shallow stream he will invariably run through the middle of it. He often makes two and three trips up and down this stream. If you can find shallow running water by cutting a hole in the ice, it is a good place to set a trap for the Mink.

—In winter a Mink will often keep a hole open in the ice and if you find such a one, look around and you will also find a hole in the bank near it and a path between the two. If you set your trap in this path and cover it with a small piece of white cloth cut to fit and sprinkle a little snow or fine dirt over it, you will have learned one more good method.

—In setting for Mink on land, I go about it in this way: I prepare my traps by boiling them in hemlock boughs. Then I dig up the ground with a trap-hook (a place two feet across) and set the trap in the middle and cover lightly with fine leaves, putting some under the trap to keep it from freezing to the ground. Don't be afraid to dig up the ground thoroughly, as a Mink will always stop and investigate such a place. Have your hook long enough so that you will not have to walk on the new ground. Fasten your trap to a springy bush or bush drag. After the ground freezes you will have to shelter your traps. I have used the following method: Take two large sized chunks of wood and lay them about six inches apart, leaving both ends open. Set a No. 1½ trap at each end. Put your bait between the two traps and cover with small bush or grass. The entrance to a hollow log is a good place to trap. You can use these two sets all winter.

Red Squirrel, chicken, rabbit, partridge, muskrat and turtle are all good baits. Fish is good when it is fresh but it does not last long. The best bait I ever used was turtle. I find it the best that I can use in cold weather. When you get a Mink or Rat, if alive, let it bleed, around your trap. It is also a good plan to hitch a string around your bait and drag it from one trap to another.

—For Mink, a good set is close to a bank and near the edge of the water. The bait, if any is used, should be fresh Muskrat, Rabbit or chicken. All are good. If you wish for scent, the musk from the animal you are trapping is preferable.

—In some river, brook or pond, where Mink tracks can be found in the mud or on the bank, place a flat stone in the mud at the edge of the water and about a foot away place another in the same manner, having them about an inch out of the water. Now set your trap just under water about half way between the stones and place a small piece of moss on the trap pan. This method is especially adapted to trapping Mink without bait. As the animal comes along his route, he jumps out to the first stone and, seeing the piece of moss between him and the other stone, jumps on to it to cross over, when you have by both fore feet.

The Mink.

There are probably more methods used in trapping the mink than in trapping any other animal. In localities where they take bait well, the usual plan is to set the trap in the entrance to a natural or artificial enclosure, on the bank of the stream, placing a bait on the inside of the enclosure. The trap should be nested down, and covered with some light material in keeping with the surroundings. The trap may be fastened to a light clog or a balance pole, or if very close to the water, to a sliding pole. The bait should be strictly fresh. Some good scent may be used if desired. Hollow logs and holes in drifts and under stumps make good places for sets. Some trappers do not set in an enclosure, but hang the bait about eighteen inches above the trap. I do not, however, consider this a satisfactory method. When an artificial enclosure is used, it should be roofed over with bark, or evergreen boughs to protect that trap from the snow.

For fall trapping, many prefer to set traps in the water. The following method is one of the best for a water set: find a steep bank, where the water is shallow, and runs smoothly and rapidly, make a hole in the bank, on a level with the water, making the hole about ten inches deep and about four inches in diameter. Put a piece of fresh bait back in the hole, fastening with a small stick, and set the trap in the water at the mouth of the hole. Stake the trap the full length of the chain into the water and cover with mud or water-soaked leaves.

Along the streams where little sand-bars lead out into the water select a place on one of these bars, where the water is only an inch or two in depth, set the trap under the water, close to the edge of the stream. Fix a small fish on the point of the stick, out in the stream a foot from the trap, pushing the stick down until the bait rests partly under water. Stake the trap so that the catch will drown. This is a very successful set and requires but little time and trouble to make.

Mink Set Under Log.
X X Shows Positions of Traps.

In some localities the mink do not take bait well, in which case, blind sets—traps without bait must be depended upon. In the fall while the water is still open, find a high bank where the water leads off fairly deep, leaving only a very narrow strip of shallow water, at the foot of the bank. Set the trap in the edge of the water and stake full length of the chain into the stream. Place a couple of water-soaked leaves on the trap, and drop a few pinches of mind on them to hold them in place. The steep bank on one side and the deep water on the other, will guide the mink into the trap. If, however, the shallow water extends out some distance from the bank, take a chunk of water-soaked wood, and stand it in the water, just beyond the trap, leaving the top rest against the bank. This will leave only a narrow passage over the trap, and you may be pretty sure of catching your mink. A similar set should be made on the opposite side of the stream, if conditions are favorable. This is a very good method for use in the south.

After streams are frozen, a different plan must be adopted. In such cases if you can find a jam or drift extending across the stream, find an opening, leading through this drift, close to the bank, and set the trap in this opening, covering with fine, drift dirt. In case you cannot find a suitable passage, make one and stop up all other holes. A little scent of the right kind may be used here to good advantage.

The illustration shows two traps set under an old log, spanning the stream. The log protects the traps from rain or snow, and a glance at the cut will show that it would be practically impossible for a mink to pass along the stream without being caught. The same set is good for the raccoon. If the stream is frozen fill the opening, under the log, with old, dead brush, so that there is no chance for the mink to pass, except over the traps.

Another good method for the wary mink is as follows: find a high, steep bank along the stream; if it overhangs, so much the better, and about two feet above the water, make a hole about four inches in diameter, and a foot or more deep. Leave the dirt that you dig out, rest directly in front of the hole, and set the trap in this dirt, covering with same. Pack dry moss around the jaws and cover the trap first with a sheet of paper, finishing with a thin layer of dirt. Put some good mink scent in the hole; the musk of the mink itself is best for this set. If the traps can be visited every day, it is a good plan to stake the trap, so that the mink will roll around over the ground, and the next one will be more easily caught.

Where mink travel around a lake, go to the outlet and lay a hollow log across the stream, just where the water leaves the lake. Set a trap in this log, covering with fine, rotten wood, and every mink that travels around the lake, will attempt to run through the log, and will be caught. If you cannot find a hollow log near at hand, build a covered passage-way of poles and chunks, and set your trap in this passage.

Mink may also be taken in box traps and deadfalls.

Scents are much used and there are some few which have proved attractive. Fish oil is one of the most common scents for mink and other animals. It is made by taking fish of almost any kind, cutting them into small pieces, and putting in a wide mouthed bottle. Let stand in a warm place, loosely covered, until the fish are thoroughly rotted, and in a liquid state: this scent may be used alone or combined with others.

If a female mink can be caught, during the mating season, remove the generative organs, and place them in a bottle, adding about two ounces of fish oil and all of the mink musk you can get. This is undoubtedly the best scent ever devised. It should be used without bait.

In traveling, the mink goes "the jump" and its foot-prints are always in pairs, the space between each set being from eighteen to twenty- four inches. The footprints will measure from one to one and one-fourth inches in length, with one always somewhat in advance of the other.

Although the mink is not exclusive as to locality in its wanderings, it prefers small rivers and running streams, leaving hardly a hole unexplored, or a stone unturned, in its thorough search after food.

Minks can be caught in almost any appropriate crap, but a steel trap, of the size of a Newhouse No. 1½ is the one usually adopted. When used in the water, the trap should be set in a shallow place where the water is one or two inches deep, the bait being placed right over the trap, about eighteen inches above it; for this purpose a spot may be chosen where the bank rises straight up from the water's edge, or the bait may be placed in its proper end of a stick. The mink is compelled to stand up on its hind legs or jump upwards the bait, and cannot accomplish this without treading on the pan of the trap and being caught by it. If there is deep water near enough, the trap should be secured to a sliding- but where this is not available, a spring pole is advisable, to prevent the mink from falling a prey to any other larger animals.

On the land, the trap may be set in any position which compels the mink either to walk over the trap, or, preferably, to stand up on its hind legs in order to secure the bait. The trap may be placed at the entrance to their holes, or in a hollow, so that it is level with the ground, and lightly covered with chaff, feathers, rotten wood, or even loose earth, about eighteen inches long planted in the ground, having its upper end, on which the bait is placed right over the trap, the space behind side being piled up with brush, stones anything that will prevent the bait from being taken except from the trap; or it may be laid at the entrance of an artificial enclosure, or in a sage-way. Traps may be set at intervals, along the banks of a stream, about two feet from the valor, properly concealed and baited, and a trail made, either by dragging a dead muskrat or a piece of fresh meat along the ground on the line between the traps, or by sprinkling a track with a prepared scent. As soon as a mink strikes any portion of this trail, it will be led by the nose direct to one or other of the traps. The mink is sometimes very methodical in its wanderings, forming regular beaten tracks, by repeatedly passing over the same router these may be recognized by the droppings or dung on them. These tracks, always lead to a hole, natural or artificial, and form an excellent location for a trap, sunk either in any portion, of the track, just below the level of the ground, and carefully covered with earth, or in close proximity to the entrance to the hole.

The bait may consist of anything of Which the mink is particularly fond; pieces of fish or muskrat flesh, of birds heads, for instance; hut the most effective is fish-oil, the odor of which it will scent from a distance, and seek for eagerly.

TRAPPING THE MINK

Mr. Leuhrs, an Illinois trapper, writes as follow: "To become a successful mink trapper it is absolutely necessary that one study the habits and thoroughly acquaint himself with the locality, otherwise he will not make a success. I have no particular secrets, but have been successful and have trapped form the Gulf of Mexico to the northern part of Canada. Last year I caught 121 mink from the 4th of Nov. 1905, to 20th Jan. 1906, and all within thirty or forty miles of Chicago. The rules that I follow in trapping mink are as follows:

"When going over strange ground upon which I intend to trap I study the watery shores of the takes, streams, swamps and creek for their natural haunts. I tak special notice of their runs, paths, dens, feeding places and dung heaps and make it a point never to disturb them. When placing my traps always disturb them. When placing my traps always disturb as little as possible and approach the place by way of water. Then I set my traps always level with the ground and if possible a little deeper, especially if the surrounding soil permits this. I excavate an opening the size of the trap which I pad out with leaves or similar rubbish, then place the trap there-in. If a water set is preferred the trap must be even with the ground about one-half to two inches below the level of the water. Some soft subtance must be placed below the pan, otherwise sand will fill in and the trap will not be sprung. In water sets I prefer the sliding or spring pole or wire. When

MINK SET

THIS STYLE OF SET CAN ALSO BE USED FOR OTTER. DRIVE ROW OF STAKES ACROSS A SMALL STREAM, SET TRAP UPON SOME FLAT STONE ABOUT 3 INCHES BENEATH THE WATER. PUT BAIT ON EACH NEAREST STICK.

making a dry land set I cover trap with fine leaves or other material that I happen to find in the locality. Occasionally I use tip-ups. My three best mink sets are as follows:

Set No. 1. Dig up nice, loose ground along the bank of a liake or running water so that it looks as though some animal had started to dig a den, the pile being large enough to hold a No. 1½ Newhouse or No. 2 B & L. trap. I place cotton or wool, or the hair of rabbits under the pan; never pack it under but place loosely under the pan. Of course before setting the trap I make an opening of the required size on top of pile and then when trap is set, smooth off the pile and cover trap with earth, etc. No bait is required.

Set No. 2. I find a spring or open running water. I place the traps so that they are covered by water about two inches. For bait I take three or four little fish (shiners or perch will do), which I fastern with wire to the pan, being careful not to kill them. At other times I use frog or crab. The mink will naturally go after the live bait and in so doing becomes a victim. Bear in mind that a raccoon, fox or otter may spring the trap, conseqently a strong trap is recommended.

Set No. 3. When the creeks are all frozen over with ice, take your hatchet or axe and chop a hold about four inches wide clear across the creek, then take some stakes, drive them about an inch apart from one side to the other. In the center leave an opening of sufficient size permitting the mink to pass through. If the water is too deep, fill up partly with grass, stones or mud. I use three traps in this set. Have often had three minks. I set one on each end and one in the middle. The stakes must be long enough to reach out of the ice. The bait I use is fish, birds, squirrels, rabbit, muskrat, etc. Bait however, is unnesessary. If used, I always place it in a natural position and always so that the animal in order to reach it must pass over the trap.

TRAPPING THE MINK

"I will write you my method of trapping the mink, during the rutting season, which you may use in your Trapper's Guide writes Mr. W. Snow of Boscobel, Wis.

"During the early winter, mink should be trapped by setting the traps in their runways and holes, or by making a hole at the edge of the water where their tracks are seen. For bait nothing is better than the head and forepart of the fish muskrat or a fresh fish. It should be fastened in the back part of the hole, by running a forked stick through and the trap set at the entrance so the pan of trap is about one-half inch under water. If the chain is then fastened to a sliding pole the mink will be drowned and in good condition. In case their holes near water cannot be found, make an artificial abode with stones, roots of trees, bark, logs, earth, etc., on the shore. The rust and smell of iron should be removed from the traps, first by; greasing, and horning off the grease in a blaze being careful not to overheat the springs, and then boiling them in a kettle of water and hemlock or willow bark. Place bait in hole or hollow log as before, and make a place with your hatchet to set No. 1 Newhouse trap so the jaws will be about level with the ground. Cover all up, being careful to put very fine material around the jaws so the trap will spring.

"Take all the musk from the mink you catch this way and save it until the last part of winter, during the rutting or mating season. The musk is found in small bags near the tail of minks. Put bag and all in a small bottle and cork tightly. Then if there is a mild spell late in January or in February, take a clean trap and tie a piece of muskrat skin or half rotten wood to the pan of trap and put on it a few drops of mink musk. Go to a marsh where there are a lot of muskrat houses. By this time of year the mink will have holes in some of their houses, or find a runway in a log or along the edge of the marsh. Dig out a little place with you hatchet to set the trap in and cover spring and chain completely. The best thing to cover twitch is the moss, plants and stuff from the inside of a muskrat house as they like the smell of this stuff and it covers up the smell of iron if there is much left on the trap. Place a few large leaves over the jaws and pan. If a mink comes anywhere near he is sure to smell the musk and he crazy to get at it, and while scratching away the leaves is pretty sure to get a got in the trap. Fasten the chain to a pole (not very heavy) about three or four feet from one end. This will prevent him from going under the ice; after he has pulled it a ways it will get tangles up in brush and he will be too weak to pull out."

TRAPPING THE MINK

One making mink trapping a speciality writes as follows:

"To be a successful mink trapper it is necessary to study the mink and his habits."

1. Mink follow steams, along lake shores, are found in holes, excavations, dens, crevices, and in or about muskrat house"

2. Set your trap, No. 1 or No 2 steel trap, in or about above mentioned abodes, and use chicken, rabbit or any other good bait, either scented or natural; place beyond the trap in the hold, also put above the trap. The animal will go in after the bait and becomes caught.

3. Take the captured mink (be sure he is dead) and use him as a decoy. With left hand take body about upper part of hind legs, and with your right hand pull tail back and squeeze with left hand, and allow drippings to fall about trap set, also rub hind part within abode. This will make a strong scent, and other minks will readily enter hole believing that one is inside, also drag mink on ground fgrom one trap to another.

4. Use fine grass in covering up the trap, and always place cotton, dry leaves, and similar soft substances under the part; cover lightly.

TRAPPING THE MINK

My experience in trapping dates back to 1857. During this period I must have trapped thousands of mink and large numbers of foxes, trapped and killed bears, mountain lions and in my time have seen plenty of

HOLLOW LOG STEEL TRAP SET.

When the trapper observes mink, marten, fisher, opossum or similar animals to frequent hollow logs, the entrance of which is two to five feet above the ground, an arrangement as above illustrated is strictly proper. The steel trap should be covered with moss, leaves or grass. Place bait at or about opening.

buffalo and other large game. To be successful, I have always studied the habits of the animal. Steel traps in my time were not plentiful, and I was obliged to resort to home-made contrivances very often.

Some years ago, notwithstanding my long experience, I was unable to catch a certain mink. I tried all methods, set the steel trap up-side down, used snares, deadfalls, but all to no avail. I gave it up for the time being, and my son tried his hand with the same result. He finally made a box 14 × 16 × 22 with glass on two sides; into this box was placed alive chicken, and after the first slight snow, the box was placed a live chicken, and after the first slight snow, the box, chicken and all was carried to the place that the mink frequented almost every day. The traps had been set quite a number of days before, one securely fastened to a spring pole, the other to a drag. The box was set between the two traps and a quantity of loose brush thrown over it so as to make it look natural. The same day it snowed considerably.

One of us visited the box every day. Tracks were seen the second day, but the mink did not attempt to get the chicken or neared the concealed traps, but seemed to walk in a circle about the box. Next day, however, much to our surprise Mr. Mink was hanging five feet in the air. It was a large male mink and at one time must have been nipped in a steel trap. The skin was sold for $4.00.

Supposing some trapper who has had the same kind of ill luck try this method.

R. B. A.

TRAPPING THE MINK

Mr. Frank Becht, of Webster, S. Dak., sends a few of his ways of catching mink.

"As I use the Stop Thief Wire Trap, I make a hole in bank of creek of stream, three or four inches deep and place a small bird in back end of it fopr bait, and then put trap over hold; but if trapping in common stoughs where the mink's holes can be easily found, place your trap over hole in such a way that the trigger or trip of trap will be close to the bottom of hole. The place a bunch of feathers about four inches away from trap saturated with decoy or beaver's oil, and oil of amber for bait. If a common spring trap is used, make a stick about sixteen inches high, place a roasted chicken on toop stick, and set your trap below. The roasted chicken attracts the mink, and when there he will walk about, sniffing up towards the bait, and be sure to step in the trap."

TRAPPING THE MINK

My favorite way of capturing mink, writes Mr. Patrick Laughrey, West Broughton, Canada, is to drive a row of old sticks across the mouth of small stream, leaving a small gapat center, in which gap I set my trap. I use No. 1 B. & L. which I set about one inch bwlow the level of the water. Trap should be covered in the usual way.

I have also been very successful in setting my traps along a small stream where the bank is steep. I set my trap clsoe to the water edge on one side with a level beach on the ohter side. I make a little wall of stones so that the end reaches the water. The trap is placed at the edge of the wall below the level of the water and should a mink come along he will invariably pass by the edge of the wall and of course becomes a victim. I use no bait or scent. The trap is covered. Caught seventeen mink this season.

TRAPPING THE MINK

Have had much success in trapping mink on my farm and in its vicinity, and on one occasion caught a wolf. My method is as follows: "I take a dead chicken or any large piece of meat, whether old or fresh makes no difference. Bury this in the ground so that part of it protrudes and upon this set yur trap. If yu can spare more than one trap, set these about six to eight inches from the meat. The traps are to be buried and covered up. Be sure and put some wool under the pan. The animal in locating the meat will naturally become caught.

N. C. A.

TRAPPING THE MINK

Mr. Lauersdorf, a Wisconsin trapper, writes as follows: "Take a skinned muskrat, tie a string about five feet long to it and drag it along on the ground where mink are known to run, and when you find a good place to set the trap, hand it on three stakes drives into the ground and extending six to eight inches above the ground; place your trap underneath. The mink, upon finding the track, will shortly follow it, and when it comes to the muskrat will spring the trap and become caught.

"At other times a trap can be placed about two inches under water along shores that mink frequent. My method of making decoy is as follows: I procure small fish or minnows, which I cut up into small pieces and place them in a wide necked bottle and with them about one-fourth to one-third angle worms. When bottle is three-quarters full, fill remainder with rain water. Cork up and expose bottle to the sun. When rancid, decoy is ready to use. Put a few drops of the above decoy on the bait or above the trap. Mink, marten, muskrat and coon are attracted by this decoy.

"Ascertain a den where a mink frequents and set your trap at the opening, concealing it in the usual way. A piece of muskrat or some other bait thrown carelessly in the opening ten to twelve inches, is sufficient bait. Should the animal pass that vicinity the bait will attract him, especially if he be a strange animal, and in passing into the abode to obtain the bait, will spring the trap. If the abode is inhabited, the mink in departing is likely to spring the trap, as well as the one entering."

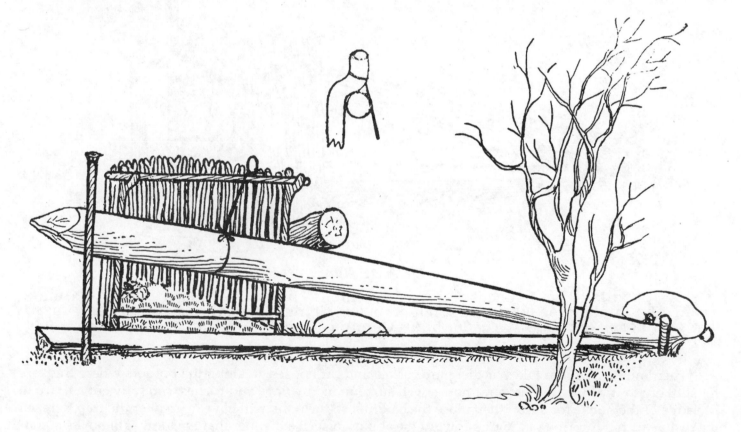

DEADFALL.

Another simple arrangement. Bait with a rabbit, dead fowl, or piece of muskrat. Bait should be fastened to the ground so as to detain the victim. To spring the trap the animal must either step on the spindle or press it down with his belly on entering the enclosure. Suitable for all classes of animals, especially the badger, skunk, wolf, fox, etc. A steel trap set in front of entrance makes the visitor's capture doubly sure.

TRAPPING THE MINK

This interesting article we received from Mr. T. Wolfe, and Iowa trapper living at Tabor.

"Perhaps this most valuable little fur animal found in most sections of the U.S. and to the far north in British possessions, frequenting lakes, streams and small rivulets, has puzzled more trappers than are willing to admit because of its keen secent and extremely cautions nature. I think I can say, who should not say it, that I have been fairly successful in trapping for mink, having caught as high as $436.00 worth in a single week, making trapping remunerative as well as a pleasure. Much has been said about the kind of bait, scent, etc., to be used. The best bait is fish, muskrat, sapsucker, prairie chicken and quail. When a mink will not pay attention to any of these it is evident that it is not hungry. Many so-called scents serve only to frighten the mink away. I once caught $436.00 worth in a week and they were not plentiful to speak of either, but did it by diligence and caution.

"Never set trap for mink that has the scent of other animals on it, for that will at once arouse their suspicion. If you are trapping on a stream it may sometimes become necessary to set in the water although this is objectionable, for the mink in trying to release himself is apt to cover his fur with mud and if cased in this condition is most likely to grade as damaged fur. The proper thing to do in a case of this kind is to carry the mink to camp get a basin of warm water and thoroughly wash and dry the fur before casing.

DEADFALL.

A peculiar yet successful arrangement in capturing various animals from the little weasel to the black bear. This deadfall is continually used by trappers, especially throughout Canada, chiefly in timber sections.

"When minks frequent lakes, if there are rushes and rat houses go along the borders where they are most likely to travel and select a rat house well surrounded by flags and rushes, carefully cut a place in the edge of the house for a trap then place the bait first so the mink will have to go over the trap to reach it. Always turn the spring of the trap toward the abit or in such a manner that the mink will not be standing over the spring of the trap when it throws as the springs are apt to throw its feet out of the jaws of the trap.

"A friend of mine once trapped for a large mink which frequented a slough the surrounding country being flat and more or less marshy. Not being able to ctch it he turned it over to me and it was with some misgiving I undertook the job as I knew him to be quite apt; but selecting a few good traps, I went up the slough one morning after a fresh fall of snow. I found the mink had been out in much evidence; following the tracks up I soon came to where the mink had struck across the bottom ; still following I soon came to where he went into a hole that apparently went straight down. Selecting a good strong trap and carefully clearing away the frost and snow. I placed the trap upside down over the hole taking care to have the pan of the trap exactly over the hold. Next morning I had a very valuable mink. I have caught quite a number of minks in this way.

"Minks like to follow old fence rows that border the banks of lakes and sloughs, making it was to take them by setting a trap by a fence post and tacking and bait to the post just above the trap. This rule will hold good along the banks of wooded streams where the trap can fastened to small saplings or trees or to a toggle. Every successful trapper should carry a good hatchet and wire staples as there is nothing better than wire staples to fasten to a toggle or other convenient things."

TRAPPING THE MINK

I find the mink a rather shy animal, but have never had any great trouble in catching him. One of my ways is to set my traps in old muskrat volts, pinning my bait down and well back in the hold with a sharp stick, using for bait rabbit, bird and fish. Always have your bait fresh and clean. I also find the outlet of tiled drainage, which seems a splendid place to catch both mink and skunk, always making a near, careful set close up to the tile, and if an extra large one, set well up in the tile without bait.

Another plan I find very good is to go to old field road bridges that are down low to the water and take up one of the planks. Set your trap in two inches of water. Leave a small nail in once of the stringers and hang your bait with a string directly over your trap, and six inches above it. Also you will find under the rots of large treed that have been partly washed out, a good place to set traps with bait.

The mink is a great traveler and hunter and he frequents every nook and corner and if you keep all these places well occupied by careful, neat set traps, you will have your share of success. You will find a great many of these plans to be good and successful ones. Also you will learn some of your best plans by careful study and practical experience, the same as in all other business. You have to adapt your plans to suit the country you trap in, such as a prairie trapper, or a timer, or mountain trapper.

CHARLES SESSIONS,
Clinton, Ill.

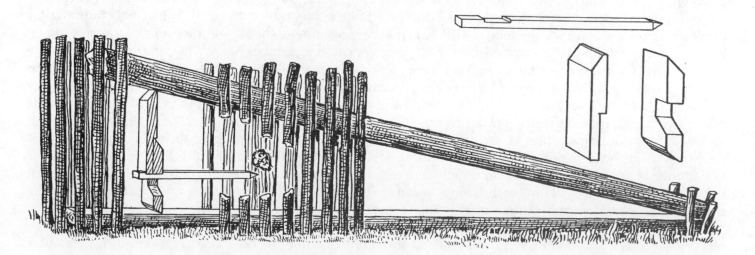

I give you herewith my method of making a trigger for the deadfall. This trigger I believe to be entirely new to the outside world, although it has been in use a good many years by two old Canadian trappers who were the originators. I got this trigger from one of the trappers and have tested it thoroughly on mink, marten, etc; and find it so far ahead of any other that I use it entirely.

Some animals go into a pen for nothing else than to smell the bait or to investigate. This trap catches these fellows, whereas the other triggers do not. The pen of this trap wants to be short so that the animal cannot get in too far. The bait should be stuck or hung up on back of pen, say six inches high, for think, marten, etc. The animal never fails to step or rub against trigger in reaching up to smell bait. Always keep the guides a distance from the trigger to prevent jamming, or use one set of guides. The treadle also wants to be slightly turned in pen.

RALPH WOLVERTON
Cascade, B. C.

TRAPPING THE MINK

To capture mink, I follow the banks of streams where the water nears a bank two or three feet high. I then dig a hole in the bank a foot wide and two feet deep. Then proceed to build a sort of wharf out of stokes. Some of the dirt I place on top of the bank and when my sets are complete I take handfuls of the dirt and strew over the setting so as to eradicate the footprints and to make everything seem fresh. The bait is placed within the abode, excepting small pieces are carefully strewn close to the water which has a tendency to attract the animal. The trap is placed a few inches within the abode, the pan facing the stream. There is no harm in dragging the bait in the immediate vicinity, finally leading it into the hole. The trap should be securely covered with rotten wood and lastly with fine earth.

For scent I use fish oil made by me during the summer time from minnows, shiners and perch. If in position to obtain a female mink during the running season, the matrix of the animal is placed in a bottle, either separate or with the fish oil. Have had good success. As much as possible I use spring poles, but if the weather is mild I arrange to fix up some way to drown the animal.

N.C.A.

TRAPPING THE MINK

"Many years have now past but I still remember one February morning at three o'clock my father yelled-"Roll out Son, if you want to go the round with me this morning." A snow storm was in full bloom. After a hasty breakfast of corn bread, venison and black coffee, we both swung out on the trail. Father was trapping for mink and promised to take me along. This was mating season and about one mile up stream, close to an pond where a small stream emptied into the Tygart we came to a small hollow log and in this log was a female mink. On the outside father had set three Newhouse traps and two of them were sprung each holding a male mink. Father up the trap line we came to a hollow tree. Inside this father had imprisoned another female mink. He had set five traps on the outside and three of them were sprung, each holding a large male mink; five minks in less than two miles trapping. I was small then but I learned a secret that morning that easily knocks out any method known to the trapping world. Brother Trapper you can readily understand why these minks were imprisoned. The next thing is how to catch the female mink, alive and unharmed.

Get four boards six inches wide and nail them together forming a long box. In one end make a trap door by inserting piece of board nine inches long; fasten the end of the board with leather hinges, thus you have a door that inclines toward the center of box. Take a stick the size of a pencil two inches long, and set upright. Now you have the door set. If you have already located den-which every old trapper knows is easily done by certain signs-insert the trap with door raised about one foot into the hole. If you cannot find such a den, make one, into which after placing the box, close up all other openings and see that box is solid. Let swing door rest on pencil. No bait is necessary. The female mink will enter in order to hide from the male and you have your mink as sure as shooting.

You will ask: "Why can't we catch the male mink by this method?" Simply because the male mink is rarely, if ever, in their home dens at this season as they are traveling and seek drifts, etc., by day.

WES RAY
Olive Hill Ky.

TRAPPING THE MINK AND MUSKRAT

For trapping mink in a water set, find a shallow place about one or two inches deep then take your bait (a piece of muskrat, bird or fish is good), run a stick through it and stake to the bottom so that the bait will just stick out. Set your trap alongside of it and cover trap with wet leaves or grass. Do not make any tracks on bank but wade up the creek in order not to disturb anything.

Second: Find a stream about two feet wide that flows into a lake, pond or larger stream; stake it off with small twigs or weeds, leaving a small open place in center about four inches wide in which place a No. 1 or 1½ trap. When the mink is traveling up this small stream he will go through the open place and get caught.

Third: Find a hollow log along the stream, and set your trap so it be level with the bottom of the log; cover with decayed wood from the same log so it will look natural Mink like to run through anything hollow.

Muskrat: A good way to catch muskrats is to make a box about four feet long and one feet wide with wire end. A roller, or movable stick is titled into each end and by gimlet hold. Wires fastened thereto large enough to timeline at forty-five degrees as shown in illustration.

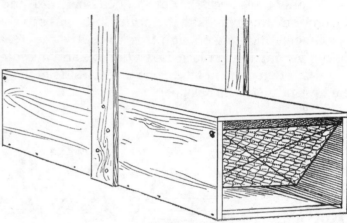

The animal hits the drops in going in from either end, but cannot get out. Set this in a small stream and arrange it so he will have to go through the box to go past. This can be clots by driving stakes into the bottom along the box. I have caught as high as five in one night in this way.

FRANK BAXDER
S. Williamsport. PA

TRAPPING THE MINK

I have been very successful in trapping mink. I give you herewith my method. Find a mink den take a rabbit or red squirrel and a small bush or tree the same kind that is near the den or hole and run the stake through the gambrels of the rabbit. Drive the stake about one foot iron the hole. Dig out a place just large enough for the trap about midway between the ban and the hole; place another trap on the other side of your bait. Sink this trap in level with the top of the ground. Put some time grass in the bottom and place trap on the grass so it will set solid and cover with leaves or grass. I preter a No. 1½ tarp. Use a bush for a stake and only trim enough to drive it in the ground.

E.N Darney
Bristolville. O

TRAPPING THE MINK

The best and most successful way to trap mink is to find where they have been running and track them to their den and if same cannot be found set your trap (No. 1) in the freshest of the tracks if they are in the sand or dig gable each excavate a place large enough to hold trap and chain and arrange to have pan level with the surrounding earth. Cover pan and trap with loose leaves and sprinkle fine earth over leaves so as to cover trap completely, but at the same time so that earth or leaves do not interfere when trap is sprung. Quite often I place the ring through a limb. Which I insert in the each to resemble a small growing tree. After this is done remove all possible traces and leave place in natural state. Bait with fish. Birds or part of a muskrat. If you have reason to believe that the mink that you are trying to capture from an old experienced trapper, that a job is before you, and in this respect a very good location in which to set you trap is in an old muskrat house, especially if the mink is in the habit of going in or about the house. If there is no opening on the top of the house, make one. Pull up some of the grasses, weeds, etc., that are usually within a muskrat house and arrange your trap about the wall and cover with grasses, etc. It is preferable to place two or three traps, the more the better-and the quicker you are likely to capture the sly thief. Bait with bird or muskrat and promiscuously strew feathers about the traps and their immediate vicinity. In addition I use Oil of Anise and the scent of the female mink.

HEINRICH BROS.,
Baldwin, N.Y.

SET FOR MINKS, COONS, ETC

Having noticed that where a tree or log has fallen or been placed across a brook or creek, any animal traveling in that vicinity will, more or less, cross upon it, led me to invent the following device:

The only tools necessary are a good sharp axe and a spade. With your tools and traps, go to the mouth of some stream or creek that empties into a lake or river. Take your axe and cut a log say eight or ten inches in diameter and long enough to reach across the creek, allowing about six inches to extend on either shore. Before putting log in place, take your axe and at center of log cut a notch just the size of trap and 1½ inches deep. Cut two more notches, one on each side of the trap notch, in shape of the letter "V," six inches wide at the top and seven inches deep.

When notches are cut, lay the log across the creek near the mouth. Take the spade and dig out each bank so the log will be 1½ inches out of water. Set the trap in the center notch and stake trap chain to bed of the creek. It is best to set trap in good shape, taking plenty of time and concealing each trap carefully.

ORRIN WICKS,
Hamilton, Mich.

TRAPPING THE MINK

I am 54 years old, and have been interested in hunting, trapping, fishing and woodcraft practically all my life. I give you my suggestive ideas as to trapping mink, also in another article as to fishing, not only for bait, but for food supply. The latter is very important for one away from home or civilization.

The time for setting traps for mink depends upon the weather and locality. In the northern and eastern states, from the first to the last of October. If your first mink skin shows dark on the inside, you had better leave your bait and take up your traps for a few days. The place to set your traps is along the banks of streams and on the shores of lakes and ponds. If possible find small spring brooks that empty into streams and lakes and at the mouth of these runs, build an enclosure with an opening in front of same, say five or six inches wide by about ten or twelve high. This end of the enclosure should stand in the water so that your trap will be about one inch under water. Now cover trap with moss or wet leaves. Never stake your trap, but use a swing or Talley pole; if the first, drive a stake with crotch on, down near the trap, and place a pole in the crotch, fasten trap chain to the small end, and hook it down to a pen driven in the ground. The built end of pole should be heavy enough to swing mink clear of the ground. Of the two I prefer the Talley pole, from the fact that one will not lose a trap if a skunk of raccoon is caught. For this, use a sapling with all limbs left on wedge chain ring on and tie the top of Talley pole to a near-by bush or small limb. There is give enough to this arrangement to prevent mink from pulling out. Now place the bait on a stick in the back end of enclosure. I have found no better bait than muskrat, fish is also good. Any meat will answer.

A good scent for fall trapping is fish oil (preferably trout) with three or four musk glands from the muskrat added; put fish and glands into a bottle, cork and hang same in the sun, use a few drops of this around the enclosure, not on the bait. Save the musk glands of the female mink (bottle, hang in the sun as before) for winter and spring trapping.

Another very good way is to set trap in a runway. If a natural one cannot be found, make one by placing an old log near a steep bank and place another log partly over this so that it will rest against the bank. If there is a space between logs and water drive down a few stakes, then they will quite likely pass through the artificial runway. Use no bait in this set; use Talley pole as before.

Skinning.—Rip down the back side of both hind legs to vent of careful and not go deep enough to cut musk glands at root of tail, use a split stick to remove bone from tail. Now pull skin off over body, cut around the eyes and ears and the skin is ready for stretching.

Stretching Skin.—This is best done on a three piece fur-board which is made as follows: First make the board from one-half inch stock, round off end and the edges. Now saw this lengthwise into three pieces; the middle piece should be a little tapering to form a wedge. Put the skin on the outside pieces first and stretch it as long as it will go and tack. Now insert the wedge. When the skin is dry, which is best done in a dark place, it is ready for market.

F.H. BASSEIT,
Waterbury, Conn.

TRAPPING MINK AND FOX

I have a very good way to catch mink and fox. My method of catching mink is this: I use a No. 3 Newhouse trap, but remove one of the springs. Thus I have a trap that catches a mink so high that he cannot gnaw or twist out. They stay right there until I take them out. I never had a mink get away yet. But a No. 2 trap gets feet and toes.

I use mink's must and mink's matrix, muskrat's musk, and oil of cumin, well mixed, and let it stand in an air-tight bottle six months and shake well before using. Four to six drops of this scent is all I need to catch the slyest old dog mink that ever walked. I certainly can get them every time. I catch three female mink in the mating season, and get the matrix of the three and put into a half-pint bottle. Then I take the must-bags of fifteen male mink and squeeze the musk into the bottle. I then catch enough muskrats to get four ounces of clear rat musk and from the druggist I get one ounce of oil of cumin. I put all into the bottle and cork it up air-tight. To bait the traps, I take a piece of muskrat skin and tie it on the pan of my trap and put four to six drops of this scent on it. Then I cover trap and chain so nothing is in sight but the muskrat skin on the pain. If there is a mink within one mile of my trap, and the wind blows in his direction. I know or no reason why I will not catch him. It is the best mink scent and bait that any living man ever used.

I have used all kinds of scent and never found any that was anywhere's near as good as this kind. I know from experience what I am saying. I never had a mink get away from a No. 3 trap yet. Anyone starting to make this scent need not make as much at one time. Make one-half or one-quarter at a time to get started. That is the way to capture the mink.

ED BREHMER,
Spring Valley, Minn.

TRAPPING THE MINK

In trapping the mink I have seldom used bait, although he will taste of almost anything that is, fish, flesh or fowl. The bait and trap in which I place the most reliance, is set in a hole—in some bank of a stream or pond; in a hollow log, among the rocks; under a root; stranded ice or overhanging bank. A mink is almost certain to poke into any hole that he comes to.

He seldom passes a hollow log or a hole in the bank without diving into it and exploring it to the bottom. If there is a log leaning from the bank into the water he will go under instead of over it and a Newhouse No. 1 or a "jumper" placed in the entrance and lightly covered with moss or leaves, will get him the first time he comes that way. I will say right here that I do not believe a mink cares any more for a naked trap than he does for a stick. If a trap is not covered, he will step over it or go round it because it is better footing that way. It is much better to cover a trap than not for the purpose of making easy footing, and if he is guided by sticks or stones onto the spot where the trap is, the catch is made more certain.

Male minks are great wanderers during the months of February and March. During their rustling about they are looking more intently for the female than for food; their errand being one of love, in their quest they leave no hiding place unexplored, and whatever caution they may have is forgotten at this time, and they will rush as blindly into any kind of a trap as a pig. The female remains more closely at home, seldom going far from the valley, swamp or water course that has been her home, so long as there is plenty of the favorite food.

Mink feed on the cottontail rabbit more often that on fish and I believe prefer the muskrat to either. I have caught a great many in traps set in the places where muskrats haul up aquatic plants to eat. Where rats are at all abundant (these places are common along water courses and ponds) they are frequently caught in traps set in muskrat houses in the winter.

A favorite set of mine has been to drive a number of stakes across a small stream, making a fence that is impassable except through an opening about six inches wide, in which a trap is set on a stone sunk to leave the trap about an inch under water. If placed where there is some current it is quite an effective set in cold weather.

I seldom use the sliding pole in trapping mink as they scarcely ever twist off a foot even on land, and when near deep water they usually become entangled in roots or other obstructions and drown.

Where bait is used, a good place to set your trap is at the junction of a small brook with a larger one; the trap is to be set in the water with the bait suspended over it in such a way that the animal must step on the trap to get at it. A hole dug in the bank and the bait placed in the back with the trap at the entrance is also very good.

For lure, the scent bags of the female preserved in glycerin has great attraction for the male, as is the case with all animals. Fish oil is good medicine-anything fishy attracts them-canned salmon, sardines, rotten shiners or other small fish, among which a few fresh ones are placed is very attractive to them.

An old mill dam is a favorite haunt of minks and there can usually be found a well-defined trail from the stream below the dam to the pond above around one or both ends.

CHARLES E. INGALLS,
East Templeton, Mass.

TRAPPING THE MINK

"I will tell you how I have been very successful catching mink," writes Mr. J. Funk of Tiffin, Ohio.

"I always used the No. 1 Newhouse trap. I did my trapping along a small creek and I would always try to set my trap on the bank where the creek made a sharp curve, especially where the water washed under the roots of trees. If there is a log near, I set my trap along this. Now I make what I call a coop. For this I procure a piece of bark or a flat piece of wood about twenty inches long and seven inches wide. Then I cut four small stakes and drive two of these in the ground six inches from the log and one inch apart; the next two I drive about the same distance from the log and six inches from the other two. Then I slip the bark down between these stakes; get two sticks, lay one at each end from the bark to the log. Another piece of bark is needed for the roof so it will cover the coop nicely. Chopping should be avoided as much as possible. After this part is completed, I put a chunk in one end of the coop as tight as possible so the mink is compelled to enter from the other end. Then I put my bait in the back end against the chunk, and I always use chicken, rabbit, or muskrat for this. Now I set my trap. This should be set as light as possible with the spring toward the back end of the coop and cover with nice dry beach leaves. I always stake my trap for minks, by getting a stake about fourteen inches long with a branch at the top so the ring cannot slip off and driving it down at the side of the coop."

We have the following from Mr. Ernest Havner of Ludlow, Montana:

"The mink eats fish, frogs and craw fish, and now and then gets into the barn and steals chickens, goslings and ducks, and crawls into the cellar and eats up the sausage meat, or whatever he can get his jaws on. He is a pilfering little animal and yet so simple and foolish that he is easily caught by a trapper that knows his habits. For the sake of sometimes to eat, he runs up strums and crosses from one lake to another, a regular renegade. He only runs along steep banks, or under old roots and around rocks.

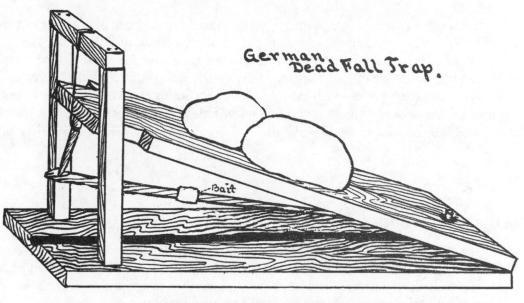

GERMAN DEADFALL TRAP.

This contrivance is chiefly used in Europe for killing mice and rats. In this country it is commonly known as the "gallow trap." Large numbers of weasels, ermines and minks are annually caught in this trap, principally in or about the chicken coop. If made on a larger scale the trap is suitable for killing mink, marten, fisher and foxes. The weight on top of upper board must be heavy, so as to break the bones and hold the animal fast. Spindle is tied to center pin by a thin string. Upper board should fit loosely about lower pin.

The young are brought forth in May or June, in litters of five or six black looking little things.

"To catch this animal you have only to be acquainted with its habits. He follows streams of water, hunting every nook and corner for something to eat. Place your trap near the edge of the water, (No. 1½ is the best for mink). Have it covered with about an inch of water, directly in front of a steep bank or rock, or something on which you can hang your bait about eighteen inches above the level of the trap, which must be so closet to the shore that the mink cannot get to the bait without stepping on it. The bait should be fresh fish or frogs, or the head of some bird or fowl, as he is very fond of brains.

"Another plan is to set your trap on the land about ten feet from the shore, covering it with a few leaves, moss grass or loose dirt, or anything that will not prevent the jaws from closing. Hang the bait about eighteen inches above it and scent it with a mixture made of equal parts of honey, sweet oil, and essence of peppermint. About a teaspoonful of this on the bait will cause them to come a long distance.

"Another good plan in which I have had good success is to set your traps about two feet back from the water, and from forty to eighty rods apart up or down stream. Then walk over the line drawing after you the carcass of a muskrat or a roasted crow or almost any fresh meat, and any mink that crosses this line or trail will follow it to the trap.

"It is also a good plan to set your trap where the mink must walk over it to get at the bait. He is a great fellow to catch muskrats, which he loves to eat, and you may bait the trap with muskrat carcass and set it in a rat house where you will often find handfuls of little fish that the mink has brought there.

"In the winter time he travels along springy brooks, pulling out frogs, and here he may be easily caught. You may also catch them in winter at the sides of big springs or along the springy sides of ponds and swamps where they like to roam."

POISONING MINKS

Gentlemen:—

Answering your letter relative to my ways of trapping permit rue to say that I use poison to a greater or less extent.

The poison is put into 2, 3, 4 and 5 grain capsules and I use equal part of powdered arsenic and carbolic crystals. The smaller sized capsules are for smaller animals and the others for fox and wolf.

I place these capsules sometimes into the carcass of dead animals, other times in small bits of meat, especially for the wolf that he can swallow. Sure death is a positive result. Never known to fail.

I have known and personally caught skunk and mink, as well as muskrat by placing a bait on good sized fish hook—the latter being attached to a wire. This may seem funny but nevertheless it is a fact. It is not more cruel to catch these animals that way that it is to catch fish. Death comes just comes just as soon as they try to escape.

Yours truly,
FRANK JENSEN.

BOX SET FOR MINK

A British Columbia trapper who wants his name withheld states that he has had continued success for three year in trapping mink, and during that time shipped at least $500.00 worth of raw furs and no small part of them were mink captured in the usual way also in his favorite Box Spring Set.

Locate a spring or some junction point where the water of a spring enters into a creek and at the most suitable place build a box of two-inch boards, two to three feet wide, three to five feet long and as deep as necessary (twelve to twenty inches). Bore many small holes into the sides or ends, so that a fresh supply of water circulates at all times. Now place small live fish as bait therein and continue to keep this stocked from the early fall or even summer. The idea is educate the mink marten, otter or even the fox to habitually come after a meal. They will soon become accustomed to come every few days.

I make a small shelf on one side or end of the box about three inches below the level upon which the mink usually stands and gets into and out of the box. I set my trap on this shelf. Trap is attached to a stone by wire so that when the trap is sprung the mink will jump into the water and pull the nearly balanced stone with him. The weight of the trap and stone will easily drown the mink. On one occasion I set two traps, one as above described the other on the edge of the box nearest to the shore. The latter trap had a regulation chain which I attached to a rope. This rope was passed over limb I balanced a stone weighing probably ten to fourteen pounds so when the fisher came during the night to obtain a bite or two he sprung the trap and evidently made a side jump, and in so doing disturbed the stone. When I came I found the mink dead in the water and the young fisher swinging five feet in the air. I killed him with my revolver. When I saw him hanging I just thought it was an otter, but his long neck and firm hold with his teeth on the chain convinced me that a lead pellet would put him out of misery and enrich me by $6.00 to $10.00

When nearing the set, even when re-stocking the box with fish. I made it a point to wade through the water and always from the opposite side.

UNIQUE METHOD OF CAPTURING MINK AND MUSKRATS

This unique way of catching mink, muskrats, even fisher and otter, is worthy of trial by anyone who finds a suitable log across a stream or reaching out in some lake.

A strong wire is attached from one end to another on stakes securely driven into the ground, the wire running parallel with the log but at a distance of twelve to sixteen inches. Fasten strong fish books to some linen lines capable of holding the desired animal, and attach to wire. Fasten securely so as not to slide. Bait hooks with small pieces of muskrat, which the animal is able to swallow without chewing. One-half of the hooks so baited should be placed on the log, the remainder just touching thee water. To prevent the victim chewing off the string, use guitar wire or gut strings. If hook is attached six inches from one end of line and to the latter a stone weighing one to two pounds is placed on the log, when the animal is caught he will jump off the log into the water and the stone will have a tendency to hold the animal down and of course be will drown very quickly. Those lines which touch the water are arranged for mink, muskrats and others coming up stream and become caught without getting on the log.

A Montana trapper has used this method successfully and at one time caught an otter, on another occasion his six out of eight hooks had a victim—three minks one marten a weasel and a fisher. It is a very good idea to arrange a stone to pull the animal below the level of the water.

C. F. G

TRAPPING THE MINK

After trying nearly all kinds of baits and scents with no great results, I hit upon a bait of my own three years ago, which I have used exclusively since and will say that I have had first-rate results. While minks are scarce in my locality, if I can find where one runs or a place they travel, I have nearly always taken them and I am going to give the readers of this article the benefit of my experience.

I am not going to tell you how to set your traps, as I find nearly every trapper has his favorite sets. As for me, I use the pen or cobby the hollow log or hole; whichever I find handiest. I take pains in setting and covering my trap. My favorite trap is the Oneida Jump trap No. 2, which I set and cover to make look as nearly natural with the surroundings as possible.

Then for bait, I use the common canned salmon and I find, in my locality a mink will take it when nothing else will attract him. The way I use it is to take a can as it comes from the store and empty the juice and about half the fish in a large-mouthed bottle with a good cork to it. After setting my trap, I dip a stick down in this bottle and place the stick back of the trap, only using what salmon adheres to the stick. This is both a scent and a bait.

I have purchased different kinds of scents, paying $1.00 for a little bottle no bigger than my little finger, also made fish oil, angle worm and all those things but give me the canned salmon. It does not hurt it if it becomes a little rancid.

F. H. SHEEP
Montrose, Pa

Take a box trap and line it with tin. Take a two-inch plank, bore a two or three-inch hole in it, drive sharp nails in about one inch from the top. Bore a hole little larger than the spindle, insert spindle in it; have the plank so arranged that it cannot be shoved in any farther. Put bait behind plank and set trap. As the mink puts his head in the hold to get bait, he will pull to get out and spring the trap and once sprung, he is yours.

Stop Thief traps are very good. I averaged one mink every day for a week by the use of these traps, which could hardly be possible with any other. Take essence of peppermint, honey and sweet oil for scent, or small fish cut in pieces and put in a bottle in the sun till oil is formed.

TRAPPING THE MINK

These animals are caught in various ways, depending upon the location, time of year, on land or in water. Some trappers consider the capturing of this animal an easy task, other contend that the annual is equally as sly and as cute as the red fox. The mink certainly and readily scents the hunter trapper or works of man, and will sly on his approach and from things made by him, especially on or about his usual paths.

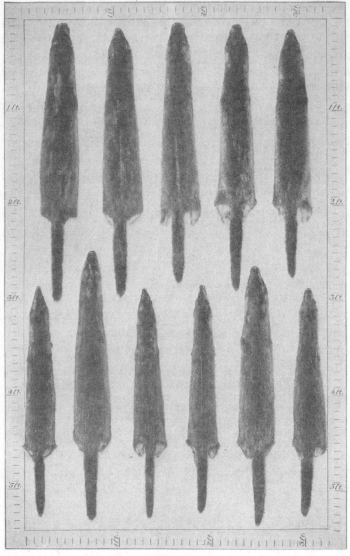

MINK SKINS. "Dressed"
All Sizes. Northern and Northwest. Scale Shows Inches and Feet.

The animal is captured by the use of snares, steel traps, detail falls, box, barrel and other home-made traps also the rule is sometimes resorted to but the trapper who makes trapping a business, is contented with the forms three methods of capturing the mink.

Snares are resorted to by all classes of trappers, even to the present day, not only in this country, but also in Europe. The snares are made out of strong linen or silk thread, silk lines, linen lines, copper or brass wire; also horsehairs. The proper way and placed to set these snares is about the paths or the front of the holes which the animal frequents. Some make an artificial abode and place bait therein, and as the mink enters become caught. Spring poles or other methods should be adapted or attached to the snares, which takes the animal off the ground otherwise the victim likely to be carried away or the fur badly damaged by such animals as the fox, fisher, wolf and wolverenc, or manage to escape.

The use of the rifle is advised, though the skins becomes more or less damages. The shot-gun is detrimental to the skin, and the practice of killing the animal with this instrument should be avoided whenever possible.

The reader is directed to carefully peruse the article under marten, fox, muskrat; also to study the art of making and setting of the various kinds of traps, the illustrations of which can be found on other pages. As this animal can be captured in so many different ways, almost any of the style can be successfully adapted in the capture of the mink as well as the marten. It is not an easy matter to kill minks, as trappers say the mink has seven lives, and naturally the animal dies hard; therefore, in hunting the animal with the rifle or short-gun the wound, in order to become effective, must be a severe one, as a inches flesh wound will only retard the animal momentarily.

The use of steel traps in preferred, but when inconvenient or the supply becomes exhausted; other home-made traps can be resorted to; but regardless of the kind of traps used, the chief aim and ambition of the trapper should be to use such traps that will securely hold the animal and retain the value of the pelt, also to cause a speedy death. Steel traps should be set along river banks, and generally where one creek empties into another, upon paths, about holes, stumps or trees and hollow logs. If the trapper cannot find a convenient place to set his traps it sometimes behooves him to dig a hole or to make an artificial adobe. If the latter is attempted, care and judgment in retaining the natural surroundings of the former conditions is essential, and the use of a good bait is recommended.

The author has set steel traps, No. 1½ and No. 2 also has seen experienced trappers set such traps in barricaded places using an old tree, stones, ground, sod, etc. to make the adobe. The making of such an adobe is simple, effective an successful although the trapper is sometimes obliged to wait for days or weeks for a victim. The traps should be set at a convenient place about the opening, somewhat below the level of the earth, and covered with find bits of loose earth or leaves; a little cotton or leaves should be placed under the pan. Bits of rotten wood or feathers, whenever the latter are handy, should be strewn about the trap and within the adobe. Great care should be taken that the animal is obliged to enter the opening left and not to force an entrance in some other vital or detrimental part of the adode.

If bait is used, the latter should be placed six to eight inches beyond the trap in the adobe. The proper bait to use is birds, fish, pieces of muskrat, or fish oil. If meat is used, same should be smokes. Some trappers burn a piece of paper or some dry leaves in the abode after the meat bait is set, thus eradication human scent, and at the same time smoking the meat. A spring or sliding pole should be used whenever possible, as the former will lift the animal in the air, the other carry the victim into deep water to drown.

Deadfalls or other homemade traps working on this principle, are often used, especially by trappers in the far interior, who find plenty of time to make them. A good way to make a trap is to procure a two-inch plank, about one or two feet long, six to eight inches wide, into which a two-inch hold should be bored, and sharpened nails driven into the plank about the hole, in such manner that if the mink places his head into the hold after bait, it cannot be withdrawn, as the nails will prevent the withdrawal, and naturally the animal is in a helpless condition. The nails must not be driven too close nor too far, and the opening must be sufficient to permit the animal will not escape by sliding clean through. See Illustration for particulars.

The mink as well as the marten can be successfully lured to the place where traps are set. Many decoys are good; the most common and easiest to procure is fish oil. Elsewhere in this book will be

Upper Row
Mink Skins

MINK and MARTEN SKINS
Center Marten Skins
Improperly Skinned

Low Row
Marten Skins

found methods of making these decoys, manner in which they are used etc. Some trappers smear some of this decoy on their boots others drag scented bait along the paths.

Wire traps can be successfully used; many trappers prefer them when they have an opportunity to set a trap in front of a hole, as a matter of fact they all recommend them in such cases. They are conveniently carried, easy to set and cost less than steel traps. Use the No. 2

A new tarp called the "Tree Trap" is being used and while some claim this trap cannot be set except on trunks of trees, others use them at different locations with good success. There are now so many makes of traps that what one trapper likes another would not have, but the majority, especially the successful trappers, stick to the Newhouse.

CHAPTER 4

Marten

(Ger, Marder, Lat, Mudtela Americana)

AMONGST the fur bearing animals of the weasel kind, the marten with its various species, is most important, especially since their skins command high prices and ready sale. In all zoological work the martens osciallate with the sable. The latter, however, is simply a large marten found in higher latitudes.

MARTEN

The Beach or Stone marten, which inhabits Europe, is distinguished from the Pine marten by its pure and large, white furred throat, also by its other external features and size.

The Pine marten of Europe resembles the American marten, but in that country like in the New World, marked contrast and difference between animals form one, to that of another section occur, but not in habits, from that found in Germany, Austria, Spain and Italy. The former is large in stature, its pelage is finer, darker, denser and in general, longer.

The sable, or Asiatic species, as the name implies, is found in Russia and northerly portions of island belonging to Japan; also equally large and similar furred animals are found in the extreme portions of North America, but these receive a sectional name and are commercially known as Hudson Bay sable. The fur of the sable as compared with the marten, has a mellow character is darker, longer, finer in texture the skin larger and more beautiful and for that reason commands a much higher price.

The Russian sable measures in body 20 to 24 inches from most to root of tail and the latter from body to extreme tip, 10 to 12 inches. Some individual hairs on the tail are 3 to 4 inches long. The latter are very glossy, dark brown or black and invariably three to four shades darker than the fur on the body.

The American marten in respect to size, resembles the European Pine marten. The animal inhabits the northerly Atlantic, as well as the Pacific states, is found in mountainous regions, principally in forests, in the latitudes extending from Maine to

Oregon, although its existence in the middle states as far south as Pennsylvania and Ohio, Colorado and Wyoming is and been established but of late years most of the skins have been received from Canada where the animal is still plentiful. Beautiful as well and high priced skins are received form Maine, Lake superior region around Lake of the Woods, Northern Minnesota, Michigan, Wisconsin, and notably from the St. Lawrence River and Hudson Bay region, also along the Canadian Pacific Railway from Selkirk to Port Arthur.

The color of the skin from Montana, Washington, Wyoming, Oregon, and extending along the Pacific coast, up in Alaska, excluding the extreme northern or inland portions, and generally of a canary or light brown, intermingled with steel-like colored hairs. Similar colored skins are also received from different sections, which are all dyed to imitate the darker kinds, but in this state are readily distinguished by the manufacturer who fails to pay the same price he would for the beautiful natural colored skins.

The Marten.

The color of the American marten during the winter months is almost indescribable, due to the endless diversities occasioned by age, sex, season and climatic conditions. Its fur is long extremely soft and full. It can be divided into three kind of fibers the fist is very short, fine, soft and downy the second about the same, but in addition wavy, ¼ to ½ inch longer, and becomes noticeable from the outside; the third represents the long as those on the mink. The predominating color of fur ranges from a light canary, orange, light brown, dark brown, dark and almost black, excepting the fur on the throat, which is rather yellowish or clear white. The legs are short and covered with black fur. The tail seems bushy and that member is very valuable in the fur trade.

The American marten, like the sable has carnivorous and arboreal habits; its home is in the forests, scarcely ever found in open sections and being of a sly and suspicious nature, it is one of the first to disappear, amongst the smaller animals, with the advance of civilization entering its woody resorts. Mr. Ross has recorded a remarkable fact of the animal's periodical disappearance. "It occurs in decades or thereabouts with regularity, and it is quite uncommon what becomes of them. They are not found dead. The failure extends through out the Hudson Bay Section at the same time, and there is no tact or region to which they migrate where we have not posts, or into which our hunters have not penetrated."

Making its home away from civilization, it is not guilty of invading the farmyard, but otherwise is very active, industrious. Cunning and predaceous, and finds its subsistence in the weaker rodents, mice, moles, insects, squirrels, frogs, birds and fish. If forced by hunger will eat nuts and berries.

Its odor is mild as compared with the musk of the mink or ermine. It rarely kills after its hunger is appeased, nor does a blind ferocity hand it to attack annuals larger than itself.

The mother brings forth a litter of three seldom exceeding six, young, which the nourishes for some time and Stellar says that the mother will readily protect them from the male by carrying them out of danger in her mouth fashion usually to some or hole in the bank of a kill, the opening of which she closes with her body and presents the intruder with a emulous look.

In the more southern portions of their range, the martens are quite pale. The finest and darkest skins come from Labrador and the country east and south of Hudson Bay, also from northern British Columbia and the interior of Alaska and the Yukon province. The marten is strictly an animal of the woods, being found only in the heavily timbered country. Their favorite haunts are in the rough, broken country, where the timber is of various kinds. They feed on rabbits, squirrels, mice, birds and eggs and probably have no trouble in obtaining a sufficient amount of food, but unlike the mink and the weasel, they never kill more than is needed to supply their wants.

The young are usually born in April, and there are from three to five at a birth. Just where they make their dens I cannot say. Some writers say they live in hollow trees, while others assert that they live in holes in the rocks or ground. I should say that the latter idea is most likely to be correct, at least as regards the marten of the far north, as in that part of the country, hollow trees are few and far between. One peculiarity regarding the martens is the fact that they occasionally disappear from a locality in which they were formerly numerous. The common supposition is that they migrate to new feeding grounds when food becomes scarce.

The marten travels mostly in the gullies and depressions on the mountains and hills. As they usually follow the same route, when one sees their tracks in such a place, he can be reasonably sure, if he sets his trap there, that he will make a catch. They are not shy or suspicious and are easily caught. In many ways, marten trapping is the most pleasant as well as the most profitable kind of trapping. As they are found only in the timbered country, the trapper does not feel the storms like he would in an open country. They are easily caught, light to carry and easily skinned. Moreover, they are a very valuable fur and if one is in a good locality, he will make a large catch in a season. They usually become prime about the 15th of October and remain in good condition until the last of March.

In countries where the snow does not fall too deep, the traps are set in small enclosures, the same as for the mink. If there is snow on the ground, I set my traps as follows. With my snowshoes, I tramp the snow down solid, at the; foot of a tree, and build a small pen of stakes, or chunks split from an old stump. The stakes or chunks, are arranged so as to form the sides of the pen and the sides are placed about six or seven inches apart, the tree forming the back of the pen. I roof the pen with evergreen boughs, to protect the trap from the falling snow. It is a good idea to leave a couple of boughs hang down over the mouth of the pen so as to hide the bait from the birds, and also to prevent the rabbits from entering the pen. I set the trap on a bed of boughs, just inside of I the pen, and cover lightly with tips of evergreen. The bait is placed on a stick behind the trap. I fasten the trap to a toggle, but if only marten is expected, the trap may be fastened in almost I any way, as they seldom escape. It is also a I good idea to bend a small twig and place it under the pan of the trap, to prevent it from being sprung by birds, squirrels and weasels.

For bait, rabbit, partridge, squirrel, fish, small birds or meat of almost any kind is good. The Indians sometimes smoke-cure salmon, pickerel, or white fish, for marten bait, and other trappers use putrefied salmon roe, but the majority prefer to use fresh bait. Some trappers advise dragging a piece of fresh, bloody meat along the line, to lead the marten to the trap.

Another very good method is the following: Find a small spruce, about three inches in diameter and cut the tree about two feet above the snow, leaving the top of the stump V shape.

Draw the tree forward and lay it over the stump, so that the butt of the tree will be three or three and a half feet above the snow. Now, about a foot back from the end, flatten off a place for the trap and set the trap on the pole. Tie the trap fast with a light string and loop the chain around the tree. Split the butt of the tree, and fasten the bait in the split. This is a very good set, possessing advantages most methods. The birds can not eat the bait, the trap is not bothered by weasels or rabbits, the marten must stand on the trap when trying to get the bait, and when caught, falls off the pole and can not get back.

In the mountains, where the snow falls deep, the traps are set on the trees, five or six feet above the snow. The most common way, is to make two cuts in the tree with an axe, and drive in two wooden pegs, about five inches apart. Set the trap and place it on the pegs, one peg passing through the bow of the spring, the other between the jaws and the bottom of the trap. Draw the chain around the tree and staple solidly. The bait is pinned to the tree, about a foot above the trap. A bunch of boughs may be placed over the bait to hide it from the birds.

If desired, a notch may be cut in the tree and a trap set in the notch. The notch should be about four inches deep and about twelve inches from top to bottom. Cut the bottom smooth, so the trap will set solid and fasten the bait in the top of the notch. Staple the trap to the tree. If desired, you can lean a pole against the tree for the marten to run up on, but this is not necessary.

The trapper should always be on the look-out for places in which the trap may be set without much labor. Sometimes a tree can be found, with a hollow in one side and this makes a good place for a set. Lean a pole against the tree, with one end resting in the hollow, set a trap on the pole and place a bait in the cavity above the trap. At other times a cavity may be made in the side of a rotten stub and a trap set in the same way.

A Marten Set.

The traps recommended of marten are the No. 1 of any make, but the No. 0 Newhouse is much used. If there are fishers, lynx and other large animals about it is best to use a No. 1½ trap. Deadfalls are also used and they

The Pine Martin

may be built on the ground or snow, or on the top of a stump, or the side of a tree. The track of the marten resembles that of the mink, except that it is a trifle larger and the footprint wider in proportion to the length. The toes do not make as clear a print as do those of the mink, the feet being more heavily furred.

One trapper says he once caught a Marten in a trap set at the foot of a tree, the Marten being up the tree at the time and watching the operation. The trapper had left his gun at the shanty, unfortunately, as he could easily have shot the animal.

In former years the marten was ordinarily captured in wooden traps of very simple construction, made by the inhabitants in the vicinity in which the animal was captured. (See illustration.) These figure-four arrangements are usually enclosed in a line of stakes driven into the ground in the form of a V or U. The marten is forced to enter and opening especially left for him, and in seeking the bait, steps upon the trigger. At other times the bait is attached to the trigger itself, and when the animal disturbs same the log falls upon his head, smashing the skull. Lines of such traps extend many miles. The bait used by Indians, half-breeds and the early trappers, was a piece of squirrel, fish, bird or rabbit.

One of the greatest obstacles that the early marten trapper had to contend with tin most parts of Canada, was the persistent destruction of these traps by the wolverine and fisher. These animals, especially the former, displayed great cunning and perseverance, and intentionally followed these lines of traps, not for the purpose of obtaining the bait but to destroy the traps and seemingly to make the marten hunters life miserable.

The marten is also captured by snares; he being an expert climber, the snares can be arranged between the forks of trees through which the animal passes in his upward flight; at other times in openings of hollow

From Painting. Property of   AMERICAN AND CANADIAN MARTEN OR SABLE   U. S. and Canada
Andersch Bros.   Winter Furred

trees. These home-made traps and contrivance have been replaced by the steel trap. As many as two hundred traps are attended to by a single trapper. These traps like the old figure four arrangement, are set in abodes and left there during the entire season. A Hudson Bay Trapper informed the author that these abodes are not specifically made to draw the animal into, but more so to protect the setting from bad weather, also to keep rabbits and birds from springing the traps.

Wire traps can be used, also the new Tree Traps, but from best information obtainable neither of these well with the old and experienced marten trappers.

TRAPPING THE MARTEN

"I will tell you how I trap marten." Writes Mr. C. Anderson of Cape Scott. "I go up on a hill where there is cedar and find where they have been running up and scratching the back off the trees. I then take sticks and drive in the ground to make a pen, leaving an opening where I set a No. 1 trap, and cover it up with feathers. Use fish and venison for bait. Throw the bait in the pen about eighteen inches from the trap. Drag bait when going form one trap to another as the marten will follow the scent."

In trapping marten one wants to set his traps the same as he does for mink, excepting he must take into consideration that the marten is at home on trees, perhaps more so than on terra firma. I prefer to set my traps mostly in pens, especially constructed with the idea of leaving them from one year to that of another. Set the traps in the den, concealing them in the usual way.

When it comes to bait, I use decomposed fish; probably nothing is better than salmon roe, especially if putrid. If this is unobtainable any other meat or fish will do. No artificial oil is used by me although a brother trapper of mine has used anise oil. No. 1 and 11/2 Newhouse traps are used exclusively by me. Since trapping up here, I have found that it does not pay to depend entirely upon marten, as some years the catch is so light that one would starve if he had to depend upon the returns that he received form the sale of marten skins. Therefore I spend considerable time in trapping for fox, lynx and of course mink.

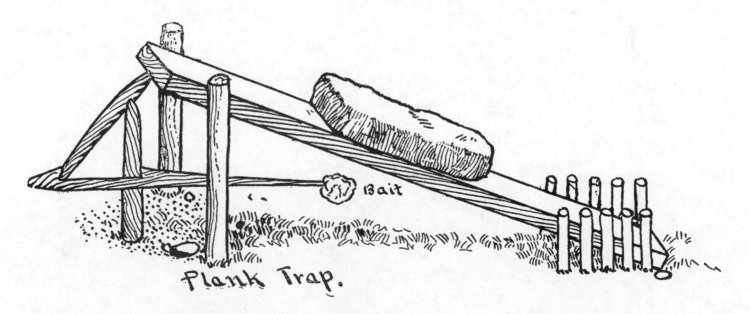

Plank Trap.

There is no particular role where marten traps are to be set. One must study the habits of the animal and during the winter time choose the place where the tracks are most numerous. My marten line sometime extends three-quarters of a mile, but 50 traps is all I care to handle besides sets for other animals.

E.L. Turner

TRAPPING THE MARTEN

Frequently marten are met with in low, swampy ground, where the timber is small and therefore there will be no hollow legs or decayed stumps. In such case the trapper will have to avail himself of the boughs of spruce or balsam fir to make a structure to keep out snow. Selecting a place where tracks are most numerous, both old and fresh, and where there are one or more evergreens growing, he proceeds to cut down a spruce and trimming off the branches cuts it into length about three feet long these he drives into the snow or mossy ground in a circle about a foot in diameter with an opening on one side about four inches wide. The stakes slant outward, making the pen wider at top. The bait, which may be any kind of meat or bird is fastened inside the pen with a peg put through it. The trap is placed in the opening and two twigs are stuck in the ground on both sides of the trap thus insuring success. The twigs also should slant outwards next the sides and top of the pen are covered with spruce boughs, heavily on the top and letting the ends come down so as to almost conceal the opening. This is for keeping out meat birds and other vermin. The marten will find the opening without difficulty and of course when he steps in to get the bait becomes caught.

T. GULLICKSON.

CHAPTER 5

Sable

As I have already remarked, the Sable is closely allied to the Marten. It is classed with them in Natural History under the scientific name of *Martes Zibellina*. Two species are known: the *Maries Zibellina* or Russian Sable and the Japanese Sable The latter is marked with black on its legs and feet. It is thought by some of the Hudson's Bay Company's agents that a Marten exists in the northwestern part of British America and in the late Russian Possessions, which, if not the same, is very closely allied to the Russian Sable The Russian Sable is spread over a vast extent of territory, being found from the northern parts of European Russia eastward to Kamtscliatka. Its size is about equal to that of the Marten, being about eighteen inches in length exclusive of the tail It is not very prolific, seldom bringing forth more than five at a birth and generally only three. This takes place in March or April. They make their homes chiefly near the banks of rivers and in the thickest parts of the woods. They usually live in holes which they burrow in the earth. These burrows are commonly made more secure by being dug among the roots of trees. Occasionally they make their nests in the hollows of trees and there rear their young. Their nests are composed of moss, leaves and dry grass, and are soft and warm. Their food varies with the season and is partly animal and partly vegetable. In the summer, when hares and other small animals are wandering about, the Sable devours great numbers of them. But in winter, when these animals are confined to their retreats by the frost and snow, the Sable is said to feed on wild berries. It also hunts and devours the Ermine and small Weasels, and· such birds as its agility enables it to seize. Sometimes, when other sources of food fail, it will follow the track of Wolves and Bears and feed on the remnants of prey these animals may have left.

The Russian Sable

The fur of the Sable is in great request and is the most beautiful and richly tinted of all the Martens. The color is a rich brown, slightly mottled with white about the head, and having a gray tinge on the neck; it varies somewhat according to locality, and in some regions is very dark. The best skins are said to be obtained in Yakootsk, Kamtsckatka and Russian Lapland. Atkinson, in "Travels in Asiatic Russia," says that Bagouzin, on Lake Baikal, is famed for its Sables. No skins have been found in any part of the world equal to them. The fur is of a deep jet black, with points of hair tipped with white. This constitutes their peculiar beauty. From eighty to ninety dollars are sometimes demanded by the hunters for a single skin.

The Russian Sable is monopolized by the imperial family and nobility of that country. Only a few skins find their way into other countries. Some, however, are obtained privately in Siberia, by Jewish traders, and

brought annually to the Leipsic fair. The fur of the Sable has the peculiarity of being fixed in the skin in such a manner that it will turn with equal freedom in all directions, and lies smoothly in whatever direction it may be pressed. The fur is rather long in proportion to the size of the animal, and extends down the limbs to the claws.

The best method of capturing the Sable is by the steel trap, the same as I have already described for taking the Mink and Marten.

The Sable can be domesticated with success.

CHAPTER 6

Fisher

(Pennants, Marten, Pekan, Lat, Mustela Permants.)

The Fisher is strictly a North American animal and naturalists claim that he forms the connecting link between the Mustela and Gula. He is rated as belonging to the weasel family, of which with the exception of the wolverine. He is the largest and strongest of the entire species. The scarcity of the animal can be noted by reviewing the table found elsewhere in this volume. They are chiefly found in Canadian timber section are very scarce in the heavily timbered sections of the northern states. A few skins are annually received form the timbered sections of Washington, Oregon, Montana, Minnesota, Wisconsin and Michigan but as above notes, the animal is chiefly found in Canada. It weighs from 12 to 16 pounds.

In his habits he resembles the marten, being arboreal, carnivorous and occasionally seen in the early morning or later in the afternoon preying after small animals, but as a rule the fisher possesses nocturnal habits. He is known to rob traps of their victims, and is occasionally nipped himself. The are scarcely ever seen in open sections, but like the marten live in forests and away from civilization.

The specimens before us now indicate that the animal measures 24 to 30 inches from tip of nose to root of tail, the latter measuring 14 to 19 inches, the tail in the larges specimen measuring 16½ inches, in the smallest 13¼ inches. Its black furred legs are stout and one the larges specimen 4 to 5 inches long.

In color the pelage varies unusually much, and each individual skin viewed, indicates a variation from light steel grey on the head and fore part of the body, terminating and blending into a rich brown, nicely topped with long black guard hairs. The long slender tail is considerably darker furred. The undergrowth or fur fibers are shorter by ¼ to ¾ of an inch, as compared with the top guard hairs, which are much coarser but gradually become more pointed at the tip. The nature of the fur is mellow and soft, and furriers say that it works up handsomely.

FISHER

Late Fall Scene
Eastern Canada

THE FISHER

From Original Painting.
Property of
Andersch Bros.

The following account form B. R. Ross, covering the experience in the Mackenzie River region (Canada), is interesting; "In this district it (the fisher) is not found except in the vicinity of Fort Resolution, which may be considered as its northern limit. In the numerous deltas of the mouth of the Slave River it is abundant, frequenting the large grassy marshes or prairies, for the purpose of catching mice, its principal food. In appearance it bears a strong family likeness to both the marten and the wolverine. Its general shape assimilates more to the former, but the head and ears have a greater similitude to those of the latter. It is named by the Chippewayan Indian 'Tha Cho' or great marten. Its legs and feet are stouter in proportion than those of the marten, and its claws much stronger. In color and size it varies greatly. Young, full-furred specimens, or those born the previous spring, can scarcely be distinguished from a large marten except by a darker pelage and a less full, more pointed tail. As it advances toward old age, the color of the fur grows lighter, the long hairs become coarser, and the grayish markings are the greater extent and more conspicuous.

"The largest fisher which I have sent was killed by myself on the River de Argent, one of the channels of the mouth of the Slave River, about 15 miles from Fort Resolution. It was fully as long as a Fulvus fox, much more muscular, and weighted 18 pounds. In the color of its fur the grayish tints predominated, extending from half way down the back to the nose. The fur was comparatively coarse, though thick and full. The tail was long and pointed, and the whole shade of the pelage was very light and had rather a faded look. Its claws were very strong and of brown color and as if to mark its extreme old age the teeth were a good deal worn and very much decayed. I caught it with difficulty. For about two weeks it had been infesting my marten road, tearing down the traps and devouring the bait. So I resolved to destroy it. I made a strong wooden trap. It climbed up this, entered form above, and ate the meat. A gun was next set with no better success, it cut the line and run off with the bone that was tied to the end of it. As a dernier resort I put a steel trap in the middle of the road, covered it carefully, and set a bait at some distance on each side. Into this it tumbled. From the size of its footprints my impression all along was that it was a small wolverine that was annoying me, and I was surprised to find it to be a fisher. It showed good fight, hissed at me much like an enraged eat, biting at the iron trap, and snapping at my legs. A blow on the nose turned it over, when I completed its death by compressing the heart with my foot until it ceased to beat. The skin when stretched for drying was fully as large as a middle-sized otter, and very strong, in this respect resembling hat of wolverine.

"In their habits the fishers resemble the martens. Their food is much the same, but they do not seem to keep so generally in the woods. They are not so nocturnal in their wanderings as the foxes. An old fisher is nearly as great and infliction to a marten trapper as a wolverine. It is an exceedingly powerful animal for its size and will tear down the wooden traps with ease. Its regularity in visiting them is exemplary. In one quality however it is superior to the wolverine, which is that it leaves the sticks of the traps where they were planted; while the other beast if it can discover nothing better to hide, will cache them some distance off. It prefers meat to fish, is not very cunning, and is caught without difficulty in the steel trap."

Its habits, as will be noticed, are arboreal, carnivorous as its name implies, is an expert fisher, but this is again forcibly contradicted. One trapper claims that the fisher will crouch down with head slightly in the water and lie in wait for the swift pickerel or trout three to five hours at a time, seemingly without moving a muscle. It favorite position as claimed by this trapper, is on a fallen log across a brook or stream on a bank where the water is shaded by willows. Nevertheless all agree that one of his principal articles of diet is fish, notably the speckled Mountain trout.

The breeding season is in the early spring, and the female brings forth a litter of 3 to 5 young, which are kept away form the male until they are able to defend themselves and live upon their own resources. Strange to say the father will kill his off spring and for theta reason the mother takes the young to some isolated place and protects them against all foes, and readily risks her life to protect the young from all intruders.

Fishers are taken in steel traps by the same methods as the Mink and Marten. The barricade around the trap, however, should be stronger, and the entrance larger. The trap in all cases should be fastened to a spring-pole of sufficient strength to lift the animal clear from the ground, as he is pretty sure to gnaw off a leg, or the pole, if left where lie can touch the ground. The Hudson's Bay Company's trappers sometimes used the same methods in trapping the Fisher as those employed in Fox trapping. Messrs. Holland and Gunter, trappers of many years experience in the Laurentian Hills of Ontario, describe their mode of trapping the Fisher as follows:

"For capturing the Fisher we always draw a trail composed of the oil of anise, assafœtida and the musk of the Muskrat, mixed with fish oil and placed in a deerskin bag about the size of a mitten, pierced full of holes with a small awl. If drawn along the line of traps the scent is sure to attract the Fisher's attention and when an animal once finds it, he will follow the trail till he comes to a trap. Mink are sometimes caught along trails of this kind and it is a good plan to set a trap for Wolves on the line, as they are likely to be attracted to and follow it. In setting the trap we either place it in a hollow log or build a strong house and place the trap at the entrance. In the latter case the bait should be placed in the brick part of the house, about two feet from the door. The trap should be covered with finely powdered rotten wood. A spring-pole should be used, as all animals of the canine family will follow the trail and rob the traps. Deer-meat, Muskrat-meat, or fish, make good bait for Fisher, Marten, Mink or Wolf."

The Fisher is an exceedingly powerful animal for its size and will tear down wooden traps or "dead-falls" with ease. It frequently annoys the trapper by robbing his Marten traps of their bait, or the animals they have caught. Indeed, the Marten trappers of the Hudson's Bay Territory consider an old Fisher as great an affliction as a Wolverene. It will follow a "line" of traps for miles and visit them with exemplary regularity. Some trappers prefer to catch Fisher by a fore foot.

For its size, the fisher is an exceedingly I powerful animal, and is rather hard to hold in a trap, as it will struggle as long as life lasts. The animal possesses a musk, having a peculiar, rank odor, which it ejects when alarmed. The food of the fisher consists principally of rabbits, partridges and other small animals and birds, I but it will scarcely refuse anything in the line: of flesh, occasionally eating mink, weasel, etc., I out of traps. It also preys on raccoons in the parts of its range where those animals are found and sometimes kills and eats the porcupine. Neither is it a strictly carnivorous animal, as it feeds largely on the berries of the mountain ash and in seasons when these berries are plentiful, the fisher does not take bait well. At such times the Indian trappers will often use a bunch of mountain ash berries for bait.

The Fisher

They are found most plentiful on the higher ground, where the land is fairly well timbered, and the surface of the country is very ragged. They are great travelers and follow the wooded ravines whenever possible. Like all other animals of a rambling nature, each individual has its: regular route of travel, and when you see a track, especially in a ravine, you may be sure j that the animal will come that way again. The fur becomes prime about the first of November and remains in good condition until the first off April, or sometimes longer. They are not very prolific, there being only from two to four in a litter. The young are usually born in April.

Usually, the fisher is easily trapped and will enter the trap as readily as the marten, but there are "off seasons" when food is plenty and the animals are rather shy. On such occasions I have seen them refuse to cross my trail in the snow. In most cases, however, they will jump into the trail and follow it to the trap. When trapped, the animal struggles violently and if the leg is broken, is likely to twist off the foot and escape. It will also chew up everything within reach and the traps must be well fastened. The use of a balance pole is advised, but where, for any reason, it cannot be used, the traps should be fastened to a heavy log. The most common method for trapping the fisher is by setting a trap in a pen of stakes or a natural enclosure, the same as recommended for marten, but the pen should be larger. It should be two feet high, wide at the top and just wide enough for the trap at the bottom.

The bait should be placed on a stick in the back of the pen and the trap should be covered with some light material. The pen should be roofed with evergreen boughs, to protect the trap from the snow. It is the custom among the Indian trappers to make the trap pen of green wood, splitting it and placing the stakes so that the split side will be inward. The object in this is to enable the animal to more easily locate the bait, for sometimes when the fisher scents the bait but cannot find it at once, he moves on. If however, the pen presents a bright interior it attracts the animal's attention and leads to an investigation. This method is used generally, but should not be employed when setting for the more wary animals.

The Indians also at times hang the bait by a piece of light wire, in preference to placing on a stick. This is so that the little wood-mice can not reach and destroy the bait, and I have found it to be a very good plan. A small twig should be placed under the pan of the trap to prevent squirrels and birds from springing it.

For trapping the fisher, I recommend the No. 1½ traps of all makes, also the No. 2 Victor and Oneida Jump traps, Mr. Charles Carner, a noted trapper of California, uses the following method. Find somewhere on the fisher's route of travel, a small bushy evergreen tree with limbs coming down to the ground, cut away a few of the limbs, on one side, so as to make a sort of enclosure. The limbs that are cut away should be stuck in at the sides and back to make the pen tighter. The bait should be tied to the stem of the tree and the trap set a short distance in front of the bait, so as to catch the animal by the fore foot. The trap is fastened securely to the butt of the tree. Mr. Carner recommends the use of the following scent. Fish oil, oil of anise, assafoetida and muskrat musk, thoroughly mixed. He saturates a rabbit with the scent and draws it from trap to trap, and on the last trap uses the rabbit for bait. This scent is also used by some other noted trappers.

I have also caught fishers by building a pen on an old log, lying with one end above the ground. I would make some splits in the log with my axe, drive in a few stakes and weave evergreen boughs among the stakes, roofing the pen with boughs. The trap should be set the same as in the first method and should be stapled to the top of the log, so that when the animal jumps off on either side, he can not get his front feet or the trap down to the ground. The above methods are all very good, but if a particularly shy animal refuses to enter the pen, try setting in a natural enclosure, and if this fails, try the following method:

Under some thick evergreen tree, scrape up a cone shaped pile of snow, making it two feet high and pack the snow solid. Have the trap fastened to a clog and bury the clog in the snow. In the very top of the mound, hollow out a place for the trap and line this place with evergreen tips. Set the trap in this nest, cover it with a piece of paper, and brush a half inch of snow lightly over the paper. For bait, use a whole partridge or rabbit and hang it by a string from a limb of the tree, so that it hangs about two and a half feet above the trap.

Brush your tracks shut with a bunch of boughs and when looking at the trap do not go too close. This method is very good for the shy ones but is too much trouble to use as a regular set, when putting out a long line of traps. The best places in which to set for fishers is in the timbered ravines, especially where two ravines join. Other good places are at the ends of lakes, the points of swamps, and in narrow strips of timber connecting larger bodies.

The track of the fisher is very similar to that of the marten but is larger. The length of jump is about three feet and the footprints from one and a half to two inches in length.

The remarks about the tracks and signs of the mink, apply also to the fisher; the mink, marten and fisher being led by their voracity into very similar habits in their search after food, rendering them reckless and incautious, and causing them to fall an easy prey to almost any kind of trap or dead-fall, provided only that they can obtain what their appetite craves.

While in Winnipeg I spoke to an old Hudson Bay trapper in regard to trapping fisher, and was informed that spring poles should be used in preference to any other appliances in connection with steel traps; but the author believes equally as good results can be obtained by having traps attached to more modern appliances for lifting the animal from the ground and beyond harm of the wolf and other animals. For bait the author suggests the use of fish, rabbit, or a decapitated bird, and if the fisher is to be lured or attracted to the trap, beaver decoy mixed with fish oil and a little oil of anise, should be smeared in vicinity of the trap. Some trappers place this preparation on the sole of their shoes or boots and walk to the traps, while others place the decoy in a buckskin bag which contains some cotton, the latter absorbs the decoy, and as the bag is drawn over the earth, the smell protrudes through the small openings which have been previously made in the bag.

The bag should be drawn towards the trap, not away from the trap. The trapper will sometimes find a trap sprung by a fox, mink, or a marten, and in some instances by a wolverene, but the latter are usually caught by following a line of traps and while in the act of devouring a previous victim. The mink trap will hardly hold fisher or wolverene, unless the trap is attached to a strong spring pole, and then it is doubtful, as the weight of the animal will cause its leg to slide through the jaws of the trap. Deadfall traps are very practical and are continually used by hundreds of trappers, especially by Canadian Indians and half-breeds. Both snares and deadfalls should be set in places where the animal frequents. The same bait and decoy used with steel traps can be advantageously applied to snares, deadfalls and other homemade traps. It is necessary that the steel traps be buried in the usual manner; spring poles or other appliances should be used, in preference to drag or clog, yet some trappers prefer a clog or drag fastened to a long chain or to a stationary object. Sliding poles can be adapted in some places, while sunken barrels or box traps can be used to advantage in certain localities. The latter must be strongly built, otherwise the fisher will escape unless so arranged that if captured he will drown in short order.

CHAPTER 7

Wolverine

The Wolverine is a typical animal of the north. It is found only in the north woods and in the timbered districts of the Rocky Mountains, and not in large numbers in any one district. It is a strong, vicious and cunning brute, and is the greatest plague that the trapper of the north knows.

Its home is a burrow, and here the female brings forth her young once a year, from three to five at a birth. Perhaps the only good side to the character of the Wolverine is the affection the female has for her young, and her fearless and ferocious attacks oil any man or beast that threatens their safety.

The Wolverine does not hibernate, but is about at all seasons.

It is a carnivorous animal and feeds on insects, reptiles, rabbits, mice, lemmings and some of the smaller Fur-bearers. It is a fairly good climber, and game hung in a tree is not safe when a Wolverine is around.

The Wolverine is a great wanderer and will travel from twenty to thirty miles in each direction from its home den. It is not fleet, however, and a man can outrun it. It is a good swimmer.

The Wolverine is also known under various other names— Careajou, Mountain Devil and Skunk-Bear.

It inhabits the whole of British possessions in North America, is sparingly found in the United States, but has been known and still exists in some of the Northern States from the Atlantic to the Pacific Coast, especially in the regions of the Rocky Mountains. Has formerly been seen and was captured in Maine, Masschusetts, very recently in Michigan, Wisconsin and Minnesota, and in the Rocky Mountain regions of Wyoming and Montana; and specimens are still in existence showing that it inhabited to a greater or less extent the states of Utah and Colorado. Very few skins are now received from the northern states and the supply principally comes from Canada. The European species, which is still in existence, resembles that of the American to a great extent.

The wolverene is a night prowler and makes his home in burrows, hollow logs and crevices of rocks; often he partakes of sleep in dens of foxes as well as former dens of wolves, and in fact, seeks rest and sleep wherever it may be found.

WOLVERINE

Eastern Canada
Full Furred.

THE WOLVERENE

From Original Painting
Property of Andersch Bros.

Its principal food is mice, rabbits, mink, marten and similar animals. It follows the wolf and the fox in the hope of obtaining a portion of their prey. Is known to climb low-limbed trees from which it pounces upon its prey, and succeeds in a remarkably short time in subduing its victims. It then proceeds to devour the body, and what it cannot consume is carried away and hidden below the surface of the ground or snow. It is particularly known to follow lines of traps for many miles, partaking of the bait and victim, and even if unable to devour the food so found, it will delight to break into the traps or spring them as the case may be.

The wolverine is very seldom captured; is known to enter the huts of the Laplander and to carry away frying pans, ammunition and similar articles, which it buries, and in consequence thereof is a dreaded animal, being detested by the hunter and trapper as well as the inhabitants of the extreme north. Is known to prey upon beaver and otter. Historians greatly exaggerate the consumption of food as well as the tricks and mischief which are laid at its door.

The following story from Mr. Lockhart may be very interesting:—"The winter I passed at Fort Simpson," writes Mr. Lockhart, "I had a line of marten and fox traps, and lynx snares, extending as far as Lac de Brochet. Visiting them on one occasion I found a lynx alive in one of my snares; and being indisposed to carry it so far home, determined to kill and skin it before it should freeze. But how to cache the skin until my return? This was a serious question, for carcajou were numerous. Placing the carcass as a decoy in a clump of willows at one side of the path, I went some distance on the opposite, dug a hole with my snow shoe about three feet deep in the snow, packing the snow hard down after packing the skin in the smallest compass and putting it in the bottom of the hole which I filled up again very carefully, and then strewing loose snow over the surface till the spot looked as if it had never been disturbed. I also strewed blood and entrails in the path and around the willows. Returning next morning I found that the carcass was gone, as I expected, but that the place where the skin was cached was apparently undisturbed. 'Ah, you rascal,' said I, addressing aloud the absent carcajou, 'I have outwitted you for once.' I lighted my pipe and proceeded leisurely to dig up the skin to place in my muskimoot. I went clear down to the ground, on this side and on that, but no lynx skin was there. The carcajou had been before me, and had carried it off along with the carcass; but he had taken the pains to fill up the hole again and make everything as smooth as before."

Mr. Lockhart also relates that the wolverine habitually sits on his haunches and shades his eyes with one of his fore paws, just as a human being would do in scrutinizing a dim or distant object. On one occasion he was drifting down stream in a canoe, and came within a short distance of one of the animals on the bank; it stopped on perceiving him, squatted on its haunches, and peered earnestly at the advancing boat, holding one fore paw over its eyes in the manner above described. Not seeming to take alarm, it proceeded on a few paces, and then stopped to repeat the performance, when Mr. Lockhart, now sufficiently near, fired and killed the beast.

At times the wolverine displays more boldness than this in the presence of man. It has been known to seize upon the carcass of a deer, and suffer itself to be shot rather than relinquish possession, though the hunter had approached within twenty yards of his game. When pressed by the pangs of hunger, still bolder exploits are sometimes performed, as in the instance narrated by Capt. J. C. Ross. In the dead of an Arctic winter, his ship's company were surprised by a visit from a wolverine, which clambered over the snow wall surrounding the vessel, and came boldly on deck among the men. Forgetful of its safety in the extremity of its need for food, the animal seized a canister of meat, and suffered himself to be noosed while eating.

The animal is of great strength, but lacks activity of body, being heavily and clumsily supported on thick-set, rather low legs and rests upon large feet. The animal resembles that of a small bear. The palms and soles are generally furred, but the digits are naked. The back is high and arched, the figure in general, drooping both before and behind, the head and tail being carried low while in locomotion, similar to a bear. The head is broad and rounded on every side, with a rather short, stubby nose, low ears, and eyes sunk rather deeply into the skull.

On the body the fur is of a blackish, deep dusky brown color. The length of the fibers beginning at the extremities where they are very short, gradually increase to 3½ to 4 inches on the sides and hips, thus giving the well-known shaggy appearance of the animal. There is a light grey patch between the ears and eyes which is extended from the shoulders on both sides and forms the ruff or shaggy aspect heretofore noted. The two broad bands on the animal's sides are occasioned by the variation in color, being of a chestnut or yellowish brown, or even fading to a dingy brownish white, starting at the shoulders and running along the sides and turning up, meeting its fellow on the rump near the base of the tail and forming a rather indistinct lyre-like connection. The claws are sharp, strong, much curved, and about an inch long. The tail resembles more that of the badger, excepting that it is twice as long; the hairs on this member are from five to seven inches long, rather coarse, and the entire member is of a brushy instead of a plume-like appearance.

The fur is used for various purposes and owing to its scarcity brings fairly high prices, but the principal use is for robe or mat purposes. The total number of skins annually collected and marketed rarely exceed 3,000, one-half of which are marketed by the Hudson Bay Company, at London. The price varies considerably as the darker skins bring much better prices, generally from $3.00 to $10.00.

The Wolverine also has the habit of following a trap line, robbing the traps of their bait and of the captured animals. For this reason it is thoroughly hated by the trapper of the north. Once the Wolverine has found a trap line, it will follow the trail to the end, springing the traps, stealing the bait and taking out every animal that has been caught. If the animal is not dead, the Wolverine kills it and pulls it out of the trap; if dead and frozen, the animal is violently jerked until the trapped leg is torn off the body. The Wolverine will eat all it can, and what it cannot eat, it will carry some distance, dig a hole in the snow and cache the dead animal at the bottom. Then replaces the snow in the hole, tramps it down and neatly smooths over the surface, after which it defiles the snow over the cache and goes its way. By these signs a trapper can tell where to dig for his stolen Furs.

Sometimes the Wolverine will enter a trapper's cabin, during his absence. Then it is in its glory. It rips open every sack and parcel, scatters flour, coffee, sugar, tobacco, matches, bacon, soap, etc., in one confused mass upon the cabin floor, and wallows in it all with the greatest joy. At last what it cannot carry away, it defiles to the utmost and departs.

When a Wolverine finds a trapper's line, it is either give up the line for a time, or catch the Wolverine. However, trapping this animal is no easy matter for it is slyer than a Fox and very wary.

A No. 4 trap should be used. It must be well concealed and fastened to a heavy clog, "spring pole" or a "balance pole."

A rabbit, squirrel, muskrat, a piece of goat or any kind of flesh is excellent bait. Beaver Castor is very attractive to the Wolverine and is the best scent for this animal.

One way of trapping this sly and wary creature is to hang a large piece of venison or other meat in a tree. Set traps around the tree carefully concealed in the snow, fastened to a heavy clog and the clog must also be hidden well. Do not disturb the surroundings any more than is absolutely necessary.

Another method is to place a rabbit in a trap and set traps all around. Be sure to cover the traps well and fasten to heavy clogs.

The fur is long, soft and tolerably fine, overlaid with larger and coarser hairs which are about three inches long on the rump but shorter in front. The Wolverene is a great mischief-maker for the trapper in the region where it dwells, especially the Marten-trappers of British America, who use the old fashioned "dead-fall" One of these animals will follow a line of traps for miles, tearing them down, devouring the bait and the animals that have been caught. They are also very troublesome in destroying *caches* of provisions. On account of its destructive propensities, and great cunning and sagacity, the Indians call the Wolverine the Evil One or Devil.

The Wolverine.

The wolverine is also known under other fancy names, the most common of which is "carcajou". In Europe it is called the "glutton" from its supposed gluttonous appetite. Among the Indians of the northwest it is known as the "mountain devil" and in British Columbia is sometimes called the "skunk bear."

The animal really does bear some resemblance to the skunk in its appearance and actions, the most noticeable of which is its habits of raising its tail when disturbed or when it stops to listen to some noise. Sometimes it will stand on its hind legs in order to get a better view of some object which lias aroused its interest.

TRAPPING THE WOLVERINE

This great mischievous animal can be captured in steel traps, snares, deadfalls, etc. but owing to their cuteness, great strength, peculiar habits and training, they will seldom fall a victim.

A Canadian trapper relates that after a single wolverine had destroyed hundreds of dollars worth of his furs, following and releasing traps for a period of three months and practically the entire season, he was fortunate enough to capture him. He set a No. 1 ½ steel trap in the usual way for mink and marten, and surrounding this trap he placed three No. 3 steel traps properly arranged with spring poles. The wolverine visited the scene many times, and on two occasions the trapper found signs of his usual depredations, but the third or fourth time the wolverine sprung one of the traps and was lifted high from the ground.

The wolverine is detested by professional trappers, who spend weeks following this horrid creature at the expense of other work.

An aged hunter and trapper, upon his return from the civil war in 1865, settled in the upper part of Michigan, where he continued his vocation. On one occasion he relates that he captured this marauder after a fruitless effort of three weeks' continued watching, and at one time this wolverine led Mr. Graham for thirty miles, who upon return to the cabin in three days, found fresh tracks of the animal, and upon setting six nests, (three steel traps to each nest), placed at intervals, baiting with pieces of beaver, otter, muskrats, parts of fur scented with castoreum, finally captured a large wolverine.

He invariably used deadfalls and No. 3 steel traps attached to spring poles, and "Of all voracious animals," says Mr. Graham, "the wolverine is the hardest to trap, but by running him down and skillfully manipulating the traps for his reception, by no means become discouraged, and you will triumph and bring the evil-doer to the end of his rope."

Poison can be successfully applied if placed within a carcass of a marten, mink, bird or muskrat; also small pieces strewn about.

The following is borrowed from Mr. Lockhart: "At Peel's River. on one occasion, a very old wolverine discovered my marten road, on which I had nearly a hundred and fifty traps. I was in the habit of visiting the line about once a fortnight; but the beast fell into the way of coming oftener than I did, to my great annoyance and vexation. I determined to put a stop to his thieving and his life together, cost what it might. So I made six strong traps at as many different points, and also set three steel traps. For three weeks I tired my best to catch the beast, without success; and my worst enemy would allow that I am no green hand in these matters. The animal carefully avoided the traps set for his own benefit, and seemed to be taking more delight than ever in demolishing my marten traps and eating the martens, scattering the poles in ever direction, and caching what baits or martens he did not devour on the spot. As we had no poison in those days, I next set a gun on the bank of a little lake. The gun was concealed in some low bushes, but the bait was so placed that the wolverine must see it on his way up the bank. I blockaded my path to the gun with a small pine tree which completely hid it. On my first visit afterward I found that the beast had gone up to the bait and smelled it, but had left it untouched. He had next pulled up the pine tree that blocked the path and gone around the gun and cut the line which connected the bait with the trigger, just behind the muzzle.

Then he had gone back and pulled the bait away and carried it out on the lake, where he laid down and devoured it at his leisure. There I found my string. I could scarcely believe that all this had been done designedly, for it seemed that faculties fully on a par with human reason would e required for such an exploit, if done intentionally. I therefore rearranged things, tying the string where it had been bitten. But the result was exactly the same for three successive occasions, as I could plainly see by the footprints; and what is most singular of all, each time the brute was careful to cut the line a little back of where it had been tied before, as if actually reasoning with himself that even the knots might be some new device of mine, and therefore a source of hidden danger be would prudently avoid. I came to the conclusion that that wolverine ought to live, as he must be something at least human, if not worse. I give it up and abandoned the road for a period.

"On another occasion a wolverine amused himself, much as usual, by tracking my line from one end to the other and demolishing my traps as fast as I could set them. I put a large steel trap in the middle of a path that branched off among some willows, spreading no bait, but risking the chance that the animal would 'put his foot in it' on his way to break a trap at the end of the path. On my next visit I found that the trap was gone, but I noticed the blood and entrails of a hare that had evidently been caught in the trap and devoured by the wolverine on the spot. Examining his footprints I was satisfied that he had not been caught, and I took up his trail. Proceeding about a mile through the woods I came to a small lake, on the banks of which I recognized traces of the traps, which the beast had laid down in order to go a few steps to one side to make water on a stump. He had then returned and picked up the trap, which he had carried across the lake, with many a twist and turn on the hard crust of snow to mislead his expected pursuer, and then again entered the woods. I followed for about half a mile farther and then came to a large hole dug in the snow. This place, however, seemed not to have suited him, for there was nothing there. A few yards farther on, however, I found a neatly built mound of snow on which the animal had made water and left his dirt; this I knew was his cache. Using one of my snowshoes for a spade. I dug into the hillock and down to the ground, the snow being about four feet deep; and there I found my trap, with the toes of a rabbit still in the jaws. Could it have been the animal's instinctive impulse to hide prey that made him carry my traps so far merely for the morsel of meat still held in it? Or did his cunning nature prompt him to hide the trap for fear that on some future unlucky occasion he might put his own toes in it and share the rabbit's fate?"

CHAPTER 8

Skunk

EARLY historians, naturalists and travelers, pointed to the American skunk as the most detested animal on the face of the globe, and many are even to this day so deeply impressed with the distant horrible experiences that he or she will refuse to wear a manufactured garment made out of skunk skins, and the manufacturer is obliged to call the skins from which the garment is made "Black Marten." Thirty and forty years ago the animal was detested by the hunter, trapper and farmer, and it is surprising to note the change in conditions, due largely to the enlightenment of the rural population as to the benefits of the skunk, also to the rapid increase and value of

SKUNK

their pelts. Many skunk farms are in existence, the owners making a business of raising these animals for their pelts. While this may be a queer business, nevertheless it is perfectly legitimate, and as far as know, profitable. A ready sale of the pelt is to be had, and the skins from these domesticated animals generally bring higher average prices, being well handled and killed at a time when the fur is at its best.

The skunk is by no means confined to North America, as the animal is also found in southeastern Europe, South America and in Africa. In these countries he is known under Stinktiere, Surilho, Cape Zorillo, in fact his nomenclature covers a wide range and is still greater confused by naturalists disagreeing on certain species. Mr. Gabriel Sagard-Theodat, the prominent French writer, in his history of Canada, (r636), designates the animal "enfan du diable" which apparently was the recognized Canadian French name for this animal; others mention the "devil's own beast." Te Cree Indian knew the animal under Seecawk, Sometimes he is erroneously called polecat, fitch and chinche. He belongs to the weasel or marten family.

The skunk is found in nearly all the states and territories of the Union and climatic and geographical conditions are responsible for the great variation in size and color of its pelage. There are very few fur-bearing animals as plentiful, and especially so in the civilized sections, that bring such a handsome income to the trapper as does the skunk. As noted, the chief difference in character, besides the size of the animal itself, lies in the color of its fur, and the animal from the outward appearance is closely described in the following pages.

The body is 16 to 22 inches long, its tail from root to farthest point of fur, 12 to 16 inches, the latter being covered with hair, the color of which varies, depending upon the color of the fur on the body. For instance, the fur on the tail of a black or short striped skink is black or nearly all black, while that of the broad or narrow striped skunk is interspersed with black and white hairs. While the skin of the animal is very valuable, the tail is rarely used, though manufacturers of late years have consumed the hair in the manufacture of brushes and similar purposes. The legs are short and close to the body, the paw is naked, and the five toes on each foot are closely grown together like that of the badger. The foot is well adapted to digging The toes are not webbed; the head is small, with short, rounded ears and rather long, projecting nose, with two small piercing eyes. Audubon describes the animal in the following words; "The skunk, although armed with claws and teeth strong enough to capture his prey, is slow on foot, apparently timid, and would be unable to escape from many of his enemies if he were not possessed of a power by which he often causes the most ferocious to make a rapid retreat, run the nose into the earth, or roll and tumble on the ground as if in convulsions; and not infrequently even the bravest of our boasting race is by this little animal compelled suddenly to break off his train of thought, hold his nose and run as if a lion were at his heels."

The skunk in general appearance is always neat and clean, and in walking seemingly takes special pride, as when promenading, its tail is erect and its back peculiarly curved. Very few animals are as harmless as this creature and were it not for the peculiar odor which it distributes when in danger, it would be more hunted and probably eradicated in sections. Its principal weapon, as heretofore noted, is a peculiar secretion and fluid possessing a very disagreeable odor. This fluid is of a pale yellow color and is discharged by the animal when in danger, in thin-like streams and wit such accuracy and aim as o strike any object within 6 to 12 feet. The fluid is secreted in two anul glands from which by the contraction of the sub-caudal muscles and by uplifting of the tail it is discharged in the form as above stated. Trappers who are familiar with this secretion state that the discharge of this perfume looks like a puff of steam or white smoke. Dogs and other animals are adverse to attacking a skunk and only inexperienced or so-called "tenderfeet" will view this animal from the rear unless at a great distance.

Mounted Male   **THE SKUNK**   Iowa Matured

The animal is carnivorous, nocturnal, not entirely terrestrial, as occasionally he is known to climb trees, perhaps not of choice but rather compulsion, being forced to this fancied secure position by the hunter of his dog. Consequently his arboreal, like his amphibious habits, are rather undeserved credentials. The theory that the animal climbs trees in search of food and birds, is discredited. The animal is beneficial in many ways to the farmer, and his eradication from any farming community should be prevented, and laws prohibiting the wanton destruction encouraged.

The contrast in size of the animal and the important variation in the color in the color of its pelage, due to climate and geographical differences, cannot be denied. The breeding and inter-breeding of the different colored furred species is the principal explanation why the young of a litter are so much unlike in color. A Michigan trapper recently sent my firm eleven skunk skips, two larger than the others, presumably one from the male or father, the other from the female or mother; the balance were from the offspring and were all much smaller. All were dug out from under and old granary. The skins graded as follows:

1 Large Narrow	Striped	Skunk	Skin	"Father."
1 Medium Short	"	"	"	"Mother."
3 Small Short	"	"	"	"Cubs."
4 Small Narrow	"	"	"	"
1 Small Broad	"	"	"	"
1 Small White	"	"	"	"

The largest of the skunk species are probably found in Manitoba, where a few years ago four animals were killed and weighed by me; the average weight of the male was 15 pounds and that of the female 11⅓ pounds. All of the animals had two long white, furred, rather narrow stripes extending from neck, over body, terminating at the tail. The average weight of the northwestern male skunk is from 6 to 10 pounds, that of the eastern or southwestern animal 4 to 6 pounds.

The predominating color of the fur of all species is black and white with the exception of the Texas skunk, which due to a peculiar soil, is of reddish cast. Some of the animals have a clear coat of fur, others are all black excepting a small white star, but the majority have two stripes, some terminating at the center of body, on others the stripe continuing from the forehead over the body, terminating at the tail. The stripes on many are so wide that very little black fur is left, and quite a number of skins are annually received that have practically no black fur at all. The white fur is usually of clear color, but occasionally skins are received that have a yellowish cast.

This carnivorous and nocturnal animal is unlike most every other animal possessing these habits. He can be seen in the early morning returning to his haunts, and once in a while in the middle of the day: at no time is he in a hurry, or will he discommode himself by getting out of your sight or especially away from your path and it is not to be wondered at that the farmer, as well as he hunter, will give the animal the right of way. His made of locomotion is slow, and rarely will he be found away from his haunt a greater distance than one or two miles. His abode is usually in a hollow log, under some old barn or granary, or in a hole on the sunny side of some hill. He enjoys a sun bath, probably more than does the bear or the badger. His meal is made up by free consumption of worms, bugs, grasshoppers, mice, birds and eggs. In some sections he is known to be quite a vegetarian, consuming as he does, roots, berries, vegetables, and fruits. Occasionally frequents the hen roost, not only for eggs, but for the hen as well.

In enemies he has to contend wit the hunter and trapper, the fox and he wolf; but the latter two must be in an extreme state of hunger before they will disregard the pungent fluid and devour is body. Dogs are rather skeptical in attacking the skunk unless it is their first experience. In this respect they are no different than the hunter.

The animal passes the winter season in a state of incomplete hibernation, and at regular intervals he will arise, come out of his abode and expose his body to the sun, and judging from the effluvium, empty its distended pouches, but the stench thus caused, soon ceases, which is not the case when it is spurted under irritation or in self-defense. Dr. Coues states "that the animal uses this secretion in the relation of its perpetuation of the species, though overshadowed by its exaggeration into a powerfully effective means of preservation of the individual, is evidently the same as in other species of Mustelidæ, each one of which has its own emanation to bring the sexes together, not only by simply indicating their whereabouts, but by serving as a positive attraction. In the case of the skunk, it would seem that the strong scent has actually tended to result in a more gregarious mode of life than is usual in this family of mammals; and it is certain, at any rate, that the occupancy by one animal of a permanent winter abode serves to attract others to the same retreat. Burrows are sometimes found to contain as many as a dozen individuals, not members of one family, but various adult animals drawn together. One other effect of the possession of such unique powers is seen not so much in mode of life as in the actual disposition of the creature. Its heedless familiarity, its temerity in pushing into places which other animals instinctively avoid as dangerous, and its indisposition to seek safety by hasty retreat, are evident result of its confidence in the extraordinary means of defense with which it is provided.

The White Skunk has a clear, white-furred pelt is very sparingly found, in fact so seldom, that many consider it a freak of nature and not a distinct species. It is common to receive skins which are commercially called "white skunk skins," but these have some black fur, either on the shoulders; neck or legs, and occasionally a few black hairs or an extremely narrow stripe of black fur in center of the skin, beginning about the shoulders and terminating at the tail. In length, quality and texture, the fur compares favorably with the other species. The skins have little value. The range of prices depends somewhat upon the size of the skin, primeness, density, quality and texture of the fur fibers.

The white skunk is found in common with the black, short striped and narrow striped species, chiefly in the localities where the black and short striped species are more plentiful. Are unknown in the locality that the large, narrow and long striped skunk inhabits. Are found in the eastern, Atlantic, middle and western states, but the percentage of white furred skunk skins, including those also commercially called "white skunk skins," is small. Trappers dislike this species, and are aggravated to find a white skunk instead of a black or short striped animal in their trap.

The Black Skunk has a black coat of fur is found in many states, those of New York, New Jersey, Pennsylvania, Michigan, Wisconsin, and eastern Canada, are better furred, and in consequence command better prices than those coming from the central states. The black skunk is also found in Illinois, Indiana, Kentucky, Arkansas, Virginia, North Carolina and South Carolina, in fact in every locality excepting in the northwestern states, also northwestern parts of Canada. The animal cohabits with the other species, and there is no apparent rule governing the breeding and interbreeding and the probable coloration of the offspring. Somewhat disregarding the color of the parents, the litter contains black, white, short, narrow and broad striped youngsters. The fur of the black skunk, especially the eastern variety, is soft, wavy, and of a deep lustrous black. Those animals that have only a small white furred star at the forehead are commercially called "black skunk." The tail of such a skin is invariably covered with long, black hairs. The animal that inhabits the southern and southwestern states is rather small and the fur inferior, consequently the skins command a lower price as compared with those found in the middle or eastern states.

The Short Striped Skunk inhabits the same section as the black skunk, the only difference between them is that the small white star of the former develops into prongs or two distinct white-furred stripes, starting at the forehead and terminating at or-about the shoulders or center of body. Quite often the forehead is entirely covered with white fur, and immediately beginning at the top of head the white hair continues in two prongs, each varying in width from three-eighths to three-fourths of an inch. Should the white stripes continue clear across the body and terminate at the tail, such skins cannot be classed as short striped but are known as long, narrow or broad stripe.

Short striped skins are second in value, the price being about one-third less than that of the black skins. The white stripes are of no value to the manufacturer, these are cut out by him, and for the reason the skin that has the greatest amount of black fur is worth more and the value lessened by the increase of the white stripe. The fur of the tail is black with intermingled white hairs. The disagreeable odor is removed by the dresser (tanner) and by the time the skin reaches the manufacturer, it is cleansed from all impurities and ready to be made into garments.

The Narrow Striped Skunk animal inhabits nearly every state and territory of the Union and greater part of Canada, and is the true American skunk, the one that is so much detested by the traveler and the early historians. His coat of fur is black, excepting two white stripes beginning at the forehead and terminating at the tail. The width of these stripes varies somewhat, depending upon the size of the animal, usually three-eighths to three-fourths of an inch. There is always a goodly portion of black fur between these stripes. The white stripe is of no particular value, and after the skin comes back from the dresser, the manufacturer removes the white stripe and sews the balance of the skin together. The white stripes are narrow and close together, but widen apart at center of back and again narrowing when close to the root of tail. The largest animals of the skunk family come under the longer or narrow striped species. Some of these animals are as large as the badger and raccoon. The smallest skins come Texas and other southern states; the fur is rather coarse and such skins have little value.

The Broad Striped Skunk. is found in common with the previous species, and its difference is only in the width of the white stripe which is wider, and the quantity of black fur on the skin is lessened, thereby diminishing the value of the skin. This species is found more plentiful in the southern and southwestern states, is quite numerous in the Atlantic, western and northwestern states. On some specimens the white stripe is so broad that very little black fur is lefts. Perhaps this is more true of the smaller skins received from Texas and other southern states, and, of course, these have little value. There is not apparent iron-clad rule, or a dividing line between, or just where and when a skin should be called broad stripe and not a narrow striped skin.

This naturally must be left largely to the judgment and discretion of the buyer or the manufacturer, who, in grading, seeks and average more than any particular dividing line. The tail is covered with white hairs with occasional interspersed black hairs.

The One Striped Skunk. has a long, horizontal white stripe extending from forehead, continuing over the body, terminating at root of the tail; the latter is covered with white fur and is probably more bushy in proportion to its size, than the other northwestern species. He is found only in the lower tiers of states bordering Mexico, probably more numerous in California than any other portion of this country. The skin is of no great value. The fur is rather coarse and the skins undesirable.

A story related by one of the perpetrators of a joke upon a young Russian deserter located in North Dakota, is very interesting. In company with three others, he was taken on a hunting expedition in quest of foxes and coyotes, the latter for the bounty, and the former for his pelt, which was worth $4.00 to $5.00. He was impressed with the great value of silver or black fox skins and their color, etc. During the forenoon each of the three succeeded in killing one or more foxes and wolves, but the young Russian was rather unfortunate and depressed in spirits, he not having had any success. A little later on he perceived a large stone pile, and upon nearing it some black furred animal entered therein. Apparently this movement was also noted by the others, but the Russian became excited, thinking that he had seen a black or silver fox enter the stone-pile. The others, however, knew that the animal he had seen was a skunk. It was agreed that whatever the animal might be, the Russian was entitled to its capture. The others gradually withdrew, but before departing, cautioned him, also intimated that the probable capture of the black looking animal might place hundreds of dollars in his pocket, especially if it happened to be a well furred black fox, and if he could be captured without injuring the skin. The companions in withdrawing chuckled to themselves and left the "tenderfoot" to his wits and at the mercy of the skunk.

The ambition of the Russian was to capture the fox alive and immediately rolled a large stone at the opening so as to prevent sudden egress. Stone after stone was now rolled and thrown aside, he working like a Trojan for about 20 minutes, before he reached what he thought was the den. There was no fox in sight, and more stones were removed, and while so occupied a skunk came out from one of the excavations; turning his tail to the enemy, who at that moment perceived the supposed fox and started to grab him, but in return received one or more charges from the concealed battery. Perhaps this was too sudden for both, at least indications pointed that both were surprised, but as neither party gave quarters in the battle that followed, as may be expected the Russian became the victor, but much to his sorrow immediately thereafter. Holding the skunk by the neck with both hands he begged assistance, claiming he could not see and had difficulty in breathing. He finally dropped the skunk, which decamped back to the stone pile, while he reached for his handkerchief, wiped his face and eyes, spat, and acted as if demented. His face, hands and clothing were full of perfume, which became unbearable to him, and upon being told that the animal was a skunk and not a fox, he cussed the skunk, stone pile, country and his companions, but all to no avail. The hunt ended right there and then, and they all departed for home. Upon arriving home his clothes were removed and burned. His style of action in battle was criticized and the probable result is that when he again enters into a fight of this nature, he will attack the enemy "face to face."

The Skunk yields a handsome Fur, which is very fashionable and in great demand. It is one of the staples of American Raw Furs, and every season trappers make good money trapping this Fur-bearer.

The Skunk is a nocturnal animal, but occasionally it is seen during the day. It is sluggish in movement and has but little fear of man, sometimes coming close up to barns and outbuildings.

The Skunk is wholly a terrestrial animal', that is, it does not climb trees nor swim, and lives in burrows in the ground, dens in rocks, decayed logs or stumps, or any natural shelter that is not away from the ground. They occasionally even take up quarters under a haymow or a barn. The burrows and dens sometimes contain as many as a dozen Skunk, not members of one family, but grown up animals attracted to one another. They hibernate only during the severest part of the winter.

The Skunk is carnivorous, that is, its food consist of worms, insects, frogs, mice, young birds, birds' eggs, and it will sometimes eat rabbits and even kill and eat young poultry.

The Skunk is very prolific, bringing forth from five to ten young at a time, which is usually in May.

That which particularly distinguishes the Skunk from other animals is its peculiar and powerful means of defense. It ejects a very foul-smelling and vile fluid when excited or attacked. This fluid is not the urine of the animal, as is commonly supposed, but a peculiar secretion contained in two large glands located near the root of the tail and covered with a dense mass of muscle. The fluid is ejected by the contraction of this muscular covering, which so forcibly compresses the glands that the fluid may be ejected to a distance of six to twelve feet. The bite of the Skunk is capable of causing rabies.

No great skill is required for the capture of the Skunk, as it is not a cunning animal and is not suspicious, therefore, trapping Skunk is an easy matter. The best suited traps for Skunk are the Nos. 1 and 1½ sizes.

The following are good baits for Skunk: Young chicken, birds, mice, rotten eggs, a piece of tainted Skunk or rabbit meat. Tainted bait is preferable. The scent of the animal itself is about the best to use. However, Skunk are so easily caught that a bait or scent is not essential.

The best way of trapping Skunk is to set the trap just in the entrance of the den, but if the entrance is small, set the trap just outside. The trap should be set with the jaws lengthwise, so that the Skunk will step between the jaws and not over one, as by stepping over the jaw the foot might be thrown out of the trap, by the rising jaw, as the trap springs. Sometimes Skunk will only look into a den and turn away without entering, therefore, when trapping at dens, it is well to put a piece of bait inside of the den.

If you cannot find a den, dig a hole under an old stump and place a bait inside. Set the trap in front of the hole and cover lightly. Sprinkle a little scent on and around the stump and ground.

Another good set, is to make a small pen of rotten wood, stones, etc., setting the trap in the entrance and placing a bait in the pen beyond the trap.

A hollow log, a hole in the bank, or in a wall, or any natural enclosure is a good place in which to set a trap for Skunk.

Fasten the trap to a clog, "spring pole" or "balance pole"

There are various methods of killing a trapped Skunk so that it will not eject its scent. However, trappers who trap extensively for Skunk are not particular about getting scent on their clothes or hands, and have no time to bother with fancy methods of killing. They merely hit the animal a good blow on the head and are indifferent to getting scented. For the benefit of those who have objections to becoming scented, the writer will give several methods of killing.

One way, if the trap is fastened to a clog, is to approach the animal slowly, without making any quick movements, and when within striking distance, hit it a good, smart blow across the back with a club. In this way the back is broken, thus preventing the animal front emitting its "perfume."

Another way is to drown the animal, if there is water nearby. Fasten the trap to the end of a long pole, ten to twelve feet in length. When the Skunk is caught, approach carefully arid pick up the pole. By moving very slowly and making no quick motions, the animal can be led to the nearest water, where it can be drowned. Lift the animal up easily and let it down into the water, pushing the pole down until the animal's head is drawn under. Hold it under water until nearly drowned, then let it up to breathe, and push it under again, keeping it there until dead.

Still another method is to cut the animal's throat. Attach a small, very sharp, pointed knife blade or lance to a long pole, about ten or fifteen feet in length. Approach the animal carefully and place the point of the knife or lance against the side of the animal's neck, low down, then give a good, quick jab, and in most cases it is all over with the Skunk.

If the trap is fastened to a "spring pole" or "balance pole," the animal can be killed by a blow across the back.

When skinning Skunk smear your hands with grease. After the animal is skinned, wash your hands with hot water and soap, and there will be no scent on your hands.

To remove Skunk scent from clothing, use benzine or gasoline, or bury the clothes over night in damp ground.

Skunk should be skinned, "cased" and shipped flesh side out.

J. W. BENCK,   WORTH, ILLINOIS
A very successful trapper

As accidents are liable to occur the following recipes by an old trapper may prove useful:

"To get rid of Skunk scent or other offensive odors, wash the hands in hot cider vinegar."

"To remove odor of Skunk from clothes, rinse in gasoline, wring out and hang in open air to dry and evaporate."

Gasoline is very inflammable and should never be used near lighted matches, lamps or fire of any kind but in the open air by daylight.

PRACTICAL SUGGESTIONS BY TRAPPERS

—Hang a Skunk's carcass or a dead hen to a limb or bush about a fool from the ground and set a trap below it.

—The musk of the Skunk and rotten eggs, with a piece of tainted meat, will attract Skunks, showing that not only their odor, but their sense of smell is peculiar.

—In November Skunks re-visit old dens looking for winter quarters. Place your traps in these holes, with bait of Muskrat, Rabbit or chicken placed beyond the trap at each setting.

—Skunks hunt over old logs in search of grub-worms. Set a trap beside such a log and bait with a piece of chicken. A chicken's head, a Skunk's carcass or a piece of fish makes a good bait for Skunks.

—I will tell you how I make a novel set for Skunk or Mink: I take an old wooden churn—the bigger the better—make holes through hoops and fasten each stave with small nails and nail staves the bottom; then with a saw rip the churn lengthwise and divide it into halves. Take one of these and lay it flat side down in a place where you think there is game and cover with leaves or sand, making everything look as natural as possible. Throw a piece of Muskrat carcass in the back end and set a No. 1 trap at the mouth and you have a set hard to beat. It is some trouble to make this set but you can use it for years.

In the northern states the skunk becomes prime about the last week in October, while in the extreme south they are probably not prime until the last week in November. In the north they commence to shed their fur about the tenth or fifteenth of March, while in the south they shed still earlier. During very cold weather, when the skunks have been confined to their dens for a considerable length of time, the warmth of the dens has a tendency to injure the fur. The males also fight among themselves and their fur is often injured in this way. At other times the fur is spoiled somewhat, because of too small an entrance to the den, the fur having a rubbed or woolly appearance. It is the fine black skins taken when in the best condition, that are the most valuable. Skunks are, perhaps, found in the greatest numbers in the eastern states, and the trappers from that section, make more money from skunks than from any other animal.

In winter, one may track them to their dens, and if the den is a good one, may find any number of skunks, up to a dozen, in the same den. It is a common practice to dig the den open and kill all the inmates, but as this method means the destruction of a good den, it is not advisable to do so. The best way is to trap them, as in this way the den will not be injured, and it is almost certain that you will find skunks in the same den each season. Such a den is worth money to the trapper. The oil of the skunk, if rendered carefully, without burning, is useful, and is often used by country people as a remedy for croup.

The most common method of trapping the skunk is to set the trap in the entrance of the den, without bait, but where there are many dens, or where the dens are hard to find, it is best to use bait. In setting the trap in a den, it should be set just inside the entrance, unless the mouth of the den is small, when it should be set just outside. The trap should be set with the jaws lengthwise of the hole, so that the skunk steps between the jaws, and not over them, as by stepping over the jaw the foot is likely to be thrown out of the trap, by the jaw,

The Skunk.

as the trap springs. This rule also applies to all traps set in dens or enclosures of any kind. The common way of fastening is to stake the trap or fasten to a clog, but the balance pole is better.

No great care is necessary in covering the trap, as the skunk is not suspicious, but it is always best to use care, especially in setting baited traps, as one never knows what animal may come along. On one occasion I caught a fox in a trap set for skunk.

It is a good idea also, when trapping at dens, to put a small scrap of bait inside of the den, as many skunks that are traveling about, only look in and turn away, and if the trap is set inside, will not be caught. If, however, there is a small bait inside the den, the skunk will attempt to get it, and will be caught in the trap.

The traps most used for skunks are the No. 1 and No. 1½ There are also some special traps manufactured for these animals, having double jaws or webbed jaws, to prevent the animal gnawing off its foot.

Traps set for skunk should be visited every day, as otherwise the captured animals are likely to escape. They seem to struggle more on dark stormy nights, and during such weather, one should get around to his traps as early as possible in the morning.

Sometimes one can find a well-defined trail leading away from the mouth of the den. In such a case, several traps may be set in the trail, thus doubling or trebling the chance for a catch.

When good dens cannot be found, dig a hole under an old stump, and place a bait inside, setting the trap directly in front of the hole and cover with dry dirt. Sprinkle some scent about, on the stump and ground; use care in setting as you are likely to catch a fox, providing the trap is carefully set and covered, and the stake driven out of sight. For bait use tainted meat of almost any kind.

Another good way is to find a spot of sandy ground, and set the trap in a small hole, covering with sand. Cut the bait into small pieces and scatter it all around the trap, also, if you have it, sprinkle some scent around. The trap may be fastened to a brush drag, and the brush set up to look as though it were growing there.

If you can find a tree or stump with two spreading roots, set the trap between these roots and fasten the bait on the side of the tree, about ten inches above the trap.

Still another way is to make a small pen of old, rotten wood, stones or stakes, setting the trap in the entrance, and placing the bait in the pen beyond the trap.
Any natural enclosure, such as a hollow log, a hole in the bank, or in a wall or pile of stones, makes a good place in which to set a trap.

Skunks may also be taken in box traps, deadfalls and snares, and they seldom become scented when caught in such traps.

For bait, the following are all good: muskrat, skunk, chicken, birds of any kind, rabbit, squirrel, mice, rotten eggs or fish—tainted bait is always to be preferred for skunks, fresh bait being second choice.

To make a good decoy, take one-half dozen rotten eggs, and the scent of one skunk, and mix thoroughly. A mixture of the male and female scent is probably best. Many of the decoys recommended for the fox are also good for skunk. The scent of the skunk itself, is one of the very best to use with a club, as they are certain to throw their scent if killed in this way.

If the fur of the skunk has become scented, I use the following method for removing the scent: Build a fire and throw an armful of evergreen boughs on it so as to make a dense smoke. Hold the scented animal in the smoke for about five minutes, using care to keep it away from the fire or the heat will curl the hair. After the skunk is skinned hang the skin in an airy place for a few days, when there will be practically no smell left.

The track of the skunk is peculiar and is not likely to be mistaken for that of some other animal. Although a member of the weasel family, it does not travel by a series of jumps as does the weasel, mink, marten, etc., but maintains a steady walk, and the foot-prints will be an even distance apart and spread considerably so as to make a wide trail. The length of step is about five inches and the footprints will measure from one to one and a half inches in length, according to the size of the animal.

The trapping of skunk is one of the most profitable branches of trapping, especially for the farmer and members of his family, on their own and adjoining lands, and it is only natural that the younger element should pursue these practices during the winter months.

The fur of the skunk usually becomes prime November 1st, and during that month, also December, his skin brings the trapper more money and probably he is caught then with more ease than later in the year when one has to resort to digging them out. The Skunk can be caught with the assistance of a good dog during the night, also by setting fraps in their dens which may be in some side of a hill, under a root of a tree, in hollow logs, under old out-buildings, barns, etc. Quite often, if such places are not found, traps may be set in some small enclosures made by stakes driven in the ground. Baiting is quite essential but anything will do for the skunk.

During January skunks are somewhat harder to trap, but just as soon as the sun gets warm, which is usually the case during the month of February, the skunk will begin to run from one hole to that of another and their hibernating habits cease. The buck skunk will usually travel much farther, but I find that the female skunk does not confine herself to her abode as is the practice of the female mink. Should the weather be cold the running season does not begin until March. At that time, you will find skunk on the go might and day. Quite naturally the male skunk knows every den in the immediate vicinity and in his haunts visits one after another and, seemingly, he is not detained very long in any one of them, but passes on to another within a very short time. This is the time when the farmer boy should devote a week or two to trapping skunks, because soon thereafter the skins are unprime, the fur begins to shed, and the fur dealer is obliged to class same as No. 2, No. 3, and shedding.

Place your steel traps in front of their dens. Don't confine yourself to steel traps entirely but obtain wire traps, either the Stop Thief pattern, or those made by the Oneida Community Co. Better results are sometimes obtained by using home made traps, especially when you can get five to six

1   Red Fox in a Jump Trap
2   Young Raccoon in a New House Steel Trap
3   Raccoon in a Jump Trap
4   2 Skunks Caught in Steel Traps

Caught and Photographed
by H. O. Ingalls,
West Haven,
Vermont

skunks at one time. At this time of the year, when skunks are plenty, I never stop to dig them out; time seems to be too precious. If the weather should turn unfavorable, then I revert to digging.

Last year I caught over three hundred skunks within three weeks, besides other furs, and if anyone can beat me, he will have to show me because I come from Missouri.

JACK MORROW.

TRAPPING THE SKUNK

From a trapper in Missouri we have the following article on catching skunks:

"To find the skunk's den look for a hole at the side of a hill or rise of ground, or under rock piles and rocky bluffs, and sometimes in old wells. Now examine the holes to find if black and white hairs are sticking to the entrance, which is often the case when the holes are to small. Skunks are lazy animals and when possible, they take possession of holes made by other animals. If they have occupied the hole long, you will find a manure pile nearby.

"If their den is found in the side of a hill where digging is easy, dig them out, but never start where there are too many rocks. Their bed is usually placed above the rest of the hole in such a manner that makes it very hard to drown them out. With these points in view it is best to trap them either with steel traps or with what is commonly known as a "deadfall" which consists of a lot about twelve inches each way closed on three sides. On the fourth side lies a pole which sets upon the "triggers" and which is baited with hog-liver, if obtainable; if not, with fresh meat (preferably rabbit heads). When the skunk touches the bait the trigger rod releases the pole, and falling, it breaks the back of the anima, and consequently, when found the next morning, he is dead. These traps should be placed about five feet from the hole in the run, and baited carefully. Should you wish to use the steel traps rub them with hog-liver. Place the traps in the hole and cover all but the plate with leaves; then fasten the trap securely to some clog or stake. Take the fat from some fish and fry it out and pour into a bottle. Leave the cork out expose it until the oil decays and becomes very strong. Place a few drops near the hole and some on the plate of the trap. Cover the trap with fine leaves, fasten securely, and visit your traps each morning. This decoy is also good in trapping other animals.

"The skinning is the next process; to do this, cut from the foot of one hind leg to the foot of the other and detach them from the flesh. Next cut form both sides to the root of the tail, carefully avoiding the "musk bag." Then after skinning the tail, put your feet on its two hind feet and pull steadily the tail, have detached the hide. Be very careful not to cut any holes in the fur as this slightly injures its selling value. Stretch and dry the hide in a cased shape and always have the fur next to the board or stretcher, so as to keep the flesh part exposed to the air to dry: Scrape the fat from the skunks and render just as you would lard. This makes a very good medicine for people suffering from colds. Ship your furs to a reliable company and do not sell to the home dealer as he usually pays an inferior price. Go to your traps daily and skin as fast as caught."

TRAPPING THE SKUNK

A Pennsylvania trapper, who wishes his name withheld, writes as follows:

"My experience in catching skunk is a follows: The time to start out is during the fall (November or December) when there is a light fall of snow which enables me to follow the skunk by his tracks to the den or his feeding place, and at these places I set the traps. Their holes are found generally on the south side of a hill under stone piles, and when you have found such a place examine the sides of the holes and look for black and white hairs, that generally adhere to the sides. If you find these hairs you can bet that the hole is not an old one and that skunks inhabit the same.

"Another way I can always find out whether the hole is occupied of inhabited is in looking about the opening and if I find a pile of their manure which has a fresh appearance, I know that hole is inhabited, and I set my trap on the pile or thereabouts. I use a steel trap, No. 1 or 1 ½, but in front of holes often use Stop Thief traps.

"You will find all the way from two to twelve skunks in a den. They are not shrewd at all will readily walk into uncovered steel traps. I like the Stop Thief trap better for the reason that it kills the skunk and does not leave the disagreeable odor on the pelt."

TRAPPING THE SKUNK

I well remember the first skunk I ever caught, in fact, I shall never forget it. I had heard a lot about people catching them, and selling skins for a good price and as I wanted some money, I concluded I would catch skunks.

One warm day in January, I started out with an axe and spade on my shoulder. (Skunks are nearly always dug out in this vicinity.) I had gone about a mile and came onto a track and followed it till it went into a hole under a stump. As it was afternoon when I started, it got dark before I got Mr. Skunk, I concluded to plug the hole up and leave him till morning. I went back the next morning, but he had gotten out, so off I went on his track, following about two miles, to where he had stopped for the day. I set to work again and as it was a short shallow hole in a sheltered place, I soon came to him. I got a long stick and pounded him till he ceased to struggle. Then I got him out and he proved to be a big broad stripe. I certainly was pleased to think I had got him and came home feeling great. Everything went fine until I got home. Then the trouble began. I had to change my clothes, wash my hands good, and put my boots outdoors. You will all know why. I sold his pelt for 40c and that ended my first winter's skunk-hunting. But I did better afterwards, as I got along without any smell in either killing or skinning. I will give my method for the benefit of those who dig skunks out. First, when you get a skunk tracked to a hole, look all about to see if there are two or more entrances. If there is only one entrance all the better. If more than one, run a stick down below the frost in all but one, so the skunk cannot get out. Then begin to dig at the mouth of the hole and follow right along. If there are branches off of the main hole, dig them out too, unless you have a good dog. If you have, he will soon show you where your game is. The most delicate part of the digging-out process is when you come to his skunkship. When you get right close to him, be careful not to disturb him, but quietly shut the hole up in front of him and dig over top and past him. Dig till there is not more than an inch of dirt over top, then gently begin to press the dirt down on him. After you get him nicely covered three or four inches

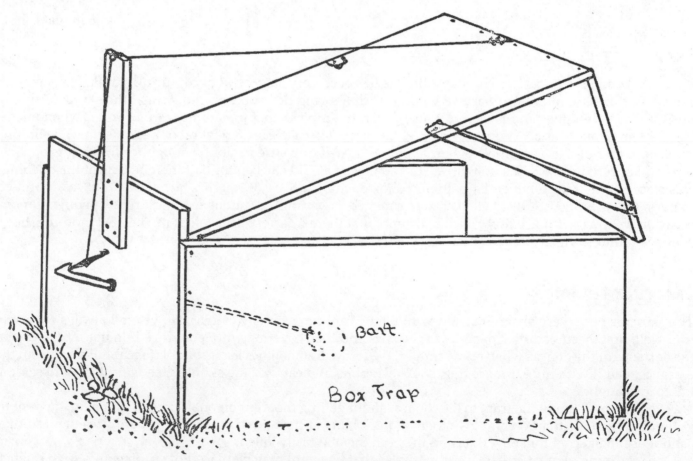

BOX TRAP.

A very simple arrangement especially adapted for capturing animals and birds alive. The cover or lid can be raised much higher if preferred. A similar contrivance was used some years ago for capturing a large African lion that was taken to England.

deep, begin to tramp the dirt in solidly. Cover about eighteen or twenty inches deep and leave for fifteen or twenty minutes and he will be dead.

Skinning is the next operation. I always begin at the heels on the inside of hind legs and cut to the root of tail. It is best to use a very sharp knife for this. Loosen the skin around the hind legs and take tail-bone out. Sharpen a stick six or eight inches long at both ends and fit through the large cords just above the heels and hang over a limb of convenient height. Then use your hands and a somewhat duller knife to pull the pelt over his head. Be careful cutting around the eyes and not leave a big hole as it injures the pelt. Be careful around the ears also.

Stretching comes next in order. This is a very important part of handling too. I use the one piece stretcher most, although I sometimes use the three-piece, which I believe is a little better as you can stretch the skin a little more. It is hard to get the one-piece stretcher just the right size and the three-piece stretcher can be vaned a little to suit the size of the skin. There is danger of stretching the skin too hard with the three-piece stretcher, which makes the fur appear thin.

Selling our catch is important to the most of us too. Well handled skins always bring a good price and everybody likes to buy them. Poorly handled, the buyers try to buy them cheap. The trapper, as well as the buyer is displeased with his returns for poorly handled skins. Some travelling buyers pay good prices and some very poor prices, so taking everything into consideration, it is better for the trapper to ship his own catch to some reliable company.

ROY ABRAY,
Highgate, Ont.,

TRAPPING THE SKUNK

Mr. A. A. Lamb, Buchanan, Mich., states that he has been very successful in capturing skunk. "I sometimes use two or three joints of ordinary stove pipe with a swing door on one end, which the skunk is able to push inward; the other end is closed. I also fasten the pipe so that the animal cannot roll it when inside. Have taken as many as six skunks is one night. For bait I use a piece of muskrat or part of some old stinking chicken. Either of these are good. A neighbor and myself dug a trench long enough for four joints of stove pipe and covered these joints up with earth and placed an old chicken for bait therein. One of the openings was closed, and in the other end a swinging door, opening inward, through which the skunk was supposed to pass, was arranged. A dead chicken was dragged in various directions leading to the opening. On one occasion we dragged this bait for such a distance that there was very little left of it. The next morning, however, we found thirteen skunks in the stove pipe."

TRAPPING THE SKUNK

The skunk is not a very sly animal and with a little care can be easily caught. However, I always cover my trap well, first by spreading a paper over the jaws and then covering with loose dirt. I do not set my trap at the entrance of the den, as when one is caught, the rest will sometimes leave, but place it about a rod from the entrance, bait it with mice, prairie dog, squirrel, or bits of meat, and the skunk, greedy for bait, will seldom fail to get caught.

After getting them in the trap, to kill them without getting the scent on one's person, come up, if possible, without attracting attention and give them a quick blow at the root of the tail. This paralyzes them so they cannot use their scent for some time and they can then be easily killed.

Or, if trapping along a stream, set the trap so that a weight may be placed over the water, so that when the skunk is caught he will be thrown into the water and drown; in this way no scent will remain about the hide.

FRED D, ABBOTT.
Ft. Pierre, S. D.

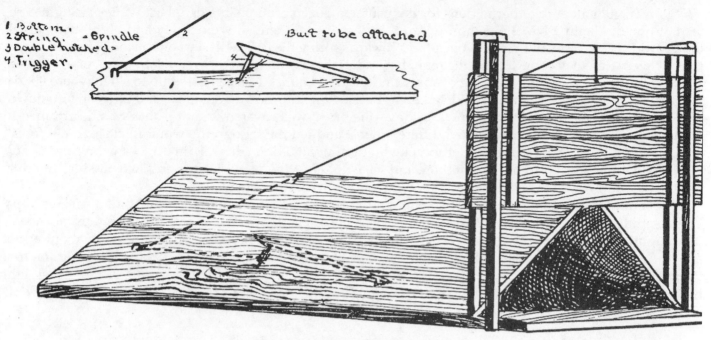

TRIANGLE BOX TRAP.

The triangle should be from 3 to 4 feet long, and for bottom take 2-inch plank 14 inches wide. Lower plank should be 3 inches longer on each end. Securely fasten wire screening or laths on one end and arrange drop door as per illustration. Tie a string to door, pass over beam through upper portion of triangle, then slanting to staple, and fasten to figure four arrangement by using lower plank as a part of the contrivance. The spindle should be arranged to hold upright stick to which string is attached by a notch made into the plank. Bait should be attached to spindle. The animal by partaking of the bait disturbs the spindle and the door drops.

TRAPPING THE SKUNK

We have the following interesting article from Mr. William Plummer, of Rochester, Minn.

"I was once told that skunks were the most ignorant of all wild animals and the most easy to catch. Probably, that is pretty near the truth, for, as a rule, it does not require much skill and experience to catch the ordinary skunk. But like everything else, there are a few of them that get wise by experience; at least, I have found it so.

"During the winter of 1901, a neighbor's boy told me where several skunks were in the habit of frequenting. He had been trapping for them but could not catch them. They would get into his traps but always pulled out some way. He showed me his traps. They were No. 0 rat traps. Well, I told him I would try my hand, so I went to work with a No. 1½. The ground was bare at the time so I had to got somewhat by guess. I set at least half a dozen traps, using smoked bacon for bait. I kept this up for a week but got no skunk. Finally, one evening, there fell a light soft snow. Now, I thought, I will get my skunk. I was out early, found a track and followed it to within six feet of my trap where it turned off. I followed it further and found where some sheep had been killed by wolves. Just part of one leg and some wool was left. Mr. Skunk had feasted on that and gone on. I set two traps right there, covered them up carefully, brushed out my tracks best I could. Next morning I went to get my skunk but he was not there. He had come for another meal but having discovered danger, turned when within ten feet of the trap and left. Several others served me the same way during the week, so I gave it up. That neighbor's rat trap had educated them, but they are not all wise.

"I have caught them by turning over a nail keg, placing a steel trap in the front end, and laying a small bit of bacon at rear end. I have caught them by setting steel traps in paths uncovered; have caught them by the neck by placing a bit of meat under the pan of trap.

"Skunks will gather together in dens for the winter, a dozen or more in a den. Last winter I caught eighteen at one den with a No. 2 Newhouse trap. I kept that trap there all winter, day and night. Sometimes, though, one or two only with stay at one place. Towards spring the toms will start out on long journeys, stopping at every den they come to, and the man that undertakes to run them down must prepare for a long trip.

"One morning last winter in going over my line of traps, I noticed a track going up to a den where I had a trap set but the skunk had turned aside when he noticed the trap, so I made up my mind to run him down. A soft snow had fallen during the previous day—the brush was covered with it—but I was determined to get that skunk. He stopped at a dozen different dens, and led me though the worst thickets in the forest. Finally, about three o'clock in the afternoon he brought up at a den where skunk tracks were coming and going in all directions. I stopped right there and set a No. 2 Newhouse in the den and two outside, and during the next few days caught seven skunks right there—five of them females.

"I generally use No. 2 double spring steel traps, I find it pays as they sometimes pull out of smaller traps. When setting in dens, I use no bait and seldom cover the trap, but in paths away from dens, I usually cover them lightly with dried grass or leaves, and bait with smoked bacon under the pan or hang about a foot above. To kill them without scenting, I take a foot of fine brass or copper wire, make a loop of it, tie to a twelve foot pole, slip the loop over the skunk's head, and pull him quickly off the ground. If caught just right he dies in a few minutes, if he continues to wriggle I hang the pole over a bush, stump, rock or whatever is handiest, and look after the rest of my traps; when I come back he is always dead."

TRAPPING THE SKUNK

An Iowa trapper relates his way of killing skunk without the animal throwing its essence over him.

"Take a stick three to four feet long, and when I see a skunk in the road or about his hole. I simply walk right for him, pointing the stick at his nose, and it's surprising that the animal with stand in a hypnotized manner, and when you get within reach will try to grab the stick. Then is the time to give the animal a sharp blow over the head. This will settle him. I never trap or kill skunk until about the first of December, and not later than February."

BOX TRAP.

Especially adapted for capturing skunk, badger and similar animals. The box is about 18 to 20 inches long, 12 to 14 inches deep. The door is conveniently hung on a rod penetrating from one side to the other, as per illustration. This trap is recommended only when trapper desires to capture the animal alive. Bait with meat or dead birds, rabbits etc.

TRAPPING THE SKUNK

"Last winter I caught sixteen skunks by setting No. 1½ steel traps just at the opening leading to an old graveyard.

"I barricaded all other openings, excepting two, and set a trap a little on one side in the opening and every morning I had one or two of them caught. I killed them with my twenty-two rifle by shooting them in the head or eyes.

"My brother, who makes a business of trapping each winter, helped me to take the skins off and I will tell you how he did it. He calls it 'his lightning way,' and sure enough, it didn't take him any time to take the skins off from the first three skunks. He has had great experience trapping for the last ten or fifteen years, and selling $300.00 to $500.00 worth of fur every year, all being his own skins.

"When I told him to help me, he went into the barn, brought two knives, a hatchet, two knife-like pieces of wood made out of oak, a rope, a few pieces of string cord, a small hand saw, some nails, and stretchers. This constituted his outfit for skunks.

"He tied a string to each hind foot, raised the animal off the ground, hung it against a tree in which he first drove a ten-penny nail with his hatchet, and then took the small knife and made a slit from the vent to where the strings were tied on the legs, cut around each leg jus below the string, and then proceeded to skin out the legs. He then skinned as far as possible down the body, severed the tail from the body, and pulled the skin down, using the knife as little as possible. In no time he was down to the front legs. He cut the legs off just by the knee, and with one hand against the body, the other holding the skin, freed the legs, then he pulled the skin down to the head. He cut around the ears, eyes and mouth, and the skin was off. I don't think it took him five minutes. He later removed the string and placed it on another skunk, and proceeded the same way as he did before.

"When it came to stretching, he took an ordinary single board stretcher and with his hatchet drove four nails—two on each side of the tail and two on belly portion—and proceeded with his hatchet to scrape off the surplus fat and later used the two hard-wood knife-like pieces, and in no time had the skin freed from fat. He also split the tail open and by attaching a string to the tail-bone, pulled the bone out; at another time he simply ripped the tail open and removed the tail-bone by cutting it out. When he was through with all the skunks we took the skins home and he placed them for me on regular wedge stretchers. After the skins were thoroughly dry, I shipped them to you at Minneapolis and you allowed me from 85c to $1.30 apiece -they being narrow striped skins—and the average price I realized after freight was deducted was nearly $1.05 each."

PEDAR OLSON.

TRAPPING THE SKUNK

This animal belongs to the weasel family, and is nocturnal in it habits, but unlike other fur-bearing animals of the weasel family, lacks alertness. It is unable to climb trees, is exceedingly slow in locomotion as compared with other animals, and naturally falls an easy prey to the average hunter or trapper.

The only drawback and reason why this animal was not extensively hunted or trapped and the skin marketed twenty or thirty years ago, was the danger of being sprayed with their peculiar essence, which is its only weapon and upon that the animal relies to distract the hunter, trapper or poacher and, naturally, the strong odor becomes speedily effective and answers the purpose only too well.

The fur is fine and eagerly sought after, especially the black furred skins, which bring high prices. As many as 500,000 skunk skins are marketed in a year, and if the demand is good, the skins bring 75 cents to $3.00 each, depending on size and quality of fur.

The skins are generally divided into four or five distinct grades, and each grade is then assorted accordingly to quality and size. The black, short or half-striped, narrow or long striped, broad striped and white, are the common grades, but the skins vary considerably in value. The fur of the former is all black, the second, or half-striped are such skins as have two short, white stripes descending from the nose over the head and reach to about the center of body, while the stripes on the third class extend clear along the body and run well into the tail. The broad striped, or fourth order, as above enumerated, is similar to the third order, excepting the white stripes are broader, thus lessening the value of the skin considerably, as the white skunks, have little by

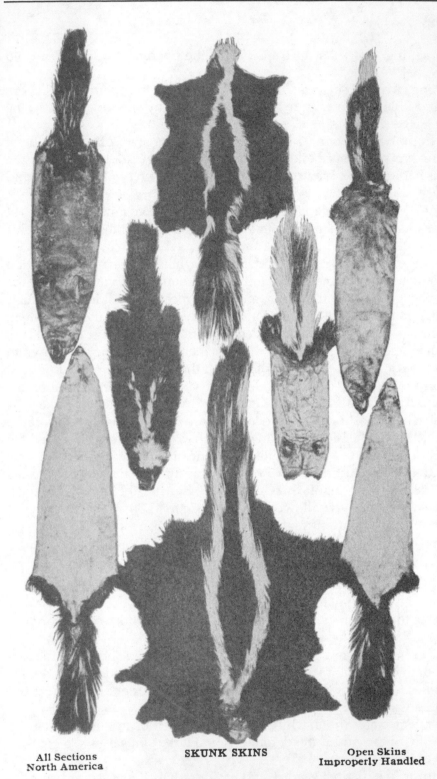

SKUNK SKINS

All Sections
North America

Open Skins
Improperly Handled

manufacturers. The fifth order, or white skunks, have little value, as the back, in fact, nearly all portions of the skin is covered with white fur, and such skins are only used after the fur is dyed, for cheap garments or trimmings.

Skunks should not be killed for the pelt out of season, but this is true of all animals, where the furred skin has a market value. The open season for Minnesota, Dakotas, Iowa, Wisconsin, Montana and northern sections, is from November 1st to February 15th, varying somewhat upon the weather. South or middle states the season opens somewhat earlier, and naturally closes on approach of warm weather. The fur of the skunk is the first of all fur-bearing animals to become prime, and is also first to suffer the loss of its lustre and primeness. There are many ways and methods in common use for capturing and killed this animal, but probably the best is the use of steel traps, though a long stick is equally as good, providing the one who holds it comprehends his business and uses same advantageously. The author has known two lads to kill and skin forty skunks in a day. Of course, great care must be exercised to kill the animal without receiving a discharge of the perfume. A six to eight foot long stick, one and a half to two inches in diameter is the proper weapon and instrument to use in killing skunks. A smart blow on the back about one to two inches beyond the tai will readily fell the animal. This blow will paralyze and benumb the muscles and nerves employed by the animal to distribute its obnoxious fluid. An additional blow is necessary, and the latter should be given on top of head.

Steel traps are used with good effect. They should be set just before the hole and be covered with loose bits of dirt, leaves or other vegetation. Some prefer to use bait, the latter can be a beef head, a chicken, or, in fact, any chunk of old meat or carcass. Drag same in various ways and drop in a conspicuous place or in center of a nest of traps. The trap should be attached to a clog, or loose bushes, never attach two traps to the same article. Skunks often spring traps set for mink, wolf and other animals, but seldom devour or even touch a victim should they come upon same while making their nocturnal visits.

The usual bait for skunk is birds, bits of meat, pieces of chicken and rabbit, whether old or fresh. A good method and trap is to bury a large dry goods box; see that the top is even with the surface of the earth, place light brushes, leaves, hay or straw across the opening, upon which sprinkle a little loose earth. Some prefer to make an artificial opening in top of box after same is buried, into which the skunk will descend, rather fall in, but cannot get out. Some strong smelling bait should be placed in the box, which is to attract the animal from a distance. As many as eight skunks have been caught during one night by the use of this style of box trap.

Another method is the so-called barrel trap. A sugar, vinegar or whiskey barrel will answer. Remove the head and securely fasten the bait on inside bottom of barrel. Place the barrel in a slanting position, open part toward the earth, and arrange by balancing the barrel in such a way that when the skunk enters by crawling up in barrel, being attracted there by the bait, the barrel with the skunk will tip over and Mr. Skunk fall on his nose inside of the barrel and be a captive. This is a good and cheap trap and the victim cannot get out, though only one animal can be caught at one time. Some trappers dig the skunk out, others dig until they reach the cavity in which they usually have their nests and are found huddled up together in a bunch. If found in such a position it is an easy matter to suffocate them, thus obliterating all possible chances of the animals distributing their obnoxious perfume. All that is necessary after one sees the animals is to them up with soft dirt, which should be lightly tamped every two inches of filling and continued until about fifteen to eighteen inches is securely tamped. In about fifteen to twenty minutes the trapper can uncover the den by removing the earth, and he will find the animals suffocated.

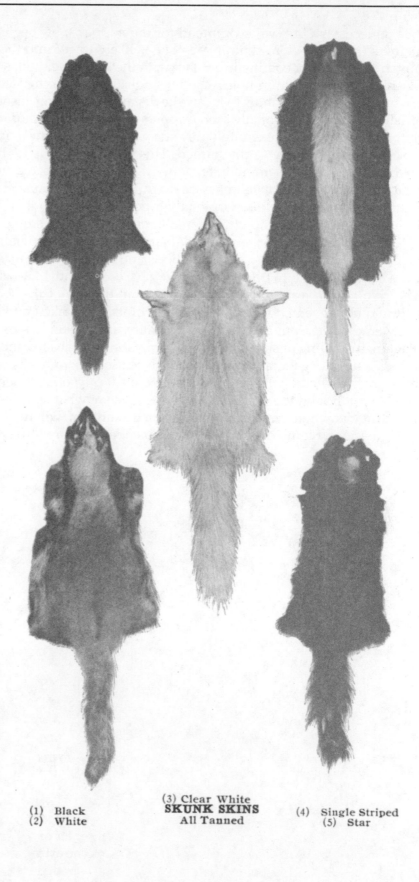

(1) Black
(2) White

(3) Clear White
SKUNK SKINS
All Tanned

(4) Single Striped
(5) Star

It is unnecessary, but we recommend for the trapper, (new beginners) or hunters, to remove the perfume containers (glands) before skinning, as one is likely to cut into the bags and distribute the perfume, but it removed all danger of coming in contact with the liquid weapon is of the past.

Skunks, when located in holes, can be smoked out or suffocated, either with common smoke or vapors arising from burning sulphur. To locate the distance of digging, insert a long switch or telegraph wire into the hole. The author has personally seen trappers dig down for a short distance and then reach after the animals with their hands, and sure enough they succeed in bring-in the animals, one by one, from their den. Strange as it seems no perfume was discharged. This is probably due to the fact that the other trapper assisted by knocking them senseless immediately after their heads appeared through the hole. A piece of ¾-inch round iron, about twelve inches in length, was used. Trappers relate and claim that it is a positive fact that the skunk will refrain from biting or discharging their perfume while in their holes.

Deadfalls, figure four and other home-made traps can be employed, though the animal must be skinned promptly, and often the fur becomes damaged from the instrument itself or by long delay and exposure to the weather. There are many other methods and ways to capture and kill this animal, but by the foregoing anyone contemplating to trap or hunt will have the essential knowledge.

The rifle can be used whenever possible, but the use of the shotgun is detrimental to the skin, and its use should be prevented when the question of its fur is taken into consideration. The animal should not be entirely eradicated from any particular locality, as the skunk is more beneficial than harmful to the farms, and again, the killing of skunks out of season is entirely absurd and uncalled for, the animal being harmless. The meat while not generally consumed, can be used, though when fried, it is dry and tough, resembling bull meat in that respect. The fat is used for medicinal purposes, though of recent years, substitutes are placed before the public and the demand consequently somewhat lessened.

The druggist who formerly handled refined skunk oil, will now satisfy the purchaser with adulterants or cheap imitations. Skunk oil is highly recommended for sore throat, croup, etc.

CHAPTER 9

Civet Cat

Little Striped Skunk. Lat. Mephitis (Spilogale) Putorius.

AMERICAN civet cat must not be confused with the animal inhabiting Africa or Southern Asia known as the African civet from whose pouch a perfume, commercially known as "Civet" is extracted. This little four-striped skunk, under which name it is also known, belonging to the skunk family, possesses carnivorous and nocturnal habits. The animal is found in nearly all southern, central and Pacific states: is scarcely found in the states bordering Canada, and is unknown in the latter country. The animal is quite numerous in the central states, and especially so in Iowa. Missouri, Kansas, Indiana, Illinois and Nebraska. A large number of skins are annually received from the southwestern and western states, also from Florida and Texas. The animal Measures from 23 to 28 inches from end of nose to tip of tail and stands four to five inches high from the heel to top of shoulder. The construction of the animal's body is such enabling it to be quick in action and the body proper weighs three, not exceeding four pounds.

The fantastic, harlequin-like coloring is seldom duplicated in any two species, and in fact, no two skins in a lot of three to five hundred can be found alike—due to change and number of spots and the peculiar formation of the stripes. The animal possesses a coat of soft, black fur, having a white star in the center of the forehead, and four parallel and almost equi-distant stripes, beginning on the uppermost portion of the head between the ears, and ending at or about the center of the body. Another stripe-like formation on each side of the stripes heretofore mentioned being curved in hard or lyre-like shape, encircling and ending about the center of the body. This concludes the stripes and the remainder of the black fur is intermingled with 6 to 8 other small white spots. The tail possesses a growth of hair usually 4 to 5 inches in length, while that of the tailbone proper seldom exceeds 7 inches, usually 5 to 6 inches, a total length of 10 to 15 inches, (four-fifths of body).

CIVET CAT

From Drawing owned
by Andersch Bros.

THE CIVET CAT

Winter Scene
Southern Iowa

The animal's wide geographical distribution most naturally results in marked differences in size of the animal, and color of its pelage. The habits, however, are the same. The black fur is quite pure and glossy with the exception of animals from certain parts of Texas where the soil has a tendency to give the fur a reddish hue. The skin from animals above denoted possess four to six white stripes with numerous white sports, and its tail is covered with long, black and white hairs. The skins are used natural or dyed black, and chiefly for lining purposes. The price of skins varies considerably, usually I5c to 35c. The fur is not as staple as that of mink, skunk or muskrat.

In respect to habits the animal closely resembles that of the skunk. It is nocturnal and carnivorous, better adapted to climbing trees and more readily covers distances than does the skunk. His favorable abode is under some old building, shack, crib, etc., at other times in some hollow log or burrow made by other animals. Such is generally on the side of a hill facing the morning sun. His principal food is worms, bugs, grasshoppers, frogs, mice, birds and rats. In some sections it is claimed the animal is a great vegetarian.

By the two anul glands from which by the contraction of the subcaudal muscles and by the uplifting of the tail, a fluid ranking in odor to that of the skunk, is discharged. The animal can discharge this obnoxious fluid at its pleasure.

These skunks are not a very suspicious or wise animal, and any boy knows how to catch, one but the great trouble is to know hot to "uncatch" him without serious consequences. They have the same means of defence as their larger cousins, though in a less degree in proportion to their size. They delight to make their home around some old barn and are said to be very useful in destroying mice and rats, in fact some farmers have taken pains to protect them in this pursuit and in some instances they have become quite tame.

The No. 0 steel trap is strong enough for these animals, though No. 1 is more sure. They are sometimes taken in the common wire spring rat trap also.

TRAPPING THE CIVET CAT

This carnivorous animal, feeding on rats, mice and gophers, frequently makes a visit to the farmer's poultry yard. They are not very cunning, readily entering a trap. If you set the trap at their dens you should have the trap staked back from the hole so if one gets in they will not pull the trap back into the hole thus making it hard to kill him without getting scented. Set traps along creeks, hedges, fences, etc. Before setting traps take a piece of pork and hold it over the fire until it gets good and brown, also take along some fish oil (which can be purchased at any drug store), put a few pieces of the pork and a few drops of the fish oil around your traps and you are pretty sure of every civet cat that comes that way. I prefer a No. I trap for them, for if you get a skunk in a trap set for them he will stay there while he would be apt to pull out of a No. o. Skin them as you would a mink, taking care not to cut the scent-glands; it is best to remove them. If you take them out, commence back of them, cutting into the flesh underneath until you have them cut entirely out. Stretch your skin on a board like a mink; always flesh part outside. Leave tail attached. They are ready to take off the board in two weeks.

OBREY L.WOLFE,
Malvern, Iowa.

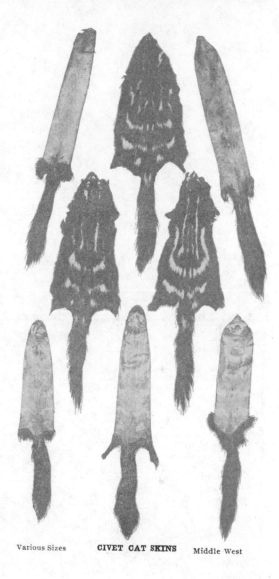

Various Sizes   **CIVET CAT SKINS**   Middle West

TRAPPING THE CIVET CAT

Civet cat are as easy to trap as skunk. The only experience I have had in trapping civet cat especially, was some years ago on the farm, and having nothing to do one December day, I fixed up an old smoke stack from an engine, which was discarded, arranged a trap door at one end and the other end I pounded together. This I carried about half a mile and placed it along a fence where I had previously seen skunk and civet cat. I dragged an old hen, from which the feathers were previously burned off, along the ground in various directions and finally threw it in the stack. The next morning I took out three skunks and two civet eats and continued to catch one or two of these animals every day.

A. L. BERRENS.

BADGER

CHAPTER 10

Badger

This animal is plantigrade and also belongs to the Bear family. It is found in America, Europe and Asia. Four species are recognised: the American Badger, the common Badger of Europe, the Indian Badger and the Anakuma Badger of Japan. The European species is the most important in the fur trade, furnishing 53,000 out of the 55,000 skins which annually find their way into the fur markets.

Though spread over a large portion of the globe, the Badger is nowhere numerous, except in a few localities on this continent. It is omnivorous, feeding chiefly on roots, fruits, insects and frogs. It also destroys the eggs and young of partridges, and other birds which build their nests on the ground. It is fond of the nest of wild bees, which it seeks out and robs with impunity, its tough hide being comparatively impervious to the stings of these insects. The Badger is a quiet, inoffensive animal, except when attacked, when it is a terrible, antagonist to the dog or man who comes in contact with its sharp teeth and formidable jaws. Its length is about two feet six inches from the nose to the root of the tail. The tail is short. The head is small, flat, and has a long snout. The height at the shoulder is about elevan inches. The body is broad and flat as though compressed. The legs are sturdy and powerful. The feet, before and behind, have each five toes strongly set in the flesh, and armed with powerful compressed claws, adapted to burrowing, in the ground, digging for roots, and unearthing the marmot, ground-squirrel, and other small burrowing animals.

The Badger chooses the most solitary woods for his residence. It lives in burrows, where it makes its nest and rears its young. When pursued, it commences digging in the earth, and, if pressed too closely to be able to hide by burrowing, it makes a hole large enough to cover its body, backs into it, and faces its pursuers with claws drawn in an attitude of defiance; and woe to the dog that attempts to dislodge it from its fort. If it has time to get its body fairly buried, it is secure from any dog, or even a man with a shovel, as it digs so rapidly that it will work its way into the earth faster than dog or man can follow. It is said that Badger are very numerous in some parts of the State of Washington, where the farmers protect them because they devour the ground-squirrels, which are such a pest, destroying the crops. These squirrels breed very rapidly and were they not kept down by the Badger would be a serious problem.

The European Badger

The American Badger was at first supposed to be a mere variety of the European Badger, but has proved to be. Its teeth are more adapted for carnivorus subsistence than those of the European Badger, and it preys chiefly on small animals such as marmots, which it pursues into their holes in the sandy plains near the Missouri and the Rocky Mountains. It is in that region that it abounds over a considerable range of latitude. Its prevailing color is hoary gray in winter, yellowish brown in summer, the under parts generally yellowish white. A white stripe runs from the nose over the forehead to the neck. The hair becomes not only very long but very woolly in winter. It sometimes makes burrows 6 or 7 feet deep running under ground for a distance of 25 or 30 feet, and rendering the surface dangerous to persons on horseback.

The fur of the Badger, when properly dressed, is said to make the best pistol furniture, and the coarser hairs are used for the fine brushes of the oil-painter. The hairs of the upper part of the Badger's body individually have three distinct colors: Yellowish-white at the root, black in the middle, and ashy-gray at the end. This gives a uniform sandy-gray color to all the upper parts. The tail is furnished with long, coarse hair

of the same color and quality. The throat, under parts, and legs are covered with shorter hair of a uniform deep-black.

The female Badger brings forth from three to five young in the early spring, suckles them for five or six weeks, and then turns them off to shift for themselves.

The American Badger differs considerably from the European species, to which the foregoing description applies. Its snout is less attenuated, though its head is equally long. The claws of its fore-feet are much longer in proportion, and its tail shorter. Its fur, both in color and quality, is different. It is also more carnivorous. Audubon describes its color and fur as follows: "Hair on the back, at the. roots dark-gray, then light-yellow for two-thirds its length, then black and broadly tipped with white, giving it in winter a hoary-gray appearance; but in summer it makes a near approach to yellowish-brown. The eyes are bright, and piercing black… There is-a white stripe running from the nose over the forehead and along the middle of the neck to the shoulder. Legs, blackish-brown; chin and throat, dull-white; the remainder of the under surface, yellowish-white; tail, yellowish-brown." The fur on the back in winter is three inches long, dense and handsome. The body is broad, low and flat.

The American Badger is found on the plains of Minnesota, the Dakotas, Nebraska and Kansas and in the timberless regions of the Yakima River Valley, in Washington. It is not found east of the Mississippi. It has been traced as far north as latitude fifty-eight degrees, and south into Mexico, where a distinct variety is found.

Badgers can be taken by setting traps at the mouths of their holes, or by the method prescribed on a preceding page for taking the Raccoon. The trap should be carefully concea led, as the Badger is somewhat

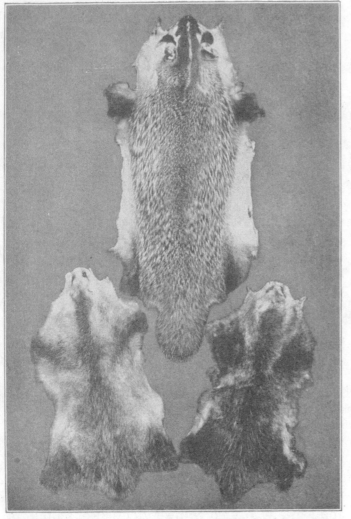

Opossum Skin   Badger Skin   Opossum Skin

cunning, and disposed to be suspicious of such apparatus near his haunts.

Wisconsin is sometimes called the "Badger State" because of the numbers of these animals found there by the early settlers.

They feed on the small burrowing animals mainly, such as the prairie dog, the gopher and the pouched rat, and they are. enabled to capture many of these animals by digging them out of the dens. They also eat mice and reptiles and the eggs and young of ground-nesting birds.

The animal is of a rather timid nature, and when alarmed seeks safety in the den if possible, but when surprised far from the den, will hide wherever possible and failing to find cover will flatten down close to the ground and by remaining very quiet, will try to escape notice. However when pursued, and finding escape impossible, they will fight desperately.

The fur of the badger is used for making brushes of various kinds, its peculiar texture making it especially desirable for this purpose. It is not used for wearing apparel.

The No. 3 trap is the proper size to use for this animal, and only the stronger ones should be used. They are caught and held occasionally in smaller and weaker traps, yet such cases are exceptional.

As the animal is not a valuable one and is not found in large numbers in any one locality, they are not much sought by the trappers and the most of the skins which reach the market are from the animals caught in traps set for other game. The wolf and coyote trappers catch them occasionally, as they may be captured by any of the methods used for those animals.

Perhaps the best way in which to capture the badger is to set the trap at the entrance to the main burrow, that is, the one showing the most use. The trap should be set just outside of the entrance and should be securely staked, using a long stake driven out of sight in the ground. The jaws of the trap should be parallel with the passage, so that the badger will step between the jaws, and not over them. It should be bedded down so that the covering will be flush with the surroundings.

Traps may also be set with bait. On the plains, material for enclosures can not be found but the traps may be set between clumps of sage brush or cactus, placing the bait behind the trap, the setting being so arranged badger will be obliged to walk over the trap in order to reach the bait. The trap should be securely staked in all cases. For bait, rabbit, sage hen, prairie dog or almost any kind of fresh meat may be used.

Like the bears, the badgers do not lose much flesh during their long winter retirement for on coming abroad in the spring they are observed to be quite fat. As they pair however at that season they soon become lean.

Early in the spring, when they first begin to stir abroad, they may be easily caught by pouring water into their holes; for the ground being frozen at that period, the water does not escape through the sand, but soon fills the hole, and its tenant is obliged to come out. The American badger appears to be a more carnivorous animal than the European, as in a female which had boon killed, a small marmot and some field-mice nearly entire, with some vegetable matter also, were found in its stomach. The badger is quite a cunning animal;

and is, therefore, net easy to catch without considerable precaution being taken. The best place for setting the traps for them is at the mouth of their holes, carefully covered: or in the paths which they make in the cornfields. They may also be caught, in the same manner as other animals, in traps laid in enclosures or dead-falls; in this case the bait required may be a mouse or a piece of meat, as anything in the shape of flesh is food for the badger.

TRAPPING THE BADDER

A great many badgers, owing to their size and slow locomotion, are dispatched by the use of the rifle in the hand of hunters and trappers.

Snares cannot be used effectively, though if attached to a spring pole of sufficient strength to hoist the animal off the ground, a strong line or wire may be arranged for his capture.

Deadfalls and other home-made appliances can be used, but the animal must be immediately killed. It would be a foolish hunter to use box trap or pitfall for a badger, as in the course of no time the animal will free himself.

Steel traps should be placed slightly within the abode or den and if the latter cannot be found, the traps can be placed in his paths. As the badger has many holes it is quite necessary that all excepting on be closed up, within which a No. 2 or No. 3 trap should be set. Bait is unnecessary though if desired, can be used.

There is probably no animal that is as easily captured as the badger, since he can be approached without danger, and anyone having any courage at all, can knock him on the head with a five or six foot stick. Quite often he is dug out the same as skunk, but this a tedious job, especially during the winter. Digging them out is not recommended, as badgers are likely to have many passages and quite often the skins are poorly furred, due to their hibernating habit. The skins of the badger are only good during the winter time and only from those that have exposed them- selves to the severe weather a good share of the time.

WILD CAT

CHAPTER 11

Wild Cat

THE WILD CAT OR BAY LYNX

The American Wild Cat is a species of Lynx. It is about thirty inches long, with a tail of five or six inches, and weighs from seventeen to twenty pounds. Its general color above and on the sides is a pale reddish brown, overlaid with grayish; the latter color most prevalent in spring and summer. The throat is surrounded with a ruff or collar of long hair. The under parts are light-colored and spotted. On the sides are a few obscure dark spots, and indistinct longitudinal lines along the middle of the back. The tail is marked with a small black patch above at the end, and with half rings on its upper surface. The inner surface of the ear is black, with white patch. The legs are long, the soles of the feet naked. The fur is moderately full and soft. The ears have a pencil of dark hairs in winter.

A variety of the American Wild Cat exists west of the Rocky Mountains, which was called by the early settlers in that region the Red Cat. Its color is somewhat darker than the common variety, being a rich chestnut-brown on the back; sides and throat, a little paler; fur soft and full.

The Wild Cat is cowardly, rarely attacking anything larger than a hare or young pig or lamb. The pioneer's hen-roost sometimes suffers from its nocturnal visitations. It feeds on grouse, partridges, squirrels, mice and other small birds and quadrupeds. It is fond of the dark, thick cedar swamps, where it preys on Rabbits, pouncing on them from an overhanging cliff or tree. In the Southern States, it frequents the swamps and canebrakes bordering on rivers and lakes, and also the briery thickets which grow up on the old fields and deserted cotton lands. In dry seasons, or during the sultry weather of summer, it explores the courses of small streams, to feed on the fish that are left in the deep holes as the water dries up.

Wild Cats are taken in the same way as Raccoons or Mink, by baiting with meat, and covering the trap smoothly over. The best way is to find a place where they have killed a Hare, grouse or other game, and have left a part of the flesh for a second meal. Set your trap there, and you will be pretty sure of a visit.

The European Wild Cat is a distinct animal from the Bay Lynx. Goodrich, in his "Illustrated Natural History," gives the following account of this Cat and its relations to the common Cat:

"There are many kinds of Wild Cat, but that from which the domestic Cat is supposed to have sprung is called the *Common European Wild Cat*, and is found in most parts of that quarter of the globe, as well as in Asia and Africa; it is also sometimes met with in this country. When America was first discovered, this species, either tame or wild, was not found here; all our domestic Cats, as well as the wild ones occasionally found in the woods, are the descendants of those brought hither by the Europeans. The Wild Cats of the European Continent are either the descendants of the original races that have continued untamed from the beginning, or of domesticated Cats that have wandered from their homes and living apart from man, have relapsed into barbarism. It is said that the wild and tame Cats, in their wanderings, sometimes meet; when this is the case, the females of the tame breed are well treated by the savage Cats, but the males are rudely set upon and sometimes torn in pieces. The wild and tame Cats sometimes breed together, and produce the kind called *Tiger Cats*. Some authors hold that the Wild Cat is a distinct species, because its tail is shorter and more bushy than that of the domestic Cat; but this opinion seems not well founded, for still greater differences are found in dogs which are acknowledged to be of the same race."

The European Wild Cat is common in France, Germany, Russia, Hungary and some other parts of Europe, and is found in Northern Asia and Nepaul. It was formerly found in England and a few yet linger among the hills of Scotland. It resembles the tame Cat, but is rather larger and more robust and has a more savage aspect. Its fur is long, soft and thick. Its color is gray, darker on the back than below, with a blackish stripe along the back and paler curved stripes on the sides. It is a very shy animal; lurks in the woods and preys on hares, squirrels and birds and is for the most part nocturnal m its habits. It makes its home in clefts among rocks or in hollow trees. The female brings forth from three to six young at a time. A full-grown male is about two feet and a half long from the nose to the root of the tail; with a tail of considerable length. The female is smaller.

This Wild Cat is of great strength, and when pursued and hard pressed exhibits daring and ferocity in an extraordinary degree. When caught in a trap they fly without hesitation at any person who approaches them, without waiting to be assailed. The directions given for trapping the American Wild Cat are appropriate for the capture of this species. St. John, the author of a work on "Highland Sports" gives the following plan for taking them: "Like other vermin, the Wild Cat haunts the shores of the lakes and rivers, and it is, therefore, easy to know where to lay a trap for them. Having caught and killed one of the colony, the rest of them are sure to be taken, if the body of their slain relative is left in some place not far from their usual hunting-ground and surrounded with traps; as every Wild Cat that passes within a considerable distance of the place will surely come to it."

THE BAY LYNX, OR WILD CAT

THE Bay Lynx replaces the Canada Lynx throughout the greater part of the United States. This animal is known to the fur trade as the wild cat and is also known in some localities as the Catamount and the bobcat.

The true wild cat is not found in America, being a native of Europe and Northern Asia, and resembling the domestic cat, somewhat, in appearance. Such cats are also found in certain parts of the United States but they are only the descendants of domestic cats which have strayed into the woods and become wild, and are not the wild cat of Europe.

The Bay Lynx is found throughout the rough timbered portions of the eastern, northern and western States, also in the swamps and cane brakes of the south. The International Boundary is about the northern limit of its range. They are quite plentiful in parts of the south, also in the foothills of the Rocky Mountains where they have become so destructive to sheep that the stockmen pay bounty on those that are killed.

The animal is somewhat smaller than the Canada Lynx, but resembles that animal in general appearance. It is about thirty inches in length, with a tail of five or six inches, and weighs from eighteen to twenty-five pounds, in some instances exceeding these figures. Its color on the back and sides is of a pale reddish brown, overlaid with grayish, the latter color being most prevalent in fall and winter. The throat is surrounded with a collar of long hair. The under parts are light colored and spotted and a few dark spots are also found on the sides. The tail is tipped with black and has half rings on its upper surface. The ears are also tipped with black hairs, but this tip is not so conspicuous as in the case of the Canadian Lynx. The hair is also shorter and coarser, and the feet smaller and less heavily furred.

The food of this animal consists of rabbits, partridges, sage hens, and any other small animals and birds which they can capture. They are fond of poultry and have been known to kill and devour the raccoon. As before mentioned, they are partial to mutton. In all probability they capture large numbers of mice, moles, prairie dogs, etc.

In the West, as in parts of the East the wild cat dens in natural holes in the rocks. In the swamps of the South they no doubt, nest in hollow trees.

They are, as a rule, shy and retiring animals, but when brought to bay show considerable courage and fight desperately. The fur of the Bay Lynx is not as valuable as that of the northern lynx. It becomes prime in the north about the first of November; in the south three or four weeks later.

The wild cat resembles the Canada Lynx so closely in habits, etc., that I do not consider it necessary to give any special methods for capturing it. The bait methods recommended for the lynx will also do very well for the wild cat, and the same bait may be used. In the south it would probably be better to set in natural

COMBINATION STEEL TRAP AND SNARE SET.

enclosures whenever possible. In the foothills of the Rockies the Bay Lynx is frequently caught in traps set for coyotes, although they may be captured as easily there as in any other section, and if the trapper wishes, he can set his traps in hollows in the rocks, or in enclosures of brush, cactus, etc.

Some trappers prefer to hang the bait above the trap, and it is a good way, but I think that the enclosure is more certain.

I would recommend the Nos. 2 and 3 traps for these animals. Although they may be held at times in smaller traps, any trap having less strength than the No. 2 should not be depended on.

The track of the wild cat resembles that of the lynx, but is much smaller. The footprints will seldom measure more than one and a half inches in diameter, and the step is a trifle shorter than that of the Canadian Lynx.

TRAPPING THE WILD CAT

We have the following on trapping the wild at from Mr. John A Lien, of Wisconsin:

"The wild cat (or bob cat sometimes called) finds its home in thick woods or swamps, particularly dense cedar swamps. To trap these animals no great skill is necessary as they enter a trap readily if properly covered with some soft material, such as powdered wood, fine grass, or tissue paper is all right when it is slightly sprinkled with snow under the open sky.

"This is the way I go at it: l build my camp or shanty away from any settlement in the centre of my trapping territory so that I trap four different ways, to save walking, I generally string my traps our four or five miles either way, and so that I can see them every other day. I set them about twenty to thirty rods apart and three traps at a place in the following manner: First, I cut stakes, (or longs, if more convenient) and build a kind of house or pen, one side open large enough for the cat to enter I place three traps in the opening. Then I get balsam or spruce boughs and make a roof large enough to shield the traps form rain to snow. I clog my traps (I never stake them fast) and cover them with any material I find handy,—feathers are very well, I then put the bait in the bottom of the hones or pen, and all is ready, I use very seldom any odors, but oil or any attraction for mink will do for the wild cat. Any kind of bait will do—rabbit is as good as any. I make my trail as close to the setting (as I call the place where I put my traps) as I can walk. The better I get my trail the surer I am of getting my cat. It is a good plan to take a proper log and drag after you to make your trail more even. Never make any sharp turns on it, as a cat will follow a trail for any length if it is fine and the snow is deep, and if once on your trail she will visit every setting until she is caught.

"A good plan is to place several traps where you see some remnants of a cat's former meal as she is most likely to return. Leaving a dead cat surrounded by traps is also good, for if there are any cats in the vicinity you are sure of a visit. The reason I set there traps to each setting is because there are always more or less squirrels, birds or rabbits coming into them and when you have several traps close by, you are more sure of getting your cat when she comes.

"The traps I have used are various, from a poor rat trap to a beaver trap. I caught the most of them in mink and muskrat traps. I never lost one that got in the trap, and even if only caught by one claw it generally holds her. However, I lost several traps from lack of better fastening to the clog. A Newhouse trap No. 1 is good enough but a No. 1½ the kind I prefer."

TRAPPING THE WILD CAT

From a trapper residing in Utah, Mr. Wm. R. Green, Jr., by names, we have the following:

"I herewith send my experience in trapping wild cat. I first get a location in a canon or valley with a stream running through

SPRING POLE.

it. Then I get some sort of game meat such as rabbit, chicken or venison and drag it across the canon or valley from mountain to mountain at intervals about a mile apart. I set a No. 2 to No. 4 steel trap at intervals along these paths about two hundred yards apart. I will place the trap in a pen of a rectangular shape, the point of pen being made in some bush or bunch of willows or against a tree, and I then place the bait in the bush or hang it on a limb of the tree a little above and a little back of the trap and make it fast and solid with a wire or some strong cord. The trap should be made fast to a clog or stick of wood about there feet long and about three inches in diameter. This clog should be covered with leaves or dirt whichever may be handiest. The wild cats generally travel up the down a canon or valley, and I will guarantee that I can catch mine out of every ten that crosses my path in the way above described.

"N. B. The traps should be covered with leaves or trash so that nothing is visible and so the they will not freeze down."

TRAPPING THE WILD CAT

W.H. Hendershot, a trapper of twenty-five years' experience, writes as follows:

"I generally hunt wild cats and lynx by using a dog to follow the tracks of the cat. I assist him very often as the cat walks logs, climbs trees, etc. But when the dog starts the Animal, one must be on the lookout and ready to shoot as the cat will run here and there and all around, dodging the dog, and in order to save the dog one must shoot the cat; otherwise the dog would become useless for further hunting, should a fight ensue.

"In trapping this animal, I find, if possible, remnants of his former meal and set traps about his leavings, or place where the cat buried the remaining portion of his victim.

"The trap, of course, must be covered with leaves, bits of rotten wood, and if snow around, I cover with snow but always have leaves, etc., under pan. If any cats or lynx are around you will catch them, and sometimes a wolf or fox.

TRAPPING THE WILD CAT

It is quite easy to catch these animals. They have their dens In cliffs and when these are not handy, they are in holes in the ground where they have their young. As a rule, they stay near their dens the year round. Find where their tracks are quite plentiful, which usually, is near their dens. Now make an enclosure in a V-shape, or find a natural one and improve it a little, so there is only one side for the animal to get in at. For bait, take a rabbit, put him in the pen, and jerk his intestines out so it will cause an order. This is the best bait a trapper can get out in the wilderness, with the exception of deer liver, lungs, and intestines, which is the best bait on earth for these animals. Sometimes sheep carcass is also good bait.

Now, if the enclosure is narrow, use one trap. If it is wide, use two or three traps. Set them in front of the enclosure two feet apart, and by using three traps, set them in triangle shape. If I trap in a country where there are mountain lions, I use the set with three traps, hut if there are no lions. Just one trap is plenty.

A No. 2 Newhouse, or Hawley and Norton, will hold a cat but if you trap in a country where there are lions, be sure to use No. 4 of the same make, for I have caught as many lions with this set, as I have wild cat and lynx.

WM. Weibel.,
La Porte, Colo.

HOW TO HUNT AND TRAP THE WILD CAT

This animal, like the lynx, can be caught in traps but generally tracked by dogs and is brought to bay with the rifle. Traps can be set about the shores of rivers and lakes, or in paths. If a place is found where the cat has lately devoured its victim and left a few remnants, one or two traps should be set about the location. Traps should be covered up in the usual manner. Any of the baits used for lynx will answer the purpose. Bait placed within hollow logs and the traps concealed in the usual manner will often result in his capture. One or two dogs are seldom equal to a cat and generally are put into misery and the cat escapes. Many traps set for coon or mink are sprung by the wild cat and if strong enough, detain the animal.

Quite often steel traps are set on each side of a log, or edges thereof over or along which the animal is known to travel. If a good, strong trap is placed at the entrance of a V or U shaped enclosure and a piece of rabbit is thrown further into the den. The result quite often is favorable to the trapper. If one is successful in locating their habitual paths, traps should be set thereon. Exercise great care in leaving the surroundings natural and always cover traps so that nothing of the human work is visible.

Another good place to set traps is where the animal has previously enjoyed a former meal, and especially if some leavings remain. Place three or four traps in the immediate vicinity. The cat will return to this place the same day, or in a few days, and in so doing is very likely to spring a trap.

CHAPTER 12

Lynx

There are several species of Lynx. The Canadian Lynx and the European Lynx are the most important to the trapper and fur dealer. The former inhabits North America from the latitude of Northern New York to the northern limits of the woods, or within the Arctic Circle. It is not found in the Mississippi Valley, but occurs west of the Rocky Mountains and is supposed to exist in the northeastern part of Asia. Its size is between that of a Fox and a Wolf. Its length from the tip of the nope to the tip of the tail is about three feet. The tail is shorter than the head and is densely furred and tipped with black. Its feet are large, thickly covered with fur, and armed with strong claws. The ears are pointed, not large, and tipped with a pencil of long black hairs. The color in winter is silver-gray on the back, paling toward the belly, which is sometimes white. A rufous under-shade mixes with the tints. It has a ruff on the sides of the neck and under the throat. In winter its fur is long and silky. The average weight of this Lynx is about twenty-five pounds.

The Canada Lynx lives in the darkest woods and swamps, preying on hares, mice, squirrels, grouse and smaller birds, and rarely attacking the deer. When pressed with hunger it prowls about the pioneer's cabin in search of lambs, pigs and poultry. It is an active climber and frequently seizes its prey by pouncing upon it from an overhanging tree; at other times it crawls stealthily like a cat within springing distance, or leaps upon it from a cliff. It pursues birds to the tops of the loftiest trees and kills fish in the streams. It also feeds on carrion, and when pressed with hunger on its own kind. It is said to have a strong passion for perfumes, particularly the castoreum of the Beaver. This is the principal scent or "medicine" used by trappers in capturing the Lynx. The female brings forth generally two young ones at a time and hides them in hollow trees or caves until they are large enough to follow her.

The Canada Lynx is a stupid animal and easily caught. It readily enters a trap that is properly set and baited with meat. The general directions already given for trapping various carnivorous animals are applicable in this case. The Hudson's Bay Company's trappers practice the following method, according to Bernard Rogan

LYNX

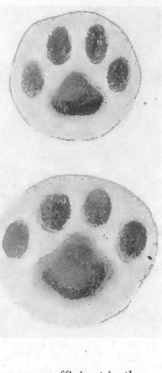

Ross: The trap is covered, inside the jaws, with a well fitting "pallet" of birch bark. On the "pallet" a piece of hare skin, well rubbed with the "medicine" or scent, is tied. The trap is then placed indifferently either under or on the snow. The Lynx, scenting its favorite perfume, endeavors to withdraw the skin with his paw, and consequently springs the trap. It does not, like most of the fur-bearing animals, make violent efforts to escape, or drag the trap to a distance; it generally lies down until aroused by the approach of the hunter, when, instead of attempting to escape by flight, it springs at him.

The European Lynx closely resembles the Canada species; its habits are also similar. Its fur is valuable. Its general color is a dull reddish-gray above, whitish below, mottled with black. On the sides are dark oblong patches. In winter the fur is longer and lighter colored than in summer. The keenness of its sight has long been proverbial. It is found from the Pyrenees to the far north, and throughout Northern Asia. The directions given for trapping the Canada Lynx are sufficient in the case of this species.

They are very "cat like" in appearance but the legs are rather long, the feet large and the tail very short. The feet are heavily furred and the toes connected with a web, the whole forming a sort of snowshoe, which prevents the lynx from sinking in the loose snow.

The young are born usually in May and there are from three to seven in a litter. The entire family will be found living in the same locality and although each will have its own particular route of travel, they frequently travel together along the border of certain swamps and occasionally the entire family will start off together and look for a better feeding ground. They live mostly in the swampy parts of the more open country, being rarely found in the great bush. In the west they are found in the timbered parts of the mountains. In the North, you will find their tracks leading along the edges of the swamps and alder or willow thickets.

Pen Drawing   CANADA LYNX   Month of August

Their food consists mostly of rabbits and partridge. The snow shoe rabbit falls an easy victim. They have been known to kill small deer and caribou, but only in very rare instances.

There has been considerable controversy among naturalists regarding the courage of the lynx. From my own observations, I should say that they are very cowardly, as a rule, but all rules have exceptions. I know of two instances in which the lynx has stood his ground for a man, and in one case, for a number of men. This lynx was killed by an axe thrown by one of the men at a distance of twelve feet.

In traveling, the lynx usually walks, only running when in pursuit of some animal, and always traveling the same route. They are active all winter, but travel most in fall and spring. They become prime about the first of November and if the spring is late, will remain in good condition until the middle of April.

The European lynx closely resembles the Canadian in habits and appearance. Its general color is a dull reddish grey, mottled with black. In winter the fur is longer and lighter colored than in summer. It is found from the Pryenees to the Far North, and eastward throughout northern Asia.

As a rule, the lynx is easily taken with the steel trap, unless food is very plentiful, when they do not care for dead bait. Almost any trap will hold them as they do not struggle much, and I have caught a number of them with the No. 1 trap, but because of their large feet, I would advise the use of a larger trap. The Nos. 3 and 4 traps are perhaps the best sizes to use.

There are various methods of trapping them but the most common, as well as the best is to set the trap in an enclosure, with bait. I prefer to make the enclosures of split wood, placing the split side inward. I make the pen about three feet in height, about two and a half feet long, wide at the top and just wide enough to receive the trap at the bottom. The pen should be well roofed with evergreen boughs to protect the trap from the snow, and the trap should be just inside of the entrance. If there is snow on the ground, I make a bed of green boughs for the trap to rest on. It is not necessary to cover the trap but I prefer to do so. The bait should be placed on a stick in the back of the pen.

Rabbit and partridge is the best bait, but it must be fresh, as the lynx does not care for stale food. Some scent should also be used as the lynx's sense of smell is not so highly developed as that of some other animals. Beaver Castor is perhaps the best, but fish oil is much used by the western trappers. Muskrat musk is also good.

The trap should be fastened to a stout clog. I use a small spruce or balsam tree, about three inches thick at the butt and fasten the trap by stapling or by looping the chain around the clog, leaving some snags to prevent the chain from slipping over the end.

The rabbits are a great nuisance, they being found in great numbers in the northern swamps. The scent of the hands left there while setting the trap, also the fresh cutting, attracts the rabbit into the pen and it is sometimes difficult to keep the trap in working order until the lynx journeys by that way again. The best way I have found to keep

Furred   YOUNG CANADA LYNX   From a Photo

The Canada Lynx

The Lynx.

them out of the trap is by dropping some dead brush in front of the enclosure, as the rabbits do not like to jump through the dead brush.

Squirrels and birds are also troublesome, and I have found it a good idea to place the bait well up under the roof of the pen so as to be out of sight of these creatures. I also place a small springy stick under the pan of the trap, which will sometimes prevent the squirrels and birds from springing it. I sometimes make a trap pen by standing up a number of small evergreen trees, cutting the boughs away on the inside. This is a very good method.

When lynx do not take bait well, some trappers make a long pen or passage, open at both ends and high enough so that the lynx can walk through easily. The trap is set inside and some beaver castor or other scent is placed on a stick in the passage. Others put scent on a piece of red cloth and fix it in a pen of brush, setting the trap in the entrance.

As the lynx's eye is more keen than its nose, I have found it a good plan to hang a rabbit skin from a string near the setting, so that it will swing about in the breeze. This will attract the animal for quite a distance, and is a good method to use when setting traps along the shore of a lake, as the lynx walks the ice and will sometimes pass outside of scenting distance of the trap.

Lynx are easily killed by a blow from a stick but when caught in small traps it is safer to shoot them, using a small caliber pistol or rifle. Another good way is to choke them by tieing a snare to the end of a ten or twelve foot pole. Slip the snare over the animal's head, draw it tight and hold the pole; the lynx will die in a very short time. The advantage of this method is in the fact that the skin is kept clean and free from blood.

The Wildcat, or Bay Lynx.

The track of the lynx resembles that of the cat but is much larger. A large specimen will make a track three and a half inches in diameter and the length of step is from sixteen to eighteen inches.

One trapper who worked for years in British Columbia, relates an experience probably seldom witnessed by man:

While inspecting a line of traps set for mink, marten, and occasionally one for a fox, he came across a partly devoured rabbit that had evidently sprung a marten trap and had been found by a lynx, which was in the act of devouring the rabbit when disturbed by the approach of the trapper. Knowing the habits of the lynx, and feeling assured that the animal would return to finish his meal, the trapper set two of the largest steel traps he had with him, "No. 2½" about the remaining portion of the rabbit, and departed for the other side of the creek. While crossing the creek, he noticed, at a distance, two wolves evidently following his trail. He felt somewhat aggrieved at not having attached the chains to a drag to detain the wolves in case one or both should spring the traps. Apparently the lynx was in the neighborhood all this time, as only fifteen minutes expired before Mr. Lynx came back to the rabbit. He sniffed around and acted as if something was wrong. Apparently he was desirous of finishing his meal, but was afraid to approach too close, he crouched and lay motionless on his belly, then he would ascend near-by trees, only to leap at once to the ground, acting in a very frenzied manner, indicating to the observing trapper that he wanted the rabbit very badly and was endeavoring to discover some way of obtaining it without delay, and without being obliged to venture too close to the spot where it lay. After the lapse of nearly ten minutes, he suddenly leaped from a tree, ran to the place where he had left the rabbit half an hour before, grabbed it, and turned about and off he went. But, alas! His forefoot sprung one of the traps. He yelped, dropped the rabbit from his mouth, took hold of the chain, and twisted it and whined. His hasty action, disregarding his usual trait of caution and alertness, was prompted by his eagerness to obtain the food that he thought belonged to him, rather than to let the approaching wolf have it. Having viewed all this from a tree, the trapper slowly descended, crossed the creek and taking his rifle, first killed one of the wolves and then the lynx. The bodies were skinned and about them three Newhouse traps were set; the next day a wolf (probably the other) had sprung the trap, and a rife ball ended his misery.

HOW THE LYNX IS HUNTED AND TRAPPED

In the first place I had one tied up by the side of my door so I could study their habits. I find by all kinds of treatment they are vicious and untamable. Will eat all kinds of game but no vegetables or bread or any kind of cooked food. Will eat sparingly of fish if starved to it. Rabbits are their general food. Where you find great numbers of rabbits you will find lynx. They will kill young deer, also young calves; will follow a trail for miles. Drag a small piece of deer paunch as you walk along, or if you have no paunch, get five or six pounds of beef liver, hang up behind the stove for two or three days or a week until it gets tainted and the blood begins to drop out of it. Then mash up to a jelly, put in jar and set away, where it won't freeze. If you happen to be in possession of a beaver carcass, take all fat off of it and try out in lard pail; do not search it. When cool, take say five or six tablespoonfuls of the beaver oil and a small teacup of the mashed liver and mix both together. Have this in a bottle to carry with you. Every half mile, on going the rounds of your traps, put a little on the soles of your shoes or moccasins; and the lynx when he comes to your trail will never leave it until he comes to your trap. If your trap is properly set, you will have the lynx. I use four or five drops of anise oil in the mixture also.

Now a lynx as general thing is quite a genius and is also very inquisitive. Never try to make a lynx get in a trap if he has just had a good meal for he will not do it. But he will follow your trail for miles and look into each house you have got on the trail, and will keep on going until he gets hungry. In order to catch them while on these rounds, I have adopted the "gate on the trail," or the "double stick racket." I found by close study that lynx will always step in your tracks, that is, if you do not step too far. I never step over ten or twelve inches. Do not make your trail too wide; keep it as narrow as you can in the snow. I have had as many as five to seven lynx follow me for over a mile, just looking into the houses and go on to the next one. So I made a little brush fence for a couple of yards or so on each side of trail; leaving a small passageway for myself and the lynx to pass through. Then I lay two small sticks across trail, say one inch in diameter and about four inches high and seven inches apart; then set a No. 3 Newhouse trap in center of little sticks and cover up with wild grass that I find around of the sticks and into the trap. I caught no less than lynx in one trap this way.

I make my lynx houses out of old brush and poles. Find a good tree that sheds snow as much as possible and make a lynx house by leaning sticks about five feet long, up against it, enclosing it quite tight and leaving an opening about fifteen inches wide facing the trail. Put bait back in house and tie it fast, and set a No. 3 trap about three inches outside of entrance and a little to one side. I use for bait a small piece of rabbit with three or four drops of anise oil and some of the liver mixture mentioned before.

JOHN A. BLEEKER

TRAPPING THE LYNX

Lynx are not difficult to trap. I have had pretty good success, and your probably know that as well as anyone else by the number of skins I have sent you. I do not expect to stay in British Columbia much longer, therefore will give you my methods of trapping in this section.

As far as traps are concerned, I prefer the Newhouse, nothing smaller that No. 2½, larger ones preferred, although I have caught a lynx in No. 1. He would have escaped were it not for the fact that the jaws held him one of his toes, and he had sense enough not to struggle.

DEADFALL.

The lynx will follow the trail of other animals as well as that of the trapper. I set my traps in my own path, as well as those made by cattle or wild beasts. A hole is made of sufficient size to hold the trap. A piece of dry limb is laid on each side of the trap, so when the lynx comes along he will prefer to step between the two pieces of wood and of course in the trap. At other times I make an artificial abode and set my trap within it. Such sets require bait. The lynx is not very particular as to what kind of bait it is—rabbit, grouse, duck, goose, or, in fact, any kind of birds or animals or parts therefrom. Occasionally the traps are fastened to some drag. At other times I arrange chain to spring pole. None of these are essential, as traps fastened on a stick answer the purpose. I do not think much about decoy but have used beaver castors mixed with whiskey and asafetida. Have killed as many lynx with the rifle as with traps, and probably all due to the lynx coming pretty close to the cabin at night. I usually shoot from the roof of the cabin.

Snares are also very good, but the cheapest and best, next to steel traps, and probably the surest, are deadfalls. In your first edition, you had my favorite deadfall (pages 218–227). You also had a good one on page 230, but in addition I always drove stakes about the front edges of logs, thus forcing all animals to get in between the logs. Last year I caught one of the prettiest black bears I ever had my eyes on in one of the last described traps. His head was flattened and he died almost instantly.

J.H. DONNLY.

TRAPPING THE LYNX

Select a large tree close to where lynx travel and fasten, bait, which may be a rabbit or the skin therefrom stuffed; tie to trunk of tree about three feet from ground and set up a few dry branches or stakes on both sides forming king of shelter for the pang on the trap. Set your trap about two feet in front of the tree, and if rabbits are numerous, throw a few branches outside of the trap to keep them out. Towards the latter part of February trappers should have all traps out set for lynx that they can possibly attend to, as at that time the lynx will go more readily for bait than at any other time in the year, and when one is caught its carcass should be thrown into the pen for bait.

T. GULLICKSON.

TRAPPING THE LYNX

The lynx like the mountain lion, can be caught in traps, but whenever opportunity presents he should be killed with the rifle. Steel traps and deadfalls are responsible for most deaths, and it is to be regretted that the animal is not as easy to trap as one may imagine.

He is not numerous in any parts of the United States, but formerly was found quite plentiful in the western mountainous states and in the timbered sections from Minnesota down along the Canadian border as far south as the Alleghany mountains and northward into Canada. As aforesaid, deadfalls and steel traps are chiefly used in killing this carnivorous cat. When using steel traps nothing smaller than No. 2½ will securely hold the Canadian lynx, but instances are recorded where this animal sprung a No. 1 trap and the jaw held the brute by one of his toes until the hunter released him from his misery. The Newhouse traps are much preferred over any other steel traps—No. 3 or 3½ probably best adapted. The former is a double spring trap, the other a single spring with four prongs. Either of them will hold Mr. Lynx. By all means fasten the chain securely to some spring pole and if this cannot be done to some limb which he is able to drag a short distance.

As the lynx is found principally in dense forests, it is quite natural that the traps must be set in some place that the animal frequent; quite often in a trail or open place; if the latter, choose a good-sized tree against which make an artificial abode. The lynx is known to follow lines of marten traps, and follow the trapper from one place to another, anticipating a carcass, bait, etc., and occasionally steals the bait placed by the trapper for mink and marten. The traps should be covered in the usual way. Steel traps can

LYNX SKINS

also be set underneath the snow, but a sufficient quantity of wool, leaves or other material must be placed beneath the pan. He has also been caught in traps set for wolves and foxes. Is known to favor the smell of castoreum and many a trapper lures the lynx to his death by the use of this decoy. His presence is made known to the trapper during the night-time by the peculiar yell that he gives from time to time.

The deadfall has been successfully used probably for at least 100 years. In fact, the early Canadian trapper confined himself almost exclusively to this variety of trap. These were set in conspicuous places and the bait so arranged that the lynx, in touching the trigger, caused the upper log to fall upon his head, killing him instantly. The snare can be advantageously used if the paths of the animal lead through brush. The ends of the wire or line should be fastened to some spring pole. One shrewd trapper was accustomed to set his traps in his own path, especially when the ground was covered with snow. He took pains that the path should be fairly smooth and placed a small, dry piece of a limb between the traps over which the animal was expected to step, and in so doing stop upon the pan and spring the trap, thus becoming a victim. The chain was invariably attached to some limb. or permanently to some near-by brush. He managed to trap many lynx in this way. At other times he made an artificial abode against a tree and set his trap at the entrance. To prevent rabbits, squirrels and similar animals from springing these traps, it is advisable to place some dry brush in front of the opening over which the small animals will hardly climb; the lynx, on the other hand, will shove this aside: so will the wolverine and fisher.

| Mink | **CANADA LYNX** | Mink | Squirrel | Young Beaver |
| Northern Species | | | | |

A full-grown Canadian lynx is equal to two or three average dogs and in a fight, should any of the latter escape, they are usually so badly wounded that they die thereafter; other times are killed by the owner to stop their painful sufferings. The lynx, on the other hand, often escapes.

CHAPTER 13

Mountain Lion

THE COUGAR

WITH the exception of the Jaguar, which will average a trifle larger, the cougar is the largest representative of the cat tribe to be found in America.

This animal is known locally under various names. In the mountainous districts of the Eastern States, where they were once found in fair numbers, they were known as the panther or "painter" from a fancied resemblance to the panther of tropical Asia. In the far West they are most commonly known as the mountain lion, and in other localities as the cougar, while in the Southwest they are sometimes called the Mexican lion. Throughout the whole of South America they are known as the puma.

This animal has probably become extinct in the Eastern States, but they are still found in the South, from Florida, westward throughout the wild, swampy sections of the Gulf States, into the lowlands of Texas, and southward. In the West they are found in all of the mountainous portions from northern British Columbia southward, and in South America are to be found as far south as southern Patagonia. They have at all times been more abundant in the West than in the East and are still plentiful in portions of British Columbia, Idaho, Wyoming, and Colorado; also in the Pacific Coast States, especially in northern California.

In size, the average, full grown cougar will perhaps measure seven feet in length from the nose to the tip of the tail, certainly not more, and large specimens will weigh from a hundred and fifty to a hundred and seventy-five pounds. Occasionally larger specimens are found, but they are exceptional. The tail will measure from two and a half to three feet.

MOUNTAIN LION

The color of the cougar is usually of a yellowish brown on the sides, a trifle darker on the back and white on the throat and underparts. The tip of the tail is dark, almost black in some specimens. This is the prevailing color but some will have a grayish cast. While there is very little difference in the specimens from the

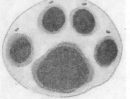

various sections, some naturalists claim that the cougar of Florida and other parts of the South is a distinct variety.

Cougars prey largely on deer, also in some sections on the wild sheep and goats. They also kill small animals, and when pressed by hunger they will not hestitate to attack larger animals than the deer; even the moose is sometimes killed by the cougar. They are very destructive to stock in many parts of the West, particularly to horses, and many of the Western States, as well as the stockmen pay bounty on cougars. In South America they kill large numbers of wild cattle.

Their method of securing game is by creeping cautiously to within springing distance, or by watching a runway from the branches of a tree, or a ledge of rock from which position they spring upon the unsuspecting victim, breaking its neck by a twist of the head. When they can get plenty of food they only suck the blood of the captured animal, and do not return to the carcass. When food is scarce they make a meal of the flesh and cover the remains. In such cases they may return for a second meal.

It was only after the panther became rare in the Eastern States that the fabulous tales of their daring, and their inclination to attack human beings, originated, and such stories are never credited by those who are acquainted with the nature and habits of the animal. While it would be an easy matter for the cougar

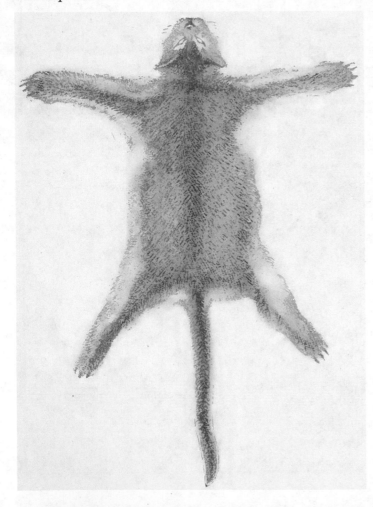

to kill an unarmed man, they are by nature, timid animals, and not to be feared by human beings. While individual animals may attack man on rare instances, such occurrences are very rare, and it is safe to say that nine-tenths of the "panther stories" have no foundation whatever. The western mountain men consider them very cowardly animals.

In the mountainous districts the cougars live in natural dens, or caves in the rocks, in places that are almost inaccessible to other animals. In the swamps of the South they make I their home in dense and almost impenetrable thickets and cane-brakes, where they make a nest of sticks, grass, moss and leaves.

The young animals are born in early spring, I there being from two to four at a birth, but as a rule, only two. The mother animal displays I considerable anxiety for the safety and comfort of her kittens.

There is no method known by which the cougar may be successfully trapped. Owing to their, rambling habits one never knows where to place a trap for them, and as they prefer to kill their own game, they will seldom touch bait. As a rule they do not return to the carcass of their victim, but if one can find an animal freshly killed, it is a good plan to set a trap by the side of the remains, and in case the animal should return for a second meal, its capture is likely.

Practically all of those which are trapped are taken in this way. The No. 4 Newhouse trap is I used but the No. 4½ is better, for being a larger and stronger trap it is more certain to hold the animal. The trap should be fastened to a heavy clog, and the trap and clog carefully concealed, for the cougar is wary and suspicious.

On rare instances when the trapper has been certain that there were cougars in the near vicinity, they have been captured by setting a trap in a natural enclosure, placing a fresh, bloody bait behind the trap, also by hanging the bait about five feet above a carefully concealed trap.

They are most commonly hunted by the aid of dogs, and in this way the capture is a comparatively easy matter. When pursued they usually take to a tree and remain there until the arrival of the hunter when a rifle bullet ends the game. The animal will take to a tree readily for any dog which has the courage to follow it.

The Cougar.

Photographed Springtime Along N. P. Ry. in Mont.

YOUNG MOUNTAIN LION

Courtesy of N. P. Ry. Co.

The skin of the mountain lion is not valuable as a fur, and is used principally for rugs, but as before mentioned many of the states pay bounties on the animals, so that hunting them may be made a profitable business in certain localities.

The tracks of this animal resemble those, of the wild eat but are much larger. The footprints will measure about four inches in diameter.

When the lion has seized a victim, he tears open its neck and laps the blood before he begins to eat. Small animals are devoured entirely, but the larger ones he eats only in parts, usually the neck and shoulders. The other parts are sometimes covered up with leaves, branches, grass, etc. His sense of smelling and of hearing is acute. His skin is used chiefly for rug, robe or mounting purposes, and unless head, feet and tail are perfect and attached, the skin becomes undesirable. Any hunter who is fortunate in bringing down this monster and desires the skin mounted should not fail to obtain the skull and leg bones.

Mounted. 4 to 6 years old   **MOUNTAIN LION**   Middle West. September

TRAPPING THE MOUNTAIN LION

"Some years ago while at home near my uncle's place in the mountains of Pennsylvania," relates Mr. Hassinger, "a large American tiger (mountain lion) made his existence known by peculiar cries, and later, became visible not only to myself but others.

"We were often followed when returning from work by this brute, and my uncle prepared and set a thirty-four pound double spring steel trap in his path and he felt sure he would follow us some day from the mountains and get into the trap.

"Some few days later his capture was made known by the terrible yells that caused chills to overcome those that heard him. My uncle, being an expert shot, visited the scene accompanied by his two little boys—four to six years old. He took careful aim and fired, and much surprised was he in missing the animal. The bullet struck the trap, breaking it, and at the same time freeing the brute. If there ever was a time that be wished his second shot to count, the time had come and he prayed that his aim might be good and he be relieved from responsibility of taking the children with him for such a task. Before the animal was able to use his benumbed paw, my uncle again took careful aim and fired, and his prayers were answered by the bullet striking the animal in the head and the brute reeling over to the ground.

"Careful investigation showed that after the brute was caught in the thirty-four pound trap he made various leaps in the air—the greatest of them was when he cleared thirty-two feet without touching the ground, carrying with him in the air a weight of thirty-four pounds.

"This tiger is the largest I have ever seen and adorns the back parlor of my uncle's mountain home."

TRAPPING THE MOUNTAIN LION

My experience in trapping the mountain lion is limited, as I prefer to bring him down with the rifle. I came across these brutes many times while in the Yukon country. It seems to me that the brutes there are much larger than those in Colorado. They tell me that the animal is very plentiful in parts of Alaska.

While in Colorado we caught one of these animals in a wolf trap. It was either No. 4 of 4½ trap and the lion sprung it with his front paw. The trap got a good hold of him, and notwithstanding that he dragged

MOUNTAIN LION
Killed with a Savage Rifle, by
A. McLeod

Length 9 ft. 9½ in.   Weight 180 lbs.

the trap and the post to which it was attached, for miles, we finally got him, though spending the best part of the day to find him. He was vicious brute and none of us dared to go near him. We finally had to kill him with the rifle.

One of the largest lions I ever killed in the Yukon country must have weighed 125 to 150 pounds, and measured from nose to tip of tail at least eight and one-half or nine feet. I would take my chances any time with a bear instead of one of these brutes.

C.J. LOOMIS.

CHAPTER 14

Jaguar
(Ger. Unse, Laf. Felix Onza.)

Photo by Prof. Hornaday   The Jaguar

WHAT is true relative to ferocity, habits etc., of the Puma, is also true of this animal, the largest of the cat species found on this continent. Although its home is chiefly in South America, it was formerly found in large numbers in the southern states, especially in Louisiana and Texas, and it is still numerous in Mexico. It is safe to say that this cat has been driven away or captured, and that very few, if any exist at the present time in the United States.

A full-grown jaguar will measure 55 to 60 inches from nose to root of tail, the latter being 25 to 30 inches in length. The fur is soft and spotted similarly to that of the leopard, although the coat of the animal varies considerable in color, from a light brown and reddish hue to a dark, almost black appearance, all having peculiar spots upon the body and portions of the tail. The end of the tail however, possesses a dark plume-like tip followed by seven or eight ring formations similar to that of the raccoon, alternating black and brown and corresponding in color with that of the body.

Its favorite haunts are in swamps and jungles, bordering close to sections of timber and dense brush, and it is a frequent visitor in pastures, often lying concealed for hours near a path or trail where cattle, horses, mules or wild beasts are known to travel. He becomes master in a remarkably short period, rarely exceeding fifteen minutes, of the largest steer, cow or mule, and it is safe to say that whenever his teeth and sharp claws are imbedded in the animal's back and neck the monster has the prey at his mercy and every effort and the strength of the victim to remove the jaguar is of little avail. Small animals are downed with one of his paws—the animal possessing unusual and enormous strength—and often his victim is torn asunder by one stroke.

The jaguar will follow animals into the water, but seldom climbs trees after animals or birds, though is able to climb and remain on trees and their branches for an indefinite period. Is known to swim a long distance and to go on board of anchored boats seeking food. Brehm relates having seen a jaguar near a stream in a crouching position looking into the water and succeeding in catching fish by a sudden movement of the paw, similar to our domestic or other species of the cat family, in that respect.

Rengger relates that the male, also the female, jaguar live alone during the greater portion of the year, and only during the months of August and September do the two sexes seek each other's companionship. A litter of two or three cubs is brought fourth in the den or pit, the latter being protected from the sun or rain to a greater or less extent, generally in a thicket or forest.

Drawn by
Ernest Thompson Seton   **ROCKY MOUNTAIN COUGAR**   Courtesy of N. P. Ry.
(For illustration of Jaguar see page 8)

The skins are used largely for rug purposes and have little or no value unless the head, claws and tail are perfect. Many mounted specimens can be seen in this country, also in Europe. Prominent southern planters and hunters possess skins as well as mounted specimens, the former made into rugs, the latter decorate their dining rooms or libraries.

Though scarcely equalling the Cougar in extreme length, the Jaguar is stouter and more formidable. This animal has a large head, a robust body, and is very ferocious. Its usual size is about three-fourths that of the Tiger. Humboldt, however, states that he saw Jaguars which in length surpassed that of all the Asiatic Tigers which he had seen in the collections of Europe. The Jaguar is sometimes called the American Tiger. Their favorite haunts are the swamps and jungles of tropical America. There they subsist on monkeys, capabyras or water-hogs, tapirs, peccaries, birds, turtles and turtle eggs, lizards, fish, shell-fish and insects. Emerging from these haunts in the more open country, they prey upon deer, horses, cattle, sheep and farm stock. In the early days of settlement of South America the Jaguar was one of the greatest scourges the settlers had to meet. They haunted the clearings and plantations and devoured horses, cattle and sheep without mercy. Nor were the settlers themselves and their children free from their attack. For many years where Jaguars abounded, the settlers had an arduous warfare before they could exterminate the ferocious marauders, or drive them from the vicinity of their habitations.

The Jaguar is a cautious and suspicious animal. It never makes an open attack on man or beast. It approaches its prey stealthily, and pounces upon it from some hiding place, or some position of advantage. It will follow a herd of animals for many miles in hopes of securing a straggler and always chooses the hindmost animal, in order that if turned upon it may escape with its prey the more easily. In this way it pursues men. A Jaguar has been known to follow the track of travelers for days together, only daring to show itself at rare intervals. A full grown Jaguar is an animal of enormous strength and will kill and drag off a horse or ox without difficulty. They commit vast havoc among the horses which band together in great herds on the plains of South America. Full grown colts and calves are their favorite prey. Goodrich in his Natural History describes their operations as follows: "Frequently two Jaguars will combine to master the more powerful brutes. Some of them lie in wait around the salt-licks and attack the animals that resort to these places.

Their habit is to conceal themselves behind some bush, or on the trunk of a fallen tree; here they will lie, silent and motionless for hours, patiently waiting for their victims. When they see a deer or a mule or mustang approaching, the eyes dilate, the hair rises along the back, the tail moves to and fro, and every limb quivers. When the unsuspecting prey comes within his reach, the monster bounds like a thunderbolt upon him. He fixes his teeth in his neck and his claws in the loins and though the dismayed and aggravated victim flies and rears, and essays to throw off his terrible rider, it is all in vain. His strength is soon exhausted and he sinks to the earth an easy prey to his destroyer. The Jaguar, growling and roaring in triumph, already tears his flesh while yet the agonies of death are upon him. When his hunger is appeased he covers the remains of the carcass with leaves, sticks and earth to protect them from the vultures; and either remains watching near at hand or retires for a time until appetite revives, when he returns to complete his carnival." The Jaguar makes its attacks upon the larger quadrupeds by springing upon their shoulders. Then placing one paw on the back of the head and another on the muzzle, with a single wrench it dislocates the neck. The smaller animals it lays dead with a stroke of its paw.

The Jaguar in external appearance and in habits closely resembles the Leopard of the Old World. The female produces two at a birth. The ground color of a full grown animal is yellow, marked with open figures of a rounded-angular form. In each of these figures are one or more black spots. The figures are arranged longitudinally and nearly parallel along the body. The belly is almost white. There if considerable variation in color among Jaguars, some being very dark or almost black, with indistinct markings. The richly tinted skins are highly valued and are exported to Europe in large numbers, where they are used by the military officers for saddle coverings.

For capturing the Jaguar in steel traps the directions given for the Cougar should be followed.

CHAPTER 15

Wolf

TIMBER WOLF

THE WOLF belongs to the dog family and is found throughout the greater part of North America, also in Europe and Asia, and parts of South America. There are many varieties, varying greatly in size and color. Of the timber wolves, we have in this country, the following varieties; the small dark grey or black wolf of Florida and southeastern United States, the red wolf or southern Texas; the brindled wolf of Mexico, the light grey wolf of the central plains region; the dark grey wolf of eastern Canada; the white wolf of northern Canada and Alaska and the large black or dusky wolf of the northwest coast region.

Of the large species, the common grey wolf, of the western stock region, is probably most abundant, and the most destructive to stock and game. The grey wolf varies considerably in size, the largest specimens weighing sometimes more than one hundred pounds. The fur is long and heavy and good prime skins bring usually from two to five dollars each. In former times, when the buffalo was abundant on the plains, they formed the chief food of the wolf, but since the buffalo has become an animal of the past, the wolves depend on stock for food. They are very destructive to cattle, horses, hogs, goats, etc. Occasionally a herd of sheep is raided, but this is of rare occurrence, as the sheep are always guarded by the herders.

In the north where there is little or no stock raised, they prey on game of almost all kinds, being very destructive to deer and even killing moose, at times. They also follow the herds of cattle, which range in the mountains during the summer and in winter are found in the foot hills. The coyote preys on young deer and antelope and on small game, such as rabbits, prairie dogs, sage hens and badgers. They are very destructive to sheep, and many of them follow the sheep when they are driven into the mountains in summer.

The breeding season of the grey wolf varies considerably, some being born in the summer, but the majority are born in March and April. The mating season comes mainly in January and February. There are usually from five to eleven in a litter. They breed in the foot hills and bad lands, in holes in the buttes and rim-rock and sometimes in enlarged badger dens.

Wolves are great ramblers and range over a large section of country. Like all other animals of rambling habits, they have a regular route of travel, and while they vary somewhat from the route, you may be certain to find them using the same passes through the hills, and the same route across a flat. However, when in pursuit of game, they go far out of their course.

For trapping grey wolves, I recommend only the Newhouse trap. A special trap is manufactured, for grey wolves, No. 4½. It has an eight-inch spread of jaws and a five foot chain, fitted with a heavy iron drag, and with chain, complete weighs nine pounds. However, many trappers consider this trap too heavy and the No. 4 Newhouse trap is used more than any other. When these traps are used, they should be fitted with a heavy chain of suitable length, and a pronged drag. The length and style of chain needed will depend much on the method of setting. If the trap is to be staked, I think the ordinary length of chain is best but unless there are two or more traps used in a setting, I would not advise staking the trap.

Some trappers do not use a drag, but wire a heavy stone to the end of the chain. The stone should be fastened securely,

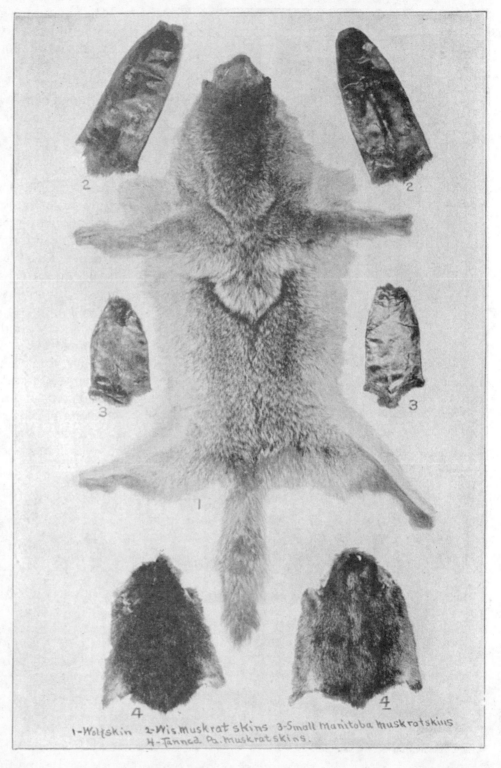

1-Wolfskin   2-Wis. Muskrat skins   3-Small Manitoba Muskrat skins   4-Tanned Pa. Muskrat skins.

for it will be handled pretty roughly, if a wolf gets in the trap. For the coyote, I recommend the Nos. 3 and 4 Newhouse, the 3 and 4 Hawley & Norton, the No. 4 Oneida Jump trap and Nos. 3 and 4 Victor. They should also, be fitted with special chains, unless the traps are to be staked. Good hard-wood stakes should be provided and they should be about fifteen inches long, unless the ground is very soft, in which case they should be longer. As good hard-wood is scarce in many parts of the west, it will sometimes be best to have iron picket pins, made by the local blacksmith.

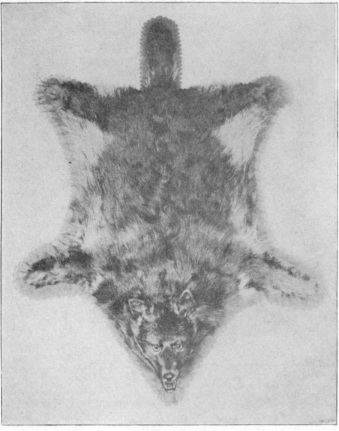

Winter Furred   **BLACK WOLF RUG**   Montana

W. B. FARNSWORTH AND BROTHER, CAREY, IDAHO
Two Successful Coyote Trappers

The bait for the grey wolf should be strictly fresh, for if food is plenty, they are pretty particular. Any of their favorite foods may be used for bait. Horse or sheep is probably best, but prairie dogs, rabbits (both sage and jack rabbits), sage hens, badgers, etc., make good bait. When using small animals for bait, they should never be skinned, for that makes the animal suspicious.

Many different kinds of scent have been used for wolves. Some have been used successfully but in using scent, one should also use good sound judgment, or he will only make the animal suspicious, and harder to trap. Beaver castor and Chinese musk are mildly attractive. Siberian musk is very attractive to both the grey wolf and the coyote. Assafoetida used alone, is worthless, but may be mixed with other scents, to advantage. The urine of the wolf, bottled and kept until it has become rancid, is a very good scent, and the sexual organs of the female, taken when in heat, added to the urine, makes it far more attractive to the male. This scent is most successful during the mating season and should be used without bait.

A very effective scent and one that is much used is made as follows: Place half a pound Of raw beef or venison in a wide mouthed bottle and let it stand from two to six weeks, or longer, or until it is thoroughly decayed and the odor has become as offensive as possible. If the meat is chopped fine, it will aid decomposition. When thoroughly decayed, add a quart of some liquid animal oil—prairie dog oil is probably best, and one-half ounce of assafoetida, dissolved in alcohol and one ounce of tincture of Siberian musk, or if this can not be obtained, an ounce of pulverized beaver castor or one ounce of the common musk used as perfumery. Mix thoroughly and bottle securely until ready for use. This scent is attractive to both the wolf and the coyote, also to cattle and horses and in using it the traps should only be set in places where they are not likely to be disturbed by stock.

This method of trapping, as well as the above scent formula is given by Mr. Vernon Bailey, who made an investigation of the wolf trouble in the interests of the Biological Survey and the department of Forest Service.

ON The Trail. To A.B. Shubert.

HUGH CHALFANT. JAYEM. WYOMING

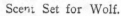

Scent Set for Wolf.

"The best anchor for a wolf trap is a stone drag of 30 or 40 pounds weight, to which the trap is securely wired. A long, oval stone is best, but a triangular or square stone can be securely wired.

The trap, stone and chain should be buried out of sight close to a runway, where the wolves follow a trail or road, cross a narrow pass, or visit a carcass, with the trap nearest the runway and when covered, flush with the surface of the ground. To keep the dirt from clogging under the pan, the pan and jaws should be covered with a clean, oval shaped paper, and over this should be sprinkled fine earth until the surface is smooth and all traces of paper and trap, have been concealed. The surface of the ground and the surroundings should appear as nearly as possible, undisturbed. The dust may be made to look natural again by sprinkling with water.

Touching the ground, or other objects with the hands, spitting near the trap or in any way leaving a trace of human odor nearby, should be avoided. Old, well scented gloves should be used while handling the trap and making the set, and a little of the scent used for the traps should be rubbed on the shoe soles. A piece of old cowhide may be used to stand on, and on which to place the loose dirt when burying the drag and trap. Place the scent about 6 inches beyond the trap and a very little may be sprinkled over the trap, to the trail.

If possible, place the trap between two tufts of grass or weeds, so that it can be readily approached from one side only."

As many of the wolf trappers do not believe in scent, the following methods are given. They are methods that have been thoroughly tested and are being used today, by some of the best trappers. The first method is a trail set, for use with a large bait, and is equally good for grey wolves and coyotes. It should be remembered, however, that trail sets of any kind, can not be used to advantage, if there is much stock about. Find a well defined stock trail somewhere on the wolfs route of travel and set two traps close together, on the trail, then go on from fifty to one hundred yards and set two more in exactly the same manner. Use care in setting the traps, so as to leave everything looking the same as before. You can wear gloves if you like, but I do not think there is much gained by doing so, for it is impossible to make a set without leaving some human scent. The scent will pass away in a day or two and few trappers count on making a catch until after the traps have been set a couple of days.

A large bait should be placed close along the trail and midway between the two settings. When the wolves get to feeding on the bait they will travel on the trail and will not be looking for danger so far from the bait. If desired, only one trap need be set in a place, but two are better, as the wolf is likely to step over the trap if only one is used. It is a good plan to set the traps several days before placing the bait, so as to allow time for the human scent to pass away and the setting to take on a more smooth appearance.

Here is a method that is much used for both wolves and coyotes. It requires three or four traps and they should all be fastened securely to one stout, hard-wood stake. Find a smooth, sandy spot and scoop out a little hollow and drive the stake down until the top is below the level of the ground. Fasten your bait securely to the top of the stake, so as to hide the stake and prevent the wolf or coyote from taking the bait away. If three traps are used, spread them out in the form of a triangle, if four are used, arrange them in the form of a square. Set the traps very carefully, so that when they are covered, everything will be smooth and looking just like it did before. As the bait is fastened, the wolf can not take it away, and in trying to pull it up, will step in one of the traps. He is almost certain to get in another one when he commences to struggle, and there is little danger of him escaping. If a place can be found where the traps may be set between bunches of weeds, cactus, etc., so much the better.

Bank Set for Wolf and Coyote.

Another very good method, is to set a trap on top of a straight or over-hanging bank, from four to eight feet high, so that when the animal is caught it will leap or fall over the bank and be unable to get back, where it would have a chance to struggle. The set is made as follows: Find two bunches of cactus, growing on the top of the bank, fix the bait on the very edge of the bank, between the two bunches of cactus. Fasten the bait with a small stake, and drive the stake out of sight in the bait. Stake the trap just the length of the chain from the edge of the bank, driving stake out of sight, and set the trap between the cactus and about twenty inches back from the bait, somewhat farther if grey wolves are expected. Cover the trap very carefully. If two bunches of cactus can not be found growing close together, get some and place it there, so that it will look natural, and have the appearance of having grown there.

A single trap may be set almost anywhere, and small pieces of bait scattered around the trap. In this way you can bait the trap without dismounting from your horse and avoid leaving human scent.

Mr. Vasma Brown, a noted trapper of Texas, gives the following method: "Take a large piece of fresh meat and drag it along a trail. Stop occasionally and set a trap, just outside of the edge of the trail, where the stock will not step in it. Dig out a place for the trap and set the trap, covering first with a piece of paper and finishing with sand, leaving the place looking just like it did before. Cut some of the meat in small pieces and scatter them around the trap. Use no scent; fresh pork is the best scent you can get. If you can find some animal that the wolves themselves have killed, do not fail to set traps there immediately."

When trapping around a large bait, sometimes the animals will not approach close enough to be caught. In such cases a small bait may sometimes be used to advantage, by setting traps a short distance away. The tail of a skunk is said to be an unfailing lure. Do not smoke or grease your traps or the wolf is sure to locate them at once.

Sometimes a badger will be caught in a wolf trap. If so, do not skin it, but kill it and set the trap close by. It will make a fine bait, and the trap may be set in the ground that the animal has dug up, leaving no signs of human presence.

When trapping during freezing weather, fill in around the jaws and springs of the traps with sage leaves, or some similar dry material, before covering with dirt.

Always carry a rifle with you when tending the traps. You will get shots at wolves or coyotes almost every day.

When visiting wolf traps, always go on horseback and if possible avoid dismounting near the traps.

Dark, cold, stormy nights are the best for the wolf trapper.

Use plenty of traps. The more chances you have, the better success you will have.

Sometimes a coyote will uncover a trap or dig it up and spring it. Nothing can prevent this. Your only remedy is to have lots of traps set, and if he fools you in one set, you may fool him in another.

In warm weather, if you can set out a line of traps just before a rain, your chances for making a good catch are very good, as the rain washes away all human odors, and helps to smooth over the sets. In winter, a light snow fall will often help to increase the catch.

The tracks of the wolf resemble those of the dog and fox. An average full grown grey wolf will make a foot print about three inches wide and four inches long and will step about twenty inches. The average sized coyote will make a footprint about two inches in length and the length of step is about sixteen inches.

In trapping them it is well to know that they will almost risk their lives for lard cracklings, scraps of which, scattered about, are a tempting bait.

For capturing the Wolf by the steel trap, the directions given in first method of taking the Fox should be followed, except that the honey should be left out, and the clog of the trap should be of fifteen or twenty pounds' weight. The small Prairie Wolf that is so trouble-some to the western farmer can be captured in the same way. Care should always be taken to keep at a proper distance when looking after the trap, as the Wolf's sense of smell is very acute, and enables him to detect the foot-prints of the hunter with great sagacity.

The Gray Wolf
By Courtesy of N. Y. Zoological Society.

The following plan for taking the. Wolf is given by Peter M. Gunter, of Ontario: "Find two trees standing eighteen inches or two feet apart. Place the bait between the trees, and set a trap on each side of it. The traps should be smoked over hemlock or cedar boughs, to destroy any odor of iron. After being carefully set, the traps should be covered with finely powdered rotten wood. A

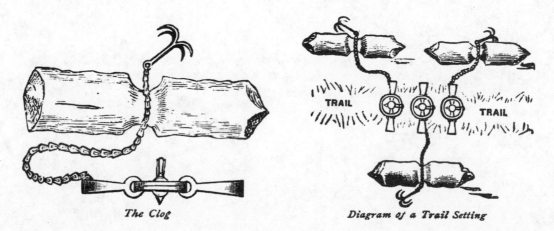

The Clog   *Diagram of a Trail Setting*

clog of hard-wood of about twenty pounds' weight should be fastened to the chain of each trap. When all is arranged, rub some asafœtida on the trees to attract the attention of the Wolves. If two trees cannot be found a suitable distance apart, lean two large logs against a tree where you wish to set your traps. It is better to use old logs, if lying about, than to make any fresh chopping."

The foregoing describes a "trail-setting." Another good method is the u "square-setting." This is made in the same manner as the first, except that it is not put in a trail, and the traps are arranged as shown on next page.

In addition to the scraps of meat that should be thrown about, a large bone or meat bait should be buried in the center of the setting.

Wolves have a habit of burying surplus provender, and also a habit of digging up what others have buried, when they chance to find the place. If a smaller number of traps than four be used in the setting, the place chosen should be where there are stones, logs or tussocks of weeds that will act as guides and compel the Wolves to step in the right spot. Care should be exercised to avoid touching any of these objects, as they carry the taint a long time afterwards. If, however, there be no weeds, etc., do not try to place any to suit. The Wolves never fail to detect and shun any artificial arrangement.

A living sheep or calf has been used with great success as a back. The animal must be staked out over night, and must be tied up very short, for otherwise, it will either get into the trap itself or large numbers will be required to surround it. In selecting a spot for the bait, due regard must be had for tussocks of sage, soapweed or rocks, as by choosing a place which has but few natural pathways to it, fewer traps will cover the ground and guard the bait. A calf or sheep that will bleat is to be preferred, and it is more likely to attract if its ears be cut so as to bleed.

The head of a beef makes a good bait, for, although the Wolves do not eat of it, they usually approach it, walk around, and water on it. One of the traps may be attached to the head itself, as it makes a good clog, and needs no burying.

A FEW GENERAL HINTS

—At night, on retiring, put on a large bone or a lump of meat in the fire; this will smoulder and roast all night, making a scent that the Wolves will detect twenty miles away, and come to, if they are very hungry.

—Never use asafœtida, aniseed oil, or oil of rhodium, as Wolf-lures. According to my experience the only effect of these odors is to render the animal suspicious.

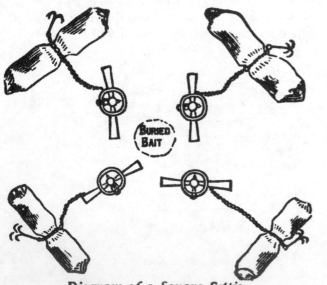

Diagram of a Square Setting

Diagram of a Setting among Weeds, Rocks, Bushes, Etc.

—The most attractive of all odors is that of a female Wolf or dog at the mating season. After this the odor of blood is the most pleasing, and in the following list the various baits, exclusive of the two just named, are given in their order of preference: Antelope, Donkey (*Burro,*) Jack Rabbit, inner parts of a young Beef, Colt, Mutton, Veal and Horse. Wolves will not eat diseased meat, and have but little liking for old or strong beef. For example, it is little more than a waste of time to bait or drag with a "big-jawed" steer.

—Never stake your traps immovably, but always fasten them to some sort of clog which they can drag away, and never put two logs in one hole, or two traps to one log.

—The cattle themselves are the great plague of the Wolf-hunter; they are attracted by the scent of blood, and come pawing about the traps, usually springing all that they discover. It is mostly the steers and bulls that do this, and fortunately, their hoofs are too large to be caught by the trap, so the only harm done is the spoiling of the setting. The only remedy for this difficulty is setting in the afternoon after the cattle have gone out from water, and are again scattered over the pastures.

—Never put your hands or fingers between the trap jaws; always work from the under side of the loose jaw, or else use your trap wrench or a stick.

—The original drag made by the meat that was trailed after the wagon will be good for about two days. The Wolves are able to follow it even on the third day, but it is better to put out a fresh drag, at least every other day. This I usually do on horseback when going the rounds.

—If the jaws of the trap do not lie perfectly flat, bend the springs towards the jaw which is held down by the "dog."

—If there is any difference, the dust over the "pan" should be a little more even than elsewhere, for the Wolves like to tread on a smooth place.

Mounted. Owned by
Andersch Bros.   **NORTHERN PRAIRIE WOLF**   Northern Wisconsin

—A piece of white cotton, or a tuft of white feathers, properly placed, often adds a good finish to the setting, as the Wolf, attracted by the general scent of blood, will at once see and examine minutely the white object.

—If a whole carcass is the bait, set the trap opposite the belly, between the legs and by the throat and tail, unless you have enough to go all around; keeping them about two feet from the bait.

—When a bait of less than fifty or sixty pounds weight is used, it is well to fix it by driving a stout stake through it.

—It is worth while spending a great deal of time in killing Antelope for bait.

—Never fail to set traps at once about the carcass of any animal that the Wolves themselves have killed.

—A she Wolf or dog staked out in the mating season is an infallible lure, and a captive Wolf that will howl, is good at any time.

—Dark, cold, stormy nights are the best for the Wolf-trapper.

—When there is snow on the ground, use more cotton wool, and place over the trap a large soft sheet of white paper, the edges of which are everywhere buried in snow. This is especially necessary when in a region that is subject to sudden thaws, for a thaw followed by a frost will freeze in the traps and render them useless. If you are quite sure the snow will continue powdery, yon may dispense with the paper, but do not neglect the cotton wool. There is nothing a: good as cotton wool, but Coyote and sheep's wool will do on a pinch.

—In going the rounds, never approach the traps unnecessarily; if possible, avoid dismounting at all.

—For small bait, scraps of rabbit with the skin on are better than simple meat, for the skin keeps the bait from drying out.

—A Wolf's track is not distinguishable with certainty from that of a large dog; it averages perhaps a little narrower in proportion. The forefoot of course makes the largest print; a forefoot track that measures 4½ inches from the point of the claw to the straight line behind the heel pad indicates a good sized Wolf.

From Painting
Property of Andersch Bros.   **GROUP OF TIMBER WOLVES**   Rocky Mountains
Winter Scene

4¾ inches means a large Wolf. The largest I ever measured was 5½ inches long. With fair accuracy I used to reckon that a Wolf had 20 pounds of weight for every inch that his forefoot was long.

—Remember that the chief purpose of the "Grab-hook" is to make a trail that can be easily followed. See therefore that it has free play.

—When a Wolf goes off with one of the traps and clogs, it is useless to seek for his trail within a hundred yards of the spot whence the trap has been dragged, for in the frantic struggle that ensues as soon as he is caught, he rushes and leaps about in every direction; and when at length he finds he cannot shake off the trap, he generally goes in a tolerably straight course towards the nearest cover. It will usually then be quite easy to follow his track and kill your Wolf.

It may be said in conclusion that our Newhouse No. 4 is often used as a Wolf trap, and for small Wolves even a Newhouse No. 3 will answer. In all cases, however, when these smaller traps are used, they should be provided with a special chain and "grab hook".

CHAPTER 16

Coyote

Description: General color, dull yellowish-grey, some specimens grizzled with black and white hairs, under parts ashy white, tail full, tipped with black.

Range: Entire Western and Southwestern United States north to Canada, also found in extreme Northern Michigan, Wisconsin and Minnesota.

Coyotes are small, slinking wolves, very numerous on the plains of the United States and Canada. They are fleet of foot, cunning and wary, but very cowardly.

As a rule, Coyotes run, hunt and live in pairs.

They are very destructive to sheep and cattle, and prey on young game, especially deer, elk and antelope.

They never attack cattle or deer, unless in packs of six or eight. They also eat rabbits, ground squirrels, mice, prairie dogs, sage hen, grouse, Badger, etc.

They live in burrows, natural holes in the rocks, or enlarged Badger dens. The young are born in the spring and there are from five to eight in a litter.

Practically every state where Coyotes are found, as well as some of the provinces of Canada, pay a bounty for the capture of this animal. The bounties, the bounty laws and the methods of obtaining the bounty money vary in the different states. Coyote skins are often ruined and greatly reduced in market value by the requirements of bounty laws, especially when the head or ears are cut off. Most of the Coyote skins, particularly from the better sections, are used in imitation of Fox. They are dyed and made up into scarfs. If the head of the animal is cut off, it cannot be used in imitation of Fox, therefore, the value of the skin is reduced materially. The skin of the Coyote has a market value, and in recent years very high prices have been paid for perfect skins, with heads on.

Coyotes are very suspicious and difficult to trap. For bait, any of their natural foods may be used. A good portion of a horse or sheep, or a prairie dog, rabbit, sage hen, Badger, etc., make good bait. If small animals are used for bait, they should not be skinned.

There are many different kinds of scents that may be used advantageously in trapping Coyotes. Beaver Castor is fairly attractive. The urine of the animal, bottled and allowed to stand until it becomes rancid, is also a very good scent. The sexual organs of the female, taken when "in heat," added to the urine of the animal, make a scent that is strongly attractive to the males, and is most successful during the mating season, which is January and February. Another good scent may be made by cutting up about half a pound of raw beef into small pieces and placing in a bottle, allowing it to stand until it is thoroughly decayed. Add a quart of prairie-dog oil or any liquid animal oil. Then add one ounce of pulverized asafetida and one ounce of pulverized Beaver Castor. Mix well and bottle tightly until used.

The Nos. 3 or 4 traps should be used for Coyotes and should always be fastened to a clog or drag of about twenty-five to thirty-five pounds in weight (a stone or log may be used). Never stake the trap unless absolutely necessary. If the trap is staked, the chain should have a swivel at each end. The trap, chain and clog or drag should be carefully buried. The surface of the ground and the surroundings should appear as nearly natural as possible. Do not touch the ground with your hands, nor spit near the trap, and avoid leaving human scent as much as possible. While setting traps, well scented gloves should be worn and scent rubbed on the soles of the shoes. A piece of old cowhide or sheepskin may be used to stand on and to place the loose dirt in digging the hole for the trap and clog.

A good method of trapping Coyotes is as follows: Find a well defined trail. Set two traps close together on the trail, then set two more in the same manner about fifty yards beyond. Place a large bait close to the trail and about halfway between the two settings.

Another method is to drag a large piece of fresh meat along a trail. Set traps some distance apart from each other on the trail and cut some of the meat in small pieces and scatter around the trap.

Still another method is to place a bait on a stick about three feet high, driven into the ground. Set traps on each side of the bait and about ten feet from it. The Coyotes will become suspicious and will circle around the bait and in that way step into one of the traps.

If an animal is found that has been killed by Coyotes, it is well to set traps around it.

Traps may also be set between chimps of brush, weeds, cactus or between two trees. A few drops of scent may be applied to the grass, weeds, ground or trees.

The best time to set traps for Coyotes is just before a rain or light snow fall, as this will help take away the human scent.

Coyotes should be skinned "cased" and shipped Fur side out.

"Much has been written concerning the famous polyglot serenades of the coyote, by those who have been unwilling listeners, but it is difficult to convey an adequate idea in words of the noisy confusion. One must have spent an hour or two vainly trying to sleep before he is in a condition to appreciate the full force of the annoyance. It is a singular fact that the nowing of two or three wolves gives an impression that a score are engaged, so many, so long-drawn are the notes, and so uninterruptedly are they continued by one individual after another. A short, sharp bark is sounded, followed by several more in quick succession, the time growing faster and the pitch higher, fill they run together in a long–drawn, lugubrious howl in the highest possible key. The same strain is taken up again and again by different members of the pack, while from a greater distance the deep melancholy baying of the more wary lobo breaks in, to add to the discord, till the very leaves on the trees seem to be quivering to the inharmonious sounds. It is not true, as asserted by some, that the coyote howls only just after dark and at daylight. Though they may be noisiest at these times, when the pack is gathering together for a night's for aging, or dispersing again

JOSEPH BILL, MINIDOKA, IDAHO
Another "Satisfied Shubert Shipper"

to their diurnal retreats, I know that they give tongue at any time during the night. They are rarely, if ever, heard in the daytime, though frequently to be seen, at least in secluded regions. Ordinarily however, they spend the day in quiet, out-of-the way places, among rocks, in thick copses, etc., and seek their prey mainly at night, collecting for this purpose into packs, as already noticed.

"The coyote, although a carnivore, is a very indiscriminate feeder, and nothing seems to come amiss which is capable of being chewed and swallowed. From the nature of the region which it inhabits, it is often hard-pressed for food, particularly in the winter season. Besides such live game as it can surprise and kill, or overpower by persevering pursuit, and force of numbers, it feeds greedily upon all sorts of dead animal matter. To procure this, if resorts in great numbers to the vicinity of settlements, where offal is sure to be found, and surrounds the hunter's camp at night. It is well-known to follow for days in the trail of a traveling-party, and each morning just after camp is broken, it rushes in to claim whatever eatable refuse may have been left behind. But it cannot always find a sufficiency of animal food, and is thus made frugiferous and herbivorous. Particularly in the Fall, it feeds extensively upon 'tunas,' which are the juicy, soft, scarlet fruit of various species of prickly pear (Opuntia); and in the winter upon berries of various sorts, particularly those of the juniper (Juniperus pachyderma), and others.

Coyotes are so annoying that a variety of means are used to destroy them. They may be shot of course, but hunt them in the daytime is uncertain and hardly worth the trouble, while night shooting is still more laborious and unsatisfactory. Their cunning, inquiring disposition is ordinarily more than a match for man's ingenuity in the way of traps. The most certain, as well as the easiest methods of obtaining them is by poisoning the carcass of a dead animal or butcher's offal with strychnine. There is no doubt, also, that the odor of asafetida is attractive to them, and a little of this drug rubbed in to the poisoned meat greatly heightens the chances of their eating, it. Since, after eating the poison, they suffer greatly from thirst, it is well to place a tub of water conveniently at hand, which generally keeps them from making off for water, and so being lost. There is considerable difference in the fur, both as to quality and color, according to the season. In the winter it is fuller, thicker and softer than in the summer, and has much less tawny or rufous about it, being almost black and grizzled, grayish white.

Except under certain circumstances, there is a chronic feud between our domestic dogs and these dog-wolves. A good-sized dog will easily whip a coyote, though he may not come off unscathed from the sharp teeth and quick snaps of the latter. I have known a smallish terrier even to kill a coyote, of which he caught a throat-hold, enabling him by vigorous shakes to beat the wolf's skull against some boulders between which the conflict took place. Notwithstanding, there is abundant evidence that the coyote will cross, and bear fertile offspring with the domestic dog; and I believe that the female of either will take the male of the other. During the season of heat, which is in the spring, I have known dogs to disappear for several days, and return in such a dilapidated condition as to leave no doubt that they had been decoyed away by some female coyote and received hard treatment from her or her relatives. The hybrid is said to possess the bad qualities of both parents, and the good ones of neither, as usual with bastards, and to remain snappish and intractable, in spite of severity or kindness. The gestation of the species, as is well-known, does not differ materially from that of its allies. It brings forth in May or June, in secluded places, usually under or among rocks. Five or six puppies are ordinarily produced at a birth.

A variety of absurd stories regarding its re-production pass current even among the best-informed back-woodsmen; many affirming that the pups are born shapeless, inchoate masses, to he afterwards licked into proper shape by the mother."

The mating season occurs during the Spring months, varying somewhat upon the altitude and climate. After 60 to 65 days the mother bears four to eight young. The birthplace is usually in a hollow log, cave or burrow, and sometimes in dense brushes. The young are born blind and remain in this state for a period of twenty-one days. Their growth seems retarded until they reach the age of forty-five to sixty days, when they develop by astounding degrees. The mother attends to them carefully, and her love does not cease until late in the fall when the young drift away and begin life upon their own resources. In their playful mood they resemble the actions of a litter of pups.

The average age of the prairie wolf or coyote is from eight to twelve years, though individuals have lived as long as fifteen and twenty years. As a rule the large northern timber wolf attains its enormous size only after three years and continues, and probably not earlier than to years does his age begin to show in his tactics, and shortly thereafter he is left behind if he finds himself in a chase with younger brutes.

The female is invariable smaller than the male, and her depredations are more noticeable during the season when with her young. At times she takes very desperate chances, apparently disregarding her usual cautiousness in her endeavor to procure food for her young.

TRAPPING THE WOLF OR COYOTE

"I will relate a successful way to trap the coyote." Writes Mr. Lothamer, a Canadian trapper residing at Heather Brae.

"The coyote is a very cautious animal, and is hard to trap, yet be can be caught in several different ways. The trap should be bid in a small pile of ashes or leaves, and should be smeared with lard or blood. Fasten the trap to a small clog or log, so that he can move about when caught. Obtain from the female of the dog, the matrix, in the season of coition, and preserve it in alcohol, tightly corked, when it can be had. Leave a drop here and there around the trap and put some on your shoes when visiting the traps. Take a piece of raw flesh and draw it in several directions from the trap and squeeze the blood out every little while. Leave everything as natural as possible near and around your traps.

"Here is another method. Find a place in the woods or in the brush where the coyote has made a trail and set your trap in it. Then hang a piece of meat off to one side of your trap to draw his attention away from the trap. The reason why I hang the meat to one side is because a coyote never goes directly to the bait, but circles around, it first, and in making the circle will naturally follow his old trail, at the same time keeping his eye on the meat, and walks into your trap. Use your own judgment to advantage, and you will be successful. Use Newhouse traps No. 1½ or No. 2."

TRAPPING THE WOLF OR COYOTE

We quote a trapper, H. Miller, living at Redding, Cal who writes an article on the coyote:

The coyote is a very shy animal, and it requires considerable care and attention in setting the traps. This is one of my plans and is nearly always successful if the coyote is pretty hungry. I first find out about where he runs; then take the entrails or any part of the sheep, deer or goat (entrails from hogs will sometimes do). Select a place where there are a few brush, near a trail or road; fasten if you can the bait to the bottom of a tree or spreading tree at the end; must be old brush, make no new work that will show when brush is in shape. Then set our trap about four feet from bait and near the entrance of the pen; cover nicely and leave no part of the trap in sight. Chain can be fastened to the butt end of a large limb or bush sunk in the ground so as to admit of being smoothly covered. Pen should be about a foot wide at the entrance. If work is done well and trap rightly set, when he come—whatever he is—and is hungry, you will catch him. No need of smoking traps to catch such animals; that is nonsense.

"I have tried all plans in my 13 years of trapping and can safety say that I never could see that smoking or handling with gloves did any good, as the scent on traps will go away of its own accord in a few days, This plan is the best I have found when meat for bait is used."

TRAPPING THE WOLF OR COYOTE

"In trapping for wolves," writes Mr. Chamberlain, "take en -trails of a hog or beef to a place where you know wolves frequent, and throw, upon an ant-hill or some mound, and set steel traps about 3 to 6 feet away on some other high elevation if possible. The wolf will go around and around the bait, sniffing and gradually reaching closer and closer, until he gets caught. Attach chain to a 5 pound, not heavier than re-pound clog."

TRAPPING THE WOLF OR COYOTE

The way I trap wolves is to find where they hand out. One will find them near some river, creek or lake. Horse manure or old barn yard litter will take away the scent of traps. I cover traps with manure or chaff. To attract wolves, I kill some animal and roast the carcass ; this is done at the place where I expect to set my traps. The carcass will roast and smoulder for quite a while and the odor therefrom is smelled by the fox or wolf as a great distance and I am sure will attract these animals for miles. Before starting the fire, have your traps set in the manure and hide them in the usual way. Where there are plenty of wolves I set from four to six No. 4½ wolf traps about the bait. My reason for using No. 4½ traps is on account of the long chains and pronged drag. If a wolf springs the trap he will try to get away and in the space of time will become tangled up. The trail made by these pronged books is very easy to follow.

The wolf is a cunning rascal and very suspicious when he detects any artificial arrangement.

PITFALL.

At the same time he is so inquisitive that he will shortly investigate everything and will come to the same place right along for a period of weeks. If you cannot prepare a roast for the wolf obtain fish; these even if badly decayed are better than if fresh. The stronger the scent the greater the distance it will be carried by the wind. I never go to my traps on foot, usually look over the line on horseback. The advantage of placing such a set upon some slightly elevated place, especially during a snow storm, is to be taken into account. I prefer to place such sets close to cattle trails.

I hope the brother trapper will get many pelts and enrich his pocketbook by the bounty which the state offers.

CHAS. H. ZEIGLER

"IN a level country at is sometimes more difficult to set traps during the winter months when snow is drifting and the wind has sufficient power to disturb even haystacks as well as piles of manure that may be hauled in the open prairie. In starting out to trap wolves, I pay particular attention to my traps. Instead of smoking them I use a compound made out of tallow, Spruce and cedar needles. These I boil up together and then pour contents into a fruit jar. When I have located place that the wolf frequents, I drive or ride in the vicinity where I intend to set my traps and seatter a few branches smeared with this preparation. My favorite place is to set traps around a straw or hay stack. In a few days thereafter I take the stomach or intestines of some calf, sheep, bog or beef, and throw it close to the stack. I now take two No. 4 or 4½ double spring traps and set them 12 to 14 inches on the outside of the bait. These traps are set level with the ground, and concealed with earth, rotten wood, etc. The chains fire securely fastened to some old limb, or loose fencepost. The latter makes an excellent drag. If traps are skillfully set and concealed and if there are any wolves or foxes in the neighborhood, you will get them. Do not be disappointed if you are not successful the first few days, as the fox and wolf are both suspicious and sometimes will loiter in the vicinity for hours of a time and two or three days before they will approach the bait.

The funniest experience that I have had was in Manitoba Along on the Red River, where two of the afore-mentioned sets were placed on the opposite sides of a haystack. In one trap I got a large buffalo wolf and in the other a stray dog. During that same season and with the same three traps, I caught 6 wolves, 8 foxes (for one of these skins I received $85.00) and one dog.

J. R. BARTON

TRAPPING THE WOLF OR COYOTE

A favorite set is to bury part or all of some dead carcass on an elevated mound or lull. From 15 to 20 inches on each side, place one or more steel traps, which are to be buried and covered in the usual way. Occasionally I place poisoned pellets of meat in the immediate vicinity.

Just before leaving I obtain one or two armfuls of straw, which I place four or five feet away from the center of bait, start it afire, and just as soon as I am sure the fire is all out, go away. The wolf or fox will come the same or next night, and if the set is a natural one, he may go to the bait the first day. If not he will go in two or three

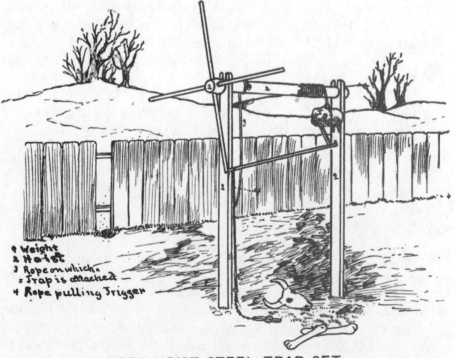

1 Weight
2 Hoist
3 Rope on which
  Trap is attached
4 Rope pulling Trigger

BEEF HOIST STEEL TRAP SET.

days. The wind has a tendency to distribute the ashes and by so doing overcomes any and all human scent that the trapper may have left.

R. B. A.

WENT FISHING FOR WOLVES

A Nevada youth, not having any traps, caught many wolves by promiscuously baiting three pronged trolling fish books with small pieces of meat attaching them to ordinary baling wire fastened on limbs of trees, so as to hang tour feet from the ground. The wolf in jumping for the bait snaps just like a dog, and the prongs very readily find themselves imbedded in his upper and lower jaws.

TRAPPING THE WOLF OR COYOTE

Coyotes, unlike the wolf, are not very great travelers. Generally unless driven out, they remain in the vicinity where they were raised, and on their range, areas familiar as a clerk in a store. They travel on trails, wherever they lead, in the direction they are traveling. It is as natural for them to travel on a trail as it is for a cow or horse, because their feet get sore from traveling over rough ground covered with rocks.

Find a cow trail where you see coyote tracks quite often. Locate a small bush about 2 to 15 feet from the trail. Now take three traps, No. 3 or 4 Newhouse or H & N. Always use large traps, for there is no felling what kind of an animal is going to get caught accidentally. Have a grapple on each trap. Now put a trap on 3 sides of the bush. Put the grapple of each trap in the center of the bush and cover with leaves. Bury each trap down level with the ground. Put 2 or 3 grass stems cover fightly with fine, dry dirt. Treat each trap this way. Everything should look so natural that you, yourself, cannot see the slightest alteration. Now put some cracklings in the center of the bush and over all sprinkle fish oil, especially on top of the bush so the wind can carry the smell a long ways. A coyote can smell this set if the wind is blowing in his direction, for one-half mile and will then come straight for it.

Always use clean buck skin gloves when handling yore traps. Traps for coyotes should be set horse-back. Take along a piece of hide large enough to stand on. Tie a 6-foot rope on it, throw this on the ground, step off and set your traps. When through, get on your hors, and pull the hide up with the rope if you are trapping in a country where there are deer or antelope, use their hides in place of a beef hide. This leaves no human scent on the ground and fools the smartest coyote.

The way I make my fish oil is to cut up fish and put them in a bottle, cork up and let stand in the sun for two weeks. It is then ready for use.

This is the best set I have over used and is used by the best and most successful trapper in Wyoming, known as Rattle-Snake Jack. I have taken 3 coyotes at one set, in one night. If this set is used in the vicinity of a dead horse or cow, a person is sure of success the first night.

WM. WEIBEL
La Porte, Colo.

TRAPPING THE WOLF OR COYOTE

Will herein give you my experience and method in trapping the wily coyote and grey wolf, which are very troublesome to the stockmen of the country, or other stock-raising countries. The bounties paid for these friendless animals by state, country, and stockmen, pay the trappers very well for pursuing them both winter and summer. The country bounty, is $6.00, state, $3.00 and the bounties paid by stockmen in different parts of the state vary from $5.00 to $20.00 on a single wolf; so between the bounty and his skin, it is worth while looking after Mr. Wolf. But let me tell you, boys, the trapper has to deal with an animal of almost human intelligence and sometimes it seems to be more so than that of man. I have, before now, set my traps for wolf

DEADFALL.

and on going back afterwards have found the trap taken up and thrown out of concealed place, not even being sprung.

For trapping the wolf, always use the Newhouse No. 4 beaver trap. Instead of using a drag, I use an iron pin, 2 feet long, driven into the ground out of sight. This is not so heavy to pack and does just as well.

First, have you traps smoked over cedar boughs or feathers of any kind. This kills the odor of iron. When setting traps, always dig out a hole in the ground about two and one-half inches deep to fit a trap, with springs a little bit turned to let jaws down even. Now place your trap and cover with a piece of paper large enough to cover jaws of trap and cover all with fine, dry dirt one inch deep. Also cover chain and pin. See that the latter is just even with the ground. The idea in using paper is to prevent dirt getting under the pan of the trap, then when any animal steps on the pan, your trap is sure to spring. If the dirt taken out of the hole is too lumpy, have a sack or something to carry the lumps away, and bring good dirt. Leave everything looking just as it did before you came. When covering traps, never use your bare hand, always have on mittens or gloves and brush away your track, or you will get no wolf.

This, in my experience, is the best method for catching the foxy old wolf. When looking after traps, keep from 10 to 15 rods away, unless you have something in your trap, or it is sprung.

After catching a wolf, always clean and change your traps, because you will never catch two wolves in one place in this country where there are so many cattle. I set my traps in trails where cattle go and come from water. I set them at cross trails or in forks of trails. This makes lots of work as the cattle often spring your traps. Where there are lots of rabbits, cattle and stuff for wolves to eat, no bait, is necessary as this would only arouse the wolf's suspicion and cause him to walk away.

Another good way where bait is to be used: Find a place where there are a few mounds. Now, conceal your trap as before stated on each mound and throw your bait between mounds. He is certain to get upon these mounds to look around and you will get him, or the trap will.

When you think a snow storm is near at hand, don't cover the traps deep, as the snow makes a good covering with just a little dirt under it.

I think this method of concealing the traps will also answer for taking other land animals. But the trapper will have to use his own judgment in covering the traps, with regard to the size of the animal he expects to capture, as a small animal would not spring a trap with so much dirt on it. I have caught skunks and badgers in this manner.

I never use the chains that come with the traps, as they will not hold a wolf in cold weather. I remove same and make chains from chain tugs, and have same a foot long.

ROBERT ROBERTS,
Harding Gove, S. D.

TRAPPING THE WOLF OR COYOTE

The Wolf is the most cunning animal with which the trapper has to deal and to trap him successfully takes both care and patience, but with my method, I have good success.

First, if the traps are rusty or stained. Boil them in willow Bark and water. This will remove any odor, rust or blood, when handling, use buckskin gloves. Set the traps where there are signs or wolves.

I use No. 4 Newhouse traps, and for scent I use,

1 oz. Anise Oil.
½ oz. Skunk Scent.
1 oz Essence of the Wolf

Mix and apply to pan and spring of traps.

Now, cover the trap first, by placing a paper over the pan and jaws, then cover with dirt enough to remove all traces of the trap and chain.

For bait, I use squirrel prairie dog, rabbit, or birds, and alive when possible. To fasten the bait, bury a stake in the ground and fasten the bait to it by means of a short chain attached by one end to the stake and wire the other end to the leg of the bait.

Now, set a trap on each side of the bait, and about six feet from it, and when the wolf sees that the bait is fast, he will begin to sniff and walk in a circle around it and so get caught.

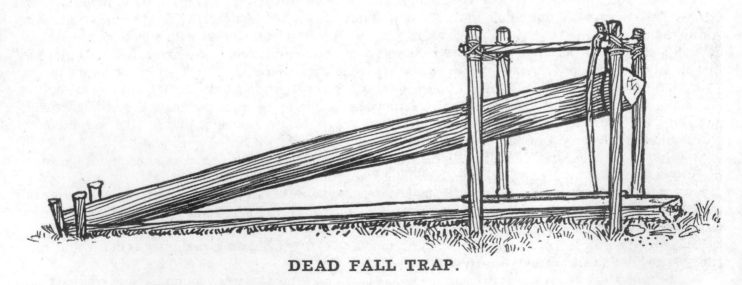

DEAD FALL TRAP.

I have seldom known this to fail when the wolf came near enough to see the bait.

F. ABBOT,
Ft. Pierre, S. D.

TRAPPING THE WOLF OR COYOTE

In such states where a good bounty is offered it is more profitable to capture young wolves for the reason that they are more plentiful and easier captured. When they are three or four months old they can be seen going away quite a distance from their abode. Then is the time to bring some dead carcass in the vicinity and to place No. 2, No. 3 or No. 3½ traps thereabouts. Nine times out of ten the mother will be suspicious, but she cannot prevent the cubs form nearing the bait, due to their over-zealous desire to satisfy their carnivorous appetites. The cubs, as they become captured, will of course make a big disturbance, and the mother will approach them timidly. Sometimes will carry them away, trap and all. On one occasion four cubs and three full grown wolves were captured at one setting, presumably the larger ones went to the assistance of the cubs or probably for pure deviltry. At other times, notwithstanding the suffering of those captured, others will come and devour parts or all of the bait.

N. C. A.

TRAPPING THE WOLF OR COYOTE

The wolf is probably the most cunning animal of the dog family. If he was as easily captured and killed as is the buffalo he would now be extinct a hundred times. It is a well-known fact that a wolf is not as cunning in a new country as be is in an old settled community, and he does not feel out of place to travel in good society in an old settlement. What methods are good in one place may not be worth the paper written on in another.

I was fortunate enough to catch one of the slyest wolves that ever lived in southern Minnesota. He was known for years as the "three legged wolf" and seemingly had an encounter with a double spring trap years ago. Since then he baffled everything in the trap line and no one in the vicinity was able to bring him to bait. There was no use to set traps around a home as it would have saved many the worry and trouble of looking after them. I took the bones of an old carcass and hauled them out in the open and left tem there for some time. Mr. Wolf came and smelled round the hones for two or three days and then watered upon them. Probably the wolf had no idea that a map would be so foolish as to expect him to eat dry bones, or that one would place traps thereabouts; but nevertheless I got him.

To set your traps when going into a wolf country, drive if possible, tie a big piece of meat (lung or liver is good) behind your wagon and drag it along. Smear the drag with three parts of asafoetida, beeswax one part, and thirty drops of anise oil to one pint of mixture. If you get off the wagon smear your soles with this preparation, also your gloves. I usually take along a pail of blood which I sprinkle in the immediate vicinity in places where I set my traps. I also dip the traps in the pail before setting them. Traps should be set in some cattle trail near some bush, and if possible at some intersection of another trail or road. Traps should be covered with leaves and grass and make the setting look quite natural with the surroundings. Occasionally I cover my traps with rabbit for. At other times when the weather is real cold, I dip the traps in water and roll them in loose feathers or rabbit fur, which of course becomes immediately attached to the trap. If the weather continues cold, set this trap in the trail without any additional covering. The wolf will come along and ninety-nine times out of a hundred, paws at it.

Young cubs are easily caught. Place traps around their feeding place and if you cannot locate the feeding place, make one by bringing some dead carcass there. The cubs are not very shrewd and in their over-zealous desire to satisfy their craving appetite, they near the bait and of course become a victim.

ANDREW DAVIDSON,
Bathgate, S. D.

TRAPPING THE WOLF OR COYOTE

A Wolf is the most cautious and keen animal I ever tried to trap. A person has to go some in order to fool him. The only successful way to trap him is to use a blind set at a dead horse or cow, for he will not go near it as long as there are any live cattle on the range. A wolf travels in a large circle and manages to get around this circle once every four or five days. They generally, unless very hungry, lay around in cliffs and washouts in the daytime and when night comes, come out of their dens and prowl about all night in search of prey.

Find a place where you see his tracks in a cow trail or old deserted road. Watch the place where you have seen his tracks and see if they occur there more than once. If they do, you have found a place where he travels regularly. Now take five No. 4 Newhouse or Hawley & Norton traps, with an eight-inch chain and a good swivel, and a twelve or fifteen-inch pin if the ground is frozen, and if not a twenty-inch pin is none too long. Use one pin for each trap. Take a calf, antelope, or deer hide, tie a six-foot rope to it. Do not touch the hide or traps with bare hands, but use very clean buckskin gloves. They will leave no human scent on traps. Now take your traps and hide and get on a horse and go where the set is to be made. When the place is reached, throw the hide down on the ground, step off on the hide.

Photo by Vasma Brown   The Coyote

You should also have a small piece of hide, one foot square, so you can stand on it with one foot and move the other hide to a convenient spot. Under no conditions get off the hide, as you will then leave a scent. Take the traps and drive the stake of each trap so that when the traps are set they will cover about thirteen feet of the trail. The stakes should be driven so deep that they will not show. The traps must all be buried level with the ground. Put two or three straws over the jaws, then a piece of paper. Now cover them with fine dirt. Cover enough so the paper will not show. When you are through take fine dirt and throw it up in the air so it will light on the covered traps. Make everything so natural that it looks no different where the traps are than it does fifteen feet away from the traps in the trail.

Use no scent. Experience has taught me not to, as it will make him suspicious and he will walk around your traps and your work is all for nothing. When all is ready, get on your horse and pull the hide up. Now the next time he walks along you have got him for it is impossible for him to walk over this set without stepping in one or more traps. This is the only successful set I have ever used or have seen used and works when all others fail.

WM. WEIBEL,
La Porte, Colo.

CHAPTER 17

Foxes Red, White, Black, and Blue

There is no scarcity of well-authenticated instances of this animal's cunning. One of recent occurrence will suffice. A farmer possessed a large number of fine turkeys, which usually roosted in the branches of some tall Scotch firs, immediately adjoining the farm-yard.

Reynard had an eye on them, and made several visits during the moonlight nights, but unsuccessfully, as they were perched too high for him to reach them. He was, therefore, obliged to resort to stratagem, and this was the plan be adopted: He first scratched the ground beneath the tree with his fore-feet, and then the base of the tree itself, in order to attract the attention of the turkeys, at the same time looking up to mark very movement. He then ran round the tree in rapid rings. The turkeys, aware of their danger, followed his quick movements with their eyes, and became confused and dizzy. One fine bird fell to the ground, was instantly killed, and carried off to the earth. The scheme was repeated, with equal success. The loss of turkey after turkey induced the farmer to watch in ambush, and the truth of the stratagem was fully established; but the cunning animal paid the forfeit of his own life, for he was shot dead while decamping with his last booty.

THE various members of the fox family are found in almost all parts of the world but are most abundant in the Northern Hemisphere. There are many species and varieties, but it is those of North America that are of the most interest to the trapper.

Those found on this continent are the red, the gray, the kit and Arctic foxes, and there are a number of varieties of the red and gray species.

The black, silver and cross foxes are supposed to be only color varieties of the red, but why this occurs, and only in the North, is a mystery.

RED FOX

Mounted Specimens. Owned by   NORTHERN SWIFT FOX   NORTHERN RED FOX   Both matured
Andersch Bros.   Winter Furred

The Silver or Black fox is the most beautiful and most valuable of all the foxes. It is found in the high, northern latitudes of both continents. In this country, it is found as far south as the northern tier of states. They are most abundant in the interior of Alaska, the Northwest Territories, Ontario, Northern Quebec, Labrador and Newfoundland.

At the London fur sales, specimens have been sold at over one thousand dollars each, but the average price is probably about two hundred dollars, f Wherever the Silver fox is found, the Cross or Patch fox is found also, and they also range somewhat farther south. They are always found in greater numbers than the Silver variety.

The Red fox is the most common and is distributed over a larger territory than the other varieties. They range from the northern timber line, to well down in the Southern States. They are probably most abundant in the Eastern provinces of Canada and the England States, but they are found in fair numbers in parts of New York, Pennsylvania, West Virginia, Tennessee, Arkansas, Missouri, Michigan and the larger part of Canada and Alaska.

The Gray fox is one of the least valuable, and is most abundant in the Southern States. In the East they range as far north as Connecticut. In some places they have supplanted the Red species, and in other places the grays have disappeared and the reds have taken their place.

The fox, as well as the wolf and coyote, belongs to the dog family. The different species are all practically the same size, but the same varieties vary in size in different localities. The average weight is from nine to ten pounds. In general appearance they somewhat resemble the dog, being rather light of build, considering their height. The ears are erect and pointed, the tail thick and bushy, and the muzzle small and pointed. The fur varies in the different species, being coarse and rather short on the Gray, while that of the Silver fox is extremely fine and soft.

The mating season comes in February, and the young are born usually in April, there being from four to nine in a litter. They make dens in the sand hills and in rocky districts, den in the rocks. Except during the breeding season they spend very little time in the dens, but lie during the day in some clump of brush or weeds, or often on top of a stump or log. In mountainous sections they lie during the day, somewhere on the mountain side and come down into the valleys at night in search of food.

The fox is not strictly a carnivorous animal. When food is scarce they often feed, on apples and other fruits, but their regular food is flesh. They are fond of partridge, rabbits, mice, skunk, muskrat or opossum flesh, carrion of almost all kinds, fish, eggs, poultry, and often they come around the camps and gather up the scraps, bread, bacon rinds etc. If they are given time and not disturbed they become quite bold in coming to such places for food and the trappers sometime take advantage of this peculiarity by baiting them awhile before setting the trap.

The fox in the North becomes prime in the beginning of November and remains in good condition until the middle of March, when the fur begins to take on a rubbed and woolly appearance. In the South they do not become prime until the last of November or the beginning of December and go out of prime in February. Most of the foxes are trapped in the fall before the ground freezes too hard for dry sets, and of course, many of them are not prime.

The traps recommended for the fox, for dry land use are the Nos. 2 and 3 Oneida Jump and Blake & Lamb, the 1½ Newhouse and Hawley & Norton and the No. 2 Victor. For water and snow trapping, the Nos. 3 and 4 Oneida Jump and Blake & Lamb, and the 21½ and 31½ Newhouse will be found most desirable.

No Place Like Home   **RED FOX AND FAMILY**   From a Photograph

In places where there are springs and small streams, there is no better method than the old water set, which is made as follows: It is best to find a spring which does not freeze, but for early fall trapping a brook will do. The rise and fall of the water in small streams sometimes makes trouble, and a spring or small pond gives best results. The spring should be at least four feet in diameter and should be prepared for the set in the summer, but if care is used, may be fixed up during the trapping season. A moss covered stone, or a sod (according to surroundings) should be placed about a foot and a half from shore, and should rise about two or three inches above the water. This is the bait sod. The trap is set half way between the sod and the shore, and the jaws, springs and chain should be covered with mud, or whatever is found in the bottom of the spring.

The pan of the trap should just be covered with water. Now take a nice piece of moss or sod and place it on the pan of the trap, so that it will rise an inch above the water. When properly placed, this sod will look natural and will, apparently be a safe stepping place for the fox. The pan should be so adjusted that it will not spring too easily. A small piece of bait and also some scent should be placed on the larger sod.

In making this set you should wade up the outlet of the spring, and stand in the water while making the set. Do not touch the bank or any of the surroundings. The trap should be fitted with a chain about three feet in length, with a two prong drag attached, but most trappers simply wire a stone of eight or ten pounds weight to the end of the chain. The drag, whatever is used, should be buried in the bed of the spring.

Water Set for Fox.

I recommend the flesh of the muskrat, skunk, opossum or house-cat for bait, and it should be allowed to taint by remaining about a week in a glass jar. This method was first used by William Schofield a famous fox trapper of the Eastern states. Two men have been known to catch over one hundred foxes in a season with this method, besides considerable other furs taken in the same traps, for the method is good for many other animals besides the fox.

One trapper recommends setting the trap in exactly the same manner, except that the bait sod is omitted, and the bait, a bird, is fastened by means of a stick thrust in the bottom of the spring. The stick must be entirely out of sight, and the bird, apparently, floating in the water. Both of these methods are very good, and are especially recommended for the novice, as they are the easiest and surest methods to start on.

The water sets given above, can of course, only be used in certain places, for in some of the best fox countries, springs cannot be found, and even the streams are not suitable for trapping. For this reason many professional fox trappers prefer to use dry land set, and the blind set will be found to be one of the very best.

Look for fox tracks in old stock trails, foot paths, old roads in the woods, openings under fences, etc., and having first cleaned the traps by boiling or washing, find a narrow place in the trail and dig out a nest for the trap. Make this nest so that when the trap is set in it, the jaws will lie lengthwise of the trail. Line this nest with dry grass or leaves, and having attached the trap to some sort of a drag, set it and place it in the place prepared. Fill in all around the outside of the jaws with dry dirt, and cover the springs. Now lay a piece of clean paper over the trap and cover all with about one-fourth inch of dirt, making it look like the other parts of the trail as much as possible. The chain and drag must be carefully concealed.

It is best to have a basket or piece of canvas in which to place the dirt while making the set and to carry away what is not needed. Do not spit near the trap, and do not leave any signs of your presence. It is not necessary to wear gloves, but the hands should be kept clean. This is an excellent method, especially for the old, sly animals.

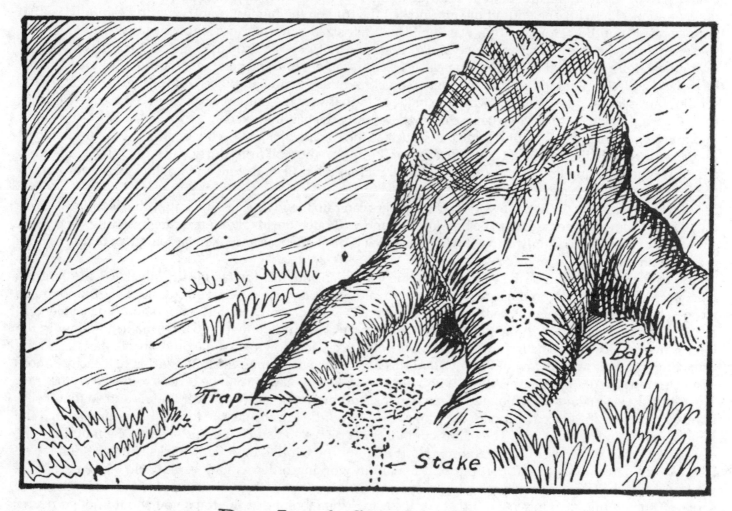

Dry Land Set for Fox.

The professional trappers of the East use the bait method, mostly, and although the different trappers use different baits and scents, the methods of setting the traps are all, practically the same.

Prepare you bait about a week before you want to set the traps, by cutting into pieces about half the size of an egg, and placing in a clean jar to become tainted. Put a little bit of scent on each bait before placing in jar. There are different ways for preparing the traps; most trappers prefer to boil them in hemlock boughs, or lay them over night in running water. Wear clean gloves when handling the traps and carry them in a clean basket. Now find an old stump or a rock along some hillside, and dig a hole under it making the hole four or five inches in diameter and ten or twelve inches deep. Stake the trap solid, driving stake out of sight, and set the trap about ten inches in front of the hole. Cover the trap first with a piece of clean paper and finish by about one-fourth inch of dirt dug out of the hole. It should look as if some animal had dug the hole and scratched the dirt out in front. Use a small shovel made for the purpose, or a sharpened stick to dig the hole, and keep your gloves on all the time. Do not walk around, but stand in the same spot until the set is complete. Now put a piece of bait in the back of the hole, using a sharpened stick to handle the bait and put just a little scent by the side of the hole. When you catch a fox, kill him without drawing blood, and set the trap back in the same place. Your chances for catching another fox are doubled. Skunks, coons and other animals will also be caught in these sets."

The following method is a good one to use in settled countries, as it is not so likely to catch dogs and other animals, as other methods are. Find an ant-hill, a small, pointed knoll, an old rotten stump, a moss covered rock, or an old log with one end off the ground. Set the trap on the highest point, covering carefully, so that it looks just like it did before the trap was set. Place a fair sized bait, such as a skunk or muskrat about eight feet away from the trap. The fox is always suspicious of a bait, especially a large one, and will always get on the highest point to look at it before going close. Of course, there must be no other place for him to get up on, near the bait. In the winter, traps may be set on muskrat houses, and bait placed on the ice. I think it best to set the traps several days before placing the baits, as in that way the human and other scents have a chance to pass away. When baiting, go just close enough to throw the bait into place.

Some trappers set traps around large baits, such as the carcass of a horse, cow or sheep, but I think it best to place the bait by the side of a trail and set several traps on the trail from thirty to seventy five yards from the bait. When feeding on the bait the foxes will travel on the trail, and they will not be looking for danger so far away from the bait.

Comparatively few of the professional fox trappers can trap the fox successfully after the deep snow come on; but the following methods are the best known, and will catch the fox if you use care in setting. Of course, snow sets of any kind can only be used when the snow is dry and loose and likely to remain in that condition for some time.

The first method given is the one used by the Canadian Indians, for taking the silver fox in the great northern wilderness. Out on the ice on some frozen lake, or on any open, wind swept piece of ground, make a cone-shaped mound of snow, beating it solid, so that it will not drift away. The trap should be fastened to a clog, and the clog buried in the mound. Make the mound about two feet high, and make a hollow in the top for the trap to set in. The hollow should be lined with cat-tail down, or some other dry material, and the trap set in the hollow and covered first with a sheet of white note paper, finishing with a half inch or more of loose snow. Do not handle this snow with your hands, for if you do it will be certain to freeze on the trap. The best way is to take a bunch of evergreen boughs, and brush the snow up over the mound so that it sifts lightly over the trap. The covering on the trap should be a little lower than the top of the mound so that the wind will not uncover the trap. The bait is cut into small pieces and stuck into the sides of the mound.

After the trap is set it will only require a short time for the wind to drift your tracks shut and remove all traces of human presence, and the trap will remain in working order as long as the cold weather lasts. If water rises on the ice it will not reach your trap, and if there is a snow storm, the first wind will blow the loose snow off the mound, leaving just a little over the trap. When looking at the traps you should not go nearer than fifty yards, and do not turn off your route, but walk straight by. This is a splendid method for use in the far north where the snow never melts or freezes during the winter months.

For use in the settled countries I have been very successful with this method. Find where foxes travel on old wood roads and with our traps clean, and with drags attached, go and break a trail in the snow by walking back and forth on the road, and set the traps in this broken trail without bait. The traps should be set and covered, as in the other method, and the chain and clog pushed under the snow at the side of the trail. Do not let it appear that you have stopped at all, and when looking at the traps you can follow the trail and step right over the traps. In settled localities, the fox will follow the trail because the walking is better, but in the wilderness where the track of a man is seldom seen, they not only refuse to follow the trail, but often will not even cross it.

I believe that scent is more used for fox trapping than for trapping any other animal. Some of the best trappers, however, do not use any scent at all, but I believe that if the right kind is used, that it is a great help. One of the best scents known for dry land or water sets is prepared as follows: Remove the fat from one or two skunks, chop it fine, and take a sufficient quantity to almost fill an ordinary pickle bottle. Take two mice; cut them up and add to the fat and let the bottle stand in the sun until the mixture is thoroughly decomposed; then add the scent of two skunks and five or six muskrats. The bottle must be kept covered so the flies will not blow it, but it must not be tightly corked. Different trappers have different ways of preparing this scent, but I think this way is the best.

Another very good one is made by allowing the flesh of a muskrat to rot in a bottle, and adding about four ounces of strained honey and one-half ounce of essence of musk,

Pure fish oil is attractive to the fox, and is used by some very good trappers. We believe that one of the most successful scents, especially for winter use is made by taking the generative organs of the female fox, when in heat and preserving it in alcohol. The urine of the fox is also good, but in using these two scents, no bait should be used.

The brine from mackerel or other fish is claimed to be a good scent for foxes, but if there are any porcupines, or snow-shoe rabbits about, it will make plenty of trouble as the salt is very attractive to these animals.

The Red Fox.

When making blind-sets, or when setting on a trail some distance from a bait, do not stake your traps, but fasten to a drag of some kind: a brush, a stone or a grapple. By so doing the fox will not spoil the trail for the next one, and the trap may be set back in the same place. For a bait set on dry land, the trap may be staked to advantage, for if one fox is caught and rolls around over the ground, you are more likely to catch another one there.

Do not start out with a dozen traps and expect to make a success of fox trapping. You should have all the traps that you can look after.

Do not depend on one method of setting, as a fox will sometimes learn your method, but some other method, even if it is not so good, may fool them.

When killing foxes in traps, do so, if possible without drawing blood. One of the best ways is by piercing the heart with a wire dagger. Another good way is by breaking the neck, which may be done as follows: Strike the fox a light blow over the head with a stick, just hard enough to slightly stun him, and when he drops down, place your left hand on the back of his neck, pinning him to the ground and with your right hand pull his nose backward against his back. It requires some practice to do this right.

The track of the red fox resembles that of a small dog, being perhaps a trifle narrower. The length of step is about twelve or fourteen inches, and the foot prints of an average sized fox will measure about one and a half inches in length.

The track of the gray fox is rounder and more like that of a cat.

Some hunters claim that they can distinguish the track of the male fox from that of the female, the footprints of the female being smaller and a trifle narrower in proportion.

There is no difference in the footprints of the black, silver, cross and red foxes.

CROSS FOX

Description: Color varies greatly, from a light red, scantily mixed with grey and black hairs to a darker red, very liberally interspersed with grey and black, especially on the rump. All examples have a black or very dark red band across the shoulders and another along the back. Belly and legs are black, tail bushy, varying in color according to color of body, tip white.

Range: Same as Red Fox, but no further south than Michigan and Wisconsin, in western states as far south as Nevada, Utah and Colorado.

The Cross Fox is merely a color variety of the Red Fox. The foregoing remarks about Red Fox regarding habits, characteristics, difference in quality of Fur, trapping methods, etc., apply equally to the Cross Fox.

However, the Fur of the Cross Fox is more valuable than that of the Red Fox.

Cross Fox should be skinned "cased" shipped Fur side out.

SILVER FOX

Description: Color black, interspersed with silver-grey hairs, underfur dark drab, belly generally black, sometimes a spot of white is found, tail thick and bushy, tip white. Some examples have more, while other less of the silver-grey hairs. Those that have but few or no silver-grey hairs, are called "Black Fox."

Range: Alaska, Canada, Newfoundland, extreme northern United states, also high altitudes of western states.

The Silver Fox is the scarcest of the Fox family, and its Fur is of greater value than any of the others. The black variety (Black Fox), outside of Sea Otter, is the most valuable of the North American Fur-bearers.

On account of the great value of each individual skin, this variety of Fox is being raised in some parts of Canada, especially eastern. However, the farm skins have not the lustre and fineness of Fur possessed by the wild animal, consequently, do not command as high a price.

Like the Cross Fox, the Silver Fox is merely a color variety of the Red Fox, and the remarks about Red Fox regarding habits, characteristics, trapping methods, etc., apply equally to the Silver Fox.

Silver Fox should be skinned "cased" and shipped Fur side out.

GREY FOX

Description: General color grey, the back being covered with long hair of two colors, black and white, underfur is dark drab or blue, throat white, chest and sides reddish, belly white, tail long and silvery, same color as the back, much coarser than the tail of the Red Fox, reddish underneath, tip black.

Range: Entire United States, also British Columbia.

The Grey Fox is more dependent on the forests than the Red Fox, and is very rarely found in a cultivated country, not for the reason that it hates civilization, because the Grey Fox is gifted with much natural trickery and is sly and cunning, but it lacks the amazing shrewdness and wiliness of the Red Fox, and is more easily outwitted by the trapper.

The Grey Fox is smaller than the Red Fox and not as bold and fearless, but equal to the Red Fox in speed and endurance.

They seldom live in burrows, preferring to make their dens in hollow trees and old stumps. Sometimes they like to sleep in the open air and lie hidden among the bushes and undergrowth.

They eat insects, reptiles, rabbits, mice, fish, birds and almost every small creature that lives in the forests. The same baits, scents and trapping methods may be used for the Grey Fox as suggested for the Red Fox. Grey Fox should be skinned "cased" and shipped Fur side out.

KITT FOX

Description: Smallest of all Foxes, general color yellowish-grey above, darker on the back, mixed with longer whitish hairs, under parts white, sides light yellow, tail full, yellowish-grey with longer black hairs, tip black, black patch on each side of muzzle.

Range: Western plains and northward to southern districts of Canada.

The Kitt Fox is a much smaller animal than any of the other Foxes. Its range is restricted entirely to the western plains.

It lives in burrows in open parts of the plains and at a distance from the wooded country.

It is very fleet of foot and is sometimes called "Swift Fox." Kitt Fox should be skinned "cased" and shipped Fur side out.

WHITE FOX

Description: Color pure white, ears and muzzle shorter and less pointed than Red Fox, black nose, underfur varies from ashy to a light drab.

Range: Alaska, Newfoundland, Labrador and extreme northern parts of Canada.

The White Fox is not a lover of solitude, but is fond of company and lives in a community of twenty or more burrows adjoining each other, dug in places where the soil is light and sandy. Here the White Fox lives from year to year, and brings forth its young, from three to five at a time.

It eats lemmings, White Weasel, hare, mice, wild fowl, eggs, etc. In the summer the White Fox lives in luxury, food is plenty and hunting is an easy matter, but the little animal, though it lacks some of the wily shrewdness of the Red Fox, is a very intelligent creature. It realizes that the summer will soon be over and that the lemmings will be safely hidden in their dens beneath ice and snow, and the birds all driven south before the cold. The White Fox knows that it must make provisions for the long winter with its wild snows, screeching gales and intense, bitter cold, so it hunts diligently while game is yet abundant, and brings back the fat lemmings and mice to be packed away in cold-storage for the winter. It burrows down through the light soil until it reaches a temperature just above freezing. (In the land of the White Fox the frost never wholly leaves the ground.) Here it deposits a dozen or more fat lemmings and mice, then it covers them up with grass, roots, moss, sods and light soil. The White Fox establishes a number of these caches and when the summer is at an end and the hour of need arrives, the question of food gives the White Fox no anxiety.

The White Fox is very neat and clean, both in the care of its burrow and its Fur.

Although the White Fox is a crafty little animal, it is not as sly as the Red Fox, and is not as clever in avoiding traps.

The No. 2 trap is about the right size.

For bait, lemming, hare, ptarmigan, etc., may be used.

A good set for White Fox is to make a cone-shaped mound of snow, beating the snow solid, so that it will not drift away. Fasten the trap to a clog and bury the clog in the mound. Make a hollow in the top of the mound, and line with paper. Set a trap in the hollow, place a piece of clean white paper on the trap and cover with loose snow. This snow should not be handled with the hands or it will freeze on the trap. A piece of bait should be cut into small pieces and scattered on the sides of the mound.

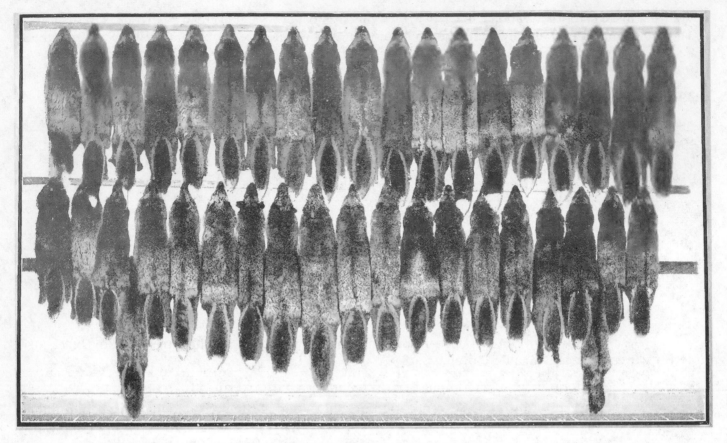

A COLLECTION OF SILVER FOX VALUED AT $17,500 00.

Another good set is to find a bare point, jutting out into a lake or pond, or a clump of bush-growth where the White Fox are known to travel. Pack the snow down a couple of inches, making a small hollow, line it with a piece of paper, and set a trap therein, place another piece of paper over the trap and then dust snow over it until the trap is covered lightly. The trap should be fastened to a stick about three or four feet in length. A trench the length of the stick and about a foot deep is cut in the snow, the stick laid in, covered with snow and packed hard. A piece of bait should be chopped up and scattered around, beginning some distance from the trap and leading to the trap.

White Fox should be skinned "cased" and shipped Fur side out.

BLUE FOX

Description: Same form and size as White Fox, color is slate drab or darkish purple.

Range: Alaska, Newfoundland, Labrador and extreme northern Canada.

The Blue Fox is merely a color variety of the White Fox. Some persons, and even some naturalists, wrongly suppose that the Blue Fox is the same animal as the White Fox, and that a Blue Fox turns white in the winter. This is not true. The Blue Fox does not turn white in the winter, but always remains a Blue Fox.

The form, size, pelt, food, mode of living, habits, etc., of the Blue Fox, are exactly the same as the White Fox, the only difference being the color—the Blue Fox being merely a color variety of the White Fox.

The same bait, trapping methods, etc., may be used for the Blue Fox as are suggested for the White Fox.

Blue Fox should be skinned "cased" and shipped Fur side out.

THE BLUE FOX

This is strictly an Arctic species, and is found in the same see lions as the white and black fox, apparently distinct from them, but resembling them in size and habits. The animal is eagerly sought after, as its fur is quite valuable. The notable difference is entirely in the color of its pelage, being of rather indistinct of bluish hue. There are no blue foxes in the United States.

TRAPPING THE FOX

If every other method fails, the following, if properly done, will crown you with success.

In some out-of-the-way place, which foxes are known to frequent, away from the public road and from dogs, on side of small hill out of view of roads, houses and other places of habitation, drop a load of barn manure from a wagon or sled but do not step off the wagon or sled. In unloading the manure make a round pile somewhat flat on top. In a few days drive to the place again and drop from the wagon or sled the stomach and intestines from a freshly butchered hog, sheep or other animal. Place this on top of the pile and slightly cover with manure. Now take two or three fox traps and set them twelve to fourteen inches outside of bait. Before setting traps see that they are in good working order, and either have them soaked in blood or smoke them. Fasten chain to some drag, which may be a limb, piece of fence post or any object weighing ten to fifteen pounds, unless it be a limb, in which case it can be much lighter. Cover every part of the trap and chain with old manure, and take especial pains in covering the trap with fine grass or rotten wood, leaves or feathers, in fact, anything that is light and yielding. If one prefers a few drops of anise oil or other decoy may be used about the trap. Have known foxes to be attracted three or four miles, apparently the wind taking the

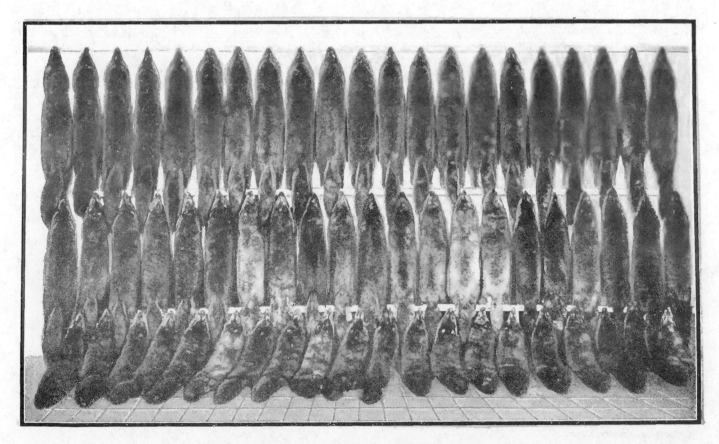

A COLLECTION OF BLUE FOX VALUED AT $8,000.00.

smell such a distance, and where the fox or wolf once sniffs the odor he is sure to locate the bait and of course becomes caught. The manure has a tendency to overcome the human scent, and again, manure piles, such as above described, are natural signs to the animal.

N.C.

TRAPPING THE FOX

Mr. Patrick Laughrey, West Broughton, Canada, uses the following method in trapping foxes: To trap the fox I use a No. 4 B. & L. trap. I usually provide a place to set these traps two or three weeks or a month before time to trap. My favorite place is to go to a small stream or spring and choose a place where there is no bank; take a hoe and dig a place in the side for trap, so that the water will be one and one-half inches deep when trap is set. Place some sod on pan so as to be level with the remaining shore. Then I procure another piece of sod that has long grass on. This I place about twelve inches from the shore in the water. The sod should protrude a little above the water. After making everything natural, I leave the place. In a few days I return and place the bait on the little island and within the tall grass. It is a good policy to sprinkle water all over the set before you leave it the first day. Any bait will do, but I prefer that made as follows:

"Take a quart screw-top jar, into which put the carcass of a muskrat finely cut up. Also the fat of a skunk and their scent bag and the entrails of three field mice. Screw on cover, not too tight and then bury the can in a pile of manure which has heated for three weeks, and leave it for several weeks; then it is ready to use. I usually take a clean stick and smear part of this mixture on the grass or lay some of

Taken from Original Painting   THE BLACK FOX   THE WHITE FOX   Arctic Region
Property of Andersch Bros.

it between the grass on the sod. I assure the trappers that this is a very good bait. Caught twenty-seven foxes last season."

TRAPPING THE FOX

Sir Reynard has not only a very fine scent, but is an exceedingly acute observer. He notices everything that has been moved or laid amiss and cautiously steers clear of all objects that have the least suspicious look; yet for all this, he can be easily trapped in several different ways. By using judgment, and exercising patience, and as the object of this article is to tell how that can be done successfully. I will not dwell on his peculiar characteristics further than is necessary to tell how he can be caught.

One way to bait traps for red foxes is with live rabbits. Make a chain two and one-half or three feet long out of small wire. Put a small leather strap in one end and buckle or tie this around bunnie's neck. Drive a

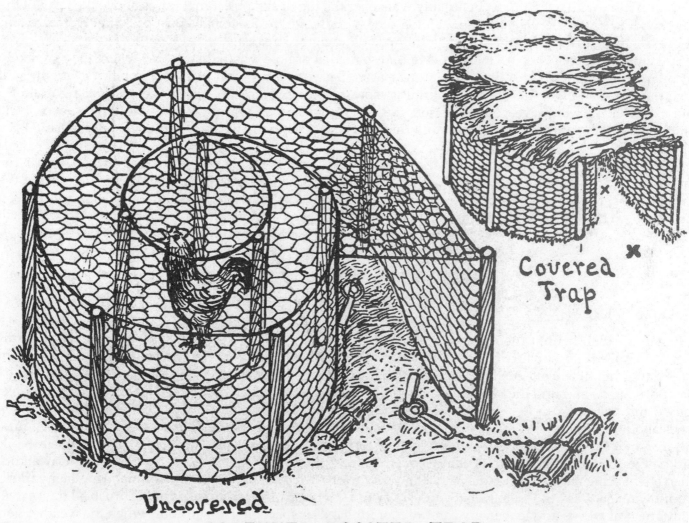

SCREENED ROOSTER TRAP.

An original practical and worthy contrivance, suitable for capturing mink, fox, wolf and other similar sized animals. If this contrivance is placed where wolves, foxes and minks are very numerous, it is well to set additional traps. A snare properly placed immediately at the opening may also be effective, but should be used only in connection with the spring pole. Newhouse No. 1 to No. 2 traps are recommended.

stake in the ground where the fox is in the habit of passing and fasten the other end of the chain to the top of the stake, which should be on a level with the ground to keep the rabbit from winding the chain up. Set one-half dozen steel traps far enough from the stake that the rabbit cannot throw them. When Mr. Fox sees bunnie hopping around, he forgets all danger and makes a rush. In his effort to get the rabbit, he gets in the trap. This method has its drawbacks, as it is difficult to keep a rabbit alive after the second night, if tied by the neck.

Another way of baiting for the red fox, is to go to some stream, where they are in the habit of travelling on the ice. Take a half rabbit, split open lengthwise, and nail or tie it to a stump, log, root, or perpendicular bank, with the lower end resting on the ice. As soon as the ice is sufficiently strong, set a steel trap on the ice in front of the rabbit. The first snow that falls, the fox will take to the ice, stop at your rabbit and get his foot in the trap. It does not matter if there is nothing left of the rabbit except the hide and bones.

Another very good method is to go to some stream where they are in the habit of travelling on the ice. Find a rock that protrudes a few inches above the surface, or a log that lays lengthwise up and down the stream, and half above the water. Set a trap at the upper and lower sides of the rock , or at the ends of the log. Then wait until it snows. Foxes almost invariably walk over the top of any object that raises above the level of the ice when it is covered with snow. A small log can be placed on the ice for this purpose, after it freezes and before it snows. The log should always point up and down the stream.

Still another very successful method is to find some den or hole where they are, or where they are likely to congregate during the running or mating season. Set your traps clear outside the hole, where he will have to walk up to look in. Then wait until it snows. Foxes examine these places especially right after a snow fall. Then if you have your traps set, you get Mr. Fox. Foxes seldom go into these dens, except the females after the mating season is over. But they all visit these places. just before, during, and just after the mating season.

When trapping for foxes. I always use a common No.1½ trap. I always fasten a trap that I set for a fox with wire or a grape vine, ten, twelve or fifteen feet away from the trap and two or three feet from the ground to a springy bush. Never go to a trap that is set for a fox, unless it is absolutely necessary, until you catch the fox. Pass by near enough to see if all is right. Let well enough alone. Have patience and you will be successful.

E. G. ALLDREDGE,
Russellville, Mo.

TRAPPING THE FOX

"I first locate their haunts, then when trapping season is about in (around December 1st). I take a little straw or hay and pile it up, say fifty or one hundred yards from their dens or passes, and burn it. Let it lay two or three days until the burnt smell is gone, then set your traps in the ash pile, as many as you like. I use No. 1½ Newhouse traps and find they are large enough for fox and smaller game. Put ash piles about four or six feet square and five or six inches deep. This makes a good set in all kinds of weather. Set three or four traps in ashes about one or two feet apart and fasten about two traps each to a little pole or stone just big enough so they can move it a little; in this way they are not so apt to get loose. Set traps in form of circle in the ash pile and bait with chicken in centre of ashes, covering your trap lightly with ashes, also your drag or weights. Then strew some feathers around ash pile and over traps, using caution not to spit or make too many tracks around your sets, as Mr. Fox has a cute nose, in fact, he is cute all over; when set is made brush all tracks over with brush or weeds and leave very carefully for Mr. Fox's inspection. He will come when the weather gets cold and stormy, and you will get him sure; try it, boys.

"I have had good luck with this kind of sets, catching twenty odd each winter for the past three winters. Try it, using care in making your sets, and you will have success in catching fox on the prairies of the Northwest."

R. B. A.

Concealed Steel Trap.

CONCEALED STEEL TRAP.

The above is an excellent set for fox, raccoon, also aquatic animals. Set one or two traps on some artificial island, 16 to 18 inches from the shore,, cover in usual manner and place bait on a stick 18 to 20 inches above the set. Attach chain to spring pole or drag. One or more steel traps can be concealed at the nearest approach to the island from which the fox usually jumps to obtain a foothold upon the island. If clog is used same must be buried.

TRAPPING THE FOX

Mr. Martin Brenner, a Minnesota trapper, favors us with the following:

"I have trapped foxes, minks, wolves, etc., in Beltrami county, Minnesota, and I must admit that there is no grander sport than the trapping of foxes. "But, before continuing my narrative, I must say a word or two about myself. I am an old trapper and woodsman with considerable practice.

"In the fall of 1899 I found myself, together with a hunting party, in Beltrami county, and there I saw 'signs' which led me to believe that I could find no better place for my winter trapping.

"I at once sent for a supply of traps, ammunition, etc., and set to work on a cabin. It was slow work, and it was November 15th before it was ready. I then received a goodly supply of traps, ammunition and provisions.

"I now began cutting logs and building log traps, which, as all woodsmen know, was also very slow work. By November 25th I had built eight log traps, seven feet square at the bottom, tapering to four feet square at the top, and five or six feet high. I did this work almost for nothing, as I caught only one fox in them all.

"But log traps were not my only resource. I had ordered two dozen mink traps, one dozen fox traps and one dozen otter traps with teeth. These latter, though the most expensive, proved also the most effective.

"I set traps around the carcasses of foxes and sprinkled thereon a few drops of oil of rhodium and oil of bergamot, mixed half and half. These oils have a wonderful attraction for foxes, wolves, minks, etc., and I once caught four foxes around a fox carcass—all within a week.

"I also caught a great many foxes by setting traps in their holes. I first smeared blood on the traps, and after setting them, sprinkled water all around.

"That winter I caught twenty-seven red foxes, nine cross foxes, nine young foxes, four wolves and seventeen minks. I shot one red fox, one mink, and a number of rabbits and other animals, which I used for food.

"By shipping the furs to the best fur establishments in Minneapolis I realized nearly twice what I could have got in towns near where I camped."

TRAPPING THE FOX

The following fox set has been used by me for the last three years and is original as far as I know. Am also sending you herewith two photos. Have had good success with this earth set and I recommend it to your consideration.

This set can be made in the pasture, fields or in woodland. Choose places as free from small stones as possible; when there are stones, they should be carefully picked out, as they are very apt to catch between the jaws of the trap and prevent them shutting close.

The sod and stones should be removed from a place eighteen inches in diameter and with a hoe, or some tool, dig, chop, and work the dirt until you have it fine, and free from all roots, sticks, etc., to a depth of six inches. The finer the dirt, the better. Have a piece of cloth of some sort three or four feet square to put sods, stones, etc., on. When the bed is finished take up the cloth by the four corners and carry away to a distance, say ten rods, and dump in some inconspicuous place.

Beds should be made several days before setting traps. In placing the trap, set it at a distance; have everything you will need with you; walk directly to bed. Dig a hole in the center deep enough to hold grapple, chain and trap. Place the creeper with one prong down on bottom of hole and press down till the other two prongs lie flat on bottom, coil chain top of creeper, put in a little dirt, and bed trap firmly in this. Put a little paper, leaves, or something over trap to keep out loose dirt, then gently level over the whole trap, about one-half inch of dirt. Smooth the whole bed level with bush or stick; drop four or five drops of decoy six or eight inches from, and on each side of trap. Now pass *straight oil* to next trap. Do not move the feet, or step about, while making the set. Walk up, stop, and *stand still* while you work. All movements leave signs that are hard to efface.

Decoy: To one ounce of pure, home-made trout oil, add ten or twelve drops of skunk musk, and the scent glands of two or three muskrats (males, and must be taken in the springtime). When tending traps, go only near enough to see that everything is all right. If trap is gone, there will be a distinct hollow in bed. The B. & L. No. 3 or 4 is especially good for this set.

L. J. WRIGHT,
Collinsville, Conn.

TRAPPING THE FOX

In order to trap foxes in snow, you must first find where they travel or the places where their traces are most numerous. Look up and down old wood roads, and in and around swampy places. When you are sure you have found where they frequent most, follow along their tracks until you come to a small bush or tree twenty or thirty feet away from their path. Notice the bush and the surroundings carefully so you can find it when you come to set your traps. As soon as you feel a snow-storm coming, take three or four Blake & Lamb traps, and a hen, or leg of a horse or cow, and cut some limbs four to six feet long with the branches about three inches long to fasten your trap chain to for a drag. Go to the bush and tie your bait securely about twelve inches from the ground and about ten feet away set your traps forming a circle. Dig out the snow just deep enough to set your trap in. Put large, dry leaves in the bottom of the trap hole and set the trap on top, also put leaves on top of trap and brush just enough snow over it to cover lightly. Cover the chain and lay clog or drag in the snow out of sight. Set your traps about ten feet apart, forming a circle around the tree. Now about one hundred feet away put a few drops of scent on some old dry limb, up as high or highter than your head if you can.

Take some muskrat's musk, and mix it well with foxes' musk and honey. This is a good scent.

Now, when the snow comes, it will cover your traps, and tracks, and the scent will entice the foxes in there, and when they are there, they will be attracted by the bait. If they are hungry, they will walk around and around it, coming closer each time around, and are very liable to step in one of the traps. Attend your traps about every other day and don't go any closer to the traps than you can help. The farther you keep off, the quicker you will catch foxes. Take plenty of time in fixing your traps, and use care about smoking and spitting around or near the setting.

ED. BREHMER,
Spring Valley, Minn.

TRAPPING THE FOX

L. M. Pickens, Mooresville, Tenn., writes: "For trapping foxes around pastures and fields, the following method can be relied upon, and is familiarly known as the path method:

"Look for fox tracks in stock paths, about the fields, pastures and woods, old roads not much used, places under fences, gullies and washouts, sand-bars along the streams, and chances are you will see fox tracks going and coming. Then select narrow places and dig a pit just the size of trap to be used, having the springs laid lengthwise in the path or trail—not across it—just deep enough so the trap will be a little below the surface level when put in the pit. Cover over the springs and around the outside of jaws with soft dirt, put wool, cotton, or soft dry moss inside of jaws and under pan, or lay flat leaves, thin paper or a small piece of cloth over entire trap, then pulverize fine some dirt and sprinkle enough over the trap to entirely conceal it, always finishing to look natural as before the set was undertaken. Complete the set by laying a dead weed an inch or two from the trap so the fox will step over it and into the trap. Fasten your chain with bailing wire to the middle of a green cut limby brush, the size and length of a hoe handle, and conceal the chain. No bait to be used."

5 Red Foxes

Excellent Result
Courtesy of Nat. Sportsman

TRAPPING THE FOX

"Here is my method of catching and trapping the red fox. It may seem queer, but nevertheless it is very effective.

"Take a common house cat—whether it is your wife's pet or not, doesn't make any difference. Tie a wire around the cat's neck, either before you kill it or after the cat is dead. Then roast the cat with the skin on over an outside fire until the cat is fairly roasted, being brown and juicy. Then insert in a sack and carry it until you are in the vicinity of the place that you anticipate setting your trap. Then drag the bag in various directions about the trap, and proceed to make a hole about six inches deep, into which insert the cat, leaving part outside. Cover portions below the surface with earth and make a small mound around the other portion, leaving an opening in the centre, so as to make the appearance similar to a gopher hole. Now take two No. 2 steel traps, fasten to a stick driven in the ground or to a clog, both covered up and made invisible. Place one trap over the hole, covering up both springs and placing a little dirt on pan. The other trap set on windward side. The fox will go at bait from that side. Remember to cover the trap up and leave the surroundings very smooth, so as to be natural. In case of snow, don't go near the trap until it is sprung unless you have reasons to believe that the setting is not proper or frozen under. The trap night not be touched for some few days, but generally the fox seeks the bait after a little snow.

"In my time I have caught over one hundred red foxes—nineteen of them last year. My fifteen years' experience certainly amounts to something. Tell your friends about, it but don't use my name."

TRAPPING THE FOX

"I thought I would write a little of my experience in hunt-and trapping the fox." writes Mr. A. Carpenter, of Witoka. Minn.," as I have made it a business for several years past, and know something about their habits.

"I have made a business of still hunting without any dog, and have made good success of it in the Southeastern part in the State of Minnesota, where the foxes are very plentiful in the bluff country along the Mississippi River and Root River Valleys; both red and grey foxes are found here.

"I start in the morning after a new snow and go out over the hills until I strike a fresh fox track. Then follow it until have got on the bluffs, for no care is needed in being quiet while the fox is running on the flat. There is where he goes to hunt for mice, of which he is very fond, especially the common meadow mole or grass mole, which also makes very good bait to use in trapping. This is also a safe bait to put out with poison in, as dogs will not touch it. The right amount of poison to use is about one dram bottle to six baits, if moles are used for bait. As the mouse will freeze very hard, it takes more poison to do the work

UNCOVERED STEEL TRAP SET.

An easily constructed contrivance, having a live rooster, hen, squirrel or rabbit for bait. If properly made and placed no better all-around set exists for capturing the barnyard thief, as well as raccoon, skunk, mink, and is suitable for all animals possessing carnivorous habits. The steel traps should be covered, also the clog. Use No. 1½ Newhouse traps. If set for wolves or foxes, a larger size trap must be used.

quickly, and if that amount is used he won't go over 40 rods from where he eats the bait. I killed 55 last winter this way. "But to go on with hunting the fox. After the leaves the flat and goes on the hill or brush, then some care is needed in going still, and if you see the fox is walking you can make up your mind the fox will not go much further before he lies down and he is almost sure to lie down in a bunch of red grass or in hazel brush, if there is any to be found, and always on the south side of the bluff or point. If there is neither brush nor grass, he is pretty sure to lie down behind some small stone, with his back against it so he can't be seen from the lower side of the hill and so he can watch the upper side and his back tracks. Consequently, lots of care is needed to move quietly, for they are very quick to hear and very cunning. I have known a man to walk up within two or three rods of one and then scare him up and yet never see him sneak away in almost clear ground for 20 rods, and without the hunter knowing that he is quite apt to do, he will always lie down with his nose pointing down hill, and it is easier to get up to him by coming down the point on him.

"In trapping them the best way is to take a sack of oat straw or chaff and throw down in their paths or where they run frequently, and after it has been there for a week or so, the foxes will be sure to come there to play and look for mice. You want to set the traps in the chaff and cover them and the clogs with chaff, and you will be sure to catch some foxes this way. Powdered fetty is a very good thing to put on the traps and around the chaff, as they like the smell of it. About the first of January catch a female fox and cut the entire sexual part, which smells very strong and drag it along over traps and around the bait, and the male fox will be sure to follow it.

"Well, I have written about all the main points I have found out through experience in my hunting and trapping the fox for the last six or seven winters, and what I write here I know to be true and I hope it will prove to be of some value to my fellow friends."

TRAPPING THE FOX

Mr. G. Halvorson, of Arvilla, writes that he has been very successful in trapping. Read what he says below:

"Have been very successful in trapping foxes. Procure a dead horse or colt, drag it to a place where red foxes are known to roam. Leave it there for a time until you have evidence of foxes partaking therefrom. Then is the time to set your traps about the animal; attach each trap to a clog or drag (must not be too heavy). Cover with weeds, grass and snow. I'll bet my farm that a No. 1 imitation Newhouse trap will not hold him every time.

"Other times when setting traps, I use ashes from burnt wheat straw. I take a piece of newspaper, just enough to cover the trap, and sprinkle ashes about one inch on the paper which covers the steel trap. On top of this I take snow and just sufficient to make everything look natural.

"I've caught foxes in traps set in a pile of ashes. They come to a burnt straw stack because large numbers of mice are generally found there, and these the foxes eat with a relish."

TRAPPING THE FOX

Elsewhere will be found his article on skinning the red fox.

Note the article below from G. Miller, of Conway, about red foxes.

"The trap should be well smeared with blood or beeswax to destroy the odor of the iron. Set it in soft earth, packing moss or leaves lightly around the pan and jaws. Bait with fried meat. To make the allurement doubly sure, obtain from the female of the dog, fox or wolf the matrix in the season of coition and preserve it in alcohol, tightly corked. Leave a small portion of it on something near the trap, also when visiting the traps put some on your boots.

"Another method is to make a bed of chaff in the open field in a locality the fox frequents, but when it will be least likely to be visited by passing hunters. Visit it daily and stir into chaff every old scrap of meat made fine or toasted cheese, using utmost caution not to change the appearance of the bed or its surroundings, and make as few tracks as possible. The materials of which the bed is composed should not be handled any more than is absolutely necessary. Too much care cannot be taken in making the beds, for if foxes are plenty and you get several to visit it, it will last for sometime and will afford you a great deal of amusement. As soon as you are satisfied the fox has visited the bed regularly for five or six nights you may put in your trap. It should be fastened to a clog light enough for a fox to drag, but heavy enough so that he cannot get too far away, though if there is no snow on the ground there will be some difficulty in finding him if he goes some distance. He may be caught the first night, but more likely than not, will dig out your trap or show his contempt in some other way, compelling you to bring into force all your ingenuity before your efforts are successful.

TRAPPING THE FOX

J. Stephen, of Hart, writes the following on foxes:

"I will give you my two best methods of catching Reynard, The Fox.

"First find a place in the woods where there is a fox run-way and follow it until you come to a small knoll or where there has been a tree turned out and rotted away: then as a fox most always leaps over it, set your trap just under the snow on the opposite side, and as he jumps over he is quite likely to jump into one of your traps (it is a good plan to have about three).

"Another good method is to take about four good traps (I use Newhouse), and go where there has been something killed (the slaughter house is a good place), and soak your traps in the blood. Then take a hen (one that is dead will do), and drag it along the trail until you come to where he goes through some bushes. Then hang the hen up by a wire around her head; set your traps under the snow, or under the ground, and cover them with leaves or grass so that all looks natural. When the fox comes along he sees the hen; he lies down on the ground about five minutes and watches the hen, then jumps for her neck, which he gets, and the hunter gets the fox."

TRAPPING THE FOX

From Sherwood Shattuck, of Pepperell, Mass., we have the following:

"I find the senses of foxes are acute, especially those of hearing and of smell: their limbs are exceedingly pliant, and their tail is so flexible that they can roll it around their nose. They are shy, cautious, exceedingly cunning and patient.

"This is the way I catch the fox: One of the most attractive objects to the four-footed midnight marauder is a well-stocked hen-roost, and its attractiveness may be turned to good account by turning the tables on the fox, mink, skunk, or, indeed, any animal that has a constitutional predilection for poultry. The following ingenious but very simple arrangement will be found entirely successful in not only fully protecting the chickens, but also rendering the capture of the intruder sure. The contrivance consists of two parts, independent of the trap. The first is a box without a lid, and one of its ends taken out. This is inverted as seen in illustration, and a piece of the bottom cut away at one end, corresponding in size to the inside measurement of another similar, but smaller, box; this latter is also without lid, open at one end (see illustration), and large enough to furnish a place for a dead hen. This smaller box constitutes the second part of the affair; instead of a lid it is fitted with laths or slats across the width, the ends of the slats being secured to cleets nailed one on each side along inside of the box. To make these arrangements available, the larger box is placed on the ground inverted, with its open end against and inclosing the entrance to the hen-roost—the latter being allowed to remain invitingly open. Inside the box, and just facing the entrance, a steel trap is placed, set for effective service, and lightly covered with buckwheat shucks. Smoke trap by burning hens feathers to prevent smell of steel, as foxes have a keen scent, as has already been said. The chain of the trap is attached firmly to the ground. A chicken is next placed inside the smaller box, and this inverted exactly over the hole which has been made in the bottom (now the top) of the larger box. Any enterprising fox, or other hen-roost thief, passing by will take advantage of the open entrance, survey with feelings of unmixed satisfaction the chicken overhead, take just one step nearer to secure his prey, to find his whole energies enlisted in fruitless endeavors to depart, without his anticipated feast, his captivity rendered almost unendurable by the tantalizing sight of his supper 'so near and yet so far.' I use No. 3 Newhouse traps for foxes."

TRAPPING THE FOX

How an Idaho trapper captures the grey fox:

"Find some trail where the fox is most apt to pass along, empty a gallon of wood ashes out in a round pile and set your trap in the centre of the pile. The fox is sure to step in the ashes for I have never seen it to fail. The only kind of bait I ever use for trapping fox is burnt meat skins; that will attract their attention for

DEADFALL FOR WILDCAT, LYNX, RACCOON, FOX AND WOLF.

The above log trap is inclosed with sticks driven into the ground, with an opening of sufficient size permitting the entrance of wild cat, lynx, raccoon, fox, wolf, and, if log is of sufficient size and weight, for bear. Set figure four arrangement with care and place bait on spindle. For bait use meat, honey, and, if consistent, smear spindle with some of the preparation elsewhere noted in this Guide.

a long distance. The kind of traps used for fox are the No. 11/2 single spring Newhouse trap; if smaller than 11/2 trap is used don't fasten trap solid, but fasten to small stick or block of wood, so when the fox leaps it will give without pulling off his foot."

TRAPPING THE FOX

"My favorite dry land set for fox is to find some stump or some opening V shaped on the bottom, which I carefully clean out; and into which I set my trap. For bait, I generally succeed by nailing a piece of meat, such as muskrat or bird at the farthest end. Leave the surroundings in the most natural condition and always place some cotton or fleecy material beneath the pan.

My favorite water set for the fox is to find some spring, make an artificial island 10 to 15 inches from the shore. This I sometimes makes as early as July or August. The reason I choose a spring is that the water is about the same level the year round. Trap should be set on a flat stone and on top of this stone place sod two or three inches thick, but remove sufficient to hold trap so that when the trap is covered it is just even with the upper part of the sod. Place some soft material below the pan, and cover trap with grass which can be weighted down with small quantity of earth. Springs can bee covered with a thin layer of sod. The entire island thus formed should not be more than six to seven inches wide and everything below the water as much as possible excepting the pan. For bait I use piece of muskrat or bird, freshened up with some fish oil or natural scent of the female of the fox or dog. This I place on a stick beyond the trap so that the animal in endeavoring to get at the bait places his forefeet on the island where the trap is set.

J. C. O'REILLY.

TRAPPING THE FOX

Another good way to trap Mr. Reynard, especially if he is bait shy, is to set a trap near some tree or stump, if you happen to find the path of the fox and there is no tree or stump in the neighborhood, drive in a stake or a fence post a yard or two from the path. Set your trap 14 to 16 inches from the stump, tree or stake. Prefer to use two or three traps.

Now obtain from the dog a quantity of urine, which pour on the stake. The fox being of the dog kind, has the same habits as the dog, and when passing along will run up to the stake, tree or stump to urinate, and of course becomes a victim. If a tree, stump or stake is unhandy, use a boulder or flat stone; the latter should he set in the ground edgewise.

After you have succeeded in capturing one fox, especially if it should be a female, after skinning, save the animal's urine, which you will find in the bladder; run it in a bottle and use same at the

Gray Fox Skin
Kitt Fox Skin   Red Fox Skin   Gray Fox Skin
                                         Swift Fox Skin

various places where traps are set. E. L. S. After you have satisfied yourself of the kind of decoy to use, take an auger (1/2 to 1 inch), and start out to where foxes are known to run. Ascertain some old stump that has been sawed off, into which bore a hole and fill with the prepared scent or decoy. This hole is usually bored in center of stump. The fox will naturally put his front feet on the stump and endeavor to procure the decoy with his mouth or lick same with his tongue. The steel trap should be about a foot away from the stump, and he will either spring it with his front or hind fact. It is a good idea to have numerous sets in a vicinity of this kind, and if a stump cannot be found, bore a hole in some log or tree.

M. C. A

TRAPPING THE FOX

Many trappers will laugh at me when I tell them that in my experience of trapping, on more than one occasion have I set my traps upside down. They may look funny, but it is true nevertheless.

I remember distinctly 12 or 15 years ago the first time I had trouble in capturing a fox. I found his den and set a No. 3 trap in the usual way, only to find every little while the trap disturbed, either by being many feet away from the place where it was set or turned upside down, and quite a number of times the fox watered upon it. The fox on that morning had thrown the trap on one side of the hole and evidently had tried to cover it up with earth. I asked an old grey-headed trapper what to do, and he told me to set the trap upside down in the locality where I had set it previously, and sure enough the next morning the trap hold the front foot of a red fox. Of course I did not see how he disturbed the trap, but I reasoned that he uprooted the trap with his nose and then pawed it away. There was no sign on the animal that he was captured before. Have heard other trappers say that occasionally they have the same trouble with mink, and by turning the traps

STONE DEADFALL.

This arrangement was used by our forefathers, and history records its use many hundreds of years ago. It is very simple, and if properly arranged becomes one of the surest methods of killing small animals that we know of. Now sparingly used.

upside down, are able to capture them. Have set Newhouse traps over a hole with pan downwards and more than once caught mink that way. Would recommend trappers who have experienced like trouble to try this method.

WILL HENDRICKS.

TRAPPING THE FOX

This animal, like the wolf, is hard to capture or trap. It belongs to the dog or wolf family, and is carnivorous in its habits. The different variations number as high as twenty-one, but in this country eight species are commonly known to the hunter and general public, though naturalists claim as many as thirteen varieties on the western continent. As they resemble each other closely in appearance, habits, kind of food, and all possess unusually fine sense of smell, sight, hearing, and are rapid in locomotion, we shall not endeavor to place the different species when it comes to capturing the animal for the pelt or to kill for other reasons, under various headings, but under one common and generally applicable rule.

The fox can be caught in various ways, and with many different traps and ingenious appliances, common to the hunter and trapper, especially of the frontier days.

Steel traps are now commonly used; the No. 2 trap is preferable and sufficiently strong to hold any full-grown animal, though in localities where such game as lynx, wild cat and wolf exist, larger traps should be set. It is advisable in all cases, to smear the trap and chain with blood, beeswax, lard, etc., to prevent the smell of iron from alarming the animals. The chain should be attached to a clog weighing about eight to ten pounds, and be buried the usual depth. Loose bits of earth, or what is still better, wood ashes, should be strewn over the excavated portion under which the traps are buried. The smell of the ashes, especially if wet, often is sufficiently strong to overcome the smell of iron.

Traps should be nested by having three to five traps to one bait. It is advisable to set the traps on an elevation; some knoll or high ground will answer admirably.

Birds, skinned muskrats, or other small, freshly skinned or bleeding animals, will answer for bait; the latter should be fastened so as to detain the fox, and should he endeavor to pull at the bait or walk around it, the chances of his springing a trap is greatly increased. Occasionally two traps are sprung in his frantic endeavors to free himself. It is advisable to set a trap slightly in or just before a hole or excavation to or from which tracks lead; should the animal be absent, most likely he will return the following night. Bury the trap and clog in the usual manner, and smear a little of the musk or matrix from the female fox above or beyond the trap, but not on the trap, chain or clog.

An experienced trapper informed me then he was very successful in catching foxes by tying a live bird or mouse in the center of a nest of four No. 3 traps. The nice were caught in small wire traps, and

RED FOX AND WILD CAT SKINS

then a light brass or aluminum chain was tied with linen thread to one of their feet, likewise to the bird's, one or both fastened in center of nested traps and left to the mercy of the game. Sufficient nourishment was left with the mouse or bird, to prevent starvation. It is wise to try this plan, but in our judgment, a chicken or a duck would be more acceptable, especially, if the fox has frequented the roost, and the farmer or trapper desires to risk another fowl in order for the thief to become the victim.

Wool, moss, leaves, deer hair, cotton and the like, should be placed beneath the pan and around the jaws. A horse's tail or piece of sheep pelt should be used to brush away loose bits of earth from the excavation, also in visiting traps, especially when the trap was accidentally sprung, it is advisable to attach a piece of sheep skin or other fur to the boots and approach the traps in this manner. In handling traps or working about them, and in the act of setting, always wear gloves; some trappers smear their gloves with blood or decoy.

If meat be placed about the traps in small chunks, it is preferable that same is fried. Honey bait about the trap answers well, and is sometimes more successful than meat bait. Some trappers drag a piece of frest meat or poultry about the trap with the intention of leading game to it. The bait is often placed on a stick about two feet above the traps. A European Jager (licensed hunter) placed a steel trap near to a flowing spring in about two inches of water the surroundings were cleared of moss, stones, etc., and the bait arranged so that the fox would naturally step with his front feet on the pan, which was covered with moss, to keep from wetting his feet, thus springing the trap and becoming the victim.

A spring pole can be used advantageously, especially if the traps cannot be visited every twenty-four hours. Some of the northwestern farmers are unusually lucky in ridding their ranch or farm of wolves and foxes, also making a little spending money during the dull winter months, by setting traps and capturing these animals. The traps are set in various places, and both steel and deadfalls are used. The former is buried in the usual manner, and instead of being covered with earth, leaves and the like, the excavations are covered with manure taken from hen coop, which is strewn about, while the musk of the female fox, wolf or dog, taken during the mating season, is smeared about the deadfall trap.

Many farmers and trappers use the deadfall very advantageously while others prefer to snare such game in the old fashion. If snares are to be used it is advisable to attach same to spring poles.

Whenever opportunity presents the fox can be killed with a rifle, as the pelt is not damaged extensively, and seldom grades as damaged with the fur dealer.

This animal can also poisoned with stryclmine, but as a rule shuns such bait, unless exceedingly hungry. The author has known poisoned bait to lie for twenty to thirty days undisturbed, although the fox has frequented and even watered in the vicinity without disturbing same, but shortly thereafter a heavy snow storm set in, and as food was scarce, the fox scratched for the bait, which he easily located, ate same and his corpse was found within twenty-five yards. The poison should be mixed with a little honey or lard and a dose inserted in a piece of meat; five to ten such pieces should be strewn about. If you have reason to believe that one of these pieces was devoured, look carefully in the vicinity and you are sure to find the corpse.

Some of the most successful methods of catching the Fox are the following:

To prevent the smell of iron from alarming the game the trap should be thoroughly smeared with blood, which can be done by holding it under the neck of some bleeding animal and allowing it to dry. Or for the same purpose, it may be heated and covered with beeswax, which at the proper temperature will readily run all over the trap and chain. It should be set near the haunts of the Fox. A bed of ashes, chaff or light earth should conceal the trap, and it should be fastened to a movable clog or bush of six or eight pounds weight, as heretofore directed. Wool, moss, leaves or some other soft substance should be packed lightly under the pan and around the jaws. The surface of the earth in the neighborhood should be brushed with a feather or bush, so that all will seem natural. Scraps or small pieces of fried meat, rolled in honey, should be scattered over the bed of the trap, except where the pan is. Care should be taken to erase all footprints. To make the allurement doubly sure, obtain from the female of the dog, fox or wolf the matrix in the season of coition, and preserve it in a quart of alcohol tightly corked. Leave a small portion of this preparation on something near the trap; and then, putting some of it on the bottom of your boots from time to time, strike large circles in two different directions, leading round to the trap. A piece of bloody meat may be drawn on these circles at the same time. The Fox on striking this trail, will be sure to follow it round to the trap and be caught.

Fox Skins

Another method practiced by woodsmen is to set the trap in a spring or a small stream that does not freeze over in winter, placing it about half an inch under water, and covering the space within the jaws with a piece of moss that rises above the water. A bait of meat should be placed in such a position that the Fox, in taking it, will be likely to put his foot on the moss, to prevent wetting it. The essence of the skunk is sometimes used in this case, in connection with the bait, with good effect; but most trappers prefer the preparation in alcohol, above mentioned.

Another good way is to obtain from the kennel of some tame Fox (if such can be found) a few quarts of loose earth taken from the place where animal is accustomed to urinate. Set your trap in this material, and bait and smooth the bed as before. The Fox, cunning as he is, is not proof against such attractions.

There seems to be quite a rivalry amongst old trappers as to the best methods of taking Foxes. Most trappers have thought that they were suspicious of the smell of iron and steel, and that the trap must be smoked, or covered with blood or beeswax; but another tells of a Fox going through a field, under a harvesting machine, under a wire fence, and following the tracks of a steel-tired wagon. So it is probably the human scent on the traps or paths that warn the Fox. If every care is taken to remove all human scents or odors this animal can be taken with almost or quite the certainty experienced with others.

It is good practice to make a trap-bed and get the Foxes baited to it before petting the traps. When it is found that they are coming and eating the meat left on the bed, set the trap in the center of a cleared and smoothed space, eight or ten feet square covering it with wood ashes if practicable, and scatter more bait skillfully around but not on the trap. Fasten the trap to a bush, clog or light piece of pole, so that the Fox can run a little way with it. Then he will not disturb the bed, which can be used over and over again.

A Massachussetts trapper says in a letter to us: "In my 51 years of trapping I have always used skunk meat and never closed a season with less than 200 to 300 Foxes. I use 400 traps, but I never go to my traps without first putting on wooden shoes or a new pair of rubber boots. I also bury my bait in the earth for five or six days before using. Then instead of handling it with my hands I have a hook with which I take it out of the ground, using the same means to place it near the trap."

PRACTICAL SUGGESTIONS BY TRAPPERS

—Honey mixed with your scent will prevent its evaporating rapidly.

—Where Foxes are eating carcasses of dead cattle or other animals, set your trap carefully, covering it with feathers, wool, hair or chaff.

—Set two traps a few feet apart in a furrow plowed for the purpose through a buckwheat field. Place some bait or scent in the furrow between the traps.

—Musk glands from several muskrats put in a bottle with a lot of angleworms and hung in the sun through the summer will make a good scent for Foxes.

—During the summer lay tree limbs across cow paths in the woods and pastures. On either side of these obstructions will be good places to set traps without bait in the Fall.

—Find a carcass or put one in some spot in the woods or field within a few yards of a stump and set your trap on top of the stump. The Fox will get up on the stump to look the situation over.

—Half a pint of skunk's oil, the musk glands of a muskrat and the scent bag of a skunk, make a good Fox scent.

—The brine off a mackerel kit, scattered where you intend to set a trap makes a good scent

—Foxes like to walk and play on fine sand, and if you can find a bed of it which has been washed down, follow this plan: Take an old beef's head, or a hind leg, or a dead chicken or turkey, for bait, and partly bury it in the sand, letting some part stick out. Drive a stake close to the bait and set three or four traps spread out as far as the chains will permit when fastened to the stake, digging a little bed in the sand for each trap. Cover the traps and chains lightly with sand. Better put a little bunch of cotton batting under the pans of the traps. Then take a small bush and brush out all your tracks, and smooth sand over traps.

—Foxes are quite likely to use old cow and sheep paths, especially those leading around swamps or water. By scattering a little scent at points where you set your traps in or beside such paths the chances of a catch are good. Foxes, like dogs, are very apt to stop and urinate on any little mound or rise of ground when following such a path, and by setting a trap or two on the mound you may catch one. Cover the trap with a few dead leaves, or with dry grass, or rotten wood.

—If you wish to be real cunning and foxy yourself, try setting three traps, one in such an old path without any covering, and one on each side of it skillfully covered. The Fox will give all his attention to the uncovered trap and by going around it may step into one of those on the side.

—We have previously described a "water-set" for Foxes, where a bit of moss or turf is placed on the trap pan to tempt the Fox to step on it as he crosses the water. In this case see that the pan does not trip too easily. Better have it go hard enough so that if the fox tests it first by putting his foot on lightly it will not spring. Then, feeling that it is safe for him, he will trust his weight on it and get caught.

AN ELABORATE SET

First, I find a level spot of ground, at least twelve feet square; then I cut four green poles about seven feet long, the thickness of which must be three inches for the fox, four for the coyote, and five for the wolf. I take soil and bed these down level with the surface, in as nearly a perfect square as my eye can measure. I then cut the sod back beside the poles as neatly as possible, and put all the dirt not used in the center of the square. If I have any long grass (leaves will do), I make a hive-shaped heap in the center of the square, with base about eighteen inches from poles at all points. This done, I take four-one inch boards, about one foot wide and three feet long, and place a trap on each board, set, with a spring adjusted so as to let the pan be level. Now mark around bed-plate and spring, with pencil and cut out to fit the trap, leaving the jaws, to rest solid on the surface of the board, while the bed-plate and springs are let into their respective notches, so as not to hamper the springs in any way, but to hold the trap firmly in position.

Use one board for each trap and place at center of each pole so as to bring the trap, when in its notch, about half way between the pole and the grass or leaves. The surface of the board should be low enough to allow the covering on the trap to come level with the surface of the surroundings.

These boards are used to prevent the animals from turning the traps, which the wolf and the fox are both good at. They can be put into place easier, if done before the grass is put into the square. I always cut my boards so as to leave the chain end of the spring about an inch out beyond the edge of the boards. If one has no boards, use a forked branch, adjusting the trap so it will be guarded on both sides by a limb about two inches in diameter and two or three feet long.

After you have done this, let the place rest at least three days. Then get your jack-rabbits, if you can, partly peel them and put a skin on each one of your feet when you go in the vicinity of the setting. Put your gloves on before handling either bait or traps.

Have traps clean as a pin, walk right up to the side of the square and place a trap in each form and wire fast to each pole. This done cover traps and chain with fine grass. Lift off grass-pile to a height of about eighteen inches and lay a jack, or some other fresh meat on the edge of the heap next to each trap. Drive a stout stake in the center of the heap, and wire bait fast to a stake, covering up well with part of the heap you lifted off.

W. EARLY.

—Use a Newhouse regular fox trap No. 2. Use no bait or scent, but just carefully set the trap. First examine the stock paths in these pastures some morning; or if there is an old road on the farm look for the tracks there, also look in places under the gates and fences and in the gullies. If you see a fox track, that is evidence that he is traveling. Select a narrow place in the road, path or gully, and commence your work with a ready-sharpened, hardwood stick, using it to dig a hole the size of your trap and deep enough so that the pan and jaws will be a little below the surface. Cover the springs and all around the outside of the jaws, with some of the dirt you have dug up. That conceals the trap except the pan and inside of jaws. Cover these up with some good flat leaves or some paper. Then pulverize some of the remaining dirt and sprinkle over the leaves or paper until none of these can be seen. Take a small weed and smooth over your trap which completes the set. Lay a dead weed or a stick the size of your thumb on each side of the trap say, four or six inches away, and my word for it you will get the first Fox that comes along. Cut a bush and wire your trap to it securely.

B.P. PICKENS.

—I harnessed up the old nag and drove over to Plymouth to the house of a friend who kept a tame Fox.

There I got a box full of dirt out of the cage where he kept him. That afternoon taking my 2½ instead of Jim's , I went down to the pasture and chopped a hole in the sod and set the trap in it and then covered it with the earth I had brought and set the No. 2 traps as before, all around it; then I placed the bait and went away.

The next morning Jim and I went to look at the traps. We found them all sprung and the bait gone as usual but the trap set in the earth was gone.

We skirted the field and finally found the wise old Fox tangled in a bunch of briers with my No. 24½ firmly snapped on his hind leg.

—A good winter-set can be made in a spring that does not freeze up. The first thing is to hoe it out well, observing carefully the surroundings. Leave a piece of moss or grass, whichever grows in the spring, to put your bait on and get some of the same to place on and cover the pan of your trap, letting it come just above the water. The trap should be set a few inches from the shore with the bait just beyond. Put some moss or leaves under the pan of the trap to prevent any obstruction from getting there, and use a light clog of maple or iron wood and take great pains to cover it, as well as the trap and chain with loose dirt. In making this set always wade up the stream to the spring, being careful to keep in the water all the time and avoid spitting anywhere around, even in the water, especially if you use tobacco. Take great care in all your operations to have everything as natural as possible. Use a piece of Skunk, Muskrat or Rabbit for bait, and if you wish to use a scent, a good one can be made as follows: To the musk-bag of the male of one Skunk, Muskrat, Beaver and Fox, add four drops of anise oil and one pint of alcohol.

Cork tight and let stand two months in a cool place. A couple of drops of this on a stone or stick will last two weeks if there is not too much rain.

For Mink I mix it with fish oil, eel oil, the musk bag of one Muskrat, and two ounces of alcohol. Apply the same as fox scent.

—Skunk, muskrat, partridge and meadow mice are all good bait for foxes. Muskrat, meadow mice, partridge, red squirrel, beef's liver, fresh speckled trout are good mink baits. Take the musk bag of of Skunk and lay it on the ground, scuff your boot bottoms in it and start right off in the woods or anywhere you wish to travel, and Foxes are quite apt to follow your tracks. A male Fox will follow your tracks if you put the matrix scent on your boot bottoms. If, however, you desire both male and female to follow you, use the following on your boot bottoms: Take several trout or fish, put them in a glass or stone jar, add one-quarter pound salt, and one and one-half teacups of clear fresh water; let stand loosely covered in the sun four weeks, then strain off the brine (throw away the thick stuff), put the brine into another quart jar, add the matrix of the female Fox and the musk of one Skunk and add one-half pint of alcohol, then cover jar air tight. Let stand in a cool dark place from two to ten months—the longer the better.

—To allure the Fox to this bed some trappers draw a piece of meat over the ground in a circle; others leave an enticing trail by rubbing the bottoms of their boots with a preparation made by preserving the matrix of the female Fox or Wolf in alcohol; this preparation may be kept indefinitely, but only interests the dog Fox. Another way sometimes practiced is to make an excavation under an old stump or log, setting the trap at the entrance with bait at the back side. A favorite winter method is to set the trap in a spring hole where the water does not freeze, placing it just under water and a few inches from shore. A bit of moss is placed on the pan, and the Fox is attracted and led to put his foot on the moss by a piece of tempting bait hung just out of reach above and beyond the trap.

O. D. WRIGHT.

—I used a house rat. I killed him and put him in my bait box, being very careful not to get the rat bloody or the fur ruffled up. I went to a place where a Fox had been coming every night but didn't want my bait, so I got out my rat and set the trap about six inches away.

The Fox came the very first night and made a jump for the rat, and I got him by the hind foot. I then set the trap again, and the next night I got his mate in the same way. By this time the rat had got all ruffled up, and I could catch no more in this place until I got a new rat for bait. Quite often I get the Fox by the hind foot when he makes a spring for the bait, but generally he gets caught by the fore foot.

C. E. HOLLEY.

—In the Sall place bait, the carcass of some animal or any meat you can get, in a clump of bushes, or under evergreen trees, in the pastures or woods where Foxes are likely to run. Trim out the branches so as to leave an easy opening on one side, and the Foxes will get to visiting the spot, even after the bait is gone. Then, at the proper season, set two traps where two evergreens grow near together, one on each side of the passage, and you will be almost certain of a catch. In trapping for Foxes and Wolves, do not set the trap too near the bait, but back a few feet. Tainted meat is a good bait. For winter use salt fish, smoked is excellent, as it will not freeze like fresh meat, and so gives off the scent longer.

—In winter, hang the hind part of a Skunk, Muskrat, or Rabbit about three feet high on a bush growing by itself, and set under it two traps, one on each side of the bush, fastening to a drag. Put a wad of cotton or a few leaves under the pan of the trap, and carefully cover the trap with light snow. Brush out all your tracks, and leave everything looking as natural as possible. If you think best to use some scent, in addition to the bait, take one-half pound of honey, the musk from one rat, four drops of anise oil, one drop skunk's oil, one ounce alcohol. Let stand one month before using. A few drops of this in a place will be sufficient. Some trappers cut a clean sponge into small pieces on which the scent is placed, then a piece of the sponge is hung up over the trap.

—When trapping for Fox in woods, nail two pieces of bait to a tree, a foot or fifteen inches from the ground, and wire the bait under the head of the nail so that it will be difficult to remove. Nail one of the pieces a little higher up than the other, and set the trap between the roots of the tree when they are above ground.

—"Now brother trappers I am going to give you a fox method on snow. We find lots of land-sets but very few snow-sets. This one I have tested. Take a fork and throw some chaff in the sleigh box then put in your fox trap well cleaned, with a stone tied to the chain. Drive out into an old field and throw out two or three small forkfulls of chaff as you drive along. When you get to where the Fox has his trail across the field, stop and fork out some chaff. Set the trap and place it on the chaff, then cover about two inches with chaff. Place a mouse over the trap-pan and cover it all up except the head. Be sure to stay in the sleigh as the Fox is not afraid of a horse or sleigh tracks."

E. CLYNGENPEEL.

CHAPTER 18

Bears Black, Brown, Grizzly, and Polar

THE BEAR

The bear family is a large one, and its members are found scattered over the greater part of the globe, Australia and Africa being excepted. They range through all latitudes, from the equator to the poles. The following species have been described by naturalists: Polar bear, grizzly bear, European Brown bear, American Black bear, Alaskan Brown bear, Inland White bear, Glacier bear of Alaska, Asiatic bear, Siberian bear, Spectacled bear of South America, Thibetan bear, Bornean bear and Malay bear. The three latter are called Sun bears, from their habit of basking in the rays of the mid-day sun. They are the smallest members of the family and live exclusively on vegetables.

Bears differ from each other in consequences of the differences of climate, more than almost any other animal. Those that inhabit the far north and such high, cold regions as the Rocky mountains, are monsters, of great strength and ferocity, while those that inhabit warm countries are small, feeble and inoffensive. The smallest of all is the Bornean bear, while the Alaskan Brown bear is probably the largest. The Grizzly or Silver Tip, and the Polar bears are very large.

The American Black bear is probably the most numerous of the family, and is one of most interest to the trappers. With the exception of the prairie country, they are found scattered over almost all of the United States, and a large part of Canada and Alaska. The Cinnamon is only a color variety of the Black bear, differing only in color. Both kinds are found in the same litter. In some sections, as for instance in some of the northwestern states, and in Mexico, the Cinnamon bear predominates, while in the east and north they are very rare. The average weight of the Black bear, when full grown, is from two hundred to three hundred pounds, but specimens have been killed weighing far more than these figures. The fur is fine and soft and usually of a jet black color.

Bears of all kinds, with the exception of the Sun bears and the Polar bear, feed on both vegetable and animal food. The Polar bear lives entirely on fish and flesh. Bears, with the exception of the Polar species, hibernate in winter. They usually den in the ground or rocks, but sometimes in a hollow log or tree.

THE BLACK BEAR

BLACK bear is the best known species, due to its numerosity and wide geographical distribution, inhabiting as it does all sections of the globe, excepting Australia. It is known by naturalists as the Baribal, Muskwa and the Ursus Americanus. On this continent the black bear is found from the Gulf of Mexico to the Arctic regions and from the Atlantic to the Pacific ocean, differing somewhat in size, habits, quality and color of its pelage, which variations are entirely traceable to climatic conditions. He resembles the European bear very much and the animal's nomenclature is extensive and diversified, as the knowledge of his existence has reached every tribe and nation. Much has been written about the black bear that has made him very popular, his ferocious habits have at times been ignored and at other times largely exaggerated.

The black bear of the north is much larger, stronger, ferocious to a greater degree, and his pelage, especially during the winter months, is much more valuable as compared with his southern brethren. A full-grown northern black bear will weigh 500 to 650 pounds, while the large yearling or two-year-old will compare favorably in size and weight with a full grown southern species, ranging from 250 to 400 pounds. Hunters relate that during the '60's, also early '70's of the past century, black bears were killed that weighed as high as 750 pounds in the dense pine forests of Minnesota, Wisconsin and Michigan. The average yearling black bear of the north would measure forty to forty-five inches, when two years old, fifty to sixty inches, and when full grown six to seven feet long from tip of nose to root of tail. The ears are small and well rounded, being covered with a short, black fur, the eyes are exceedingly small, while the snout is short and in general the head is smaller in proportion to that of the brown or grizzly bear. Its legs area strong, while its feet are large, the latter possessing each, live long, but dull and almost immovable and unretractable claws. Thirty-five to thirty-seven monstrous looking teeth are firmly set in its jaws and the animal's power in its mouth is tremendous. Its lustrous black fur is from three to five inches in length, the undergrowth about two-thirds of the latter size. The latter quite often is way and instead of being glossy has a dull appearance ranging from a deep brown to a jet black. The fur is evenly distributed over the skin, but gradually tapers as the body terminates into legs, head and tail. Oftentimes the guard hairs about the hips become rabbed and the fur matted. The latter then becomes of a woolly appearance.

That the animal possesses carnivorous as well as omnivorous habits, cannot be denied, feeding as he does indiscriminately upon vegetation, such as grass, fruits, leaves, and when opportunity presents upon poultry, sheep, veal, rabbits and deer. Occasionally when his ferocious nature is aroused will capture and kill other live stock and many instances can be recited where the brute turned to cannibalism, although this action on the part of the animal is rare. Honey is eagerly sought by all of these species, and probably nothing is more pleasing to them than to discover a beehive. His sitting, sliding, scratching, hugging, tumbling habits, and the brute's aptitude of walking erect on his rear legs when approaching man, also his peculiar way of swinging his head when leisurely strolling, are his chief characteristics and of course these are well known to those who have come in contact with the black bear. His habitual sitting up on his rear haunches,

Michigan   **BLACK BEAR**   From a Photo
                    In a No. 5 Newhouse Steel Trap

invariably destroys the value of the skin for robe and rug purposes, also for the taxidermist. The fur about the hips becomes badly rubbed, matted, and of a woolly appearance. During the winter months the animal is conspicuous by its absence, being in some den partaking of the winter sleep. The extent, duration and period of this hibernating habit depends largely upon the weather, surroundings, food supply, and upon the animal himself; sometimes lasting three to four weeks, at other times as many months. Quite often during mild and thawy weather, the bear will awake from his winter slumbers and seek food and drink. When his appetite and thirst are satisfied he may re-enter his den and remain there for weeks, at other times he refuses to re-enter and immediately begins looking for prey, and being emaciated and run down, his requirements are large in that respect.

Bears held in captivity, unless exposed to the elements and in some large, roomy locality, with all the natural surroundings, will lose their hibernating habit. Occasionally in his wild state and in his natural home, he will neglect to partake of this periodical winter sleep. This brute is an expert swimmer, fairly good at climbing, and it takes a good man to run away from his if the animal becomes enraged. While the cubs and young bears habitually climb trees, the old ones very rarely climb them unless in search of food and then they quite often tumble to the earth on account of the claws being dull. Nature has provided him with all the facilities for escape that man has, being equal to the average man in running, climbing and swimming, hence if pursued the chances of escape are somewhat dubious unless backed with lots of nerve and good weapons.

The female brings forth a litter of two, three or four, occasionally five, and rarely one cub. The cave or den, where the mother raises her children, is generally warm, being padded with dry leaves, grass or other vegetation and is usually on the sunny side of some hill or mountain. The den is generally in some inscrutable place with impervious surroundings, which obstacles the hunter readily overcomes by manifold methods, In such cases the female will carry the young away to another obscure locality, sometimes a distance of three or four miles. While so engaged, should she meet the intruder, and cannot readily proceed in her whishes, she will turn upon the hunter, showing fight, especially if previously molested. Regardless of their clumsy construction they can outrun the pursuer, and it is not an easy matter to escape from this animal after he or she is enraged and turns upon the pursuer.

THE BROWN BEAR

This brute is about extinct in the Appalachian chain of mountains and is now sparingly found east of the Rockies, more numerous in some of the western states, about the Sierra Nevadas, Cascade mountains and along the Rocky mountains extending from New Mexico to Alaska. Idaho, Washington, Oregon and Montana have lately furnished most of the skins, but the animal is probably more numerous in British Columbia than anywhere else on this continent. This species is more or less confused with the cinnamon bear, which it closely resembles. Great variation in size, strength, ferocity and color of its pelage exists, due to the vast territory and the marked changes in climatic conditions. The northern animals are by all means the strongest, heaviest and probably more ferocious than their southern brethren. As compared with the black bear the brown bear is about his equal in size, but in certain localities, especially in British Columbia, the brown bear attains an enormous size exceeding in that respect the black bear by 100 to 250 pounds.

The fur of the southern brute is coarse, uneven, shaggy, harsh, less dense, and in color ranges from a dirty yellow to a light brown, and such skins are of little value. even when prime. The pelt of the northern brute is quite valuable, especially that from the two-year-old or three-year-old animal. The older the animal the coarser the fur, and consequently the skin is of less value unless it is extremely large and suitable for specimen purposes. The fur of the three-year-old animal is from three to five inches long, quite often of a wavy appearance, soft, mellow, and in color ranging from a light brown to a deep, rich, dark brown. Two beautiful colored and furred skins, coming probably from two-year-old animals, are before me now. In length the fur is seven to seven one fourth inches, in color light brown, with the inner fur two or three shades still lighter. The fur fibers are wavy, silky, mellow, and in general the skins area very beautiful. The animals from which they were taken were killed in the Caribou mountains of Athabasca, Canada. As to their habits, there is no distinct difference between this species and the black bear.

THE CINNAMON BEAR

The cinnamon bear (Ursus Cinnamoneous) is found rather sparingly on this side of the Canadian line, although quite a number are annually dispatched in the mountainous regions along the Rocky and Cascade mountains in the states of Montana, Wyoming, Washington, Idaho and Oregon. The brute is more numerous on the Canadian side following the Rocky Mountain chain clear up to Alaska. This is not an Arctic species as some suppose, neither is the animal found as far south as the brown bear. Being more of a northern species it is quite natural that the animal is large, strong, robust and ferocious, and it is not surprising at all that the Indians consider it a feat second in importance when a brave succeeds in killing a large cinnamon brute to that of the famous grizzly. The cinnamon bear is more or less confused with the brown bear. As will be observed he is of larger stature, and instances area recorded where the animal attained the enormous size comparatively with the grizzly bear.

Its pelage, as its name implies, is of a dark brown, resembling the color of cinnamon bark. The fur of a medium aged animal is soft, mellow and three and one half to four inches long. The body is well and evenly covered with rather a dense coat which becomes shorter as the body terminates into the head, legs and tail. Occasionally skins are received where the fur is much longer, on the other hand the fur of the older animals is short, harsh and rather uneven.

A certain Mr. McDonald, a member of the mounted police in Canada, witnessed a fierce combat between a cinnamon and a black bear. The former became the victor only after four to six hours of the fiercest combat probably ever witnessed by man. Being so evenly matched, no apparent advantage was gained by either one over the other, until the black bear was unfortunate in being rolled into a rapidly-flowing creek, and being fairly exhausted and held down by the weight of the brown bear, it required comparatively only a few minutes until the black bear was drowned. In describing the fight he states that it resembled that between two huge dogs, biting, growling, scratching, hugging, rolling, etc. The noise these brutes made while so engaged was indescribable. In habits, the animals differ slightly, if any, from the black, brown and grizzly bear.

The Grizzly Bear.

THE GRIZZLY BEAR

THIS monster inhabits strictly mountainous regions and is now sparingly found in the United States. Was formerly in large numbers in Montana, Wyoming, Oregon, Washington and southward along the Rocky and Cascade mountains. He is numerously found in British Columbia where a large specimen was recently captured weighing 2,800 to 3,000 pounds. He is also found in the extreme northern parts of Canada, and in Alaska. The largest skin that came to my notice measured eleven feet, three inches in length and average width of seven feet and six inches. The fur on this skin was poor, he being killed during the early fall months when the skin and the fur were unprime.

The pelage of the grizzly bear varies greatly in color, so much so indeed that naturalists as well as the fur trade divide the species into two grades, the grizzly and silver tip. The outer garment of the former is dark grey to black, with interspersed grey or silver hairs. The fur is shaggy, harsh, uneven, and especially is this true of the older animals while the fur of the younger brutes is even, somewhat fine, rather dense, and two and a half to three and a half, possibly four inches long. The fur of the silver tipped bear skin is more even, and tends toward a greyish color with white silvery tipped hairs, rather evenly dispersed and prominently predominating, making the skin rather beautiful as well as serviceable. Occasionally the fur on the latter is of a dark, steel grey, with interspersed white tipped hairs. Only the skins that are prime are of any value, as summer skins are unfit to be tanned and can only be used for specimen purposes. This brute is sometimes confused with the cinnamon, also the brown bear, of which he is their master. The animal has enormous strength in his legs and jaws, and with apparent ease is able to drag a horse or cow for miles. His collossal weight and size enables his to subdue any and all wild animals which inhabit this globe and in a probable encounter with the African lion or the huge elephant he would come off the victor.

The fur on this monster carnivorous brute is of a shaggy appearance. The word "grizzly" is justified in describing the condition of the fur of the old species, probably more so than the two to four-year-old brutes. The color of its pelage varies, not only in the different sections but also in the animal's age. The older the brute the more shaggy, grizzly and faded the fur.

THE POLAR BEAR

The polar bear ranks second, if not first in size of all the various species of the bear family. He inhabits the extreme polar regions where ice prevails the year round. By no means does he alone belong to the Western hemisphere, as he is found on three continents. On this continent the polar bear is found about the eastern coast along the Baffin Bay, north of Hudson Bay Strait and across the continent to Alaska.

Its pelage consists of a coarse coat of yellowish white fur of various length; but that of the body is usually three to four inches long. The ears are short, neck rather long, body long in proportion to its height and has unusually long feet. The claws are heavy and not so stubby as those of the land species. In his habits he varies somewhat from the other strictly land species, being that he is confined to the extreme northern regions the year round, living as he does amongst ice, often obliged to procure his only food from the deep seas. This bear like all others is carnivorous, also possesses omnivorous habits, and devours with voracity the carcasses of whales that drift ashore; in fact devours all dead animals that the waves hurl against the icy shores of the Arctic region.

Capt. Lyons describes the polar bear at full speed, "as a kind of shuffle as quick as the sharp gallop of a horse." Quite often the animal swims off to floating ice or to icebergs and is carried with them hundreds of miles in the direction that the wind happens to be blowing. Capt. Peary reports that the Esquimaux on the coast of Mellville Peninsula attain part of their subsistence from the flesh of the female bear, which they dig out from the snow. Mr. Graham states that the female retires to her winter quarters in November, where she lives without food until she brings forth usually two cubs about Christmas time. The cubs in size resemble those of a shepherd dog. The offspring, especially if tired, ascends the animal's back, where they ride securely, either in water or shore. The following report from Capt. Lyons is interesting:

"At the commencement of winter the pregnant bears are very fat, and always solitary. When a heavy fall of snow sets in, the animal seeks some hollow place in which she can lie down and remain quiet, while the snow covers her. Sometimes she will wait until a quantity of snow has fallen, and then digs herself a cave; at all events it seems necessary that she should be covered by, and lie amongst, the snow. She now goes to sleep, and does not wake until the spring sun is pretty high, when she brings forth two cubs. The cave by this time has become much larger by the effect of the animal's warmth and breath, so that the cubs have room to move, and they acquire considerable strength by continually sucking. The dam at length becomes so thin and weak that it is with great difficulty she extricates herself, when the sun is powerful enough to throw a strong glare through the snow which roofs the den. The Esquimaux affirms that during this long confinement the bear has no evacuations, and is herself the means of preventing them by stopping all the natural passages with moss, grass, or earth. The natives find and kill the bears during their confinement by means of dogs, which scent them through the snow, and begin scratching and howling very eagerly. As it would be unsafe to make a large opening, a long trench is cut of sufficient width to enable a man to look down and see where the bear's head lies, and he then selects a mortal part, into which he thrusts his spear. The old one being killed, the hole is broken open, and the young cubs may be taken out by the hand, as, having tasted no blood, and never having been at liberty, they are then very harmless and quiet. Females, which are not pregnant, roam throughout the whole winter in the same manner as the males.

THE BEAR

The mating season is in July and August and the young, usually two, are born in January, February and March. They remain with the mother until fall, and sometimes longer.

In sections where they are found in fair numbers, they form trails through passes in the mountains, along the bottoms of the cliffs, around points of the lakes, and in other places of like nature. These trails may be easily distinguished from the paths of other animals, by the marks on the trees. At intervals, all along the trail, the bear will stand on his hind feet, by the side of a tree, gnaw a circle around the tree, about five feet above the ground. I am told that this marking is done during the mating season. The trails are traveled more in the spring and summer than in the fall.

Bears are very fond of fish, and in the north, when fish are in the streams, spawning, the bears spend much of their time fishing, at the foot of the falls. The sucker is the first fish to spawn, and as soon as they are gone, the pike come, and the bears fare well for a couple of weeks. After that they feed on the leaves of the poplar, insects, berries and nuts, and whatever meat they can find. In some sections they remain in the same locality during the entire year; in other places they migrate on the approach of cold weather and do not return until spring.

The bear becomes prime about the first to the fifteenth of November, and remains in good condition until late in the spring. In northern sections they do not commence shedding until June fifteenth, and sometimes even later. The best time to trap them is in the spring just after the snow is gone, but many are trapped in the fall.

The traps for black bears are the Nos. 5 and 15 and the Nos. 50 and 150 Newhouse. For larger bears the No. 6 is the trap to use, although many grizzly bears are caught in the No. 5.

The most common method for trapping bears is the following: Make a sort of enclosure of old logs, brush, etc., in the form of a V, about eight feet long and two or three feet wide at the entrance. It should be three feet high, behind, but it is not necessary to have it so high in front. The bait should be fastened in the back of the pen, and the trap set in the entrance.

Take a small, springy stick, about eight inches long, and spring it under the pan of the trap, to prevent small animals from being caught. To do this, stick one end firmly in the ground, and bend the other end down, and hook it under the pan. The trap when set, should support a weight of twenty-five pounds, but it is my opinion that most trappers allow the trap to spring too easily.

Always turn the loose jaw up, and work from in under, for the sake of safety. Now drive down a couple of stakes on each side of the trap, so as to leave only a narrow passage; cover the trap with leaves or moss. It is a good idea to put a good sized piece of moss over the pan. To cause the bear to step in the center of the trap, some trappers put sharp sticks around the outside of the jaws, others lay a stick across the mouth of the pen, about six or eight inches high, and close up to the jaws. In stepping over it, the bear is more likely to put his foot in the trap. The trap should be fastened to a heavy clog of hardwood. For the Black bear, the clog should be about six or seven feet long, and just small enough to go through the ring on the chain. The ring should be slipped on to the middle and fastened with a spike. For the grizzly and other large bears, the clog should be larger.

This is the best method, but if you nip a bear once, you will have to try some other method, and it is not likely that you will catch him, even then, as they become very cunning. Do not set the trap at the same place, but find his trail, and make a blind set; preferably where the trail leads through a pool of water. Of course must be sure that no person will travel on the trail. Some trappers prefer to hang a bait about six feet above the trap and do not use any pen.

Bears may also be trapped successfully with snares and deadfalls but the objection to these traps is that the animal is killed instantly and if the traps are not visited daily the skin is likely to spoil.

For bait, there is nothing better than fish, but pork, (either salt or fresh), mutton, beef or any kind of large game is good. Even the flesh of the bear makes fair bait. Beaver, otter or muskrat meat is also good. Honey is very attractive.

There are a number of scents that are attractive to the bear, such as fish oil, oil of anise and beaver castor. The scent recommended for the raccoon is good for the bear.

The track of the bear is easily distinguished from that of other animals, because of its large size. Ordinarily, the bear's mode of locomotion is a shuffling walk. The footprints of a large black bear will measure about eight inches in length.

TO TRAP THE BEAR

The bear is a furious animal when hurt or caught in a trap, and would soon succeed in breaking almost any trap if the chain were long enough to allow it. The best position for placing the trap is at the entrance of an enclosure, constructed in the manner described on page 70, but made strong and roomy enough to suit the large size of the animal.

Trappers generally select, if possible, some spot between trees or logs which can be improved upon, and made to answer their purposes with far less trouble and labor than would be required to construct a regular enclosure; the object in view being to oblige the bear to tread on the trap in order to reach the bait. Bears appear to be endowed with a very small share of cunning, and will enter any nook or corner to gain possession of a piece of meat of almost any king; they are fond of sweets, and are strongly attracted by the smell of honey. A little honey or a piece of honeycomb will draw a bear from a considerable distance; and, if this be placed near the trap, to bring the bear within scent of the meat, its capture is almost certain.

In winter time a bear may sometimes be tracked by its footsteps to the den or hole in which it dwells, where a fair shot may be had at it. Shooting bears is, however, dangerous sport, as they are difficult to kill, and are very formidable when enraged, and the hide is also injured by the ball.

HOW TO HUNT AND TRAP THE BEAR

The bear is a coward and will not molest man, even it disturbed, many times he will seek to escape the intruder and only in rare instances will he turn upon man without due provocation. To throw a stone at him, whether the stone falls short or not, is sometimes sufficient for Bruin to turn about, other times if shot and wounded he will scamper away, perhaps, the latter occurs seldom, as he is known to go for the hunter, who must be prepared for his reception.

One who cannot await his time for bear to approach within twenty-five yards has no business to go on a bear hunt. Only those shots that hit count; perhaps the statement made by President Roosevelt when speaking of our navy "In time of war and in battle only those shots that hit, and hit well, count" is also true when on a bear hunt.

"One of the best hunters that I ever saw was scarcely five feet tall, weighted about one hundred and fifteen pounds, and a tailor by trade," says Mr. Huntington, an experienced hunter and trapper, formerly a western guide, and at one time connected with the Alaska Commercial Company. "This little fellow with one or two guides would go for weeks hunting in the most lonesome forests. At one time we struck a family of grizzlies and do you suppose lie would give me a shot at them? No sir! We Followed them for some

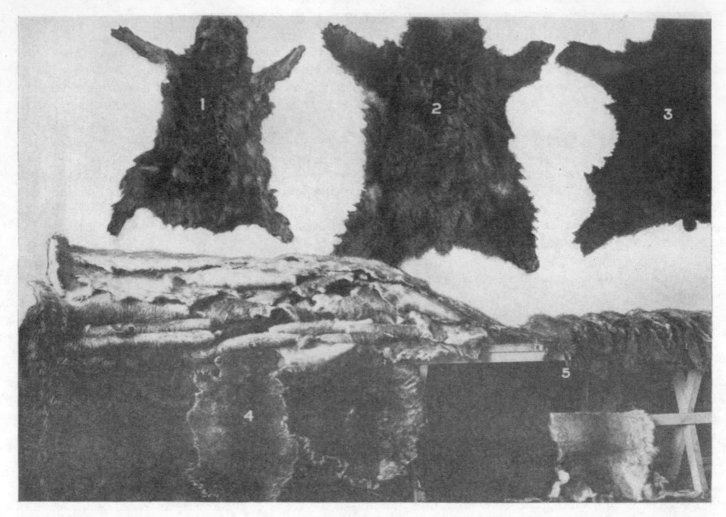

time and when within shot he bade me stay behind while be went forward. When within thirty to forty yards he darted behind a tree, rested his rifle on the side of the tree, took careful aim, and fired. The first shot hit this monster bear high on the head and glanced off; the bear turned in a circle, like if demented, stopped for a moment, and made for the little fellow who had stopped aside the tree. The bear had gone about five yards when this tailor took aim but reserved his fire until the bear raised himself on his hind legs. A sharp report, a fall and Mr. Bruin was done for, 1 rapidly ran to the scene and was requested not to approach the dead bear until our rifles were first in complete order and allowing sufficient time for the bear to pass through his death struggles. While I skinned the monster and prepared to camp for the night in the vicinity, the tailor went after the female bear but not being able to locate her returned to camp. The next morning, much to our surprise we corralled the mother and two yearlings which were promptly dispatched."

On one occasion two Wyoming cowboys chased a black matured hear from his usual abode out into the open where he was roped about the neck, each man keeping the rope or lasso stretched and bruin in the middle away from any possible harm to the horses or riders. In this manner and position he was partly pulled, dragged and run into town where the folks viewed the prisoner with unusual admiration. Towards evening a mock jury condemned the prisoner "to be shot in the head until dead."

Some years ago the government sent a special party to capture alive some of the monster grizzlies still found in the Rocky Mountain regions in Canada. This party was successful in capturing two large specimens weighing over two thousand pounds each. From their report it would seem that the grizzlies were captured in pitfalls into which cages were lowered, and animals being partly starved were driven into the cages and

WHAT DO YOU THINK OF THAT?   From a Photograph

then boisted and placed aboard a ship, and brought to the United States at an expense of about $ 10,000,00. Of course, no trapper or hunter would care to spend such a sum fitting out an expedition.

Deadfalls, log house traps, snares, pitfalls, set guns and Newhouse steel traps are commonly used for capturing these monsters. The large No. 6 Newhouse steel trap is guaranteed by the manufacturers to be of sufficient strength to hold a two thousand five hundred pound grizzly or polar bear. If steel traps are used the clog must be twenty-five to fifty pounds for an ordinary bear, and seventy-five to one hundred pounds for the grizzly or polar bear. These large traps should be with clamps, and no one man should attempt to set these powerful devices without assistance. For bait large chunks of meat or carcasses of small animals are commonly used. These should be fastened. Honey bait prepared in various ways bring excellent results. How to make this bait is noted elsewhere in this book.

If you have reason to know that Mr. Bruin is in a certain locality and you possess a large trap and are desirous of getting the skin and meat—the latter being very delicious and highly prized during the winter months, not only by trappers and woodsmen but also city people (especially in large cities where steaks often retail from twenty-five to thirty-five cents per pounds), you should first select a proper place to set the trap.

A good location is next to a fallen log. The latter will answer for one part of the "V." Drive a sufficient number of 3-inch thick stakes, twelve to twenty inches into the ground ; the stakes should protrude about three feet above the ground more or less as the surroundings warrant or require. Have stakes close together. The row of stakes should be about five feet long and the mouth of the "V" should be three feet wide. When this is done excavate immediately within the mouth of the "V" shaped enclosure—in which excavation place the trap. Arrange the trap when covered with leaves and dirt so as to be even with the surrounding ground. Be sure and place wool or similar materials underneath the pan to prevent dirt from getting under or the trap being sprung by small animals. After this is completed place bait in the narrowest part of the "V" enclosure. Chain should be attached to a clog, never to a stake or other stationary object.

An experienced hunter from the "Great Black Forest" in Europe relates that he caught a monstrous bear in an American steel trap set at the widest part of a "V" enclosure, and used a small squealing pig as a bait; the latter was fastened in the narrowest part of the V-shaped pen. The trap, (supposed to have been a Newhouse No. 6) was set in an excavation between the widest part of the enclosure and covered with earth, leaves, etc. The springs of the trap nearly touched the respective opposite stakes of the pen.

HOW THE BEAR IS HUNTED OR TRAPPED

"A Wisconsin lumberman relates an interesting story of the capture of a three-year-old black bear without gun or trap, and without previous preparation for the capture of bruin.

LOG PEN TRAP.

The old-fashioned log pen trap is still used by hunters and trappers, but owing to the large amount of labor required in its construction only those trappers that live far in the interior, chiefly in Canada, Alaska and in Siberia, construct them.

The cabin that this bear visited during his nocturnal prowls was located in dense forest, near a stream, inhabited by woodsmen. Being winter, the ground was covered with snow and the night of the capture or detention of the thief with his plunder, was clear and cold.

The men were accustomed to see game and carnivorous animals not only in the woods, but about the cabin, picking up scarps of food that were thrown out from day to day. A small empty pork barrel was rolled out during the day and no one dreamed that this barrel with its many protruding nails would make the best kind of a bear trap. The bear, in seeking food, placed his head and neck far into the barrel, and being unable to get the barrel off by sharking, rolling and tearing through the dense bushes, knocking against trees, was obliged through loss of blood and exhaustion to give way to the inevitable. When the body was found two or three days thereafter it was frozen stiff and it was necessary to break the barrel to remove it from the animal. The barrel being rather small and with its many nails did the work. The bear roaming about with such a mask must have terrorized all animals in the community.

Many bears are annually dispatched by Minnesota, Wisconsin, Michigan and Canadian woodsmen by the use of an ax, and, as a matter of fact, these men much prefer to meet a full-grown bear, either in the woods or on denuded land with an ax instead of a Winchester rifle.

While this is true with bears, it is not so with lynx, wild cat or other members of the cat family, who pounce upon the victim from some lofty place (many times unknown) and in the hunter's unpreparedness a hunting knife is about the only weapon in close quarters, unless a test of brute strength becomes apparently necessary.

HOW THE BEAR IS HUNTED OR TRAPPED

Bears are probably as much hunted as trapped, in fact, think more are captured with the rifle than by steel traps. There is probably nothing better than live, noisy, squealing bait to attract a bear. Personally I think a

BEAR PEN.

Steel trap is to be set just within entrance. For a set gun arrangement bore a hole slantingly into trunk of tree and arrange trigger with a string to bait or some artificial treadle.

small pig would make a dandy bait, but up here in Canada the closest one comes to a pig is to get some eastern bacon, and this is a better bait for the trapper than for bruin.

If one owns one or more No. 5 or No. 6 Newhouse bear traps, he should proceed to make a V or U enclosure; either of these can be made out of three or four-inch stakes about five feet long: drive sharpened end into the ground about two inches apart. The opening should not exceed three feet for large bears and two and one-half feet for smaller ones. Set trap at entrance, and cover in the usual way. Bait should be put well within the enclosure, usually in the narrowest part. A Little anise oil will not hurt. Whether the peculiar, or the strange odor, is the attraction, I cannot say, but know from experience that the anise oil does the work. Log pens with drop-doors are also being used in some parts of Canada, but up here bears are not very plentiful, not worth the time to build such strong dens.

A very good yet peculiar trap arrangement that I saw used by a friend of mine trapping in the Blue Mountains in British Columbia, and useful not only for bears, but for other large game, was a pit with a trap door. The pit was about six by seven feet square and five and one-half to six feet deep. The dirt was held in place by long stakes driven into the ground. The top was covered all up : in the Center he had arranged a trap door, about five feet square, hinges on the inner side. The catch was arranged to the bait, also if a lever were stepped upon, door would drop and with it the victim. This pit was in the woods adjoining a spring where animals came to water. It was level with the ground and the first time that he took me there, I would readily have walked into the trap had he not pulled me back, so well was it arranged by him, that no one could perceive the arrangement. This was in the summer time, and

Compliments of N. P. Ry.   **GRIZZLY BEAR**   Rocky Mountains

while there one morning, an innocent deer was taken out. He claimed to have caught five bears the preceding season.

In skinning a bear, I always take particular pains not to cut the skin and to leave everything including ears, nose, eyes and feet with claws complete, attached to hide. One thing I do, which perhaps other trappers do not, is to ship the skull of the bear along with the skin. The buyer will pay a little more for the hide, as he may have some customer who will want to make it into a rug and the natural skull is preferred over an artificial one, which I understand is made out of plaster paris.

A.R. EDWARDS.

A Grizzly Bear, shot by Captain Clark's party in the Rocky Mountain region, survived twenty minutes and swam half a mile after receiving ten balls in his body, four of which passed through his lungs and two through his heart! Records of Bear-hunting are full of perilous adventures, and those who engage in open battle with the great Grizzly Bear of the Rocky Mountains, rarely escape without loss of life or limb. But steel traps of the right size, and properly managed, subdue these monsters with greater certainty than fire-arms, and without danger to the hunter.

The weight of the clog for a Black Bear should be thirty pounds; for a Grizzly Bear, eighty pounds. The chain should not be more than eighteen inches in length, as the habit of the Bear, when caught, is to attempt to dash the trap to pieces against the trees, logs, or rocks; and with a short chain, fastened to a heavy clog, he is unable to do this. The bait should be meat, and the Bear should be invited to feast by the smell of honey or honeycomb, burnt on heated stones, near the trap. Bears seem to entertain no suspicion of a trap, and enter it as readily as a hog or an ox would do.

We here wish to call attention to the danger of setting Bear traps by levers; and the still more dangerous practice of trying to set there traps by standing on the springs. We have known of a case where the unfortunate trapper caught both hands in a Bear-trap while setting it in this way. He had first fastened or clogged the trap, and in setting it unaided caught both hands. There was no escape, and he miserable perished by starvation or was destroyed by wolves. His skeleton alone remained to tell the tale. The only safe way to set a Bear-trap is by using the Newhouse clamp.

CHAPTER 19

Racoon

RACCOON

The raccoon is a native of North America, belongs to the bear family, and is somewhat related to the South America species better known as the crab eating raccoon. This animal has all the good, and nearly all the bad habits that any other fur-bearing animal possesses. He is an expert climber, very good at swimming, a fairly swift runner and expert fighter, and his nocturnal and omnivorous habits are only too well known to the hunter and trapper. He is found in almost every state and territory of the union. Probably more so in the southern states than in the western or northern. He is scarcely found in Canada, although he does exist in the southern portion thereof. Under no circumstances is he an Arctic species and is not found in that region at all: in fact, he does not inhabit any section in which the polar bear is found.

The body of the raccoon is thick, plump and resembles that of the badger, although being shorter and differently furred, and his body is elevated four or five inches higher than that of the badger. Climatic conditions are responsible for the marked variations of the animal as compared with those inhabiting the northern, western, eastern and southern parts of the United States. While a full grown northern raccoon will weigh twenty-five to thirty-five pounds and the body measures from twenty-two to twenty-eight inches in length, to which a tail of five to seven inches is attached the extreme southern species will rarely exceed twenty pounds in weight, its body only measuring sixteen to twenty inches in length. While the former possess a coat of dark, dense, and rather fine fur, the latter has a thin, coarse and light-colored pelage. The tail is covered with dense fur of the ring formation. The rings change in color, alternating with the predominating color of its body.

The fur of the first above species as noted is very dark, long, comparatively fine and the inner coat resembles that of the beaver being dark brown, wavy and very dense. The outer guard hairs are black to dark brown in color, and extend on an average of onehalf inch above the fur fibers. The prime northern skins can be used for various purposes, the principal use being in the manufacture of fur coats, The best skins are probably picked out, plucked, dyed, or used natural, to imitate beaver. The pelage of the southern species is lighter in color, often of a brown leaning towards a reddish hue, and the fur is more thinly distributed as compared with that of the northern species. The skins of the southern, middle and western states are chiefly used for gentlemen's overcoats.

The animal possesses nocturnal and omnivorous habits, is an excellent swimmer and climber, and if chased will cover a considerable space in the remarkably short time, and when opportunity presents will seek shelter in a tree or in a hollow log, and with swiftness and precision will jump from one tree to another, and if occasion demands from the extreme height of the tree immediately to the ground, alighting on its feet, and catlike fashion attempt to decamp to a place of safety unless detained by the dogs or hunter.

His food consists chiefly of nuts grapes fruit vegetables and eggs. He can be seen in the evening rambling about marshes and streams in search of frogs, fish and turtles, and at night will chase mice, rats, birds, as well as rabbits. Besides these he readily consumes vast quantities of vermin bugs, crabs, etc. The poultry yard is often visited; and nothing is more pleasing to him than some domesticated animal, such as the pigeon, chicken, duck, and the large goose is not objected to by him. Not only is he fond of the meat but considers eggs a greater dainty and repast. The egg is artistically held in his long paws, is broken with his month and the contents gradually sucked out. He possesses the peculiar habit of dipping his foot into the water and then rubbing it between his fore paws to wash it. This is one of his playing attitudes. He is quite often seen about streams and water where the chief part of his food is found. He takes especial delight in reaching out his paw for shining objects or articles in the water, such as a tin can, piece of glass, broken mirror, etc. If the article is unprocurable with his paws, he readily dives for it. The

Northern States   **RACCOONS AT HOME**   Taken from a Photograph

old as well as the young are of a playful disposition resembling somewhat the fox or the bear. He is a keen observer, and it is a pleasure to watch him when he is playfully inclined.

He is a cheerful, handsome and lively fellow. His bear-like gait with his head swinging one way and then another and with his high arched back and dropped tail, makes a pleasing picture; but upon the slightest disturbance or the discovery of some scent, his interest immediately is aroused and especially if be perceives some harmless animal. He at once pricks up his ears, listens, sometimes stands erect on his legs, and swiftly darts after the object, while if fooled, he may revert his disposition to a playful mood and dart upon some tree with an agility for which one would hardly have given him credit. Frequently one can see him running on a horizontal branch like a sloth or a monkey, with body hanging downward. He is fond of playing tricks and is very often inclined towards an inquisitive and mischievous nature. The animal can bee tamed if captured young, and if successful the effort is rewarded by his constant cheerful disposition and ever giving enjoyment to the children. He enjoys being petted, and becomes much attached to persons. Of the qualities of the raccoon, Mr. Beckman has the following to say:

"An animal of unlimited inquisitive intrigue and obstinacy, with a tendency to search all nooks and corners. In sharp contrast to these qualities he also possesses coolness, self restraint, and marked sense of humor. His contending obstinacy often naturally brings about the queerest results as he realizes the impossibility of attaining any special object he has been striving for; the fiercest ferocity gives place to an

| Cotton Tail | THE RACCOON | Muskrat | White Weasel | Jack Rabbit |

apathetic indifference, and obstinate perseverance changes into resignation. On the other hand he often passes quite unexpectedly from a lazy sulkiness, into the best of spirits by turning a somersault, and in spite of all self-restraint and sagacity, commits the most serious blunders when once his desires have been attained."

The raccoon not only furnishes a skin that is valuable, but his flesh is also eaten by many southern people. During the latter part of April or May the mother will bring forth a litter from four to six young. The home is in some hollow tree or fallen log. The young attain their majority not earlier that two years, but are largely placed upon their own resources as soon as they are able to depart from their place of birth ; although the mother will assist them more or less until the beginning of fall when they are able to care for themselves without her assistance. It is very amusing to see the mother followed by her offspring in search of food, and especially if the mother is fortunate in obtaining some live animal, and under here supervision the animal is teased, maltreated and finally devoured by the young.

In the North they become prime about November 1st; the season being later in the South. They remain in good condition until late in the spring. The fur is used mostly for coats and robes.

The nature and habits of the raccoon, like all other animals differs considerably in different localities. In most sections they are very easily trapped, but those found in some parts of the Pacific Coast are said to be quite cunning. Any of the articles of food mentioned above, will make good bait; fresh fish however, being preferred. The traps to use are the No. 1½ Newhouse or Hawley & Norton, the No. 2 Victor, and the Nos. 2 and 3 Oneida Jump and Blake & Lamb traps. The trap should be fastened to a clog, and in some cases an iron drag could be used to advantage, as the coon will get fastened up on the first brush he comes to.

Mounted.   Owned by Andersch Bros.   **THE RACCOON**   **Full-grown.   Minnesota**

The most common method is to set the trap in the entrance of a pen of stakes, at the edge of the water where the animals travel. The trap may be set dry or under water, as preferred, and the bait should be placed in the back of the pen.

Another very good method, much used in the South, is to fasten a piece of bright tin or a piece of a white dish, on the pan of the trap and set the trap under about two inches of water, near the bank. No bait is used, but a little scent may be used on the bank to good advantage.

The Southern Trappers sometimes find a tree, stump or rock in the edge of the water, and set the trap in the water, just where the 'coon will walk, when passing around the obstruction. A fence made of brush will answer the same purpose.

Where the bank is steep and the water is shallow, dig a six inch hole, straight into the bank at the edge of the water. Fasten some bait in the back of the hole and set the trap in the water, directly in front of the hole.

Where coons are visiting a corn field, find where they go through the fence and you will sometimes find a well beaten trail. Set the trap in the trail, covered, and fasten to a clog.

If you find a log lying across the stream and there are signs of 'coons about, cut a notch in the top of the log and set the trap in the notch, covering with rotten wood or moss. You are likely to catch a fox in a set of this kind.

When a den tree can be found, cut a pole five or six feet long and six inches thick; lean it against the tree and set the trap on the pole. Cover the trap lightly with moss and staple to the tree.

Any natural enclosure along a stream, such as a hollow log or a hole under a stump, makes a good place to set a trap. When trapping for foxes with water sets, many coons will be caught in the traps.

One of the best scents for 'coon is made as follows: To a pint of fish oil, add twenty or thirty drops of oil of anise and two ounces of strained honey. Pure fish oil is used by some trappers and beaver castor, muskrat musk and oil of anise are also good.

The trail of the raccoon is somewhat like that of the mink, but the tracks are larger. The animal makes the print of the entire foot and the long slender toes show plainly. The print of the hind foot will be from two and a quarter to three inches in length.

PRACTICAL SUGGESTIONS BY TRAPPERS

—Raccoons travel about near their homes, and will make a well-beaten path to where they go to water, especially if they cross a strip of wild meadow lying between wooded ground and a creek or marsh. A trap placed in this path is a good set. Muddy flats along the streams are much frequented by the Raccoon. A low fence of brush between two adjoining flats, with a convenient opening in which a trap may be placed, is a good set.

—Take a log a foot or so in diameter, which has a hole in one end, and I lace it in shallow water near the land. Put some bait in the hole in the log, and set your trap in the mud near the bank, under an inch of water, just where the Coon will step in to go to the bait. For bait use an old salt fish skin smoked over a small fire near your trap.

—An ear of corn stuck in the mud near your trap is good bait. So is a piece of fish.

—If you find a log fallen across a stream and see any signs of Coon, chop out of the log a seat for your trap, set the trap in it and cover it lightly with fine rotten wood, then place a stick about two feet long and two or three inches in diameter across the log about two inches away from the trap. Do not have it more than four or five inches from the pan of trap. The Coon will step over the stick and into the trap.

—Use fish-oil scent for Coons, and for bait us ears of corn. Tie a piece of an ear to the pan of the trap, set trap on the ground, but don't cover the corn.

—Where you find Coon tracks in the mud on bank, lay an old log in the edge of the water. The Coon will not climb over the log, but will go around the end of it in the water. Set traps about two inches deep on both sides of log.

—Make a pen, > shape, at the edge of water, using dead sticks and brush. Place the bait inside and set your trap just inside the entrance, under water, covering it with soaked leaves. Fasten to trap to a brush drag. The best bait is fresh fish, but muskrat meat, frogs' legs or chicken will attract the Coon.

—Find where they travel along a stream, and where the bank is steep dig a six-inch hole straight in at the level of the water. Fasten the bait back in the hole by a stick thrust through it, and set the trap at the entrance. Or, find a place where the water is too deep except close to the bank, where it should be two or three inches deep, and the bank high and steep. Set the trap in the edge of the water and fasten to a sunken brush. Set in this way on both sides of the stream.

—Find where Coons have been working in a cornfield. Look along the fence to see where they go through it. Sometimes you can find a regularly traveled path. Set carefully in the center of the path and fasten to a brush drag. Use no bait.

—If you come across a den tree in the woods, cut a pole about five inches thick and six feet long, and lean it up against the tree. Set your trap on top of this pole, concealing it with moss or dead leaves.

—This is often a successful method: Put a slice of parsnip on the pan of your trap, whether you set in water or on land. In water no covering is needed, but on land hide the trap, leaving only the parsnip in sight.

—A minnow floated on a small piece of wood or cork and fastened to it, placed just beyond a trap set under water, makes a good bait.

—Sometimes you can do well in trapping either Coon or Skunk by tacking a piece of coarse cloth to a tree or stump about a foot from the ground and pouring a little fish oil on it, setting your trap directly underneath.

—Take a limber stick and stick it into the ground, catch a reed bird, tie him to the end of the stick and put the traps at the side of it. When the Coon tries to get the reed bird he climbs up on the pole a piece and the pole will bend and come down right on the trap, and the Coon will be in the trap with his hind foot.

—This animal is very much easier to trap than some. Curiosity is a weak point with it, and in hunting for its food it is sure to examine, and probably handle, anything that presents an unusual appearance. As it seizes its food with its paw, it is often caught by putting bait on the pan of the trap. Experienced trappers are able to discover places that a Coon is in the habit of frequenting, when they stand on the bank of some stream watching for frogs and crabs. Such a place as this is a very favorable one for setting a trap. Their paths also are sometimes found leading from the higher ground down towards the water: here also the trapper will many times meet with success. A hollow log, tree, or even an artificial brush-den, is a favorite place with the trapper, especially when using bait. Almost any meat will answer for bait. Even a piece of salt fish, well smoked, may be used. Some trappers are very ingenious in building little stake-houses along the stream, placing the bait (which, in this case, should consist of fresh fish) beyond the trap. This set, if properly made, answers equally well for a prowling Mink or Coon.

—We trap in their paths in this way: Set a trap within about fifteen feet of the ground den; stake the trap the full length of the chain; cover well the chain and trap. Put about three in one path, a good distance apart, and at the end of a log, or roots of a tree. You will be almost sure to get a Raccoon if he travels this road. Do not disturb the path.

—The best way that I ever found to trap Coons, was to put a piece of bright tin on the pan of the trap and fasten it there by bending in under the pan. Then set the trap about two inches deep in water where Coons are in the habit of traveling. When he comes and sees this, he thinks that it is a clam or an oyster, I suppose, and will jump at it, and is often caught by both front feet.

—In trapping, for Raccoons by the side of a stream along which they run, choose a place where a tree overhangs the bank, dig out a place the size of the trap close to the water, but not in it, so that the trap when set will be level with the surface. Take a piece of cloth and lay over the trap, and cover it very lightly with dirt. Place an old chunk or a stone at the edge of the water, so that when the Coon goes around it he will step in the trap.

—Another set would be to put the carcass of some dead fowl back in between two logs, and set a No. 2 trap in front, at the entrance, fastening it to a bush clog. Scatter a few feathers around.

—If a hollow log offers, pursue the same plan by shoving the bait into it and setting the trap in the opening.

HOW TO HUNT AND TRAP THE RACCOON

The animal is caught in traps of various kinds and often hunted by dogs and chased from tree to tree, and out of hollow logs or trees.

Steel traps should be set at the entrance of the animal's abode or in their paths. Snares and dead-falls can also be advantageously used. The bait

The Raccoon.

can be vegetables or meat such as chicken, rabbits, and fish, which should be roasted in order to extend an inviting smell and give the animal an appetizing relish. Favorable results are obtained in the late fall and early spring or before the water is frozen, by setting a steel trap in shallow water, ten to fifteen inches from the shore, with some shining object placed upon the pan, or the latter polished so the when the sun shines, its brightness is reflected to the observing coon when passing. The raccoon, in observing the shining object, becomes curious and will examine it. He will slowly step into the water, sniff and smell about, place his paw on the trap and if he does not succeed in removing the object, will go a little further into the water, the nearer he goes the more weight will be placed upon his foot, thus springing the trap and capturing the coon.

At other times the trap is set the same distance away from the shore on some especially prepared island. The bait which is put on a stick is stuck into the ground six to twelve inches beyond the island. The coon will smell about upon discovering the bait, jump upon the covered trap and become a victim. The trap thus set should be staked and can also be attached to a spring pole; a sliding pole may answer the purpose, but trappers as a rule dislike the idea of skinning a drowned coon.

A good idea is to put upon the stick a shining tin can especially polished for Mr. Coon, which will also attract him. Other times a bright, shining tin can in the water will cause the coon to leave the shore, wade to the can and with his paw, slowly roll it towards the shore or abandon it if it rolls into too deep water. A steel, trap set between the shore and the curious object will do the trick: no bait necessary.

Wire traps, as well as the new tree trap have been successfully used in trapping the raccoon. The former is set at the entrance of some hole or cave, and the latter is securely fastened on some sloping tree. Both traps are very humane, killing or choking the animal in the space of a few moments.

It is great sport to hunt the raccoon with the aid or dogs and to chase him out of hollow logs and see the animal dart out of same, get on a tree, etc., only to be brought down with the trusty rifle or be captured by the dogs themselves.

Hunting this animal by moonlight is great sport. Usually two or three hunters, one with a rifle, the other with shotgun and the third with an ax, accompanied by two good dogs constitute the outfit and party. The dogs will usually tree the coon or discover him in a hollow log; then the fun begins. Of course the coon won't come down nor will he get out. If on a tree a fire is usually built so that the smoke reaches his nostrils when he will jump down and a fight with the dogs results. Many times the coon escapes only to be treed again, other times he is killed by the dogs of hunters. A long pole is used to poke him out of a hollow log; other times the log is cut down or into pieces.

If the night is dark and your dogs have treed a coon and you are unable to see the animal, stand with your back against the moon and face tree, or build a fire close to the tree and stand off a ways and the fire will no doubt illuminate the surroundings sufficiently so when standing at a distance overlooking the fire towards tree you will see the coon crouched on some limb or between some fork or crotch. Take good aim, fire, and down he will fall.

Missouri   **RACCOON**   From a Photograph

TRAPPING THE RACCOON

Southern methods as used by R. W. Riggs in the swamps of Louisiana–The bait used and the way to set traps:

The bait: the caster sacs of a beaver put into a little alcohol to keep it. A little of this put on a stick six inches high and placed so that he will have to go over the trap to get it, is a sure coon exterminator. Next to that, something good to eat–fish, squirrel, persimmons and corn are my favorites, the first two preferred. In January and a part or February, I set many traps on logs. I look for old logs; cut in a place for my traps and cover with whatever is on the log. Then place two round sticks about one inch thick on each side of the trap. On logs I use the 2½ Oneida Jump trap, in most other places the No. 2 Newhouse. I make mostly water sets and think them the best in this section. I set where anything forces the coon to take to the water at the end of a log, behind a tree, by steep banks and like places. But my best set is at the clay roots of a tree that has blown down out in the water. I fasten all of my traps to a good-sized stake, driven into the ground at quite an angle. My stakes are two feet out of the water. I put mud on them to make them look old. To fasten the traps I slip the chain through the ring and put the loop over my stake. Set the trap between the stake and the bank in about two inches of water if possible. Cover well and put bait on stick eighteen inches above trap. Set around clay roots and you will get the coon.

TRAPPING THE RACCOON

"To catch Mr. Raccoon," writes Mr. J. Hight, of Samoth, Ill., "one of the surest and best ways is to hunt at night with dogs, a gun, and if the night is dark, a lantern is needed. The success and profit in hunting with dog and gun lies in the fact that several will be put upon the same tree. I have known as many as seven to be found up on oak eating acorns before the hard frosts came. When up a tree if the night is dark hold the lantern above your head and imitate the sound of a fighting coon or on worried by dogs, by putting the forefinger in the mouth and squealing. Zip will look down in the direction of the noise and his eyes will shine like balls of fire: then with a shotgun he can be brought down, I have made them jump out of the tree with finger in mouth where they were easily caught by the dogs. If the moon is bright you do not need a lantern, but you can "Moon" Mr. Rack by placing yourself so that the coon is between you and the moon. I have shot them on a full moon with a rifle.

"In trapping I use the Newhouse No. 1½ trap and select a swamp or slough if I see any sign there. Place the trap under water three or four inches from the edge and secure it by a stake driven through the ring in the chain or drive the wedge into something the coon cannot drag. I bait by dropping a few grains of white corn in and around the trap, or by placing a small piece of white china on the trigger plate. This latter seems to have a fatal fascination for Mr. Zip, as it seems he will investigate every one he sees. If there are logs in the swamp, I look for logs they travel on, which is indicated by their excrement, being voided on certain longs in crossing. If I set on a log above water, I chip out a place large enough to hold the set trap. I put in the bottom of this under the trap a piece of chicken or bread soaked in syrup or fish, if I can get it. I sometimes use the sexual member of the female, also asafetida. All these are good baits, and be using different baits on different traps, you can learn a great deal of Ring tail's habits. The best place I ever set a trap is on a log, some part of which goes down into the water. When he comes to the water he is sure to feel for the depth : there put your trap, log chipped a above, and you will get the coon. The coon is a Benjamite, that is, he is left-handed. Seventy-five per cent of all I or my companions ever caught were caught by the left forefoot.

"Another good way to catch Zip is with the 'deadfall.' Find, as before, the logs they cross the water on, and lay a pole four or six inches in diameter across a log, fastened at the other end between two stakes withed or nailed together at the proper height. To make level, chip a flat place on the end across the log for the upright trigger to stand on, fasten a string to the rear end of the 'fall' pole, let it he secured to the upright trigger, being drawn right enough that a slight push on the string will throw the trap. Use triggers similar to the figure 4 triggers, the string being the long trigger. Or I sometimes use a small switch about three feet long for a long trigger. The poles must be weighed by crossing poles above the log, which will compel cooney to go between the poles, push the string and die. Deadfalls cost no money, and there will be no gnawing the foot off or pulling out and getting away.

"Another simple device used in the swamps of Illinois is the two-inch auger hold. Bored three inches deep with four horseshoe nails. Driven slanting so that one-quarter of an inch of the points will be in the hold: put sugar. Frog, fish or broken china in the hold, and when coon tries to withdraw his foot he is caught.

HOLLOW LOG DEADFALL.

The captured raccoon in above illustration tells the story. The bait is placed within the log. It is best to leave both ends open, permitting the animal to see through. This arrangement is also suitable for mink, marten, fox and fisher.

"One other thing I forgot to mention in the beginning of this article, is in hunting with dogs, if I cannot 'shine' his eyes, I build two or three bonfires under the tree, which will make it so light that the whole body of the coon can be seen, and shot. This is better than cutting timber and paying fines. This has been my experience."

TRAPPING THE RACCOON

Mr. Chamberlain, a South Dakota trapper, writes "that in trapping raccoons, he always sets traps at foot of a tree, and securely nails a bird or rabbit about two and one-half feet above the trap on the tree, so the raccoon has to get upon his hind legs to get the bait. By the animal tramping about he will get into the steel trap. I use a clog of about three to five pounds, unless you can arrange to fasten trap to limb of tree, so that when trap is sprung it will lift the victim up in the air."

TRAPPING RACCOONS AND STRETCHING

I herewith give you my method of trapping the raccoon and stretching the skin : First go along the sloughs and look for their up with a little thin mud. Drive a stake a little distance back of your trap on top of which place a small piece of honey, and I assure you if you have a trap strong enough to hold him, he will be there when you go back.

Now for the skinning and stretching : First lay the coon on his back. Rip across back part of hind legs from one end to the other : then across form one fore-paw to the other : then rip straight through center of belly to chin and take off hide. Lav the hide on a table and stretch it both ways with your hands, until you get it a little longer than it is wide. Straighten out legs, then cut off hind legs even with the hide; sew up the upper edges of fore-leg along side of the skin that comes off the lower jaw.

Cut sticks about one foot longer than the hide; take darning needle (large size best) and common wrapping twine and sew in the same as a woman sews a quilt in the frames. Take dry sticks (about size of little finger)–dead hedge sprouts are good as they are stiff. Trim off thorns; when the side sticks are sewed in well, which must be stitched about one inch apart, cut your end sticks with a "V" shaped notch in each end so they will not slip out. Cut long enough so as to be fairly tight, but not tight enough to make the hide wider than it is long. Place lower one just below the end of the hide, sew in same as side sticks; place top stick in just above and across the ears; sew hide to stick from outside toward center until you reach the neck which sew on each side alike. Now, put on the stretcher sticks, one on each side running lengthwise the hide. Split a hole in end of nose and hang up. Take a coarse comb and comb the hair down nice and straight, taking out all burrs, mud, etc. Put all sticks in on the flesh side of the hide.

IRA BRADEN,
Beardstown, Ill

TRAPPING THE RACCOON

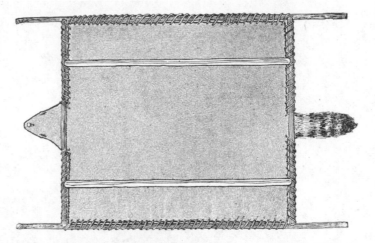

An Ohio trapper gives his method of method of capturing raccoon in the following two paragraphs: The raccoon is not a hard animal to trap. If I have occasion to believe that a raccoon is in a given vicinity, I pass along the shores of creeks and rivers and am always on the lookout for signs. Should I come across a log that is partly under water and extending to the shore, I take my hatchet and chop an opening large enough in which to set a No. 1, No. 1½ or No. 2 trap. This I cover up with leaves and moss, and to keep the wind from blowing the leaves of moss off, I usually load them down from blowing the leaves or moss of sufficient depth I arrange chain to a large stone so as to pull the raccoon into the water where he will drown. A few drops of anise on top of the moss or along the log is an attraction.

At other times I place the trap within four to five inches of water, placing a shining piece of nickel or tin on pan of trap. The raccoon seeing the reflection of the mirror-like object, will come and investigate it, and most likely when he attempts to disturb the mirror with his paw he will spring the trap and find himself a prisoner. The chain I always attach to the limb of some tree. or piece of wood and if convenient I use the spring pole. If the trap is staked fast the raccoon is likely to twist until he gets his foot out, or have seen cases where the foot or paw is left in the trap. For that reason I prefer a large limb that the raccoon can drag away and enables me to follow the trail.

R.B.A.

TRAPPING THE RACCOON

We have the following article from William Plummer or Rochester, Minnesota:

"Three years ago I went to trapping on a small scale. I borrowed a few traps from my neighbor, No. 1 and 1½ having located several dens in the rocks on the south side of a bluff. Coons will always go into rocky dens for winter quarters in preference to anywhere else. Well, I set my traps. Next morning several traps were sprung, coon hair was on the traps, but the raccoons were gone, They would pull and chew until they would get out. Finally, the one den became so covered with blood from their crippled feet that they wouldn't go in it any more. nor have I ever known a coon to go in there since. Well, something had to be done–I must have those coons. So I invested in two No. 2 Newhouse and set them in the other den. I managed to catch two small coons there during the winter.

"Last winter I made up my mind to do better at the business. So I bought half a dozen No. 3 Newhouse, and went to work at those dens. At the first den I could get nothing. They seemed to think that was a dangerous place. At the other den I did better, and caught eight during the winter. I used no bait, but simply placed the trap in the mouth of the den. One old fellow, however. got the best of me for a while–he would turn the left jaw of the trap over and walk by. So I placed another No. 2 to one side and a little behind the first one. I covered the second trap up with leaves and the next morning I had several toes, but Mr. Coon was gone. Well, that was rather disgusting, but I was bound to get him. About every other morning my traps would be sprung, and nothing there but a little fur. I got two No. 3 traps, and took the No. 2's out, putting larger ones in their place. The next morning both traps were sprung, and on the outside; Mr. Coon had got out, but left quite a chunk of his flank in the trap. How he got caught in the flank I am not able to tell unless he rolled over the traps to spring them. About a week afterward I found the coon in the trap and dead, but his fur was badly damaged.

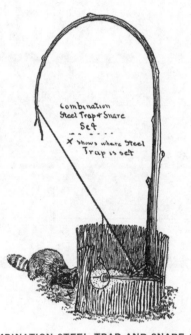

COMBINATION STEEL TRAP AND SNARE SET.

This is a very successful steel trap and snare arrangement. Bait with meat, etc.   Suitable for raccoon, badger and other carnivorous animals. Bury trap, also attach chain to spring pole. X is where trap is to be buried.

"This winter I concluded to try a new scheme. I had posted myself during the summer on the different kinds of bait for coon. I read up 'Trappers' Guides' on the subject, and went to work by placing a No. 3 trap in each path approaching the den, covered the traps nicely with chicken feathers, placing over each trap a bit of smoked codfish and scattered a little oil of anise and rhodium around. Well, the next morning I had three of the neighbors tomcats, but no coons: so I found that would not do. Then I went at the old plan, placing traps in the den. During the first week I caught two young ones, but no old ones. Then, again, my traps commenced to be sprung every night. Sometimes a little fur left but no coon. I placed a trap in each of three different paths within six feet of the den, covered them up with feathers and leaves. The feathers would be pulled off the traps and the traps in the den sprung. Well, I hardly knew what next to do, but thought I would try still another plan. I placed a No. 3 just at entrance to den, covered it up carefully, leaving the two traps on inside uncovered, and in five days caught one young coon and two of the largest old coons I ever saw. I have tried all kinds of bait I ever heard of, but never succeeded. Well, with it I have caught coons in paths by placing a stone or pole on either side of trap to make them step over and covering the trap carefully, but if they become pinched a few times they become wary."

TRAPPING THE RACCOON

"I caught hundreds of raccoons in my time." writes Mr. Hammond, now retired and living in Albany. "My trapping grounds were along rivers, creeks, canals and close to lakes in Ohio, near Deshler, and later in Missouri, south of Jefferson City. I was always upon the alert, and while fishing one spring day and sitting among bushes on the river bank, I noticed a coon on the opposite side coming up the river, and suddenly stretched his neck in direction of square oyster can (used in those days) that was about three feet from the shore in four or five inches of water. He stayed around for about fifteen minutes, at various times reaching out after the can and even moving it from one place to another, and scrutinizing it very closely. As my cork went down. I pulled in a fish, and, naturally, the coon went skipping into the woods.

"The following winter I bought a dozen coon traps, took them to the machine shop and had two small holes drilled in each pan. Then I took from an old alarm clock the nickel case and made small round disks in size resembling that of the pan. I then riveted these nickel plates thereon and polished same with wood ashes, and set the traps along the river banks, two to five inches under water. I also riveted gold plated disks upon the pans with equal results. On one occasion I placed a small pocket mirror fastened on a piece of wood slanting and shining towards the shore; and set a common steel trap just between the shore and the looking glass, but out of the water. I covered other parts of the trap with grass, leaves, etc., so when the coon tried to examine the looking glass, he stepped upon the protruding covered trap and was caught.

"I cut the skin open on the belly and stretched same in square shape. Keep grease from the fur and always pull the tail-bone out. Nicely handled and seasonable skins bring twenty-five per cent more, and that's where the profit lies for the experienced trapper.

"Before closing my letter let me relate how I captured wild cats, coons, rabbits and other animals with snares. In tramping through the woods, I often came across tracks that I did not know by what animal they were made. I set these snares, made from gut strings, wire, also cotton or linen lines, at various places, such as in front of hollow logs, passages, under brush or fence rails, and other favorable places. Arrange to lift the animal off its feet and away from harm of other animals by pulling down limbs or small trees, and if these were not conveniently situated, I often threw a long rope across a distant limb, attached a ten to twenty pound stone on end and raised it high up; the other end I fastened to the snare in such a way that if pulled by the animal the fastener would break or pull out and the weight descend and hang the victim before he knew what was up. The animal would sometimes get away if caught by front foot, but never if caught around the neck or hind foot."

TRAPPING THE RACCOON

"The raccoon is not a very difficult animal to capture. The traps should be set either in the paths in some woods that the animal frequents, or along the shores of a stream or lake. One of the most successful ways is to make a U-shaped enclosure at the edge of the water. This can be done by driving sticks in the shore; not necessary that the open part should be exposed to the water. Set trap at entrance and place some bait at the farthest end of the pen. Cover the trap with water-soaked leaves which can be held in place by a light covering of earth. I usually fasten the trap to a brush drag. The latter I know in the water, and if light put a stone on top of it to keep it from floating away. Quite

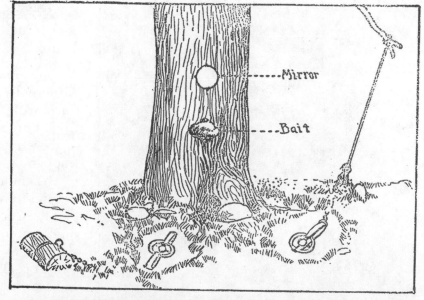

UNCOVERED STEEL TRAP SET FOR RACCOONS.

The mirror and bait form double attractions to the raccoon. A double set of this kind should be arranged near the bank of some stream or lake, or near the places the raccoon frequents. The steel trap as well as the clog should be buried.

often if the raccoon springs the trap he will get tangled up in the drag: consequently you do not have to hunt him up. This set is also recommended for mink. If the water happens to be fairly deep, the chain will become tangled up in the brush and the weight of the trap will drown the mink in short order. Caught thirteen raccoons and about twenty-five minks a year ago. Was unable to trap last year."

R. B. A.

CHAPTER 20

Ringtail Cat or Bassarisk

RINGTAIL CAT

THE BASSARISK

Among other little-known animals of the southwestern United States is the Bassarisk (Mexican Cacomixile), sometimes called Ringtailed Cat and Civet Cat, but as it is not a Civet or a Cat, neither of these names should be used by the intelligent trapper.

The animal is nearly related to the Raccoon family, and in habits and appearance it closely resembles the Coon, except that it is smaller, slimmer and much more active. It has yellowish brown sides, shading to grayish dark brown above and dirty white or salmon color below, with a body twelve to fourteen inches long and a curved, bushy tail about the same length distinctly ringed with black and white. Its ears are carried very erect and there is a quarter circle of light colored fur over each jet black eye, which gives it the appearance of wearing a pair of spectacles.

This animal ranges from Central America north and west as far as the State of Washington. It inhabits thickly wooded regions where it is very active in climbing from tree to tree. Like the Coon it is nocturnal in its habits and omniverous in its appetite, and destroys large numbers of birds' eggs and their young.

From Original
Drawing   THE RING TAIL CAT   Owned by
                                                        Andersch Bros.

The fur is quite soft and brings a higher price than formerly.

The directions given for capturing the Coon will mostly apply to the Bassarisk, although it is doubtful if it could be caught in a water set, as it is more of a dry land animal.

For bait, any one of its natural foods may be used.

The No. 1 trap is about the right size.

Hollow logs, under roots of trees, old decayed stumps, the banks of streams that they frequent, etc., are good places to set traps for the Ringtail Cat.

Ringtail Cat should be skinned "cased" and shipped. Fur side out.

CHAPTER 21

Opossum

The Opossum is the only marsupial found in America, that is, it is the only representative of that remarkable class of animals in which the young are born at such an early and undeveloped stage that the mother is obliged to carry them about in a pocket or pouch under her belly until they are old enough to take care of themselves.

The Opossum makes its den in the ground under a stump or rock. They also live in hollow logs. In cold weather they retire to their dens and only come out occasionally when the snow is on the ground. They hate the cold and are most active on warm, damp nights. They are found only in wooded districts, and can climb to the tops of the tallest trees, using their tail and hand-shaped feet. The tail is prehensile, that is, it can hold on to anything it encircles, and it is a great aid in supporting them while they gather persimmons, grapes and other wild fruit of the woods.

The Opossum is a nocturnal animal, sleeping in the daytime and seeking its food by night. It is a slow moving and stupid animal and has no particular means of defending itself. As a last resort in danger, they feign death or "play possum."

The principal food of the Opossum consists of insects, persimmons, grapes or other wild fruit, nuts, berries, roots, reptiles, carrion, eggs, small rats, mice and sweet potatoes, also poultry and corn.

Opossum are very prolific, having two or three litters each year and from six to thirteen in a litter.

Good bait for Opossum is chicken, rabbit, small birds or carrion.

This animal inhabits the warmer parts of the United States, and several species of it are said to exist also in Australia. In form it somewhat resembles the common house Rat. Its body is about twenty inches long, stoutly built, and its tail, which is generally fifteen inches in length, is prehensile like that of some Monkeys, *i.e.*, capable of holding on to anything that it encircles. The Opossum is five-toed, and walks on the soles of its feet like the Bear. Its ears are large, rounded and almost naked. The female has from nine to thirteen teats, the odd one being in the center of the ring formed by the rest. The fur is long, soft and woolly, whitish at the roots, and brown at the top.

OPOSSUM

The Opossum is omnivorous, feeding on corn, nuts, berries, roots, insects, young birds, eggs, mice, etc. It is nocturnal in its habits; hiding in the thick foliage of the trees in the daytime, and seeking its food by night. It is an active climber, and is said to spend much of its time and even to sleep suspended from the limb of a tree by the tail! The females are very prolific, producing from nine to thirteen young at a birth, and three and even four litters in a year. They are provided with a pouch under their belly, in which they protect and suckle their young.

These animals are trapped in the same manner as the Raccoon and the Badger, by setting traps in their haunts, and baiting with any of their favorite kinds of food. They have a habit, when caught, of feigning death, and will bear considerable torture without betraying any signs of life. This habit doubtless gave rise to the common by-word which calls certain kinds of deceit "playing 'possum."

The Opossum

Of the American species, naturalists have discovered three varieties, namely the Virginia opossum, the Florida opossum and the Texas opossum, all very similar.

The Virginia opossum is the most common and the most widely distributed, being found as far north as Pennsylvania and Ohio and from there westward to Nebraska and southward. In the southwest the Texas opossum is found.

In general form the opossum resembles the house rat but is much larger. The tail is almost bare and is prehensile, that is, it is capable of holding on to anything which it encircles. The muzzle is long and pointed, the ears bare.

In color this animal is generally a grizzly gray but some specimens are much darker than others. The fur is long, soft and fluffy.

The opossum dens in the ground and the abode is usually located under a stump or rock. The burrows are shallow and terminate in a larger cavity lined with dry leaves. They also sometimes locate in hollow logs. They are found only in timbered districts and are active climbers. Their food consists mainly of mice, eggs and young birds and insects, but they are also fond of poultry and almost any kind of flesh, fresh or tainted. They are not strictly carnivorous as they feed on persimmons, paw-paws, polk berries and other wild fruits.

On other occasions instead of feigning death the animal will open its mouth and present a rather fierce appearance, but there is little danger of them biting.

While the opossum is not a hibernating animal it remains in its den during cold weather. It is a southern animal and the severe winters in the northern parts of its range are not to the animal's liking. They are most active on warm, damp nights for they do not like to move about when the weather is dry and the leaves are rustly.

They are very prolific, bringing forth from six to twelve young at a litter and in some cases even more. When newly born they are very small and imperfectly formed and are carried by the mother in the pouch on the under side of the body until large enough to travel.

They become prime about the second week of November in the North and remain in good condition until March. In the South they do not become prime until about December 1st and commence to shed much earlier than in the North. The fur is not a very valuable one but there is a growing demand for the flesh which is used as food and in many places will meet with ready sale.

I recommend the No. 1 trap for this animal and those of medium strength of spring only, as the opossum's foot and leg is tender, and if the bones are broken the animal is likely to escape. They do not struggle much, however, and comparatively few escape from the traps.

I set my traps in the thick woods, usually in the gullies also along the edges of the woods, along fences, etc. The opossum is possessed of no cunning whatever, and no special care is needed in setting the traps if this animal alone is expected, however, it is always best to use care in setting for the most stupid animals, as one never knows what animal may pass that way. Whenever possible I place the trap in a natural enclosure, such as a hollow in the side of a stump or tree, a hollow between two spreading roots, an opening among rocks or in a hollow log. Failing to find any such place I construct a small enclosure of stakes, bark, stones or pieces of rotten wood, whichever is most convenient; and set the trap in the entrance nesting it down and covering with whatever is found nearby.

The Opossum.

The trap may be staked, stapled or fastened to a clog. For bait I use rabbit, fowl, muskrat or small birds of any kind. Bait may be fresh or tainted as the opossum is not particular. I have heard of many fancy sets and baits and have given some of them a trial, but find the method given above to be the most satisfactory.

Opossums will sometimes be caught in traps set for skunks, foxes and other animals and there are probably more of them caught in such sets than in any other. They may also be caught in wooden traps.

I have caught these animals in traps set on logs spanning the streams, also at the entrance of the dens, but if I were setting many traps for opossums I would use the above method mostly.

The opossum makes a wandering, aimless sort of trail, quite broad for an animal of its size and the toes are turned outward in walking. The footprints of the average opossum will measure about one and one-fourth inch in diameter-that is, the front foot-the print of the hind foot being from one-fourth to one-half inch larger.

TRAPPING THE OPOSSUM

"Below I give in a brief manner my way of trapping and taking the opossum:

"I find out where the opossum runs, then cut some sticks about one inch in diameter, about eighteen to twenty inches long, and drive them into the ground three to four inches apart, in a circle formation of a diameter of eighteen to twenty inches, leaving an opening of about six inches wide.

"Then take one or two steel traps and set at opening, using pieces of rabbit or chicken as bait which I place about twelve inches beyond opening inside of coop. I always cover the trap with leaves, bits of rotten wood and earth, having first placed loose leaves beneath pan of trap to keep dirt from falling beneath it. I also throw small bits of meat outside the enclosure.

"The best place to set this kind of trap is at the edge of a bush or thicket, bordering an old field or creek, lake or any place where the opossum comes for food or water.

"Have used snares advantageously, but always attached same to a spring pole or limb of a tree, or a young tree itself. A fiddle-string or horse-hair noose is better than copper wire, at least I always prefer it."

TRAPPING THE OPOSSUM

"The opossum has a habit of going around at night, visiting henroosts, if there are any near. If not, it catches birds, or what ever it can find, until it gets fat. Then it goes into its hole which it digs or takes from other animals. There it stays until it gets hungry and poor.

"I have had success in smoking them out. I took waste cotton rags, tearing them into small strips, putting them loosely over the hole; then setting them on fire, blowing them until they burn well. Then I put my hand or something over the hole to smother the blaze and drive the smoke into the hole as far as possible.

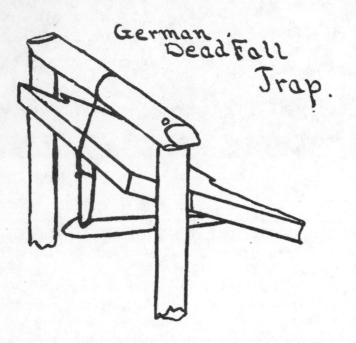

German DeadFall Trap.

"Then set the trap as you would to catch it without smoking, and you will have the opossum, as the smoke will drive it out.

"The kind of a trap I use is a No. I Victor, which always holds them if it is in good working order."

R. B. A.

TRAPPING THE OPOSSUM

The opossum, like the skunk, is an easy animal to trap. Having found out where he runs I set my line of traps on his path. Any kind of meat bait will do. Traps, however, should be covered up, and be sure and put some cotton under the pan to keep sand and dirt from falling beneath it. To keep him from twisting out, I generally attach trap to a spring pole.

A good place to set your trap is where you have seen him drink water. Also in front of his hole. I never resort to snares, although I have seen a lot of negroes brought them with ordinary fish lines. On one occasion a negro brought past our house a large male opossum that he claimed to have caught with an ordinary fish hook. He suspended the bait over a fence rail and the animal in his eagerness to devour the meat, swallowed hook and all. When the time came to go away, he found there was something tickling.

N. C. A.

TRAPPING THE OPOSSUM

The opossum is an easy animal to trap, of a lazy disposition and does not suspect danger as does the mink, fox or wolf, in this respect he resembles the skunk very much. Almost the identical methods used in the capture of the skunk can be applied to the opossum.

The best manner to trap them is with steel traps, No. I, No. 11/2, not larger than No. 2. He can also be taken with deadfalls, box traps, snares and in the use of poison. In seeking to capture the opossum one need only study his habits, ascertain his whereabouts and then by placing bait along his path which usually is beside fences, he is easily taken.

It will be remembered that the opossum feigns death and the trapper should make sure of his victim; otherwise he may trouble himself carrying the supposed dead opossum home, only to find that "the dead arise" and leave in quick order. A smart rap or blow on the forehead is sufficient. Many instances have

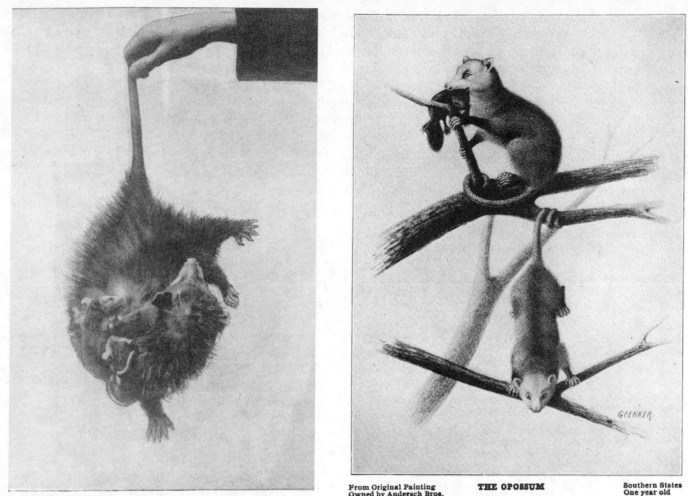

THE OPOSSUM AND HER FAMILY   From a Photograph

From Original Painting
Owned by Andersch Bros.   THE OPOSSUM   Southern States
One year old

been reported to us where the opossum, after being released from the trap, he having feigned death, scampered away.

Many prefer to smoke the opossum out if located in some den or in a hollow tree. Take cotton waste, rags or if an hollow, tree make a fire below, and you will soon have him on the limb, if such is possible for the animal to reach.

For bait use any old piece of meat as he is not very fastidious and cares little whether it is fresh or putrid. The skin should he handled similar to that of the skunk, never cut open on the belly but leave it cased; preferably to have the flesh side out. The tail should be severed from the body and all fat removed from the skin. The skin is very tender and the party in charge must exercise due judgment in skinning, scraping and stretching, especially if in the latter process one-piece stretches are used. We recommend the three-piece stretchers every time. The skin of the opossum has no value out of season and low, thrashy skins should not be marketed.

The animal is detested by the agriculturist, the fruit grower and the poultry farmer. Being a good climber he is able to hold his weight by encircling the limb with his tail and springing from one branch to another in monkey fashion. He is slightly awkward on the ground, his movements apparently lazy, his walk plantigrade, and at times the running gait resembles a series of ambling leaps. His great toes and hind paws enable him to grasp and hold firmly to the limbs of tree, while his prehensile tail assists the animal to secure a desired position and immunity from falls. He is able to suspend himself by means of his tail for hours at a time. His constant, fastidious appetite is not confined entirely to flesh, as the animal will devour quantities of fruit, vegetables and other vegetation. His favorite passages are along fences and creeks, where the frogs afford him a tolerable repast.

He is very tenacious of life, and resorts to simulation when very hard pressed. At times he will roll up like a ball, at other times lie silently, feigning death. Many a farmer in capturing the thief in his poultry yard, gives the animal one or more sharp taps on the head or body, knocking it down, in which position with open jaws, extended tongue and dimmed eyes, he will feign death; the farmer in many instances carries the apparently dead opossum in the house, shows it to the family and lays it aside with the intention of skinning, and probably eating his meat, only to find later that he has regained his liberty. Apparently the animal prefers darkness to light. He sleeps through the day in the holes in the earth or hollow trees and lives with his mate only during the pairing time, leading a solitary life during the rest of the year. It has no fixed habitation, but uses any cranny which it deseries in the morning the opossum is especially in quest of some burrow inhabited by some weaker rodent, thus obtaining food and a day's rest without great effort, and is free of all concern until the approach of another night.

CHAPTER 22

Muskrat

Muskrats that live along streams and creeks usually burrow into the banks, where high enough for that purpose. The entrance of these tunnels is under water and of sufficient depth to prevent freezing. The tunnels extend upward into the bank above the water level and are anywhere from ten to fifty feet in length, lending to a large chamber, which is lined with grass and moss.

The Muskrat is herbivorous, that is, its chief food consists of herbs, grass, roots and vegetables, but it sometimes eats animal food. In Winter the main food of the Muskrat is the roots of aquatic plants, such as pond lillies, sedges, etc., but it will also eat mussels, clams and carp. In the Summer the Muskrat eats roots, leaves, grass and sometimes they visit gardens near their haunts (doing considerable damage) where they feed on cabbage, carrots, corn, beets, onions, parsnips and practically all garden vegetables.

Muskrats are very prolific, bringing forth from four to ten at a litter and about three litters a year.

They are easily trapped. The No. 1 and 1½ size traps are the best suited for Muskrat trapping.

The best baits for Muskrat are sweet apples, carrots, parsnips, turnips, etc. A good scent is the musk of the annual mixed with a little Anise Oil and Oil of Rhodium.

There are various modes of trapping the Muskrat, the manner of setting depending upon the situation. They are usually taken at the foot of slides and trails. These trails and slides may be found along the banks of streams and ponds which they inhabit.

Find such a slide or trail and set the trap at the foot of it under a couple of inches of water. No covering is required.

MUSK RAT

Another good set is to find their holes in the banks and set a trap in the entrance.

Still another method is to find their feeding beds—beds of grass which seem to be floating on the water—set traps on these beds, under water, and cover lightly with some of the feed bed.

From Original Painting
Property of Andersch Bros.

GROUP OF MUSKRATS

N. E. States, U. S. A.
Late Fall

The floating log is also a good set. Get a log and moor it to the shore by a wire passed through a staple driven into one end of the log while the other end projects into the water. Cut shallow notches into the log just wide enough to hold a trap, set a trap in each notch and cover lightly with leaves or grass. The traps may be stapled to the log and small pieces of sweet apple and carrots scattered along the entire length. From three to ten traps may be set on one log, according to its length.

This is an animal of amphibious habits. Its head and body are from thirteen to fifteen inches in length. The tail is nine or ten inches, two edged, and for two thirds of its length is rudder shaped and covered with scales and thin, short hair, the edges being heavily fringed. The hind feet are slightly webbed, making the Muskrat an expert swimmer. Its color is brown above and ashy beneath.

Muskrats are nocturnal in their habits, but are frequently seen swimming and feeding in the day-time. They can go from ten to fifteen rods under water without breathing. Their natural food is grass and roots; but they will eat clams, mussels, flesh, corn, oats, wheat, apples and many vegetables. They thrive best in sluggish streams or ponds bordered with grass and flags. The roots of these plants are their chief support, and from the tops they constuct their abodes. These structures are dome-shaped, and rise some-times to the height of five or six feet. The entrances are at the bottom, under water, so that the insides of the houses are not exposed to the open air. The Muskrats live in them in winter, gathering into families of from six to ten members. Hundreds of these dwellings can be counted from a single point in many large marshes.

Muskrats have a curious method of traveling long distances under the ice. In their winter excursions to their feeding grounds, which are frequently at great distances from their abodes, they take in breath at start-ing and remain under water as long as they can. Then they rise up to the ice, and breathe out the air in their lungs, which remains in bubbles against the lower surface of the ice. They wait till this air recovers oxygen from the water, and then take it in again and go on till the operation has to be repeated.

The hunter sometimes takes advantage of this habit of the Muskrat, in the following manner: When the marshes and ponds where Muskrats abound are first frozen over and the ice is thin and clear, on striking into their houses with his hatchet for the purpose of setting his traps, he frequently sees a whole family plunge into the water and swim away under the ice. Following one of them for some distance, he sees him come up to renew his breath in the manner above described. After the animal has breathed against the ice, and before he has had time to take his bubble in again, the hunter strikes with his hatchet directly over him and drives him away from his breath. In this case he drowns in swimming a few rods, and the hunter, cutting a hole through the ice takes him out. Mink, Otter and Beaver travel under the ice in the same way; and hunters have frequently told me of taking Otter in the same manner.

A Muskrat House in the Marsh

In summer, Muskrats live in banks and hollow trees that stand near a stream; and sometimes, for want of suitable marshes and ponds, they remain in the banks and trees through the winter. They are very prolific, bringing forth from six to nine at a birth, and three times a year. The first kittens also have a litter, which attain about the size of house rats in September. They have many enemies, such as the Fox, Wolf, Lynx, Otter, Mink and Owl. They are found from the Atlantic to the Pacific, and from the Rio Grande to the Arctic Regions. But they do not inhabit the alluvial lands of Carolina, Georgia, Alabama, and Florida.

The modes of capturing the Muskrat are various. Some of them are good at certain seasons and in certain conditions of the ice; but for general service there is no means of capture so reliable as the steel trap. Traps should be set in the general feeding places, play-grounds, and holes of the Muskrat, generally about two inches under water. Bait is not necessary except when game is scarce and its signs not fresh. In that case you may bait with apples, parsnips, carrots, artichokes, white flag-roots, or even with the flesh of the Muskrat. The musk of this animal will sometimes draw effectually at long distances. The bait should be fastened to the end of a stick, and stuck over the trap about eight inches high, and in such a position that the animal will have to pass over the trap to take the bait. Care should be taken to fasten the trap to a stake so that the chain will lead the captive into deep water and drown him. If he is allowed to entangle himself or get ashore, he will be very likely to gnaw or twist off a leg and get away.

DROWNING MUSKRATS

An old trapper strongly urges the setting of traps where the animal can drown himself in the following manner: He stakes the ring of his chain as far out in the stream from the trap as possible, then about a foot beyond that puts another stake. The trapped Muskrat makes for deep water, and when stopped by the chain swims this way and that and very soon winds himself up on the outer stake, and drowns in short order.

The Muskrat is more likely than most animals to gnaw off, or twist off, a foot, when caught in a trap, and so escape, especially if caught by the fore leg. Old trappers say he will not gnaw through sound bone; many of them say he does not gnaw at all, but twists his leg off. However this may be, in cases where the bone has been broken, either by the springing of the trap or his violent plunging afterwards, the Muskrat is very likely to sever the cords and flesh and get away. As this is particularly true when he is caught by a forefoot, it is very desirable to catch him by a hind foot. This may easily be done by placing the bait so high and so nearly over the trap that he will have to stand up on his hind legs to reach it. Then, if you have fastened the ring of your chain to a sliding pole, or to a stake driven out in the water, the rat will drown.

A good way to trap Muskrats which are wandering up or down the banks of a stream is to dig a pocket in the bank where the water is deep, making the bench two or three inches under water, and set the trap in it. Fasten a piece of sweet apple, or parsnip, or carrot on one end of a stick, pushing the other end into the bank over the trap and at the right height.

Sometimes a landing place can be made with a large sod. Set the trap on this, a little under water.

There are many such ways of proceeding, which must be used according to circumstances and the ingenuity of the trapper.

Where it is found that large numbers of Muskrats are living in some swamp, inlet or pond, they can often be caught successfully in this manner: Take a board about twelve inches wide by sixteen feet long, and nail a few cleats across it in pairs, each pair just far enough apart to allow your trap to set between them. You could set half a dozen traps on such a board or plank. Fasten the chains to the outer edge of the board and anchor the board to some tree or stake on the bank by a rope or wire. Then shove the board out from the bank to where you think the rats will be apt to climb up on it, or near their houses. Next morning you can pull the board in-shore and examine your catch.

Muskrats are not difficult to catch nor dangerous; so they furnish boys a fine field for trapping experience. They thrive in the settled farm lands of our Eastern and Middle States, when not too heavily trapped.

FLOATING MUSKRAT SET

TAKE A R.R. TIE OR SIMILAR FLATTENED LOG, SAW OR HEW PLACES, INTO WHICH TRAPS ARE TO BE SET. COVER TRAPS, AND FASTEN CHAIN ON SIDE BELOW WATER LEVEL. BAIT WITH VEGETABLES OR MEAT.

PRACTICAL SUGGESTIONS BY TRAPPERS

—Drop sweet corn along the edge of the water where Muskrats travel, then take part of an ear and place it on the end of a sharp stick in the bank just above the trap, which should be set a little under water.

—Take a stake about two inches thick, saw the large end off square and nail a block on it large enough for a trap bed, drive in the water about eight or ten feet from shore and deep enough so that the block is an inch or so under water. Put dry grass on the block and make a nest for the trap to set in. Put some bait on the nest and fasten trap chain to the stake. The Muskrat will swim out and climb up, only to be caught.

—Take a piece of white cloth and place above your trap. Any white object attracts the attention of a Muskrat, and where they are numerous many may be caught by this simple device.

—Select a place where the bank is steep, close to where they show signs, or to their holes, and make a shelf in the bank the width of a spade, extending back in the bank four or five inches and about three inches under water. Then make a second shelf just above the level of the water in the first shelf, about three inches wide for the bait. Set the trap on the first shelf, cover nicely, and bait with apple placed on second shelf.

—When trapping in shallow ditches use a double-jawed trap, or a larger size than single-jawed No. 1, so as to take the Muskrat high enough on the leg to hold him from twisting out if caught by the fore leg. For scent, take a stick and rub over the hind parts of a Muskrat and place near the trap.

—Muskrats are very fond of catnip and a few stems of it stuck in the ground around the trap will prove useful.

—Take a piece of hay wire about three or four feet long and fasten a stake at one end, then put the wire through the trap ring and fasten the other stake to it. Put it in deep water, having the stake under the water two or three inches, so "John Sneakem" will not take your trap and rat.

—If water is shallow with now and then a stump or stone just above water, get a sod and place it upon one of them and by running a small stick through and into the mud, the sod will stay firmly in place. The sod should be so placed that it will be easy for the rat to climb up. This may be done by having one side close to the water. No bait is needed. If your traps are set in a shallow place, a good plan is to attach to each chain three feet of wire. This will give the rat a chance to get into deeper water.

—Set your traps for rats in any place where the water is not less than ten inches deep. Clear away all the brush or roots, fasten the trap chain to a stone that weighs three or four pounds, and throw the stone the full length of the chain into the stream. Use a chain that has no swivel or wire up the swivel and you will save every rat you catch, as it will drown itself at once and the pelt will not be cut full of holes as with other methods.

JEREMIAH ZETTLE.

—I have five different kinds of sets. The best I ever tried is to find where rats travel from a creek to a pond. Go along the creek and you will find a path leading over to the pond. Place a No. 1½ trap in the water at each end, just so the water will cover it an inch or two. Cover the trap well with water-soaked leaves, for you are liable to catch a Coon or Mink.

The Muskrat

—Another way is to dig a pocket in a bank where the water is deep and put a trap in it and hang a piece of parsnip or apple six inches above. The first rat along will try to get the bait and get caught.

—Still another good way is to set a trap at the bottom of a rat's slide in about three inches of water, and you will catch them by the bind legs and they will not twist out.

—In the spring you will find places along the bank where the water is about six inches deep, where the rats come out of their holes. Gather some dry grass, put it at the place where they climb or the bank, place your trap on the grass. This will cause the grass to settle down, bringing your trap two or three inches under water. When the rat comes to your bunch of grass he will try to find out what it is. It was not there the last time when he was out. He swims up to the grass and starts climbing on it. You get him in the morning, usually by both front feet.

—I find a good way to bait for Muskrat is to take a piece of apple and break it in small bits, scatter them between the jaws and around close to the trap. This makes a good set on the edge of the water, and "Johnny Sneakem," the trap thief, is not apt to notice it, because the apple soon colors.

—Muskrats should be trapped along streams or swales where you find their signs. For bait use carrots or sweet apples. Sweet apples are best. Set the trap in about two inches of water, fasten the chain at full length to a sunken limb, drive a stake on either side of the chain near where it is fastened. Set thus the rat will not "foot" himself. He will soon become entangled and drown.

—Another good set for rats is by scooping a piece out of a sod and placing it on a stone or root just under the water. Fasten the chain as before and scatter pieces of apple on the sod.

The Muskrat.

Muskrats are trapped in the fall, winter and spring, but they are not prime until mid-winter, and some are not fully prime until the first of March. Nevertheless, they are more easily caught in the fall, and as the skins bring a fair price, the most trapping is done at this time, that is for "bank rats,"—those living in holes in the banks. Where the muskrats live in houses, they are trapped mostly after the ice had formed.

In the far North the skins are in good condition until the first of June, while in the extreme South they should not be trapped after the first of April. The muskrats found in settled districts are larger and better furred than those of the wilderness, also, those found East of the Mississippi River are larger than those of the West.

When trapping for these animals, the traps should always be staked full length of chain into deep water, so that the captured animal will drown, as otherwise they are almost certain to twist off the foot, and escape, unless they are caught by a hind foot. Many trappers set their traps several inches under water, as by so doing they catch the rat by a hind foot, and there is very little danger of them escaping. Some stake their traps the length of the chain into deep water, and drive another stake about a foot beyond. The muskrat, when caught, winds the chain around the outer stake and is thus prevented from reaching the bank. Others prefer to tie a stone on the end of the chain, and lay the stone in deep water.

The traps most used are the Nos. 1 and 1½, but the No. 0 is also used sometimes. The Victor trap is a great favorite, as it does not have as strong a spring as the higher priced traps, and is not so likely to break the animal's leg. The single spring Oneida Jump traps are also fine traps for muskrats.

One of the most common methods of trapping the muskrat is to find their slides on the bank and set the trap at the foot of the slide under about two and a half or three inches of water. No covering is needed.

If you can find a log, with one end lying in the water, examine same and if there are muskrat droppings on the log, cut a notch for the trap, so that it will be just under water when set in the notch. The chain may be stapled to the log.

Another good way is to find their holes in the bank and set a trap in the entrance, staking into deep water.

If the water is still, and there is much grass in the water, look around, and you will find their feeding beds,—beds of grass which appear to be floating on the water. Set traps on these beds, under water.

If you know there are muskrats about and you can not find any of the places described above, select a steep bank, and set the trap under two or three inches of water at the foot of the bank. Pin a piece of bait to the bank about ten inches above the trap.

Where muskrats are found in large numbers as in a pond or slough, proceed as follows: Get a board about twelve inches wide and sixteen feet long and nail strips across it, arranging them in pairs, just far enough apart to let a trap set between. A board of this size will hold six or eight traps. The traps may be stapled to the edge of the board and some small pieces of bait scattered the entire length. The traps should be covered with dirt or dead grass. Attach a rope to one end of the board and anchor it in the water where the muskrats are sure to find it.

To trap muskrats in their houses in winter, cut a hole in the side of the house, and set the trap inside, on the bed. Fasten the trap to a stick outside of the house and close the opening tight, so the diving hole will not freeze. I have had best success at this kind of trapping by using a small trap, No. 0, and a good length of chain, as it gives the rat more chance to drown. The traps should be visited evening and morning.

In the spring, when the ice has just commenced to melt, you will find small piles of grass roots projecting above the ice. Move this aside and you will find a hole in the ice, with a feed bed directly in under it. Set a trap on this bed and cover the hole.

The best baits for muskrats are sweet apple, parsnips, carrot, pumpkin, corn and the flesh of the muskrat. While they do not eat the meat, they will go to smell at it, which is all that is needed. Muskrat musk, beaver castor and catnip are all attractive to the muskrat.

To this pole the chain of the trap is fastened, and the trap is placed right in their sleeping-place, lightly covered with the moss or material which forms the animals' bed. The broken wall should then be plastered up again with mud; or a hole may be cut in the side of the house, on the surface of the ice, and the trap laid inside, the chain being secured to a stout piece of stick laid outside, across the hole in the wall, the hole being then lightly repaired. In either case, the captured muskrat makes for the water, dragging the trap after it, the weight of which is sufficient to keep it under water and drown it.

The use of steel traps is a very sure way of trapping the muskrat, but it labors under the disadvantage of catching only one in a night in each trap. The following is another simple way of catching several at a time: Sink an old barrel to the level of the ground in the bank near the water's edge, and about half fill it with water; on the surface of the water, in the barrel, place two or three light strips of wood, upon which put a few pieces of carrot or sweet apple. From the barrel to the tracks of the muskrat, form a trail of small pieces of the same bait, so as to lead the rats to the barrel; they will jump in after the food, and will not be able to get out again.

TRAPPING THE MUSKRAT

I have trapped muskrats since I was twelve years old, and have had good success. I will give you my role. Trapped more than 1,000 the first month this year after the water was frozen. Chop a small hole in the south side of the house large enough in which to set your trap. Dig away a little moss on the mound so as to set the trap under water the grown rats are wise enough to fill the trap with moss and get caught and you only get the small rats.

No. 1 Victor traps are good for rats, select weak traps as the strong ones break the bone and they gnaw their leg or foot off and get away. Use the wet moss to line edges of the opening of hole, and bank up good enough to keep from freezing; then clean away about 2 1/2 inches from the level of the water, and set trap and if the water freezes one-half inch, you get a rat anyway. If you set on the mound, you don't. First trap out the small feeding houses, then the larger one. Later in the winter, a person should get five to six rats in each house.

If you wish to spear the rats, get on the house and jump till you see on and then follow him up and spear him, when the ice is first freezing. For a spear, use steel rod, like a wagon rod, sharpened to a point, tapering three to five inches, with a heavy handle. A person may spear 100 in a day. Baits are not necessary for muskrats.

In the spring is a good time to shoot rats. In a boat you may get in good shooting range. When they are pairing they are out all day and you can get then regularly two at a time, with good wages, for two or three weeks after the ice is broken up. Rats can also be trapped with a barrel at the level of the water, hall full of water with some shingles floating in it. The rat swimming up to the barrel sees the bait on the shingles, jumps down, and cannot get out. Many rats can be caught that way. If you are unable to select weak traps for capturing muskrats, you may weaken then by heating them. You lose thirty out of 100 by using strong traps, but you can catch them by the hind leg by setting about three inches in the water.

ADOLPH LIEN,
Olaf, Iowa.

TRAPPING MUSKRATS UNDER ICE

This is my method of trapping muskrats under the ice. Take two ten-inch boards two feet long, and two six-inch boards two feet long, and make a box, using the ten-inch boards for sides and the six-inch boards for top and bottom. Now make a trap door of wire for the front end of the box, which will push in but will not push out; set at an angle of about forty-five degrees. Drive shingle nails about every inch or so around the break end of the trap and weave a net across it so that any mink could not get through.

This cut shows the trap finished with narrow boards nailed to the sides, which come in handy to sink in the water for trapping muskrats. Find the muskrat runway under the ice, which you can always tell by the bubbles or riley water. Put a stone on the trap and sink. I have caught four rats in a trap made like this night after night, and I now seldom use any other trap for muskrats.

It is also a fine trap for trapping mink. Prop the door up with a short stick about 2½ inches long. Bait with rabbit or bloody chicken heads. Set under bridges or on the bank of small streams where there are stones around it, or grass overhanging sufficiently to partly cover trap.

E. J. FINAL,
Waukegan, Ill.

Muskrat Trapper   **Arthur B. Eastman**   Visiting his traps

TRAPPING THE MUSKRAT

Mr. A. S. Lamb, a Michigan trapper, writes as follows: "My method of trapping, rather capturing muskrats is as follows: Having ascertained a suitable location where muskrats are plentiful, I dig a hole in the ground into which I place a barrel halffilled with water. I place sweet apples on some laths or shingles within the barrel, and then lay a ten or twelve-inch board leading from the shore or water along to the barrel. I also place pieces of apples on the board and in the immediate vicinity on the shore, also on shingles that are fastened so as not to float away. The muskrat, on discovering the bait, will naturally go up on the board, tumble in the barrel and of course not being able to get out, will drown. So when I come along the following morning with a rake I am able to take up eight or ten drowned muskrats at a time. On one occasion I took out nineteen full-grown and three kitts.

TRAPPING THE MUSKRAT

"In trapping the muskrat on the Rush lakes of Minnesota I use a No. 1 steel trap. In the middle of winter when the lakes are frozen over, I proceed to business.

"I approach a rat-house and thrust the muskrat spear into it on the south or southeast side. If it is frequented by rats it will be found open and hollow inside. I next take my small hunter's ax and chop a V-shaped hole in the house on the south side. When the opening is reached, I take out all the moss, rushes, etc., which have fallen in and am careful to leave it just as the rats had it. By feeling around you will find a little shelf or slide which the rats climb upon in coming into the house. I now take the trap and set it on this shelf. If it is covered with water, which it generally is, it is not necessary to cover it otherwise; but if it is above water, I cover the trap with fine mossrubbed between the hands until so fine it will not present the trap holding the rat's leg. I then fill up the hold with a few rushes and moss, then cover it all with snow or moss. No bait is necessary in this kind of trapping. I visit my traps every morning and am generally rewarded by a big brown rat in each trap. I leave a trap in a house from six to ten nights, taking care to always keep it well covered so it will not freeze inside. The trap is held by a long stick stuck in the side of the house.

"In trapping the muskrat in open water in the spring I set my traps on the outside of the houses, just under the water where the rats climb upon the house. In this way I sometimes catch 5 or 6 in a single trap in one day.

"I go around to my traps in a small boat—one man can handle about 50 traps in this way.

"When a rat is drowned or dies under the water, I take the hooked end of the spear and hook it into the trap, and lift my muskrat on board. If alive, take a small stick and kill them with it. Be careful not to get them too near as they will fight, and if opportunity presents impregnate their teeth in a person's limb or body. Don't give them a chance.

"I take the skin off promptly, am careful in skinning, more so in stretching, and still greater in picking out a reliable firm to ship to."

MR. A. CRAMBLIT,
of Okabena.

TRAPPING THE MUSKRAT

The muskrat may be caught in winter by setting traps in their houses, by cutting a hole, preferably on the south side and setting traps on the inside of the houses. If the opening inside is not large enough to set the trap upon, enlarge it by means of an axe or ice chisel. At any rate the trap should be set solid so that it cannot be tipped over by the muskrat climbing on the place. The opening in the house should not be made any larger than to admit the trap, and should be stopped up by wet stuff taken from the inside, after which snow may be placed on top of the house. It is very important to close the opening and make the house as warm as possible as on this depends the success of the trapper.

Another way which is very successful in the Northwest where muskrats have holes in the banks along lakes and sloughs, is to set the traps in these holes. These openings can be readily found by taking note of the riley condition of the water at their opening. The trapper now proceeds to tramp around on the bank opposite until the earth gives way beneath his feet, then cutting a hole and setting the trap in two to three inches of water; sometimes the holes are two deep for the earth to give way, when considerable digging will have to be resorted to in order to find them. Where muskrats are numerous 10 to 15 may be caught in some individual hole.

J. R. S.

TRAPPING THE MUSKRAT

If the water is too shallow and the muskrat cannot be drowned in the place where traps are set, attach chain to small limb which the muskrat will drag into deep water and becoming tangled up will drown. If the water should happen to be very deep in the vicinity, attach a fish line to the drag which will enable you to pull in the muskrat, trap and drag, on your next visit.

The laws of many states prevent the breaking of muskrat houses, therefore it is difficult to trap the muskrat during the winter time. My method is as follows:

Chop a hole over their run-way and lower your trap with two sticks. Now make a stick with a sharp point which drive into the bottom of the lake. On a protruding branch, tie a piece of apple, carrot, etc., and arrange bait 7 or 8 inches above trap. Ring of chain should be fastened either to a string or to a pole fastened to the bottom. Sometimes I place 3 or 4 traps in one hole; in such cases I place the bait in the center with the traps all around. The chains should be staked on the outside so that if one muskrat is caught he will not spring the other traps in his struggle to get away.

F. H. C.

In the late fall and early spring, there is as much fun in killing muskrats as there is to sit in a boat and fish. Probably more. Trapping muskrat with steel traps, wire traps, resorting to deadfalls, also to boxes and barrels, is all good enough, but when these are impracticable and to get immediate yield during the daytime, I prefer the following:

FLOATING MUSKRAT SET.

Chains should be stapled upon the bottom of plank. For bait use parsnips, beets, turnips or their own meat, which should be fastened upon plank.

I provide myself with a heavy club, and my partner with a hoop net attached to a 6-foot pole. When I find an underground run-way that I think is inhabited by the muskrat. I hit the ground just above the run-way a sharp rap. If inhabited, the muskrat will immediately decamp. My partner then catches him in the net, or prevents him from coming out of the hole If one gets away I usually get a chance to put a 22 in his head. If they go into another hole, I watch, and we proceed the same as before.

A box trap with a sliding door, that can be shoved right in it. or next to the hole, or placed in a run-way under the ice, is good. I have used the box trap repeatedly. If set below the ice, nail a stick to the box so that you can raise, and locate the trap. Of course, when the water is frozen one has to chop a pretty big hole, but what trapper is not accustomed to hard work as long as it is remunerative.

Probably the best way to get a great many rats is to sink a water tight barrel into the lake so that the top protrudes two to three inches. Fill barrel one-half full of water. Weight it down with stones, but first see that the barrel rests on level or a solid piece of ground; if it is not level make it so. Within the barrel fit a lid turning on two pegs. Weight one side so that lid will always close after the muskrat is dumped into the barrel. For bait I use potatoes, carrots or apples, and if these are unobtainable. a piece of their own flesh. One of my neighbors does not seem to take so much trouble in preparing this set; all he does is to fasten the bait on a string which he suspends across the top of barrel with the bait in the center. The muskrat in trying to get at the bait jumps into the barrel, from which he cannot get out.

The only time either one of us resort to steel traps is when the weather is real cold. Chop a hole in the muskrat's house, and set on or more traps either on the shelf or on the ice within the house. These traps are covered with grass, found in the house. Cover hole up before you go away.

To prevent muskrats from twisting their legs off or getting out of the trap otherwise, I find the best thing is to set the trap on some log or railroad tie and arrange it so that when the animal jumps into the water, he will drown. Floating sets work day and night and whether the water is high or low.

About two miles from my place there is a small lake and some years muskrats are so thick that is does not take much of a contrivance or a genius to trap them. Steel traps are too slow work for me. During the fall months, I make a box three feet wide, eight feet long, and eighteen inches deep, usually out of two-inch planks. On the outside, I nail a four-inch board clear around about three inches lower than the top of the box; this is a kind of shelf, upon which the muskrat climbs with case if some food is there to attract him. The box is filled two thirds full of water and otherwise weighted down so that the outside shelf is even with level of lake. I use apples, carrots, etc., for bait; these are securely fastened upon shelf, thus forcing the animals to climb upon the shelf for the food. I do this five or six times before I want to trap the muskrat. During this time, I have boards over the box so that the animal cannot get in. When the time is ripe I remove the boards and suspend the bait on a string in center of box. The muskrat, accustomed to the shelf, gets into the box, and not being able to get out, drowns.

This is a smooth water set and not good in rough weather. Trap doors can be made within the box. These are arranged so that when the muksrat steps upon the door his or her weight drops door and the muskrat. The door of course, having unloaded its burden, goes back.

R. B. A.

CHAPTER 23

Beaver

When this country was first explored and settled, beavers were found in good numbers throughout the United State and Canada, but at present they are extinct in many of the states where they were once abundant. Today they are found in fair numbers throughout the greater part of Canada and Alaska, also in a few of the northern and western states. There are also a few beavers found in the south at the present time. However, many of the states, as well as some of the provinces of Canada, have made laws prohibiting the trapping or killing of beavers, to prevent them from being exterminated.

The beaver is an amphibious animal, resembling the muskrat in appearance but much larger. It has the same thick, heavy body, short neck and scaly tail. The hind feet are large and strong and the toes are connected by a web; the front feet are small. The tail is "paddle shaped," four or five inches wide and about ten inches long. When full grown, the beaver will weigh from forty to fifty pounds, although occasionally a much larger one is found. The under fur is very fine and soft, and is mixed with longer and coarser hairs called "guard hairs". The prevailing color is a rich, reddish brown, on the back and sides, and ashy beneath.

The food of the beaver consists mostly of bark, of such woods as poplar, birch, willow and cottonwood, as well as the roots of the water lily. In the south they also eat corn.

Beavers build houses of sticks, stones, and mud, similar in shape to the houses of the muskrat, locating usually, in the edge of a pond or lake, but often making a large pond to suit their requirements, by building a dam across the stream. Even when their houses are built on a lake or pond, they always build a dam across the outlet, so as to raise the water two or three feet.

BEAVER

The dams are built of the same material as the houses. Sometimes there are one or two small dams found below the main dam, and they are so well made that they will last for many years, and are so tight that the water usually drips evenly over the top.

The Beaver.

The houses are also very well made, the walls being several feet in thickness. There are usually two entrances, both under water. The size and general shape of the house depends on the number of beavers inhabiting it. The house of a full family of beavers will usually measure about twelve feet in diameter at the water line, but will sometimes be even larger, and the height is about six or seven feet. When there are only two or three beavers, the house is much smaller, and more pointed on the top.

A full family consists of from six to eight members. There are usually two old beavers, two or three two year olds, and two or three young. The reason for this is that the young beavers remain two years with the parents, and as it requires several years for them to grow their full size, there are always three sizes in a family. When they have reached the age of two years, they start out and make a house of their own, the beavers born the spring before, becoming the medium size, and a new litter taking their place. By autumn, the beavers that have left the main family have their house and dam completed and a store of food laid up for winter.

Many of the beavers travel about through the summer, following the streams, and return to their homes early in the fall. Sometimes, if they are late in getting back they will have to work day and night, in order to get sufficient food gathered for winter, before the ice comes. This food consists of saplings and small trees, which they gnaw off about a foot above the ground, drag into the edge of the water, where they are cut up into pieces of different lengths, stored away, under water in front of the house. Just how they cause this wood to sink, remain in place under the water, is a mystery. The beaver spends the entire winter under the ice. When he feels hungry he goes out and gets a piece of wood, takes it into the house, eats the bark, and takes the peeled stick out again. They repair the house and dam each fall and they also make holes in the bank under water, to which they can retreat in case the house is disturbed, or when they hear a noise on the ice.

Trappers who are well acquainted with the habits of the beaver, can make a fair estimate of the number of inmates of a house. It sometimes happens that a pair of young beavers, or a lone beaver that has escaped from some family which has been trapped, will locate in an old deserted house, and then it is not such an easy matter. The experienced trapper, however, is not likely to be fooled. He goes along the shore and carefully examines the stumps, where the animals have been cutting trees for food. The amount of stuff that has been cut will show, usually; but he has still a better way of determining whether the work was done by one or more beavers. He examines the teeth marks on the stumps, and if they are all alike, he decides that there is not a full family, but only two, or perhaps only one.

A lone beaver that has escaped from the trapper, is difficult to trap. I remember once finding such a one, located on a large pool of a fair sized stream. He had no dam and had only a small house along the bank. I found him in the fall, while the water was still open, and he was busy laying in a supply of food for winter. Well, I went there one rainy day and set two traps. I set the traps very carefully, fastening to sliding poles, which I had cut quite a distance away so as not to make any noise near the house. The rain washed the scent away in a short time, and I could see no reason why he should take alarm; but he did, just the same. I kept those traps set a week, but did not catch him, nor did I ever see any fresh signs there, after I had set the traps. Apparently he had left the place immediately after I had set the traps. An Indian trapper had trapped several families of beavers, near there the season before, and this beaver was one that had "given him the slip."

In cutting timber, the beaver takes the wood in small chips, gnawing all around the tree, until it falls. He knows absolutely nothing about throwing the tree in the direction in which he wishes it to fall, but lets it fall just as it is inclined to go, I have seen where a tree had lodged, refusing to fall, and the beaver had stood up and cut several pieces off the butt, and as the tree still refused to fall, he had let it remain hanging. It was a case of hard work and no pay.

When one finds a family of beavers, and expects to trap the same ground each season, he should not attempt to catch them all, as by leaving a few to breed, he is sure of getting beavers each season. The Indians, in such cases, trap the old beavers only, which they do by setting the traps a good distance from the house, for the young beavers never venture far away.

Many beavers are trapped in the fall just before the ice forms, but their fur is not prime until mid-winter. In the north they remain in good condition until the first of June; in the south they would probably not be good after the middle of April.

Beaver castors have a market value, usually selling for seven or eight dollars a pound. In preparing them, they should be dried slowly, in a shady place. Most trappers prefer to keep the castors for scent, as it is attractive to many animals. The Indians sometimes

Trap Set for Beaver — Sliding Pole.

combine the two scents by making a hole in the beaver castors, and squeezing the contents of the oil castors into them. The castors are then hung up and allowed to dry. This is more or less attractive to all animals, only a small piece being used in connection with the bait.

The best traps for beavers are the Nos. 2½, 3, 3½ and 4 Newhouse, the No. 4 Victor, the No. 4 Oneida Jump, and Blake & Lamb.

The following methods of trapping are for use in open water, in either the fall or spring. The first method given is usually considered best:

Find a place where the bank bluffs a little and the water is of good depth. Make a little pocket in the bank, several inches deep, and set the trap in the water directly in front of this pocket, where the pan of the trap will be about two inches under water. Take a piece of beaver castor and fasten it to the bank with a stick, about fourteen inches above the water, and as far back in the pocket as possible. If you are using some other scent instead of beaver castor, just dip a small stick in the scent and fasten it to the bank. Fasten the trap so that the beaver will drown; the sliding pole is best. Be sure to use a dead pole or stake, as if a green pole is used the other beavers may carry it away, trap and all. This is a very good method for spring and fall, or at any time when there is open water:

Here is another method for the same kind of place:

Set the trap under water at the foot of a steep bank, and fasten a couple of green poplar or cottonwood sticks on the bank, directly over the trap, so that the beaver will step into the trap in trying to reach them. Have the fresh cut ends of the sticks showing plainly, and make your set near the house or dam so that the beavers are sure to see it. Fasten trap so that the captured animal will be sure to drown. No covering is needed on traps when they are set under water.

Look for the beaver's slides or trails where he drags his food into the water, and if water is deep enough to drown him, set the trap under about two inches of water, just where he lands on the bank. This set is all right in the fall, when the beaver is laying in his food for the winter, but is not much good in the spring, Some trappers set the trap a foot or more from the shore, where the water is about six inches deep, as by so doing the beaver is caught hind foot, and is not so likely to escape. When using a set of this kind, it is best to use a number 3½ or 4 trap, as the No. 3 is too small for the beaver's hind foot.

Beavers usually have a slide or trail over the center of the dam, and this makes a very good place to set a trap. Set the trap under water on the upper side of the dam, just where the trail leads over. Be sure to fasten the trap so that the animal will drown, as if it is not drowned, it is almost certain to escape, and even if it does not, the others will be frightened and you will have a hard time to get them.

In the spring, after the ice has gone, it is a good plan to set a few traps along the stream, baiting with beaver castor, as the beavers are traveling at this time, and you are likely to catch one almost anywhere along the streams. When setting traps in this way, it is best to drench the set with water to remove the human scent. The beaver is seldom afraid of human scent, but there is likely to be an otter along that way, and you stand a good chance of catching him in a trap baited with beaver castor.

Beavers may be caught in mid-winter and early spring, by setting baited traps under the ice. It is not much use to set traps under the ice in early winter, as the beaver's food is still in good condition, and they will not take bait well; moreover you are likely to frighten them and make them harder to trap later on. The following methods are among the best for use under the ice, the one first given, being most used, and is probably the best:

Go close to the beaver's house where the ice is thin, and by cutting small holes in the ice, find a place where the water is about twelve inches deep. Having found such a place, enlarge the hole until it is about sixteen by twenty inches in size, making a pen the same size as the hole, by shoving down dead sticks about four inches apart. If the bottom is very hard, you will have to freeze the sticks to the ice, to hold them in place. This may be done by throwing snow in the water, and packing it around the sticks and against the edge of the ice. When the pen is completed, cut a piece of green poplar about 1½ or 2 inches thick and two or three feet long, and fasten it to a stake by one end—the poplar being placed at a right angle to the stake. This green poplar is for bait, and the stake should be driven down in one corner of the pen so that the bait is within two or three inches from the bottom, and close along one side of the pen, extending a foot or more beyond the entrance.

The trap should be staked and set well inside of the pen, and quite close to the bait, so that the jaw of the trap will just clear the bait. This set will be readily understood by referring to the cut. If the bottom is of thin mud, as is often the case, you will have to make a bed for the trap, by sinking a bunch of evergreen boughs inside of the pen. It is also best to fasten the bait near the entrance to prevent the beaver from swinging it around. When the set is completed, cover the hole with evergreen boughs, bank it with snow, to keep it from freezing.

It is best to let this set go for about a week before looking at it. The beavers will be frightened and will not approach the set for a few days, but finally one of them musters up courage enough to try to pull the bait out

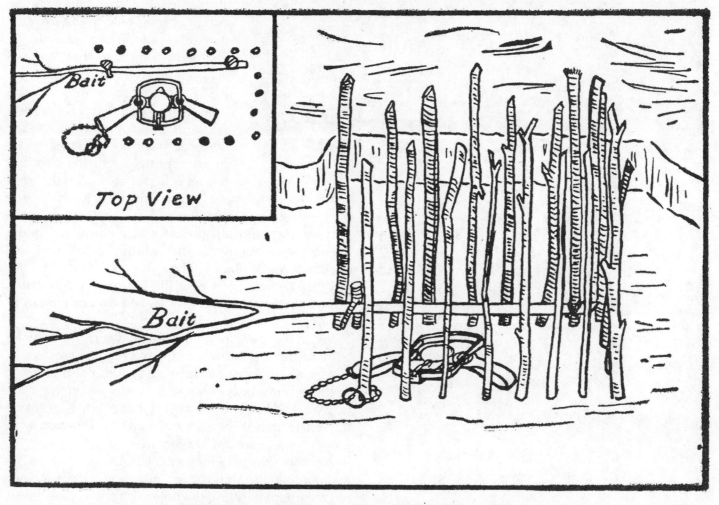

Bait

Top View

Bait

Beaver Trap Set Under Ice.

of the pen. When he finds it fast, he cuts it off at the entrance of the pen, takes it to the house to eat it; this sharpens his appetite, makes him more courageous, and he finally ventures into the pen for the balance of the bait. In attempting to cut the bait, he places one front foot on the bait and the other one in the trap. When using this set you should use three or four sets at each house.

Another good ice method is as follows: Find the proper depth of water, about fourteen inches, and make a pen of dead sticks arranging them in the form of a half-circle. Now take some green poplar and shove them down firmly into the bottom, about six inches apart, close up to the stakes, on the inside of the pen. These bait sticks must be long enough to reach above the ice, so that they will freeze fast at the top. Stake the trap and set it in the center of the enclousre, with the pan about nine inches from the center bait. Throw some snow in the hole; so that it will freeze and hold the bait sticks securely.

From Book of Dr. Spiegel, Albany   **Beaver Lodge Completed**

Beaver Cuttings

The following method is one of the best for use in deep water: Cut a dead pole about four inches in diameter and six or seven feet long. Flatten the pole at one end, and loop the trap chain around the pole; then set the trap on the end of the pole and tie it with a string, to hold it in place. Now, cut an oblong hole in the ice, and place the pole in the water in an inclined position so that the trap is about twelve inches below the ice. Pack wet snow around the pole to hold it in place, fasten two sticks of green poplar in the ice over the trap, one on either side. In attempting to cut the bait, the beaver will put his foot in the trap.

Always fasten your trap to a dead stick or pole, for if a green stake is used, the beavers are likely to carry it away, trap and all. Poplar and cottonwood make the best baits, but in case they cannot be obtained, use birch, willow or black cherry.

When setting traps near the house, in open water, make as little noise as possible, and do not remain in the vicinity longer than necessary.

When trapping in open water, never camp or make a fire near the pond where the beavers are located. In winter, after the ice has formed, it does not matter.

If you find a beaver house in winter when the snow is deep, and wish to know if it is inhabited, examine the house, and if the snow is melted on the top, you may be sure there are beavers in it.

Another way to tell whether a house is inhabited, is to cut a hole through the ice and shove down a piece of green poplar, filling the hole with snow. Examine it in about a week, and if the poplar has been cut, you may be sure you have found beavers.

The track of the beaver is seldom seen as they do not move about much in winter and on their trails their tracks are obliterated by the food which they drag into the water. The trapper does not look for tracks, but for more conspicuous signs, such as houses and dams with fresh cut wood.

TRAPPING THE BEAVER

Mr. Lewis D. Bergey, an old trapper, writes on trapping the beaver as follows:

"There are various modes of trapping these sagacious animals adopted by professional hunters and trappers. In the fall and spring the chief method is to make a small opening in the dam and set the No. 4 trap in such a manner that they will get caught when repairing the damage. The trap should be fastened by several feet of chain to a pole driven firmly at full length of the chain into the mud at the bottom of the lake; no marks must be left. Should the chain be slack, the beaver is almost sure to leave a toe or paw in the trap, since he

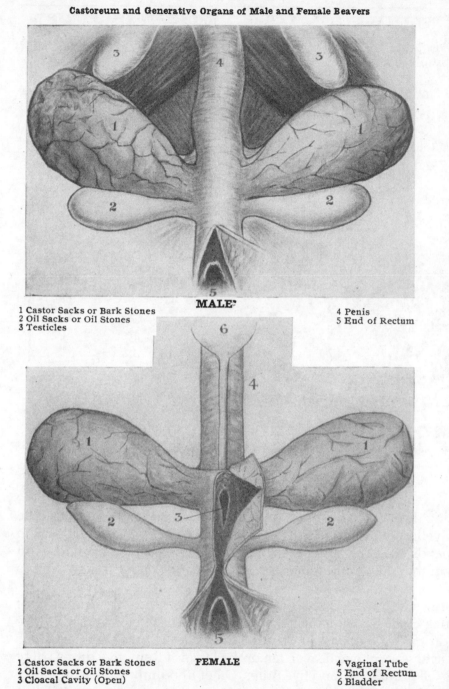

Castoreum and Generative Organs of Male and Female Beavers

MALE

1 Castor Sacks or Bark Stones
2 Oil Sacks or Oil Stones
3 Testicles

4 Penis
5 End of Rectum

FEMALE

1 Castor Sacks or Bark Stones
2 Oil Sacks or Oil Stones
3 Cloacal Cavity (Open)

4 Vaginal Tube
5 End of Rectum
6 Bladder

has a chance of resting on the dam and by twisting and using his teeth will set himself free. It is then a labor of much ingenuity to catch him. The presence of beaver and their size are judged by the freshness of the sticks and the size of the teeth-marks on them, as well as the general appearance of the works.

"Another mode practiced to catch these wiseacres is to make an opening in the dam and set the trap at some distance where he is likely to get mud and sticks for repairing the mischief. Advantage is also taken of his roads and places where he is in the habit of sitting while eating. A sort of oil called castor, used formerly for medicinal purposes, taken from the animal, is used to attract them to the trap. When setting a trap water must be splashed freely wherever the bushes or banks have been touched, as a beaver is very keen of scent, and will turn away if he suspects anything.

"The way to dress a fresh skin is to make a large hoop of birch or poplar and lace the skin tightly to it by means of holes cut all around the skin near the edge. The weight of a wellcleaned skin varies from half a pound to three pounds, according to the age and season of the year.

"Beaver are found in many places in the United States, but nowhere so plentiful as in Northern Canada. In the great stretch of lakes in Athabasca, and the north shore of Labrador, beaver are considered superior to those caught further west Beaver becomes prime about the first of October and continues to improve until about the first of May, when it deteriorates. The flesh of a fat beaver is considered by many as the most delicate of any to be procured in the bush. The tail also is a delicacy when properly cooked, and when smoked and dried it has the flavor of bacon."

TRAPPING THE BEAVER

H. Miller, of Lewistown, Mont., gives us the following article:

"The beaver is a water animal and lives in holes in the banks of streams, and in houses which it makes in the water out of mind and sticks. Its food is bark, corn, wheat, rats, grass, etc. It has its young once a year, generally in the month of April, having from two to six at a birth. They do not increase very fast, as it requires

BEAVER SET

THIS SET WAS SUCCESSFULLY USED BY JESSE McDONALD SINCE 1881 IN MICH. ALSO IN CANADA. CAN BE USED NOT ONLY FOR BEAVER, BUT ALSO FOR MINK, MARTEN, RACCOON ETC. IF UNINHABITED. TRAPS CAN ALSO BE SET ON TOP OF DAM.   USE BAIT.

about four years to get their full growth. The beaver castor or bark sacs, and the off stones, are found near the vent, in four sacs in both sexes. In taking them out, cut around them, and take out together with as little meat as possible. The bark sacs contain a yellow substance. To get the contents, tie a string around hole in the bark sacs and cub them between the hands until they are soft, then cut them open and squeeze the stuff into a cup. To get the oil of the oil stone, cut the end off and squeeze it. Keep separate and mix according as directed. You can put this in bottles.

"The baits for beaver are made as follows: 1. Take the castor of one beaver, add twenty drops Oil of Cinnamon, ten drops Oil of Anise, and urine of the beaver to make the bait the consistency of mush. 2. Take the castor sacs of one beaver add seven drops of Oil of Sassafras, seven drops Oil of Anise and ten drops of the oil from the Oil Stone. 3. Take the castor sacs of one beaver, ten drops Jamaica Rum, five drops Oil of Anise, five drops Oil of Cloves, five drops Oil of Sassafras and five drops Oil of Rhodium. 4. Take the castor sacs of one beaver, add ten drops of the oil from the Oil Stone, and beaver urine enough to make the bait like mush. These I call natural baits, and they will fool the oldest beaver that lives.

"Beavers cut small trees and build dams in streams and when you see fresh work you have beaver close by. You will find slides where they go into the water. Set your traps at the foot of the slides, three inches under the water, and cover with mud and leaves. Put the end of the trap towards the center of the stream and fasten it to the drowning pole (described elsewhere), and leave everything as natural as possible. Take your bait and put it on the end of a stick six inches long; split one end three or four times and dip it in the bait and stick it up six or seven inches above the water in the slide. Wear gum boots in setting traps and carry a tin cup—after setting a trap use your tin cup to wash away the scent.

"Skin the beaver by starting the knife in the under lip, split skin to the tail, skin the front legs whole (some skin them all whole), stretch them as near round as possible. Use the hoop stretcher to stretch the

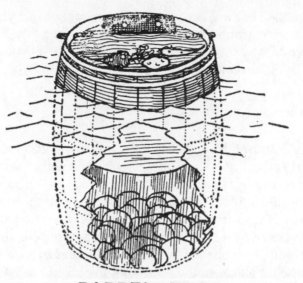

BARREL TRAP.

Suitable for muskrats. Sink so that top protrudes 4 or 5 inches above water. Fill barrel half full of water, weight down with stones. Bait swinging drop door as per illustration, with potatoes, apples, carrots, beets, etc.

beaver skin. Cut small holes close to the edge of the skin and use twine or bark. Stretch the skin until it is tight. Use a jutting-pole and knife to take off the grease and meat from the skin before it is stretched.

"I like the Newhouse trap best for catching nearly all kinds of animals. I have two faults to find with them, first, the pan is too small; second, the chain is too long—but they stand the weather.

"To set a trap for beaver, cut a pole eight or nine feet long (described hereafter), push the small end into the bottom of the creek where the water is deep enough to drown a beaver, put the chain ring over the big end of the pole, push the pole the length of the chain to one side of the slide, and sink the pole under the water and put your husk or stake straddle up the pole and drive it down solid; see that the ring can travel the pole when a beaver is caught. If he can get on land he will bite his feet off and go.

TRAPPING THE BEAVER

Southern method as used in the swamps of Louisiana by R.W. Riggs.

The bait used and the way to set the traps:

"The bait used: First mix one-half ounce of alcohol, fifteen drops oil of sassafras. Use ten drops of this mixture with the castor sac of one large beaver.

"For a set, use two No. 4 Newhouse traps. Tie the traps together by one of the springs of each trap. This is to make more weight and also to help to tangle the beaver up when caught. Now set your traps in three to six inches of water. Set so the beaver will have to come over the loose jaw of the traps. Now whatever the distance is to deep water, tie a piece of rope to the rings of the trap chains, long enough for the beaver to get into deep water when caught. If you have a piece of iron in camp you can tie that also to the traps. The stake that the rope is fastened to should have a look to it. Drive it down in the mud all out of sight. Coil up the rope and cover it up also with mud. Cover your traps so that nothing shows. Now take a small dead stick and stick it into your bait about an inch. Then stick it up in the water about six inches from your traps on the land side, with just the bait end sticking out of the water. I also tie the bait sticks to the traps with a string so when the heaver is caught he will take the bait stick with him. For if the bait stick was left after the beaver was caught, other beavers would come and smell of it and then that kind of bait would have no attraction for the them for some time. I mix up bait from both the male and female, so that I will have a change. Set your traps away from their houses or holes. Do not disturb their dams. In setting your traps wade in on one side of the place where you are going to set your traps and do all of your work from the water side. Never walk on e ground in front of your set. When you have your set made, throw water over everything near you. If there are any bushes within five or more feet of you throw water on them. If you will use care and have a little patience you can catch every one in that colony and you need not smoke your traps or use gloves either.

TRAPPING THE BEAVER

C. Steele, a trapper residing at Altamont, Mo., gives us the following good article on beaver:

"The beaver is a very shy and cunning animal, always on the guard against danger, thus making it hard to trap him unless one understands is ways and habits.

"My experience has been on the Pacific Coast, in the state of Washington. The beaver lives along streams or lakes; if streams he dams them, thus forming a kind of reservoir or lake, and even at the outlet of lakes he places a dam, thus raising the water of the lake. After he has prepared his dam and built his home, he commences carrying food. This is chiefly branches of trees or bushes, and even small trees themselves. He always chooses tender green ones. These he places in the bottom of the lake to use as desired, or in his hut or lodge, and should he be disturbed at any time he will stop work for several days and live off the boughs already sunk in the bottom of the lake or lodge, thus making it impossible to trap him until he again commences work. He usually does his work among young sprouts along the bank of his lake or stream; and float boughs down to the main lake or dam in the stream where he has his hut.

"There are many ways to catch him, but I will only give two or three of the best ways. The first thing is the trap; the best kind is a strong steel trap, the Newhouse, or some other good brand. Then the best way to trap the beaver is to procure some castoreum (which is an odorous liquid carried in, a small pouch by the male beaver). Then cut some small twigs, one for each trap, and having selected the dam of the colony of beaver you wish to trap, procure a pair or rubber boots, or remove your boots and wade up he stream along the shore of the lake or stream where they have been at work upon he sprouts, but be careful and do not step out on the land where the beaver can see your tracks or scent you, for if he does he will stay in his home for several days. When you have selected a spot where the bank is steep, secure your trap by a strong

FLOATING BOX SET.

For description see page 351.

stake beneath the water, then fasten a heavy rock to your trap and dig a flat place in the bank a few inches beneath water, placing your trap thereon. Then dip the end of you stick in the castoreum you procured and stick the opposite end in the ground, just out of the water and learning over the trap. Then your trap is ready for him. He comes out as darkness approaches and starts towards his ground where he procures food, and as he swims along he smells the castoreum and thinks a strange beaver has come into is pond or lake. He swims up to the stake or twig to get a better scout, and as his foot touches the ground the trap is sprung. Then finding he is first he springs backward into he water and displaces the rock which is fastened to the trap, and the heavy rock pulls him down and drowns him. This prevents him from making any noise to scare the rest away or front gnawing his foot off to escape, as he frequently does if left long in the trap. In this way you can sometimes catch the entire colony.

"Another way is to cut a hole or crevice in the top of the dam, and set the trap just below the surface of the water directly beneath the hole. The beaver at once starts to repair the dam and thus, gets in the trap, but this method is rarely used by experienced trappers unless they cannot procure castoreum, and in this way they procure it even at the expense of frightening the rest of the colony sometime entirely away.

"Another way is to cover the trap neatly in the path of the beaver leading from the lake to his feeding ground, but this has the same disadvantage as the last plan.

"I could write you more about their ways of living houses, etc., but think that I have told all that would be necessary to know to make a success at trapping them."

TRAPPING THE BEAVER

To trap beaver in winter when the water is frozen: Select a place close to their houses and close to a bank where the water is not more than two feet deep under the ice. If the water is too deep, cut away part of the dam and lower the water to the right depth. Now cut a hole in the ice two or three feet across, according to thinness of ice and the size of bait. Nest cut the bait, which should be the top of a poplar or birch about four inches through at the big end shove this under the ice and fasten with a-strake which has a book on it. A trap ma be placed on the bottom right below where bait is fastened by the stake, or the bait may be leit without trap for one night when in the morning the bait is usually all taken away. Now set three or four traps in the following manner, and as close to he former place as possible. Cut a number of stakes (dry) and drive into bottom in half circle about fifteen inches across, put a few green sticks of poplar inside of this half-circle and drive into bottom: set the traps on the bottom just outside of the green sticks resting firmly so that it cannot be tipped over by the beaver growing at he hark The trap should be fastened to a dry stake set sloping towards the deepest part of stream. The beaver trapper should endeavor to catch as many in as short a time as possible, as the remaining beaver will soon become shy of the place.

T. GULLICKSON
Canada

CHAPTER 24

Coypu Rat or Nutria

The Coypu Rat

Another animal apparently related to the Muskrat and Beaver is the Coypu Rat, a native of South America. It is sometimes called the Rocoonda, and it furnishes to commerce the fur known as Nutria. Only one species is known and this is found in great numbers in the La Plata region. In some seasons more than three million skins of the Coypu Rat have been exported, showing what an important item in the fur trade they have become.

In general appearance and character it resembles the Beaver. Its tail, however, instead of being flattened, is long and round and ratlike. Its favorite haunts are the lagoons of the plains or pampas, and the banks of rivers and streams. Its fur is short, fine, silky, similar to that of the Beaver, and light brown in color. Overlying the fur are long hairs of a brownish yellow color. The fur is heaviest and best on the belly. It is used for the same purposes as that of the Beaver, in the manufacture of hats and caps. The Coypu is about two feet long exclusive of tail, which is about fifteen inches in length. It is very prolific, the female producing six or seven at a birth. They feed on vegetables, are quite gentle in their character and easily tamed. They inhabit South America on both sides of the Andes; on the east, from Peru to forty-three degrees south latitude; on the west, from Central Chili to Terra del Fuego. They are also found in the small bays and channels of the archipelagos along the coast. They are burrowing animals and form their habitations in the banks of the lakes and streams. They are nocturnal in their habits and seem to be equally at home in fresh or salt water.

The Coypu is usually hunted with dogs and is easily captured. It is, however, a bold animal and fights fiercely with the dog employed in pursuing it. Of late years the South Americans have learned to catch the Coypu Rat in steel traps and this will tend to bring their fur into greater prominence in the market. Their habits resemble those of the Beaver and Muskrat and they should be trapped on the same general principles.

CHAPTER 25

Otter

OTTER

THE otter is a carnivorous animal, somewhat resembling the mink in appearance. They are found in various parts of the world and will be met with in most of the wilder parts of North America. The northern or Canadian otter is the most common, but there are other varieties known as the Carolina otter, the Florida otter and the Newfoundland otter. In habits and general appearance they are all similar.

A distinct species is found in the North Pacific, and is known as the sea otter. This animal is considerably larger than the fresh water species, and has a shorter tail. The fur is of great value.

The otter is an aquatic animal, living in and near the streams and lakes, and getting its living from them. It has a long body, short, stout legs, and webbed feet; the tail is long, thick at the base, and tapering to a point. The neck is thick, the head comparatively small, with small ears, set well down on the sides of the head. The fur is of two kinds, the under fur being fine, soft and wavy, and of a light silvery color; while the outer fur or guard hairs, are longer, coarser, and usually straight, the color varying from brown to almost black. The fur of the tail and under parts is shorter and stiffer than that on the back, sides and neck; that on the under parts having a silvery tint. Otters frequently measure three and one-half feet in length and weigh from fifteen to twenty-five pounds. The skin, when stretched, will often measure five feet from tip to tip, and sometimes even more.

The food of the otter consists principally of fish, trout being their favorite food; but they also feed on muskrats, clams, frogs, and the smaller animal life, found in the beds of streams and lakes.

They capture muskrats by entering their houses and their holes in the banks.

Otters usually make burrows in the banks of streams, lining the nest with leaves and grass. The entrances to these burrows are under the water and it is my belief that they inhabit them only during the breeding season. The young are born in April and May and there are from two to four in a litter.

The otter is a great traveler, following the lakes and water courses, sometimes going a distance of one hundred miles on a single trip. Apparently he is always in a great hurry to reach a certain place, some lake or pond, at which having reached, he may remain for several months, and again he may leave immediately after his arrival.

Otters sometimes have slides on the banks of streams, down which they slide into the water, apparently for pastime. They also have landing places on the banks of streams and on logs projecting into the water,

From Original Drawing.   Property of Andersch Bros.   **THE OTTER**   Late Fall. Northern U. S. A.

where they go to roll in the grass and leaves, or to lie in the sun. These places are seldom visited in the fall, but in the spring, they will land at almost every place as they come along.

In traveling, they usually follow the center of the stream, as they are more at home in the water than on land. In winter they travel under the ice, wherever the water is deep enough to allow of their passage. The otter's legs being very short, he has a peculiar method of traveling on the ice or snow. He throws himself forward, sliding on his belly, and by repeating the move in rapid succession, is enabled to get along at a surprising rate of speed.

Wherever there is a sharp bend in the stream, the otter will make a short cut across the point, and if the stream is traveled much, you will find a well-defined trail in such a place. Where two streams lie close together, they sometimes have a trail from one stream to another. Also wherever a long point of land projects into a lake, they are likely to have a trail across the point.

The otter appears to be on very friendly terms with the beaver, and if there are any beavers in the country, the otter is sure to find them and will spend considerable time in the same pond. When there are a number of families of beavers in the same locality, the otter will spend nearly all of its time with the beavers, visiting from one family to another. Wherever he finds beaver cutting along the stream, he examines it, and will most likely follow up the stream to find the beaver. This habit is taken advantage of by the Indian trappers of the north, as will be explained later.

In the north, the otter becomes prime about the first week in November, and remains in good condition until about the first of June. In the south they are seldom prime until the first of December, and commence to shed from the first to the fifteenth of April. The fur of the otter is valuable, the dark, straight haired ones being worth the most. Occasionally an otter is found having a decided curl to the ends of the hair, the ends being turned forward. These are called "curly" otters and are not near so valuable as the others.

Otters are found in good numbers in the swamps of the southern states; in Florida, Arkansas, Mississippi, Louisiana and the lowlands of Texas. They are also quite plentiful in some parts of Massachusetts, New Hampshire, Vermont and Maine; also in the wilds of Labrador, Ungava, Quebec, Ontario, Yukon, Mackenzie and Alaska. The most valuable otters come from the far north, but they are probably more plentiful in the south, and the southern trapper has the advantage of having open water all winter.

The best traps for otter are the numbers 2½, 3 and 3½ Newhouse; the Nos. 3 and 4 Hawley & Norton; and the No. 14 Oneida jump, also the "Seminole" pattern, Blake & Lamb.

The point to keep in mind when trapping for otter, is that they are very shy of the scent of man; more so perhaps than any other animal, and unless great care is observed, are likely to be frightened entirely out of the locality in which you are trapping. This human scent theory is disputed by some trappers, but I speak from my own experience, and from the experience of many expert trappers with whom I am acquainted. If one wall use a little judgment he will readily understand why human scent is alarming to many wild animals. Man is the natural enemy of all wild animal life, and all wild creatures realize this fact. Now you will see that any indications of the presence of man, puts the animal on its guard; especially is this the case in the wilderness where the animals are not accustomed to seeing the tracks of man wherever they go. When an animal finds human scent, he has positive proof that man has been in that vicinity.

Footprints and other human signs, if there is no scent, are not so alarming, as they are likely to be mistaken for signs made by some wild animal. Although the animals of the wilderness are more afraid of human scent than those found in the settled countries, they are just as easily trapped. The more wary animals found in settled parts, are always looking for danger because of the continued presence of man in their locality, but on the other hand, they are not likely to be frightened by human scent because it is a common thing to them.

As mentioned before the otter is sure to visit the beavers, if there are any about, so if you know of a family of beavers, go to that place and if you can find an old beaver dam, on the stream somewhere, below where the beavers are located, make a break in the center of this dam, so that all of the water will flow through this opening, and set the trap in the water, in the upper end of this passage. Narrow down the passage to about eight inches, by driving a few old stakes on each side of the trap. The trap may be staked, but it is better, if the water is deep enough, to use a sliding pole, so that the captured animal will drown. No covering is needed on the trap, but after it is set, the entire setting should be drenched with water, to remove the human scent. This is an excellent set and will remain in working order until late in the fall, as the water immediately above the break in the dam will not freeze until long after other water is closed by ice. Even in the coldest weather this set may be kept from freezing by roofing it over with evergreen boughs, and banking it well with snow.

The Otter.

Beavers and beaver dams are not found in every locality, but wherever otters are found traveling on small streams, they may be trapped in the following manner:

Find a narrow place in the stream, where the water flows smoothly, and narrow up the stream by placing a bunch of old dead brush in each side, leaving a passage of about eight inches in the middle. Lay a few stones among the brush to keep them in place. Set the trap in the opening, and splash water over the brush and banks. The trap may be staked but it is better to fasten to a clog. Cut a small sapling of such a size that the ring of the chain will just pass over the butt of the sapling. Slip the ring over the clog and fasten it by splitting the butt and drive a wedge in the split, or by driving a staple over the ring. The clog may be placed on the upper side of the brush, used to block the stream, and the top may be tied to the shore, so that it will not be carried away by high water. In very small streams, a narrow passage may be made, by simply placing a few stones in either side, leaving a narrow passage in the middle, in which I to set the trap.

When you can find a sharp bend in the stream, with a trail across the point, set the trap in the water, at the end of the trail. Use same care as advised for the other sets.

For spring trapping this method is excellent: if you can find one of the otter's landing places on the bank, prepare the place for setting in the fall in the following manner: Make a nest for the trap in the center of the trail and fill the nest with grass and leaves. Lay a bunch of dead brush or a chunk of rotten wood on each side of the trail, so as to leave only a narrow passage and cut a clog and lay it in place. The otters seldom visit these places in the fall, so there is no danger of frightening them. In the spring, before the snow is all gone, go and set your trap in the place prepared, covering with the leaves and grass, and attach to the clog, covering the entire setting with a little snow. As the snow melts, it takes with it all of the scent and signs, leaving the trap ready for the first otter that comes along.

If you do not find the landing places until after the snow is gone, set the traps just the same, washing the scent away by sprinkling with water, or set the traps in the water where the otter climbs up the bank.

Another very good method for spring trapping, is to set the trap in the edge of the water, where the bank bluffs a little, sticking up a few fresh cut, green sticks behind the trap, and at the sides. Post a piece of the dried oil castor of the beaver on a stick, behind the trap, and about ten inches high. The ordinary beaver castor is also good. The oil castor is very attractive to the otter, and the green sticks are also attractive, as the

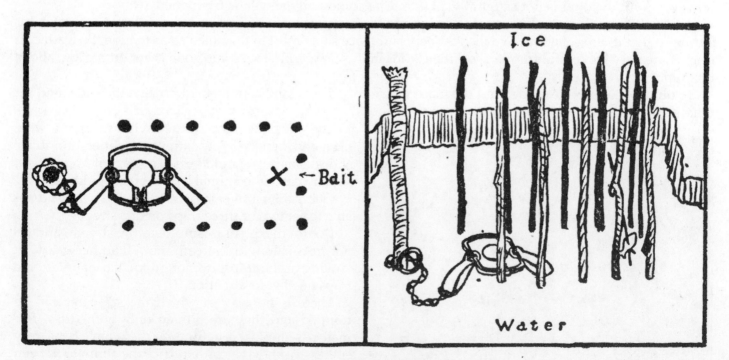

Otter Trap Set Under Ice.

otter mistakes them for beaver cutting. Always fasten the trap so the animal will drown, as you are likely to catch a beaver in this set.

One of the best methods of trapping otter in winter, after the streams are closed with ice, is as follows: Find a long pool of still water, where you are sure the otter will be traveling under the ice, and at either end of this pool, where the water is about ten inches deep, cut a hole through the ice, make a pen of dead sticks in the water, making the pen about nine inches wide, by twelve or fifteen inches deep. Now take a fish and fasten it to a stick, in the back of the pen, and set the trap in the entrance, staking it securely. Drive the stake about ten inches in front of the pen, and directly in front of the trap. The object in this is to cause the otter, in entering, to twist his body, in which act, he will put his foot down in the trap. Throw some snow in the hole, so it will freeze over. The bait should be renewed once a week. In case you cannot get fish for bait, use the head of a rabbit, the breast of a partridge, or a piece of muskrat. The bait should be skinned.

The otter will also be attracted by any white object, I know a trapper who caught one in this way by baiting with a white door, knob, and the Indians sometimes use a piece of fresh peeled poplar for bait.

If the ice has formed when the water was above its usual level, there will be an air space, between the water and the ice. In such a case, cut a hole through the ice at the edge of the water, placing a piece of beaver castor on a stick behind the trap. The hole may be closed by covering with a block of ice.

A Louisiana Otter

When the otter has been working on a lake for some time, you will find where he has been coming out at the springholes, which are found on nearly all lakes. In such places the water is always shallow, and a trap may be set on the bottom directly under the hole. Great care must be used however, for if the otter is not caught the first time he comes out, he will be frightened away.

Otters often land on the logs which project into the water. When you can find such a log, cut a notch for a trap, so that it will set about two inches deep, and place some mud in the notch so as to hide the fresh cutting. Some very successful trappers, set their traps in this way, and place some good scent on the log, above the trap.

If you can find an otter slide, find the place where the animal lands on the bank to visit the slide, and set the trap under about two inches of water.

The Otter

The Nos. 2½ and 3½ Newhouse traps were designed especially for trapping otters on their slides. The trap should be set at the foot of the slide, so as to catch the animal by the breast or body.

Otters often travel in pairs, and it is usually advisable to set two or three traps on one stream.

Do not make your camp near the stream, and do not travel along the stream more than necessary. In looking at the traps, do not go too close, unless the traps need your attention.

There is no way in which the sea otter can be trapped and they are hunted only with rifles. The methods employed in hunting them have been very successful and as a consequence the animal has been practically exterminated.

The track of the otter is peculiar, owing to their strange mode of travel. As before mentioned their method of travel is a series of plunging slides and in the snow they make a deep furrow, their footprints being from four to eight feet apart, according to the "sliding conditions". When two or more are traveling in company, they will usually all run in the same trail. Their tracks are as a rule, only seen on lakes and streams, but occasionally they will go overland from one stream to another. The footprints will measure about one and one-half or one and three-fourths inches in length and about the same in width.

TO TRAP THE OTTER

The nest, in which these animals spend a good portion of the day, and in which their young are produced, is sometimes made in a bank of earth, or in the trunk of a fallen tree; it is lined with sticks, grasses and leaves, is of large size, and well protected from the rains, and, at the same time, beyond the reach of rising floods. They have a pastime of sliding off wet sloping banks into the water, which is taken advantage of by the trappers to catch them, by placing sunken steel traps in places where the otters are thus accustomed to amuse themselves. They are fond of sliding down hill upon the snow-banks, going on their bellies, feet first, in the

TRAPPING THROUGH THE ICE.

A well-tried arrangement for trapping through the ice. Cover trap and chain with moss, evergreens and similar light vegetation. The string or wire should be loosely wound around the chain. Experienced trappers usually have two or three traps set about the hole, all attached to the same pole. Especially good for the otter, beaver and other aquatic animals.

SLIDING WIRE OR ROPE.

Take a telegraph wire (some take a ⅜-inch rope), fasten to some heavy object, which sink 15 to 25 feet from shore in deep water. Pass the other end through ring on trap and fasten to some tree or stake. The steel trap should be set at the edge of the shore or under water. Cover trap in the usual way. Good for otter, beaver, mink, etc.

manner of school-boys, "coasting" as it is called in New England, entering into the sport with intense eagerness and delight.

Otters are easily tamed when taken young; they are very playful, will follow their keeper like a dog, and become quite familiar, crouching in the lap like a cat. When tame, they eat bread and milk; in a wild state they prefer fish, but sometimes feed on birds and other game.

TRAPPING THROUGH THE ICE.

CHAPTER 26

Sea Otter

Along the northern shores of the Pacific Ocean, especially in Kamtschatka and Alaska, another species of Otter exists, called the Sea Otter or Kalan. It is much larger than the fresh water Otter, weighing from sixty to eighty pounds. During the colder months of the year this Otter dwells by the sea shores, where it is very active in the capture of marine fish. When warm weather approaches, the Kalan leaves the coasts and with its mate proceeds up the rivers till it reaches the fresh-water lakes of the interior, where it remains till cold weather again approaches. The head and body measure from three to four feet in length. The tail is about seven inches long. Their food consists of fish, crustacea, mollusks, etc. This Otter haunts sea-washed rocks, around bays and estuaries, lives mostly in the water, and resembles the Seals more than the Otters in its habits. It is very timid, and prefers the neighborhood of islands, where it can find both food and shelter.

The fur of the Sea Otter is very beautiful and of great value. Its color is variable, but the general hue is a rich black, slightly tinged with brown on the upper parts of the body, while the under portions and legs are of a lighter hue. About the head there is occasionally more or less white.

These animals have been so keenly pursued on account of the great value of their fur, that they are now greatly reduced in numbers and are almost exterminated in some sections, like the Pribylov and Aleutian Islands, where they were once very numerous. The Russian American Company took from Alaska in the year 1804, fifteen thousand Sea Otter skins, valued at fully $1,000,000. Their numbers were reduced so rapidly that at the time Alaska came into the possession of the United States, only six or seven hundred skins were obtained annually from the whole country. Now but few remain and the species is likely to disappear.

HOW THE SEA OTTER IS CAPTURED

Peculiar methods are adapted capturing this animal, and in the attempt many hunters lost their lives, but seemingly others are ready to assume the unfinished work of the former.

Capturing this otter in mid-sea is out of the question and as they possess gregarious and rambling habits, hunters usually await the opportune time, when the ramblers are about one or two miles from the shore, as many as 15 to 20 boats, each containing two or three men, one being provided with a rifle, the other with a spear or harpoon, and the third generally managing the boat. The boats usually go out in rows, following one after another, stretched out as long as a mile. If any one sees an otter the proper signal is given and a circle about the animal is formed; naturally the otter will disappear, but on its next arise the riflemen will discharge their rifles, so the bullets will strike 10 to 25 feet from the animal, thus preventing the latter from obtaining fresh supply of air. On its second descent one or two of the boats leave the circle, these generally contain the best harpoonists. All are still awaiting the next arise of the animal when he is promptly disturbed and prevented from breathing in a fresh supply of air, either by the discharge of the rifles or by splashes of the oars. If not too far, the harpoonists will attempt to spear, but if unsuccessful the former method of preventing the animal from obtaining air will finally triumph. If not killed by the harpoonists the otter will drown due to lack of fresh air. It often requires two to three hours to capture one animal.

It is very seldom, in fact, extremely so, when anyone can approach this animal in a boat while the latter is on the shore and a target for the hunter. Their sense of smell, sight and hearing is very fine.

During stormy weather hunters attempt to capture the other on the windward side of the ocean, as the animal, during such storms, generally seeks shelter on the shore, and sometimes travels quite a distance from the water. The hunter is able to approach the otter unusually close, as the noise of the wind and the even the discharge of the rifle, sound of their approach, or even the discharge of the rifle, should the aim be poor, is unheard or unnoticed.

On the Asian coast, as related by Steller, as many 75 otters were killed on one occasion. The otters, in this instance, reached shelter during a furious storm by landing on the shore. A number of hunters escape was made less possible a number of them preceded and clubbed the otters to death, the remaining guarding the outward passage. While the otter is generally considered dangerous, these men dispatched them with remarkable ease; a single, stout blow on the forehead caused the otter to place the two forepaws over the head, and another soon puts them out of misery.

The use of steel traps is little resorted to, as the sections of the coast which the otters frequent is generally uninhabited, therefore would be unprofitable, especially as the landing of the animals is an uncertainty, both as to time and place.

Mr. Anderson, an experienced seal hunter, states that the reason such a small number of sea otters are killed is because their habits, as to time and place of landing is uncertain, also the number of the animals is insignificant as compared with the seals.

CHAPTER 27

Seal

(Ger. Robben oder Flossenfuser, Lat. Pinnepedia.)

SEALS

THE seals, sea lions, harp seals, hooded seals, sea bears, saddleback seals, and other species, as well as the various kinds of walruses belong to the fin footed variety and are distinguished from other mammalian by the peculiar construction of their body, habits, actions, etc.

They are able to swim and dive with the greatest ease, often remaining ten to twenty minutes below the surface of the water, and, Cuvier says, as long as one hour, Their arteries are filled with warm blood, and the animal possesses nocturnal and gregarious habits, with a highly-developed sense of sight, hearing, smell, and inhabits all oceans of the world.

All species of the seal family frequent resorts of sandy beaches, rocks and floes, for the purpose of sleeping or banking in the sun, and for breeding. The body is adapted for continued water residence, being cylindrical and tapering gradually from centre backwards toward tail and tapering frontwards. terminating in an otter-like head, the latter being small and well rounded. The ears on certain species are well developed, while those of the Alaska fur seal are sparingly distinguished and exceedingly small, and when the animal is in the water. Same are closed by a valve, which terminates the inward flow of water, but does not retard the animal's sense of hearing. It is remarkable that the seal is able to detect slight surface noises while at a depth of ten to twenty feet below the water level. Their nostrils are completely closed when under water. and the eyes are large, and pleasingly set off the animal, as well as their intelligent nature. The mammac (teats) are on the lower rear portion of the belly, and their feet are as indicated on the illustration.

From a commercial standpoint seals are divided into two groups—hair seals and fur seals. The latter produces a skin that is worn by thousands of ladies in this country and Europe, also a quantity of oil. The hair seal is caught for the valve of the oil and skin—the latter is largely converted into leather. The latter species of seal inhabits Newfoundland, Labrador, Gulf of St. Lawrence, and portions of the White Sea Arctic Caspian and North and South Pacific oceans.

The Alaska fur seal inhabits the ocean along the coast of Alaska, and the rookeries which they frequent are situated on the islands of St. Paul and St. George, known as the Pribilof islands.

The body of the Alaska fur seal is covered with a layer of coarse outer hair, while the inner coat consists of dense, soft, silky fur fibres. The roots of the outside guard hairs penetrate deep into the skin, while the fur fibres are imbedded and terminate immediately beneath the grain formation of the skin. In the process of tanning, the coarse hairs are easily loosened in the operation of fleshing, without disturbing the adherence of the tur fibres.

A full-grown Alaska bull seal measures about seven feet, and is about equal that number of feet in circumference, and will weight about five hundred to six hundred pounds. He attain his maturity at the age of about six years. The females attain their maturity at the age of about four years. And are about two thirds the size of the male, but in weight they rarely exceed one hundred fifty pounds, usually about one hundred pounds. Their longevity varies considerably usually from sixteen to twenty years for a bull and ten to twelve years for a female. The mother brings forth a pup usually at the age of four years, and in rare cases at the age of three years.

The Alaska seal, as aforesaid, is largely captured on the Pribilof islands, the bull seals arriving from a southward direction on the rookeries as early as May and by the first of June hundreds and thousands locate themselves in advantageous position, awaiting the reception of the females, which usually come two to three weeks later.

It is extremely hazardous and requires an unusual amount of grit for the individual bull seal to maintain and defend his position. Hundreds are annually killed in combat. especially those on the water line. The fighting is done entirely with the mouth, one seizing the other by the teeth, inflicting deep wounds, their sharp incisors tearing deep gutters in the skin and at various times shredding the flippers into ribbon strips.

The skins taken from the Pribilof islands principally constitute the Alaska seal skins though numerous animals are captured along the coast of Alaska, British Columbia, along the Aleutian islands. and others when the animals return from the Pribilof islands by the pelagic sealers.

The seals are remarkably tenacious of life, but are easily killed by a bullet piercing the brain, or by a sharp rap over the head.

The seal has other enemies besides man. The monster killer whale, the polar bear and also certain species of large fishes, which usually overtake the young, but seldom attack the fullgrown seal.

The killing of seals is carefully regulated by law on the Pribilof islands and within a radius of sixty miles thereof.

The Commercial Company, which has the contract from this government, is only permitted to kill a certain number of young bachelor seals. The killing of females is entirely prohibited. The female brings forth one pup, in rare cases two pups, which are born three to six days after reaching the rookeries. Strange as it may seem, the new companion of the mother takes kindly to the pup. The bull seal usually gathers about him a number of females, sometimes as high as eight, but usually two to five. These, with the offspring of the female and her previous companion are protected by him, the father of her next-pup, which is born in about a year.

The skins taken from seals inhabiting the oceans about the Shetland islands are superior in fur qualities to that of the Alaska seal, while the latter is superior to others, especially those coming from the Copper islands, Japanese, Lobos, Cape of Good Hope and other sections.

The elephant seal that is found at various portions of the globe, and formerly along the coast of California are monsters, and historians state that the elephant seal is the largest species of the seal family, single bull seals of the above species weighing between two thousand and two thousand five hundred pounds.

Many believe that the sea lions inhabiting the are animals that produce the fur seal skins. Such is not the case.

CHAPTER 28

Gopher

This animal, called the Canada Pouched Rat, inhabits the prairie region west of the Mississippi. It is a burrowing animal and lives on roots and vegetables. Its body is firmly built, about nine inches long, with short tail and legs, the latter armed with long claws for digging. The head and neck are relatively large and the mouth has four broad, long incisors, two on each jaw, adapted to cutting roots. On the sides of the face and neck, extending back to the shoulders, are large pouches, in which to carry earth, food, etc. The Gopher digs paths or galleries of an oval form, several inches in diameter, a short distance below the surface, coming to the surface once in about a rod, where the excavated earth is deposited in little hillocks. These galleries ramify in all directions. When the animal has brought to the surface in one place as much earth as its sense of economy dictates, it closes up the hole and begins a new deposit further on, so that nothing remains but a neat little mound of earth, large enough to fill

The Pocket Gopher.

a half bushel, more or less. Gophers are great pests to the western farmers, injuring and destroying the roots of their crops and infesting their fields and gardens. They may be trapped in the following manner: Carefully cut away a square section of sod on a line between the two most recent deposits. On finding the gallery, excavate down until a trap will set on a level with the bottom of the passage. Place the trap there; then lay a piece of board or shingle across the excavation, just above the passage, and replace the sod. The Gopher, while at work, will run into the trap and be taken. The No. 0 Newhouse trap is especially suitable for catching the Gopher.

The gopher is found throughout the Mississippi Valley, ranging westward into Colorado and Wyoming, southward into Mexico, and northward into the prairie region of Canada. They are also found in Alabama, Georgia and Florida. They appear to be most abundant in those states bordering on the Mississippi River. There are a number of different varieties, but as their habits are the same, a description of the Prairie pocket-gopher, will be sufficient.

This animal measures, when full grown, about eight inches from the end of the nose to the base of the tail. The tail is about two and a half inches long, and thinly covered with hair. The color is a liver brown, somewhat lighter on the under parts; the feet white. The legs are very short; the feet armed with large claws, adapted to digging. The head is large, no neck being visible. The eyes and ears are very small. The incisors are large and chisel shaped, for cutting roots. On each side of the face and neck are large pouches, having no opening into the mouth. These pouches are not used for carrying dirt, as is commonly supposed, but are only used for carrying food. The animals known as the "grey-gopher" and the "striped-gopher" are no gophers at all, but species of ground squirrels.

Burrow of Pocket Gopher.

The gopher is a burrowing animal and is seldom seen above ground. They are working almost all of the time, during the spring, summer and fall, extending the burrows in search of food. They also work in winter, when the ground is not frozen, and it is supposed that they also work under the frozen ground, when it is not frozen too deep. They are most active in the fall when they are storing up food for winter.

The burrows will be found from six to twelve inches beneath the surface of the ground, the usual depth being about eight inches. At irregular distances along the burrow, the animal makes a short branch passage leading up to the surface, where it deposits the dirt dug from the main passage, in the form of a mound. After the dirt is all thrown out, it closes the branch passage, packing the ground in solidly, so that the only visible signs of the burrow are the mounds of ground. There is a good reason why the animal should be so careful to keep the passage closed, for they have a number of enemies besides man. Its most dangerous enemies are, perhaps, the little spotted skunk or civet cat and the bull snake, as both of these creatures, once they get inside of the burrow, follow its course until they find their victim.

The food of the gopher consists mostly of roots of plants but they often cut the roots of fruit trees. They are particularly destructive to alfalfa, and the loss to farmers, caused by these animals, is considerable, not only from the plants destroyed by having the roots cut, but also from the plants buried under the mounds, and from the fact that, the mounds interfere with the cutting of the crop. The fur is of no value, but owing to the destructiveness of the animals, land owners are very anxious to be rid of them. In many places a bounty is paid on the gopher, so that they may be profitably trapped when furbearing animals are of no value.

The traps recommended for the gopher are the No. 0 steel trap and some of the various choker traps made especially for this use. In setting steel traps, select the freshest mound, and by examining closely, one can usually tell which way the dirt was thrown out, and will know on which side to look for the burrow. A handy tool is a slender, pointed iron rod to use as a probe in searching for the burrow. Having located the passage, open it up and set the trap on the bottom, sinking it down until level. Cover it lightly with dirt, and close the hole by laying a small piece of board, or a shingle over the opening, covering with ground.

The trap should be fastened with a stick, and the same stick will serve as a marker, so that one can easily find the trap. A small spade or a heavy garden trowel will be needed for digging and for convenience, the traps, stakes, etc., may be carried in a large basket. The regular gopher traps, mentioned above, are more easily set than steel traps and printed directions for setting usually accompany the traps. They should be set at one side of the burrow, on a level with the bottom and with the mouth of the trap just even with the side of the passage. Just a little light should be allowed to penetrate from behind, and all other parts should be closed, so as to exclude light.

The gopher, in coming along the passage, sees the light and goes to investigate, when it will be caught in the trap. If too much light shows up, he does not go close to look at it, but immediately brings a load of dirt and proceeds to close the hole, thus burying the trap. All loose dirt should be removed from the burrow before setting the trap, as otherwise the gopher will gather up the dirt as it approaches the light, and shove it into the trap.

CHAPTER 29

Squirrel

HOW TO TRAP THE SQUIRREL

The squirrel is an active little animal found in great variety throughout the United States.

Its hind-legs are longer than the fore-legs, and its joints and spine very flexible, giving it great facility in springing and jumping. Its claws are crooked and sharp, and especially adapted for climbing. Its tail is nearly or quite as long as its body, very bushy, the long hair being parted in the middle all along the under side. The senses of sight and hearing are very strongly developed in squirrels, rendering them constantly on the alert, and, in consequence of their extreme agility, difficult to catch. They differ greatly in size and color in different localities.

The common Red Squirrel or Chickaree is found more or less all over the country. It is small in size, the body being about eight inches, with a tail of some six inches in length. The upper surface is of a red-brown color, the under surface being white. Though easily frightened and rapid in its flight, this species is comparatively tame, and inhabits the surroundings of civilization equally with the solitude of the forest. Its food is chiefly nuts, small fruit, and grain, laying up in the fruitful season of the year sufficient store for its winter consumption, which it buries in the ground, or hides in the hollows of the trees, the latter also often forming; its habitation. Some of these little animals, however, build nests in the clefts of the boughs or other convenient locality, using whatever they find most available for the purpose, feathers, leaves, and twigs. In northern regions, it provides a home for the winter burrow under the ground.

The common Gray Squirrel exists plentifully in the Middle and Eastern States. It is larger than the Red species, measuring ten to twelve inches, with a tail of about the same length. The upper surface is gray, varying in shade on the neck and feet; the under surface is white, like the Chickaree. In Pennsylvania and Western New York, some few of these animals are of a brownish-black, both black and gray being sometimes found among the young in the same nest.

It lives in nests built in the forks of the trees, exchanging this in winter for a hollow space in the trunk of a tree, and takes its rest in the middle of the day. In the autumn, sometimes the Gray Squirrels migrate in a body to some other locality, devouring everything that comes in their way.

There is another variety of the Black Squirrel somewhat larger than the Gray, inhabiting the country lying between Lake Champlain and Lake Superior. This appears to be a different; species from the Black variety of the Gray Squirrel.

The Red-Tailed Squirrel is peculiar to the Western States. It is about thirteen inches long, of a light gray color above, and a tawny buff below. Its tail is about the same length as its body and of a red color.

In California there are a few species of squirrel which appear to be indigenous to that locality. The Dusky variety is about a foot long, with a tail some fifteen inches. It is dark gray on the back, and a dusky yellow on the sides and belly. The Soft-Haired Squirrel is smaller, being eight to nine inches long; the fur long and soft, of a dark brown color above, and ash-color below. The Wolly Squirrel has a stout body and taill, each about a foot in length; its color is brownish above, and lighter brown below.

The body and tail of the Weasel-Squirrel is glossy black, and about an inch longer than the Woolly variety. The Gray Squirrel is also found in California, rather lighter in color than the common gray species. Some of this kind are found with a red color on the belly.

In Oregon and Russian America there is a peculiar variety called the Downy Squirrel, about the same size as the Chickaree. Its fur is thick and downy, light chestnut color above, silver-gray on the sides, and white underneath. It burrows in the earth.

In the forests of Louisiana there is found the Golden-Bellied Squirrel, about ten inches long, with a tail somewhat longer. In color it is of a yellowish-gray, and a golden-yellow underneath. Another variety, called the Sooty Squirrel, is met with in the swamps of that State, about the same size in body as the Golden-Bellied Squirrel, but with a longer tail. Its back is black, the lower part of the body as well as the legs being a reddish-brown.

The Fox Squirrel is a large variety, sometimes over fourteen inches long, the tail somewhat longer, and subject to many varieties of color. It belongs to the Southern States and is more ferocious than the smaller kinds, and is sometimes more than a match for a small dog.

The Cat Squirrel is found occasionally in the forests of the Middle States. It is rather smaller than the Fox Squirrel. In color it ranges from light gray to nearly black. The leading peculiarity is in the tail, which is broad and flat.

Squirrels are always actively on the watch, very shy, and therefore difficult to approach; but they are not gifted with a great degree of cunning, and can be caught without much difficulty in traps of almost any kind suited to their size. A No. 0 Newhouse trap placed in the neighborhood of the woods they inhabit, with a bait arranged some seven or eight inches above it, will generally succeed in catching a squirrel; a portion of an ear of corn will serve very well for the bait. If any carnivorous animals are to be found in the same locality, it is better to use a spring-pole (see page 68) for securing the trap. This little animal is not of any great value when dead, and it is generally an object to catch them alive. For this purpose some kind of box-trap of appropriate size is required, such as the Rabbit-Trap.

CHAPTER 30

Woodchuck

The Woodchuck

The body of the woodchuck is thick and squat, that the belly seems to graze the ground. The color varies in different specimens, the body being generally brownish-gray above, and reddish-brown below; the head, tail and feet are the nose and cheeks ashy-brown. Their length is about eighteen inches, with a tail four inches long. They are fond of sitting erect on their haunches, letting the fore-feet hang loosely down; they maintain an erect position when feeding, bending the head and neck forwards and sideways. During the greater part of the day they remain asleep in their burrows, coming out occasionally to look around; in the evening they go forth and feed on grass, fruits and vegetables. They are seldom found far from their burrows in the day-time; when thus surprised, the woodchuck runs very fast; and, if not seriously frightened, stops and perhaps squats on the ground and looks around slyly to see if it is noticed. In case of extremity it takes refuge in the crevice of a stone wall or rock; and, on being closely approached, utters a kind of chattering, gurgling sound, or, at times, a shrill whistle-like note, for which reason the French-Canadians call this animal a Siffleur, or whistler. In defending itself the woodchuck bites severely, and makes a desperate battle with a dog, often with such success as to affect its escape.

It usually walks on all-fours, but occasionally climbs trees and bushes to the height of a few feet, sometimes taking a nap in the sunshine on one of the branches; it cleans and combs its face, sitting on its haunches like a squirrel, and licks and smooths its fur in the same manner as a cat. The hide is loose and tough; the fur is of no value; the flesh is flabby and of rank flavor, and in summer the animal is very fat. Woodchucks become torpid about the latter part of October; they are solitary in their habits, and do not congregate in societies like the other marmots, beyond the members of one family. It is believed that they eat nothing during their torpidity through the winter season. Their burrows are usually on the slope of a hill, frequently near the root of a tree, sometimes beneath rocks, or in the crevices of stone walls. These burrows extend from twenty to thirty feet from the openings, descending obliquely at first for four or five feet, and then gradually rising to a large round chamber, which is used as the family sleeping apartment. Here also the female rears her young, producing from three to eight at a time, which grow rapidly, and in three weeks may be seen playing around the burrows. The woodchuck is extensively distributed, being found in the Canadas, and thence south to the Carolinas, and as far west as the Rocky Mountains; in some places scarce, in others abundant. In New

350

England they are common among the cultivated grounds, and. do much damage in the clover fields, not only eating the grass, but treading it down; they often make great havoc among the pumpkins, and are partial to corn when it is in the milk. The farmers in that section of the country sometimes drown them by filling their burrows with water; they are also shot with rifles, but more frequently are caught in steel traps, set at the mouths of their burrows, and lightly covered with sand or grass, a Newhouse No. 1 or 1½ being well suited for the purpose. In this manner they fall an easy prey, without using any bait.

CHAPTER 31

Rabbit

The Cottontail Rabbit.

WHILE the rabbit is classed among the fur-bearing animals, the skin having a slight market value, very few of the trappers ever market the skins as the price is so little that trapping the animals for their fur would not be a lucrative business.

The flesh is much used as food by the northern hunters and trappers, and also as bait for traps, and it is well for the trapper to know something about the animal and how to capture it.

Properly speaking there are no rabbits in North America, the animals known by that name being classed by naturalists as hares, but the name is so universally used that it would be useless now to try to bring the true name into general use.

There are many species, one or more of which will be found in almost every locality of North America, but the most important species are the common cottontail, the jack rabbit and the snowshoe rabbit, or varying hare. Of these there are many varieties, but they are so similar in appearance and habits that I do not consider it necessary or advisable to go into detail in describing them in a work of this kind.

Rabbits belong to the class known as rodents or gnawing animals, and are distinctly different in structure from all other animals of the class. The long hind legs, long ears, small tail and soft fur is characteristic of the genus.

The common cottontail is found in almost all parts of the United States, in certain parts of the north only, being replaced by the snowshoe rabbit. They are smaller than the snowshoe and jack rabbits and are of a grayish brown on the back and sides shading to white on the under parts. The fur is a reddish brown in summer.

Their food consists of grasses, fruits and vegetables, bark, and the leaves of evergreen shrubs such as the laurel. They are especially fond of fruits, sweet apples being a favorite food, and are also partial to cabbage.

Their favorite haunts are the brushy, wooded bottom lands but they are also found on the hills and mountains; in fact, in almost any place where they can find food and shelter.

The snowshoe rabbit replaces the cottontail in Canada and the most northern portions of the United States. As before mentioned they are larger than the common rabbits and like the northern weasel the color of their fur varies with the seasons. The summer coat is a reddish brown, but when the cold weather comes on in the fall they commence to take on a white color, the fur of the ears and legs being the first to change and in a few weeks the animal will be perfectly white. This is nature's provision for the animal's protection, and their color in winter is so nearly like that of the snow that when sitting under some log or clump of brush they are almost invisible. They have many enemies being preyed upon by all the carnivorous animals, also by such birds as the hawk and owl, but as they are exceedingly prolific their numbers increase rapidly.

Every few years, perhaps at regular intervals, but of that I am not certain, some disease makes its appearance among them and they die off rapidly. Some naturalists believe that this is caused by inbreeding as the rabbit's circle of acquaintance is comparatively small, and his knowledge of the country and the ground covered by his wanderings is limited to a very small area.

The food of the snowshoe rabbit consists mainly of grasses in summer and the bark of certain young growths in winter. They are very fond of salt and wherever there is a trace of it to be found, they will come nightly and dig up the soil in order to procure it. The northern settlers who use large numbers of these animals for food sometimes make a salt lick for the rabbits and watch for the animals in the early evening.

The feet of the snowshoe rabbit are very large and are heavily furred, forming a sort of snowshoe which accounts for its common name. They are very methodical, running the same route so often as to form a well defined trail, quite common in the northern swamps and hazel thickets. These trails are followed after the snow falls and become beaten several inches in depth.

It is from the skins of the snowshoe rabbit that the northern Indians make the wonderful rabbit skin blankets. The skin is ripped down the back of the hind legs and is drawn off whole and while still fresh is cut into one long strip averaging an inch in width. Immediately after cutting, the strip rolls up leaving the outside covered with fur and resembling a fur rope. These skins are wound into a ball and kept frozen until the desired number has been secured when they are woven into a frame, the ends being sewed together. It makes the warmest bed covering known, and is used universally by the northern trappers. It also was a great comfort to those who went into Alaska and Yukon in search of gold.

Rabbit Snares.

The jack rabbit is found mostly on the western plains and is the largest of the American hares. They resemble the ordinary rabbit in structure, but the ears are very long and the tail is more like that of the deer. In running they make long leaps, all four feet hanging straight down, presenting a singular appearance.

Rabbits are seldom trapped with steel traps, but almost every country boy knows how to take them in box traps baited with sweet apples. The cottontail may also be taken in a spring pole snare, such as shown in the cut. The noose is made of twine and is about ten inches in diameter. When carefully made they are almost certain in action. They should be baited with sweet apple or cabbage.

The snare used for the snowshoe rabbit is a very simple contrivance. The white trappers use No. 20 brass wire, doubled and twisted with a small loop on one end, and made into the form of a slip noose.

The snares are set on the trails, the bottom of the noose being about four inches above the trail and the loop, about four inches in diameter, is attached firmly to a brush placed horizontally over the path. A short stick is set upright under the noose and others are placed on either side of the snare. When properly arranged the noose will take the animal by the neck when it attempts to leap through, and it will be choked by its struggles.

The Indians make the snares of light linen cord but with the white man this method is a failure as the rabbit will invariably stop and bite the cord. I do not understand why they do not bite the snares set by the Indians.

Where tracks are plentiful and good trails cannot be found I have caught them by placing a few fresh twigs of birch or tamarack on each side of the snare. The rabbit is certain to find them and after eating those placed on one side it will attempt to leap through the noose to reach the others, which, of course, is the end of poor "bunny". The smallest and tenderest shoots should be selected for bait and only two or three should be placed at a snare.

At other times I have made a fence of small evergreen trees where signs of the animals were numerous, and have fixed snares in the openings along the obstruction. This is also a successful method.

I have never learned of any method of trapping or snaring the jack rabbit, but believe they could be trapped successfully where they visit the farms and gnaw the bark from fruit trees as they do in some parts of the west.

CHAPTER 32

Chinchilla

The Chinchilla

The most delicate and silken of all furs is that produced by the Chinchilla. This animal is found in South America, along the Andean region from Chili to Peru. It burrows in the valleys which intersect the hilly slopes and collects together in great numbers in certain favored localities. It belongs to the group of animals called *Jerboida*, which are characterized by great comparative length of hind legs. It is a small animal, measuring only about fourteen or fifteen inches in total length, of which the tail forms about one-third. They are very prolific, the female bringing forth five or six young twice a year. Their food is exclusively vegetable, consisting mostly of bulbous roots. They are very cleanly in all their habits. The fur of the Chinchilla is long; its color is a delicate clear gray on the back, softening to a grayish white on the under portions and its texture is wonderfully soft and fine. It is used for muffs, tippits, linings to cloaks and pelisses and trimmings. The skins which are obtained in Chili are the best. Great numbers of Chinchillas are caught in the vicinity of Coquimbo and Copiapo. They are usually hunted with dogs by boys. The true method is to take them at the mouth of their burrows with a small steel trap.

CHAPTER 33

Lion

The Lion

The principal habitat of the Lion is in Africa. Some also exist in Asia, but nowhere else. There are three African varieties—the Black, the Red or Tawny and the Gray. In Asia the dark-colored Bengal, the light-colored Persian or Arabian and the Maneless Lions exist. A full-grown Lion, in its native wilds, is usually four feet in height at the shoulders and about eleven feet long from the nose to the tip of the tail. He is of great strength and ferocity, and is commonly called the "king of beasts." Lions belong to the cat family, and prey upon all animals they can master. They approach their prey stealthily, like a cat hunting a mouse, and spring upon it unawares. Human beings are not exempt from their attack, but form their most coveted prey when once an appetite for human flesh has been established. In Africa they hang around the villages, and carry off every man, woman or child they can secure, and make great havoc among all kinds of domestic animals. Gerard, the French Lion hunter of North Africa, estimates that the average length of life of the Lion is thirty-five to forty years and that he kills or consumes, year by year, horses, mules, horned cattle, camels and sheep to the value of twelve hundred dollars. Taking the average of his life, which is thirty-five years, each Lion costs the Arabs of that country forty-two thousand dollars. The Lion is mostly nocturnal in its habits, hunting is prey and satisfying its appetite during the night, sleeping and digesting its food during the day. The Lioness is smaller than the male, and brings forth from one to three young at a time, about the beginning of the year. Lions are not numerous in Asia, and are steadily growing less so in Africa. They are now seldom found near the coasts of that Continent. Wherever the white man appears he wages relentless warfare against the "king of beasts." Its favorite haunts are the plains rather than the forests, and it is is content with the shelter of a few bushes or low jungle. They sometimes hunt in troops—several attacking a herd of Zebras or other animals, in concert. Their strength is very great, and one has been known to carry a horse a listance of a mile from where he had killed it. Their most common prey are the Deer and Antelope which abound on the plains of Africa and in India. The Zebra, the Quagga, and the Buffalo are their frequent victims.

The directions already given for taking the Cougar with steel trap are adapted to the Lion. It may also be taken by setting a trap near its haunts and baiting it with a dead sheep or other animal. Great care must be taken to thoroughly secrete the trap, as the Lion is a very suspicious and intelligent beast. It is said that when a Lion is killed all others retire from and avoid that immediate vicinity. The Lion is not a fastidious feeder. While on one hand he likes to strike down a living animal and suck the hot blool from its body, on the other, he will devour any dead animal he may find, whether fresh or otherwise. "So thoroughly is this the case" says Wood, "that Lion hunters are in the habit of decoying their mighty game by means of dead Antelopes or Oxen, which they lay near some water spring, knowing well that the Lions are sure to seize so excellent an opportunity of satisfying at the same time the kindred appetites to thirst and hunger.

CHAPTER 34

Tiger

If the Lion is the scourge of Africa, the Tiger holds that place in India and Southern Asia. The Royal Tiger of India rivals the Lion in size, strength, ferocity and activity, and excels him in beauty of form and color, and grace of movement. The Tiger is of great size, measuring in the largest specimens four feet in height, four feet eight inches in girth and thirteen feet six inches in total length. Its color is a tawny yellow, with transverse dark colored or black stripes. The under parts, the chest and throat, and the long tufts of hair on each side of the face are nearly white, and the markings on these parts are indistinct. The general make of the Tiger is a little more slender than that of the Lion. Their haunts are the forests and jungles, and they prey upon all animals which come within their reach and power. They are of amazing strength and often bound upon their prey by a single leap of fifty feet. The Indian Buffalo, which is as large as an ox, is killed and dragged off by the Tiger without difficulty. The female has from three to five young at a birth which she defends with great fierceness. The range of the Tiger is confined to Asia, and to certain districts of that Continent. Some sections are terribly infested with them, and the inhabitants are kept in a state of terror by their depredations. They are common in the wilds of Hindostan, in various parts of Central Asia, even as far north as the Amoor River, and are also found on some of the large Asiatic Islands. Portions of Sumatra are so infested with them as to be almost depopulated. Here and in some parts of India the Tiger is protected by the superstition of the people who regard it as a sacred animal, animated by the souls of their dead ancestors, and none are killed but the "Man-Eaters."

There are a number of modes adopted by the natives of Asia for killing the Tiger, such as spring-bows armed with poisoned arrows, nets, cages with trap doors, enticing them into locations where they can be shot, etc.: but they are all inferior to the steel trap. This instrument should be introduced wherever this lurking marauder abounds. The habit of returning to the unfinished carcass of the beast it has slain or found, which I have already noticed as pertaining to the cat family, is very strong in the Tiger, and can be taken advantage of in trapping them, in the same manner as described for the Lion and Cougar. The trap should be set near the hind parts of the carcass, as the Tiger always begins with those parts and eats towards the head. They may also be taken by setting traps along the paths which they make through the jungle near their lairs. In all cases the traps should be carefully secreted. A Tiger is easily killed with a bullet. Next to brain and heart, the lungs and liver are its most mortal parts. A Tiger, when struck by a bullet in the liver, generally dies within fifteen or twenty minutes. If once wounded *anywhere* they usually die, though perhaps not immediately. From sime unknown cause a wound on a Tiger very soon assumes an angry appearance, becomes tainted and the abode of maggots and finally proves fatal. This tendency to putrefaction in the Tiger renders it necessary that they should be skinned immediately after they are killed if the preservation of the skin is any object. Especially should they be removed out of the sunshine, instantly after being slain. A delay of ten or fifteen minutes will often ruin the skin by the loosening of the hair from putrefaction. The skin, after being removed, should be at once stretched and treated with a very strong solution of salt, alum and catechu.

Several other large animals of the cat kind are found in Asia and Africa, such as the Leopard, the Ounce, the Rima-Dihan or Tree-Tiger, etc. They are all carnivorous and of similar habits, and should be trapped on the same general principles as the Tiger and Cougar. Of these animals the Leopard is the most formidable and destructive. It is found in both Asia and Africa, but in greatest numbers in the latter country. It is much smaller than the Tiger, but of extraordinary strength for its size. It does not usually attack man unless wounded or pursued. It is very destructive among the herds of domestic animals, Antelope, Deer and

Monkeys. It is celebrated for the beauty of its skin and the agility and grace of its movements. Its haunts are the forests where thick, high undergrowth prevails.

Of late years the trapping of Tigers in India by the use of the Numbers 5 and 6 Newhouse Traps has given the natives new confidence and it is probable that as they become more expert in this, the number of human lives sacrificed to these ferocious beasts will be much reduced. Heretofore thousands of people have been killed by them annually. There was great rejoicing when the natives first saw the helplessness of a full grown Bengal Tiger in a No. 6 Newhouse trap fastened to a heavy clog. They saw that here was something that was stronger than their old enemy.

CHAPTER 35

Deer

This family of ruminating animals embraces a great variety of species, ranging in size from the Pigmy Musk Deer of Java, which is not larger than a hare and weighs only five or six pounds, to the gigantic Moose-Deer of America, whose height is seven or eight feet and its weight twelve hundred pounds. But the species with which American trappers are most practically concerned, are the common Red or Virginia Deer, and the Black-tailed Deer of the region west of the Mississippi. These species differ but little in habits and general characteristics, and a description of the Virginia Deer is sufficient for the purposes of the trapper. The Virginia Deer are found in nearly all of the States of the Union east of the Rocky Mountains, and abound in both provinces of Canada. They are gregarious in their habits, though frequently seen alone. Their food in summer consists of twigs, grass, berries, nuts, roots, acorns, persimmons, etc., and at that season they frequent rivers and lakes to feed on water-plants, as well as for the purpose of freeing themselves of insect pests. They are also fond of visiting the pioneer's clearing and appropriating his wheat, corn, oats, potatoes, turnips and cabbages. In winter they retire to the elevated ridges, where maple and other hard wood trees abound, the bark, twigs and branches of which are at that season their chief support. They form "yards" by tramping down the deep snows and live together in large herds, numbering sometimes thirty animals in a single "yard." These enclosures are enlarged from time to time as the Deer require more trees for browsing. Wolves and Panthers are their most formidable enemies—always excepting man. Packs of Wolves frequently attack them in their "yards" and sometimes, when the snow is deep and crusted over, whole herds are destroyed. Wolves sometimes pursue a single Deer with the "long chase." In summer a Deer thus pursued generally takes to the water and so baffles his pursuers, but in winter, when the streams and lakes are frozen over, he rarely escapes. Panthers take Deer by crawling within springing distance of them in their "yards" or elsewhere, or by watching and pouncing on them from some cliff or tree as they pass below.

The methods by which men take Deer are various. They are sometimes driven by dogs into rivers or lakes and are then over-taken and dispatched by the hunter in his canoe. A favorite method is to shoot them at night at the places by the water-side, where they resort to feed on aquatic plants and relieve themselves of insects. For this purpose the hunter prepares himself with a boat, gun and lamp. The light is set on the bow of the boat, so. that it will shine on the forward sight of the gun and at the same time conceal by its glare the hunter crouching behind. With muffled oar the boat approaches the game. The reflected gleams from the eyes of the Deer betrays his position to the hunter. If no noise is made the victim will stand and gaze at the light until it is within a few yards, and so give a sure opportunity for the fatal shot. Many are taken in this way in the early autumn and later in the season, when snow first comes, many more are taken by the "still hunt," either by following on their trail or by watching at their run-ways.

The steel trap, it must be confessed, is not much used for taking Deer, and I am not sure but that this use of it is regarded by sportsmen as somewhat barbarous. But all the ways of deceiving and killing these noble animals seem to be open to the same objection, and the necessities of the trapper often forbid him to be very particular as to the means of furnishing himself with food. There are times when the trap is the best and even the only available means of taking Deer; for instance, when the trapper is without his rifle, or has exhausted his ammunition and finds himself in the far wilderness without food. In such circumstances he might starve if he could not betake himself to his traps for supply. And even when the rifle and ammunition are at hand, sometimes in dry weather (technically called a "noisy time"), everything is so crisp and crackling under foot that it is impossible to approach the Deer within shooting distance. I therefore recommend to practical woods-men to learn how to take Deer in traps and not be over scrupulous in doing so when occasion requires.

For taking Deer the trap must be a strong one and the jaws should be spiked and shaped with an "offset," so that when sprung they will remain open about half an inch, to prevent breaking the bone. The trap should be placed in the path of the Deer where it crosses a stream or enters a lake and it should be set under water and concealed by some covering. If it is as heavy as it ought to be (say of three or four pounds weight) it should not be fastened at all, or even clogged, as the animal is very active and violent when taken and will be sure to break loose by tearing off a limb or smash the trap, if his motions are much impeded. If the trap is left loose, the Deer, when caught, will make a few desperate plunges and then lie down and will seldom be more than ten or fifteen rods from where he was taken. When the hunter approaches he will make a few more plunges, but can easily be dispatched.

Mr. Gunter, the Canadian trapper, whom I have heretofore quoted, gives the following directions for trapping Deer in winter:

"Fell a maple or basswood tree near where the Deer haunt. These trees furnish their favorite browse. Make a small hole in the snow, close to the top of the tree. Set your trap, lower it into the hole and shove it to one side, eighteen or twenty inches, through the snow. Finally take some deer-scent, obtained from the glands on the hind legs of a Deer, and which has a very strong odor, and rub it on your trap. This done, when the Deer come to feed on the twigs of the fallen tree, you will be pretty sure to take one."

CHAPTER 36

Moose

This is the largest kind of Deer, and its habits are in many respects like those of the common Deer. It is more confined, however, to the snowy regions of the north. It is found throughout the greater part of British America, ranging as far north as the Arctic Sea. In the United States it is found in Maine, Northern New York, Oregon and Washington. On the Eastern Continent it is found throughout the northern parts of Europe and Asia. Its favoriate haunts are the hardwood lands. In general color it is yellowish-brown or ashy-gray. The hair in summer is short and soft, and long and coarse in winter. The full-grown Moose weighs from eight hundred to fifteen hundred pounds, and stands seven and even eight feet high. Its horns have an expanse of nearly six feet between the tips and a palm or spade on each of a foot in width and weight from forty-live to seventy pounds. Under the throat of both sexes there is a tuft of coarse, bristly hair a foot or more in length, attached to a sort of a dew-lap. The breeding season of the Moose is in May. At the first birth but a single one is brought forth; afterwards two are brought forth annually. Moose, like the common Deer, frequent rivers and lakes in summer to feed on the roots of the water lily and other aquatic plants and retire in winter to the high ridges, to browse on the twigs of the striped maple and birch. Their height enables them to crop the overhanging branches of large trees and their weight and strength enable them to bend down small trees and slide over them with their bodies, stripping the bark and twigs to the very extremities. Like the common Deer, they form "yards" by treading down the snows, and enlarge them as fast as they strip the trees and require more. In these "yards" there are commonly found a male, female and two fawns.

Moose are taken in winter by the "long chase" on snow-shoes and in summer they are shot at their feeding places in marshes. They are, however, very wary and timid and their sense of smell is so acute that the greatest caution is necessary on the part of the hunter in approaching them. The males in the rutting season are very dangerous and will attack and, if possible, kill any person who approaches them. Moose can easily be taken either in summer or winter by setting steel traps in their haunts, as they are not cunning and enter a trap as readily as an ox or a horse. The trap should be a strong one of about forty pounds weight, and it should be fastened to a clog of sixty pounds weight.

The flesh of the Moose is much esteemed by hunters and trappers, being generally preferred to that of the common Deer. The marrow in the large bones is an excellent substitute for butter.

SECTION III

Skinning, Stretching, Curing, and Tanning

CHAPTER 1

Handling Furs and Various
Stretcher Plans

HANDLING FURS

To know the habits and the nature of the various animals and to know how to catch them is not all that is essential for success, but the trapper must also know how to skin the various animals and how to cure the skins and prepare them for market.

The loss caused the trapper by the lack of this knowledge is considerable; many skins because they have not been fully cured reach the dealer in a tainted condition, others are not fully stretched and are graded "small" and some do not have the proper shape. Some are not cleaned of flesh and fat, do not have the tail bone removed, have not been kept clean or have been badly damaged in killing or skinning, all of which has a tendency to decrease their value.

I have seen the skins of raccoon, killed before they were prime, and stretched on the side of a barn where the glare of the sun burned the life out of the skins, rendering them worthless. I have also seen skunk and mink skins drawn over the end of a thick board roughly fashioned with an axe, and hung up by the nose, the weight of the board drawing the head out until it resembled the finger of a glove. The trapper who handles his catch in that way can never expect to receive full value for his furs.

HOLDER FOR SKINNING.

There are two ways of skinning fur-bearing animals, namely, "casing" and skinning "open". The weasel, mink, marten, fisher, fox, opossum, muskrat, civet, skunk, wild cat should be cased. The raccoon, bear, beaver, badger, cougar, wolf, wolverine and coyote should be skinned open. Some dealers prefer to have southern raccoons cased.

To remove a skin by the first mentioned plan, cut it loose around the feet and rip down the back of the hind legs, to and around the vent. Peel the skin carefully from the hind legs and skin the tail by slipping a split stick over the bone, when by gripping the stick with the right hand with the bone of the tail between the second and third fingers and holding the animal with the left hand, the skin may be stripped off easily. Draw the skin downward from the body, keeping it as clean of flesh and fat as possible. To facilitate this process the animal may be suspended from the limb of a tree or other projection by looping a strong cord around the hind legs after they have been skinned. The skin should be drawn from the front legs and when the ears are reached they should he cut off, cutting downwards towards the head. The skin should be cut loose about the eyes and nose, and it will then be in the form of a long pocket, fur side in.

The weasel, mink, marten, fisher, fox, skunk, civet cat and wild cat should be skinned in this way. The otter must have the tail ripped open its entire length on the underside, and as they are a difficult animal to flesh, it is best to skin them clean with a knife, leaving no flesh or fat adhering to the skin. The muskrat and opossum should also be cased, but as the tails of these animals have no fur they should not be skinned, the skin being cut loose about the base or where the fur ends.

Some trappers do not use much care in removing the skin from the head of the muskrat, but simply pull it off by main strength. This leaves the flesh of the head remaining on the skin and a collection of such skins will usually be graded low and the skins will average a few cents less than when properly handled.

To skin an animal "open", rip the skin on the belly from the point of the lower jaw to the vent, down the back of the hind legs and on the inside of the front legs across the breast to the point of the brisket. Animals that are intended only as furs may have the feet cut off, but bears, mountain lions, wolves and wolverines should have the feet skinned out to the ends of the toes, leaving the claws attached to the skin. This increases their value for mounting or for rugs. The skin should be peeled from the body, using the knife whenever necessary.

In skinning the beaver, rip the skin from the point of the chin to the vent and around the base of the tail and cut off the feet, but do not rip the skin of the legs. Skin the animal perfectly clean using the knife everywhere, as it is almost impossible to flesh a beaver after skinning. Not a particle of flesh or fat should be allowed to remain on the skin.

After all burrs, lumps of mud and blood clots have been removed from the skin it is ready for fleshing. For fleshing all cased skins prepare a narrow tapering board of sufficient length to accommodate the longest skins and plane it perfectly smooth, rounding the edges slightly. Draw the skin over this board flesh side out and scrape all flesh and fat from it, using some blunt instrument, such as a square edged knife or a hatchet. Turn the skin occasionally and do not flesh on the edges of the board or you may score the skin; be careful not to damage it in any way. Always turn the fur side out before laying it down, so as to keep it perfectly clean.

Open skins, if they have not been skinned clean, are more readily fleshed after they are stretched.

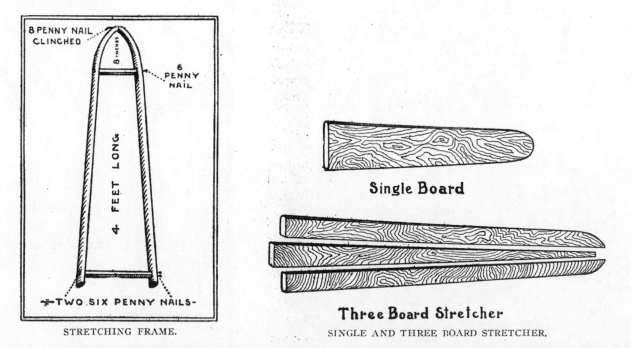

STRETCHING FRAME.

SINGLE AND THREE BOARD STRETCHER.

Single Board

Three Board Stretcher

A good supply of stretching boards of various sizes should be made in advance of the trapping season. Soft pine, poplar, basswood, or cedar boards are best, and old dry goods boxes make excellent stretching boards. They should be free of knots and should be planed smooth so that the furs may be removed easily after they are dry.

For mink the boards should be from 26 to 34 inches in length and from 3½ to 4½ inches wide at widest part, and about ½ inch narrower at the shoulders from which point it should taper gracefully to the head and end with a rounded point. For marten, the boards should be a trifle wider. For the average fox or fisher, the board should be 4 feet long, about 5¼ inches wide at the shoulder and 6½ at the base. For the otter the board should be about ½ inch wider and a foot longer. The average lynx will require a board about 7½ inches wide at the shoulder and 9½ inches at the base, by about 5 feet in length. For large muskrats the board should be two feet long by 6 inches wide at the base, ¾ inches narrower at the shoulder and with a flat iron shaped head, but more rounded at the nose. One should have several smaller sizes also. For skunk and opossum the boards should be about 6 inches wide at the shoulder and 7¼ inches at the base, 28 inches long.

Beginning at the; left, dimensions and skins stretched on the various boards are given:

No. 1. Mink board, length 28 inches and 4 wide.
No. 2. Mink board, length 28 inches and 3½ wide.
No. 3. Weasel board length 20 inches and 2½ wide.
No. 4. Muskrat board, length 21 inches and 6 inches wide.
No. 5. Opossum board, (small), length 20 inches and 6½ inches wide.
No. 6. Skunk or opossum, (medium), length 28 inches and 7 inches wide.
No. 7. Skunk and opossum, (large), length 28 inches and 8 inches wide.

SIZE OF STRETCHING BOARDS.

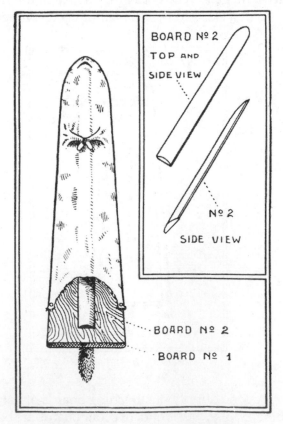

DAKOTA TRAPPERS' METHOD.

These dimensions are for the average animals, but it should be remembered that the sizes vary greatly in the various parts of the country. In the case of the skunk and the mink especially, there is a great difference in size.

For convenience and good results I advise ripping with a saw, a narrow wedge from the center of all boards except those intended for muskrats. In this way one can stretch the skins to their full size and they may be more easily removed from the boards, after the wedge is withdrawn. For large boards to be used for lynx, otter and animals of a similar size, I fasten two short strips to the base of one piece of the board, as shown in the cut. This stiffens the stretcher and prevents the pieces from turning in the skin. All boards should be beveled on the sides, leaving the edges thin, round and smooth.

The boards shown are of the Canadian pattern used universally by the Canadian trappers both Indian and white, and recommended and approved of by such large dealers as the Hudson's Bay Co. The tendency among trappers of more southern districts is to use a less tapered board with a more rounded point.

The skins should be stretched as soon as they are fleshed. In using the three piece board slip the two halves into the skin, the flesh side being out and fasten the hind legs with one or two small nails in each, then insert the wedge and draw down all slack parts and fasten with nails. Be sure to get the back on one side of the board and the belly on the other. Draw up the skin of the lower jaw and fasten with a couple of tacks or small nails. In the case of the lynx it is advisable to slip a narrow board into each front leg and a small incision should be made in the tip of the tail of all animals, to allow the moisture to drain out and the tail to dry.

The tail of the otter should be stretched out to its full width and well fastened with small nails. Some trappers also split the tail of the skunk for about one-half of its length and fasten it in the same way.

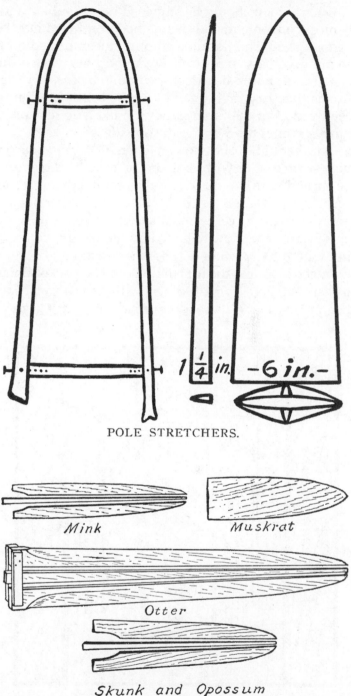

POLE STRETCHERS.

Canadian Pattern Stretching Boards.

The proper way to stretch open skins is by lacing them with twine in a hoop or frame. The beaver should be stretched round, and a hoop is most convenient. My method is to fasten the skin in the hoop at four points and then with a large sacking needle and strong twine stretch out one quarter at a time. I use a separate twine for each quarter, sewing thru the edge of the skin and around the hoop, tying the end with a loose knot. In case I find that any part is stretched too much or not enough, it is a simple matter to untie the string and give it a little slack or take up a little as the case requires.

The raccoon should be stretched nearly square and all other skins to their natural shape. A square frame is most convenient, and the method employed may be the same as for beavers. Open skins which have not been fleshed, should have all of the flesh peeled off after they are stretched and then it will frequently be found necessary to re-stretch them but this is not difficult when using the twine.

All furs should be dried or cured in a cool, airy place. They should never be allowed near the heat of the fire as they dry rapidly and become brittle and unfit for use. In camp they may be dried in some corner, removed from the fire but they are likely to take on a dirty yellow color from the smoke, and it is better to have a shelter for them on the outside.

Furs should not be allowed to remain a long time on the boards. As soon as they are sufficiently dry to prevent shrinking or wrinkling they should be removed. The lynx and all species and varieties of foxes should be turned with the fur side out as soon as they become dry enough, and if the skin has become too dry to turn, it may be dampened slightly on the stiffer parts by placing a damp cloth over it. A very little will suffice and one must be certain to allow the skin to dry out thoroughly after turning. It is best to watch the skins closely and not allow them to become too dry before turning. Some trappers turn the skins of other animals, but with the exception of those mentioned it is better to leave the fur side in.

When shipping the furs they should be packed flat and bound tightly. Those having the fur side out should be kept separate from the others so that the fur will not become greasy. I sew the skins in burlap and put a card bearing my name and address inside of the package; also tie two shipping tags on the outside.

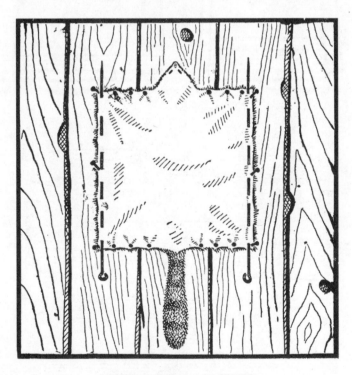

WIRE COON METHOD.

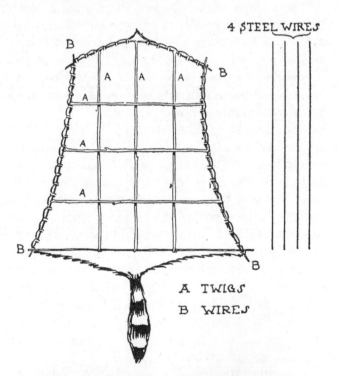

WIRE AND TWIG COON METHOD.

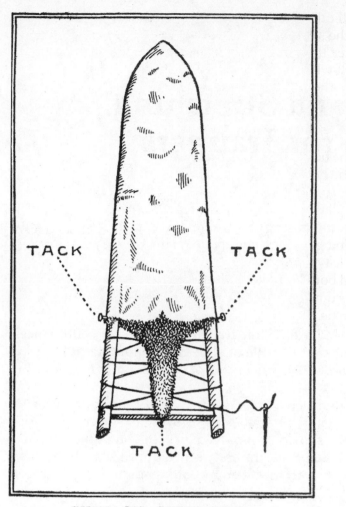

SKIN ON STRETCHER.

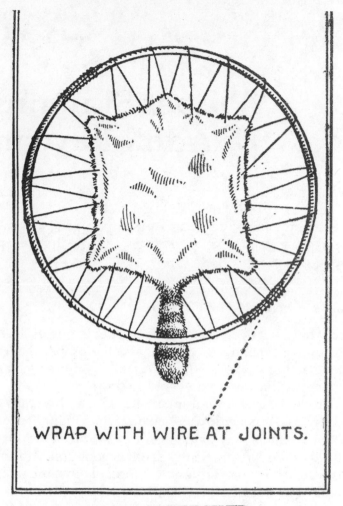

WRAP WITH WIRE AT JOINTS.

HOOP STRETCHER.

Furs handled by the above methods will always command good prices and I never have any cause for complaint if I ship them to reliable dealers, but when furs are badly handled, damaged in killing or afterwards, or unprime, one cannot expect the highest market price.

CHAPTER 2

Proper Skinning and Stretching, Add'l Revenue for Trappers

HOW TO SKIN FUR REARING ANIMALS, MANNER OF STRETCHING RAW FUR SKINS, HOW TO MAKE FUR STRETCHERS, MANNER OF PREPARING SKINS FOR THE MARKET, DRYING SKINS, ETC.

THE HANDLING OF FURS

Not only is it necessary for the trapper to posses the knowledge of setting traps, snares or other contrivances, or in what manner to poison, also the proper manipulation of the rifle or shot-gun in hunting or trapping fur-bearing animals, but he must also comprehend and master the proper care of skins in order to realize full market value and to prevent spoiling.

To be successful a trapper should visit his traps as often as possible. Every twenty-four hours or every other day is generally sufficient. If the victim lies too long in the trap the skin is likely to slip or taint. Also other animals may damage or devour the victim. The skin should be removed just as soon as the animal is dead or the fur sufficiently dry. It is poor policy to remove skin while the body is in a frozen state. If the body is warm, it is often advisable, especially in larger animals, to start the blood by cutting, permitting the blood to flow as freely as possible.

PROPER WAY OF SKINNING

In the skinning of animals that require the skin to be dried in a cased shape, such as mink, marten, otter, muskrat, red fox, wild cat, lynx, wolf, badger, opossum, etc., it is necessary to begin with the knife at the hind feet and slit down to and around the vent, strip the skin from the tailbone, in case of an otter cut the tail open but on other animals simply pull the skin over the bone. Then peel the skin from the body by drawing or pulling it over, leaving the fur inward. Use the knife as little as possible. One should have no difficulty if above method is used. Leave all claws attached to the skin, also care should be taken not to mutilate the skin around the mouth and eyes as some skins are used for mounting purposes. Heads must be complete.

SKINNING BEAVER

Take a regular butcher's skinning knife and slit from center of lower jaw down over belly to vent. Skin out jaw and carefully remove skin from head. Do not cut legs open. Remove skin from body without further cuts in skin. Be sure and scrape all fat off. (See directions for stretching beaver skins on page 244.)

LIGHTNING METHOD FOR SKINNING MUSKRATS

Cut off front feet and tail with a hatchet, with knife slit from hind legs to vent, skin around hind legs, attach a strong cord to both legs and pull skin over body.

SKINNING A BEAR

Some trappers prefer to skin a bear similar to taking of hides front cattle. This method is O. K. For the benefit of those not familiar the following suggestions will be in time.

Take knife and slit from hind legs to vent. Then from inner part of fore legs to brisket down to center of lower jaw. Then open skin by cutting straight over the belly to vent. Remove the skin from head with care. Leave ears, jaw, openings of eyes intact.

Another method resulting in Indian style handled skins, is to remove the skins similar to that of beaver, excepting the legs should be cut open so as to permit the skin to be stretched in proper shape; bear skins must not be stretched in a round shape like the beaver.

SKINNING DEER, ELK, AND MOOSE

The skin of the above animals should be removed similar to cattle, calf and horse hides. The hides should be in like shape excepting the head should never be slit open as is the practice of butchers in taking off cattle hides.

SKINNING A WOLF

To remove a wolf skin from the carcass properly, it is necessary to follow and use the same methods employed in skinning the fox, mink, or other animals whose skins should he cased and not cut open on the belly. In western states it is the practice to remove the skins by cutting clear across the belly and by following the method used in skinning bear, and removing cattle hides, though not as good as if left cased; the price for the skin is about the same.

STRETCHING SKINS IN A FRAME

The skins from such animals as the bear, beaver, raccoon, wolverine, deer and dog can be best stretched in a frame. The frame is made out of four pieces. The latter can be scantlings or one-inch boards. If these cannot be had, take saplings, which make excellent frames. The skins, however, must be green, as a part dry skin will not stretch sufficiently. After you have made a frame of sufficient size for the skin, take a large sack needle and some strong twine and sew by making stitches every one or two inches, each stitch encircling that particular portion of the frame.

Do not cut off the feet or ears; that would make holes in the skin. If same are cut off, sew such openings together before putting skin on stretcher. Some remove all meat and fat before stretching, others proceed to scrape after skin is stretched upon the frame. One can suit himself, but we believe all surplus meat and fat should be removed first, and when skin is on the stretcher, finish the work with a dull knife, hardwood stick or spoon. Shape skin with your hands before sewing in frame; do not overstretch, but make allowance for the natural shrinkage in process of drying.

BOW STRETCHERS

The use of the bow stretchers is dying out and it is well for trappers to discontinue stretching their skins in such a careless manner. A few Indian tribes and occasionally a trapper who has no tools for making other stretchers, use the bow stretcher, but only for muskrat. We recommend the discontinuance of its use altogether.

HOOP STRETCHERS

In sections where beaver are plentiful it is well for the skins to be stretched on a hoop made out of a stick of hickory or other flexible wood. If a single stick is not long enough, two small ones can be spliced together;

the over-lapping ends together with withes. See that the hoop is round, and not too large in size for the skin it is intended.

In skinning rip from center of lip to vent, gradually skin, peel and fist around the lips, eyes and ears, continue until you have reached legs. Do not rip lengthwise on legs but gradually pull them from the skin and cut so as to have smallest possible opening when skin is finally stretched. (Some prefer to sew leg holes together). When skin is off, begin at the head and fasten to hoop with twine or withes inserted about an inch apart and continue until entire skin is stretched round and a tightly as a drum-head.

Formerly bears, wolves and raccoons were stretched in this way, but of late years beavers are the only skins stretched in round shape.

SKINNING AND HANDLING RACCOON SKIN

"As I have given the main points of my experience in trapping the raccoon. I will not tell how I skin and stretch the hides. If you wish to case the skin, cut the skin around the hind legs near the heels, then slit along the back part of legs through the anus from heel to heel. Peel the skin down the legs to the root of the tail, pull the bone out of the latter, strip the skin toward the head, cutting it loose at the fore feet, and around the mouth carefully. Be very careful in skinning the tail for if it is broken the sale is injured. Take two small, square edged sticks about four or six inches long. Place the bone of the tail between them and pull steadily. To case, get a board of length and width to suit the size of the skin, the thinner the better. It should not be too sharp at the nose nor too broad at the rear. Make it nicely rounded at the nose, slip the skin, on with fur inside, pull the nose over end of board to lap on chin, tack through both, then pull for length, and tack both hind legs and root of tail.

"To remove skin with intention to leave it flat or open, slit hind legs as described above, slit fore legs across the breast from foot to foot, then entire length of belly to chin, strip skin from hind legs and tail as above; then strip to head, leaving the ears entire on skin and cut carefully around mouth and nose. To stretch, cut holes near the edge of skin along both sides from hind leg to foreleg, across the bottom, and across the top just below the ears; then insert four sticks in the four rows of holes, the length depending upon size of hide. The hide should be square or nearly so. Place a stick across the middle with the ends swallow forked to keep it in. Place another from the root of tail to end of nose. I prefer splitting the head to the back of the ears and sewing the jaw and foreleg together. This makes a beautiful figure The holes should not be more than two or three inches apart and all particles of flesh and thin pelt should be stripped off before stretching. Hang in the shade to dry with fur to the wall. When ready to ship take out all sticks, boards or stretchers, pack the skins with two fur sides together and two flesh sides alternately, as the flesh might grease the fur and give it an oily feeling. Bale or sew up in burlap and they are ready for market.

MINK AND OPOSSUM

"Opossum and mink are skinned the same as raccoons. Prepare for casing, and stretch on boards as described for cased raccoon. The tail of opossum should be cut off, that of mink left on. A slit should be made in the end of tails of raccoon, mink, otter, etc, to let out any foul matter that may gather in the cavity in warm, foggy weather. A perfect skin of a raccoon when ready for market should be nearly square. If mink, otter, or opossum, it should be nicely rounded at the nose, not too sharp, nor too wide at the tail. If the ears are hard and dry it is not a perfect skin. If the tail is hard, kinked or crooked, it is not a perfect fur. If blue behind the forelegs or under the chin, it was caught too early. If it has been whitened by salt or alum, it is not a perfect fur."

O. PULLNOW.

TO SKIN THE WILD CAT AND RED FOX

As soon as possible after the animal is dead or killed, it should be skinned and the skin stretched. In warm weather a dead animal will turn black or blue on the belly in fourteen hours. The animal should be skinned while the warmth is in the body. All skins of animals smaller than a bear can be cased more conveniently by the trapper. As to hoop stretcher and how stretcher, I do not favor them. A bow stretcher can be made in a pinch for such as muskrat.

"Hang the animal by one leg and commence by cutting down inside the hind leg to the vent and up the other leg. Cut around the leg above the claws, (I do not leave the hind claws unless for special reasons, except the mountain lion), and make a slit up the tail a little ways, pulling tail out by the help of a split stick (Tails are worthless on beaver and muskrat, and the tail of the otter should be cut open and spread out). Skin or peel down to the forelegs, break off below knee and leave paws in the skin. Cut around ears, eyes and mouth and the skin is then ready to be put on the stretcher. Always have the fur towards the stretcher and the skin part outside. The stretcher should be made in the following manner:

The Result of Knowing How to Hunt and Trap

STRETCHING.

"Get a board one-half inch thick, three feet long, nine inches wide at the wide end, tapering to about four and one-half inches wide at small end, rounded and notched out for the head. The illustration (elsewhere in this book) will give an idea of how the stretcher will look. I don't use a single piece stretcher unless I have to.

"By ripping the above stretcher into three pieces and making a wedge or three-piece stretcher there from, the result will be nicely shaped skins which can be removed without danger of tearing. I take a rip saw and cut from center of stretcher a wedge of about one and three-quarters inch to about two inches wide at lower part to a point at head of stretcher. This forms a nice wedge, and if necessary, this wedge can be run through the mouth of the skin in case the animal is a large one, and if smaller, it need not be placed clear down. This stretcher is excellent for otter, wolf, wild cat, foxes, and if made smaller, for all other animals of the weasel or marten family. The skin is pulled over the stretcher and when fairly tight, drive four nails, two on each side, into the skin to hold same firmly, and then take wedge and slowly insert until the skin attains its proper size and becomes smooth. Then take more nails and fasten skin on rear part of stretcher and wedge.

"Always stretch belly on one side and back on other side of stretcher and see that tail is exactly in center of wedge. Before putting the skin on stretcher, take a hatchet, sharp stick or knife and scrape fat from skin: when on stretcher smooth out with the same tools and remove every bit of grease, wash and wipe thoroughly dry, and then hang skin away in a shady place for five to ten days. When firmly set, stretcher can be removed. Never take stretcher off too early as skins will crumble up and get in bad shape.

"Be careful and not get fat on fur and tail. When skins are thoroughly dry and you are ready to ship, pack in burlap and ship, by express. If skins are only partly dry, they will mildew and possibly spoil; therefore, the skins should be thoroughly dry."

TO SKIN A FOX

"The body should not be frozen, if it is, thaw so that the otter portion of the body is thoroughly thawed out. The fox should be skinned while hanging up.

Scene in Raw Fur Room   **Scraping Skunk and Raccoon Skins**   Andersch Bros., Minneapolis, Minn.

"Take a small, sharp-pointed, thin-bladed knife and a large skinning knife—both should be very sharp. Cut crosswise on inside of hoof, leaving claws attached to the skin, then open hind legs by inserting small knife between the skin and body from claws to vent, following the peculiar furred line indicating the inner-most portion of leg. Now skin out the legs; use the knife to start with and pull to free the skin, in preference to cutting. Pull skin upwards so as to free the second joints of the foot before severing the skin with the claws from the leg at the joint indicated above.

"When legs are freed get spreader or gamber stick and place in position through the cords, and hang carcass up.

"Now skin on belly down about five to seven inches, then about the sides and back, leaving the tail portion unmolested until you come up from bottom.

"Now comes the most delicate job. Get an eight or ten-inch stick, three-fourth or one inch thick, split in center to about half way down. Put the body on the ground. Take split stick and place at root of naked tail, then with left hand take body and with right hand hold stick, pull steadily and you have skinned the tail.

"Now hang up again, and pull skin down over belly. Use knife as little as possible, and be very careful on belly portion as the skin is very tender and you may tear it.

"When at forelegs, take knife and open about knee and slit down to the body; but if one wants the skin of the legs left on pull skin with one hand, holding the body, and with your knife assist until you come to knee or foot, which dislodge, one leg at a time. Then pull the skin down to the head, cut ears close to the skull pull down to the eyes—cut about same way at the nose. Always leave ears, eye part, lips and nose on skin.

STRETCHING

"This requires little work. Get two think pieces of boards, have them planed smoothly, thinner on one side than on the other, also taper from one-half inch to three inches. Procure wedge one-sixteenth to one-half inch wide, same thickness as other two boards and about as long or longer. Some place fur inside and others outside. A nice prime red fox looks better if fur is outside. Place skin over stretcher, then take wedge and insert, smooth out, nail skin at tail and on belly portion, and hang up in high, shady place in the barn to dry. In a few days remove stretcher, and hang skin up until perfectly dry." From G. Halvorson, Arvilla, N. D.

HOW TO SKIN AND STRETCH MINK SKINS

Take a small, sharp, thin, narrow-bladed knife, and slit down where the fur comes together on the inner part of the leg, from heel to anus. Now take thumb and forefinger and peel the hide off the legs; take knife and slit from anus to end of tail. With your thumb and fingers loosen tailbone from skin. Some only open tail one inch from anus and then take two flat, notched sticks, fitting around the tailbone, which grasp firmly in one hand and pull skin off bone with the other. Now proceed to further remove skin from rear legs, scarcely using the knife. Pull skin over body, using your thumb and hands. When at fore legs continue to use fingers and pull forelegs out. Another pull will bring you to the ears when a knife should be used in cutting them off close to the skull. A slight pull will bring the skin off body and the knife should be used for the last time in cutting off the nose and trimming around the lips.

STRETCHING

Stretching mink skins and making them look nice and fine is more important than skinning, and, in fact, next to trapping the animal itself. Three-piece stretchers are used exclusively by me, unless in a pinch I use a one-board stretcher with a small wedge on top to take up the slack and to assist in removing the skin from the stretcher. The belly and back part of the animal should be on opposite sides and exactly even. Stretch out legs and ears, but do not tack permanently until skin is scraped.

SCRAPING

Take a dull case knife and remove all surplus fat and meat. If there is too much meat on a skin, it cannot be stretched right. After you have removed surplus fat and meat, start to stretch the skin permanently. Use pains in stretching out all parts of the skin, especially legs and tail. Take especial pains with the tail so that same is stretched, or use coarse, hollow straw, which insert so as to permit the tail to dry. Now take a dull case-knife and scrape off all fat. Don't let fat run on the fur. Wipe it off with a rag. If fat has a tendency to run in the grain of the skin, cut close with a sharp knife. Having removed all fat take a sponge or woolen rag, dampen with water, and proceed to work all grease out of the skin. All large filaments, which present a rough and ragged appearance should be removed. After skin is cleaned, put in a shady place to dry; never close to a stove, neither pile one skin on top of another. If you have occasion to force drying, put the skin in a warm room where there is good circulation of air.

N. C. A.

STRETCHING SKINS, FLAT AND OPEN

Begin at the head, nailing at the nose. Stretch lengthwise, until fairly tight and tack through the tail. Now place one nail through each leg at the foot, but not too tight. Stretch crosswise, placing nails about one inch apart. Be careful not to over stretch the hides, as it gives them a thin appearance and deducts much from their value.

FRED ABBOTT.

METHOD OF SKINNING MUSKRAT AND STRETCHING SKIN

A few remarks on skinning and stretching may not be amiss, as on the speed and thoroughness depends much of the trapper's success. Make two hooks from stout wire or ten penny nails, just large enough to fit tightly over the smallest point of the muskrat's hind legs. Tie a stout cord to each of the hooks and fasten to some object far enough apart so as to have the hooks six inches apart when the muskrat is hung up. Now take your knife, which should be slim bladed and at least 4 inches long, and insert it under the skin of hind legs, letting the point of the knife come out at root of tail. Give one quick jerk and rip the hide the whole length. Insert the knife in the other side of the tail, letting it come out at the other hind foot, and repeat the operation, but do not cut around the feet, as by so doing one is likely to cut the flesh which will come off with the hide and cause inconvenience. Take the hide between the thumb and fore-finger and pull the skin around the feet. With some practice this can be done quickly and is better than cutting. Pull the skin over the body down to the forelegs and pull them out without cutting them. On reaching the ears, take knife and cut around eyes, ears and nose.

STRETCHING

Make your stretcher out of thin boards about five inches side and tapering well to the small end. Plane and sandpaper until you have a smooth surface. Use one piece or three piece stretchers. For fleshing and to remove fat and surplus meat, take a large tablespoon and use the bowl for scraping off this fat and flesh. By this method there is absolutely no danger of hurting the skin, or damaging same by cutting, as is often the case if a knife is used. The skin is also of smooth appearance. Do not let any fat get on the fur. If you do, wipe it off with clean rag or use dry hardwood sawdust.

T. GULLICKSON.

PROPER MANNER OF SKINNING MINK AND STRETCHING SKINS

First cut down the back of hind legs from heel to anus. Now, with thumb and fore-finger peel the hide off the legs. Next, slit from anus towards the end of the tail one inch: loosen with fingers as before around butt of tail; then get a couple of flat sticks and notch them to fit around the tail bone. Grasp these firmly in one hand and pull the skin off the tail. Proceed with the knife to carefully remove hide from the hind-quarters. Having cut past the navel, you can, with a single pull, rip the hide past the shoulder. Now place your thumb between hide and fore-leg, at elbow joint, and pull fore-leg out. Another pull will bring you to the ears, where the knife comes into play again. Cut ears at the base, close to the skull and proceed to carefully skin to the end of the nose.

HOW TO STRETCH

Board being of proper length and width, proceed to pull hide over same, hair inside, belly on one side and back square on the other flat side of the board; not on the edge. If there be much flesh on hide, as sometimes happens with an old mink, pull hide tight, securely fasten with a few small wire nails, putting nails in the end of legs and one at root of the tail. With a dull case knife scrape off the surplus flesh. This will enable you to stretch properly as s fleshy hide will not stretch well. This done, you may pull out the nails and proceed to stretch out legs, nailing at edge of board on belly side. Have both legs even. Put at least half a dozen nails in each skin, so that they will not give way when the hide dries up. On the other side, put a nail near the edge of the board, taking care to keep the back even as it looks much neater than if long cornered, and cuts better when it comes to making up. Always place your nails near the edge of the hide. If you use a three piece stretcher, shove the wedge as far as it will go, but do not use too much force as you may split the hide and ruin it. Now, tack the belly and the back, pull the tail straight, and tack on the middle piece. In this position, it will dry nicely and not kink up s they are sure to do when not nailed.

MUSKRAT HOUSE.

My choice, is a flat board stretcher, with two tapering cleats. one for the belly and one for the back, the latter being long enough to allow the tail to be tacked to it. Put a nail in the belly cleat, so as to keep the hide and the cleat in place. Next, pull fore-leg up, tie with thread or twine close up to body. With a sharp knife cut about three-eighths of an inch above the string, press down with the finger, having care to turn hair out, forming a sort of rosette.

Now put away in a warm room, but not near the stove. After 8 or 10 hours, or when half-dry, it is ready to clean and polish. Use a dull case knife, scrape gently, and the fat will readily come off. If any filaments have a tendency to run into the grain of the skin, cut close, with a sharp knife. Having removed all fat, we are ready for the finishing touch or polish. Dampen a small sponge or woolen rag, don't soak, and rub all over the hide. This will lay low all the fleshy filaments which give such a ragged appearance to a skin, and will give it a neat and glossy appearance such as I have never been able to obtain by any other process. Now put away to dry, but keep away from the fire. Let it dry thoroughly, before taking off the board, as a partly-dried hide will shrink, consequently decreasing in value. When dry, always hang (don't pile up) in a dry, cool place, where mice cannot get at them. A good way is to hang them to the ceiling with a string.

J. A. DESPARDINS.

TO STRETCH A MINK SKIN

To stretch a mink skin on a three-piece or wedge stretcher, take the skin, which should be green and clean, and insert the two sword shaped pieces with the smaller ends toward the nose. To prevent nose from slipping off ends, drive a tack or small nail in each end of the board. Always have flesh part of the skin on the outside and the fur part next to the stretcher.

Now pull skin up as far as possible. Be sure tail is in center, drive two tacks, one on each side to hold skin up, then insert center piece (wedge) between the two side stretchers, shove wedge down until skin is the required shape and all parts properly stretched.

Use ordinary judgment and care and be sure not to overstretch the skin. Drive tack through tail in wedge. This completes the stretching. A medium sized northern no north-western mink skin (not including tail) stretched in this way should be twenty to twenty-two inches long, three and one-half to four inches wide on bottom and gradually tapering down to the nose.

HOW TO MAKE MINK STRETCHERS

Take two pieces of pine wood about thirty inches long, one and one-half inches wide and five-eighths to three-fourths inches thick. Taper edges from one end so as to be about three-fourths inches wide when about two inches from the other end. This again taper to one-third inch to the extreme end.

When this is done plane off from the sides so as to leave the pieces in a sword-like shape. The thickest portion when finished should be 7-16 to 9-16 of an inch on the edge while the other end about 3-16 of an inch and also tapering to a point more abruptly when about two inches from the end. Sandpaper and smooth the thin edge, also sides. Then take a piece of wood thirty inches long, the same thickness as the thickest part of the side pieces, about one and one-half inches to two inches wide and taper so as to make a wedge of about one and one-half to two inches on one end to about one-fourth or three-eights of an inch on the other end. This completes the so-called mink stretcher.

HOW TO SKIN A HEAD THAT IS TO BE MOUNTED

Many trappers often kill horned game, also fur bearing animals which they desire mounted, but in skinning invariably spoil the skin for the purpose intended. Even when skins are not desired to be mounted by the hunter, it is well to skin animal, having in view that someone else may want the skin mounted, in consequence thereof the value of the skin is increased. This is especially true in skinning the wolverene, mountain lion and cougar, also in removing the skin from horned game, such as deer, elk, moose, antelope, mountain sheep and mountain goat. In removing the skin of the latter, it is necessary to cut from the base of one horn to that of another and from center between the horns down the back of neck to the shoulder; this forms a cut resembling a "T," and the only one necessary. Never cut the skin open from the lip running along the neck to the breast as that spoils it for taxidermist purposes, and even if it does not, no taxidermist can make a good job there from. Great care should be taken in skinning about the eyes, and be sure and leave on all parts of the lip; special care should be exercised about the corners of the mouth and eyes. Leave considerable of the gristle of the nose attached to skin. If you can, turn the ears inside out. All surplus fat should be removed and the skin immediately salted. If this cannot be done, hang in a shady place to dry. All parts should be stretched so as to be exposed to the air; otherwise that portion lying next to another will become tainted.

Horns, in fact, the entire skull, should be saved and these, if good sized and well formed have always a commercial value.

ADDITIONAL REVENUE FOR TRAPPERS

It is well known that the large beef and pork packers in the operation of their plants, utilize every part of the animal. There is no waste or offal that is not turned into account; even the manure in the pouch of the animal is sold; in fact, everything is utilized excepting a "stray kick" or the "squeal" of a pig. Hair, blood, ears, tail, sinews, toes, horns, intestines, hoofs, etc., all find their way to market and bring good prices. All of these articles, as well as the flesh and bodies of fur hearing animals, could be utilized, if concentrated, as is done by the packers. Alas! it is impossible. Therefore the trapper must be satisfied in saving as many parts of the body as possible, and for which he can find a market.

Intestines

It is well known amongst old trappers that the Indians used dried intestines in sewing and patching their clothing as well as in the preparation of their furs. These were also used in the manufacture of ropes, lariats and snares, and particularly in making bow strings. Of late years, intestines, after they are cleansed and partly dried are used for musical strings.

Bear Galls

These have a commercial value, bringing from $3.00 to $5.00 per pound. Prevent leakage by tying the ends with a string and hang up to dry in a shady place; when dry, market. We have a demand for these. If you have any, write us.

Beaver Castoriums

These have been saved for the last 50 or 100 years. There is a commercial demand for them and of late years the demand is greater than the supply. These castors are found in both the male and the female beaver. The contents are of a deep orange color when dry. Hang up in a shady place and when dry, market. The oil bags that are immediately attached to the beaver castors have no commercial value. Trappers, however, use them in the manufacture of decoy.

Skunk Glands

The perfume out of these glands, as predicted by certain naturalists and scientists, will soon have a market value. If the contents of the containers or glands, are squeezed into a bottle, there is little danger of having the fluid distributed over the operator. This should be done in the open air; keep the bottle corked up. We expect a demand for this article.

Skunk Oil

Formerly there was a good demand for this oil, but of late years manufacturers have used other oils which are much cheaper and always obtainable, therefore the demand and use of skunk oil has become less and less every year. Of late years the surplus has been sold at prices comparing with aged lard or tallow.

Skunk Galls

Are used for medicinal and manufacturing purposes. Save them, and when you have a quantity, write us.

Musk Bags

The bags obtained from muskrats are salable, some years the demand is so great that the supply is exhausted and used up before half the summer is over. Handle them the same as you would beaver castors.

Animal Claws

The claws of bear, mountain lion and other ferocious animal have a market value. By no means should they be removed from the skin; if animals of this kind are killed during the summer months when the skin is of no value, they should be cut off, cleaned, and marketed.

Elk Teeth

Certain teeth of this animal are in very good demand and persons having any can dispose of them by communicating with members of the "Elk Lodge."

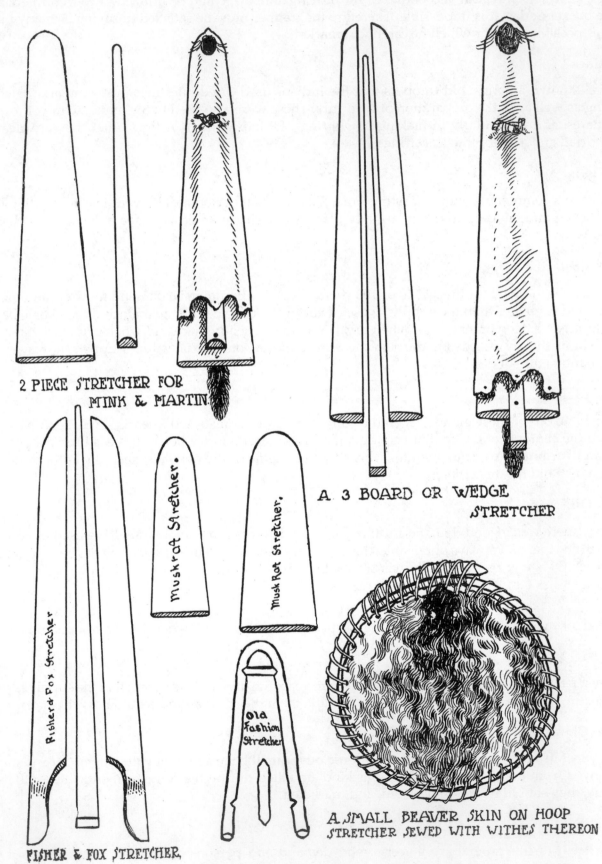

2 PIECE STRETCHER FOR MINK & MARTIN.

A 3 BOARD OR WEDGE STRETCHER

Fisher & Fox Stretcher

Muskrat Stretcher.

Musk Rat Stretcher.

FISHER & FOX STRETCHER.

Old Fashion Stretcher

A SMALL BEAVER SKIN ON HOOP STRETCHER SEWED WITH WITHES THEREON

Skulls

A ready demand for skulls exists. Trappers should save them. If skulls are saved, removed meat by boiling head in water. All fat and meat must be eliminated. The skulls from bear, mountain lion, lynx, wild cat, cougar, and occasionally those of the smaller carnivorants are wanted by taxidermists, naturalists, and others. Skulls with horns from elk, moose, deer mountain sheep, mountain goat and smaller animals are salable, but buyers insist that the skin should accompany the skulls. Thousands of artificial skulls are annually used, while the natural ones go to decay.

CHAPTER 3

How to Tan Skins

For the benefit of those who desire to tan fur skins for their own use, a few general directions are here given, which will be found amply sufficient for all ordinary purposes.

HOW TO TAN MUSKRAT SKINS

Before a skin can be subjected to the process of tanning, it requires some preliminary preparation. This consists, first of all, in washing the hide in warm water, in order to cleanse it thoroughly; after which all fatty and fleshy matter must be carefully removed.

TO TAN RABBIT SKINS

The next step is to prepare a liquor by mixing together the following ingredients:

10 gallons cold soft water.
8 quarts wheat bran.
½ pint old soft soap.
1 ounce borax.
1 pint salt.

Soak the hides in this liquor for eight or ten hours, if they are fresh; or until very soft, if the hides have been previously dried. The salt must be omitted if the hides have already been salted; and the addition of two ounces sulphuric acid to the liquor will prepare the skins in about one-half the time. The hides will then be ready for the tanning liquor, which is made of the following materials:

10 gallons warm soft water.
½ bushel bran.
2½ pounds sulphuric acid.

Stir the bran into the water until thoroughly mixed, and let it stand in a warm room until it ferments. When this takes place, add the sulphuric acid by degrees, and with constant stirring. Soak the muskrat skins in this for about four hours; then take them out and rub them with a fleshing knife. A good substance for a regular fleshing knife may be made by taking off or rounding the edge of an old chopping knife. In order to render the skin soft and pliable, it must be rubbed over a smooth beam until dry.

Lay the skin on a smooth board, the fur side undermost, and fasten it down, tightly stretched, with tinned tacks. First wash it over with a solution of common salt then moisten the surface an over with a sponge dipped in a solution consisting of

1 pint warm water.
2½ ounces alum.

Repeat the sponging occasionally for three days. Then, when the skin is quite dry, take out the tacks, roll it loosely the long way, hair inside, and draw it quickly backwards and forwards through a large smooth ring until quite soft; unroll it, and roll it again the opposite way, and repeat the operation.

HOW TO TAN ALL KINDS OF SKINS

The following is a method applicable to all skins the fur on: First trim off all useless parts, remove all fatty matter from the inside. (If the skin is dry, it must first be softened by soaking.) Next soak the skin for an hour in warm water. After this, spread over the inside of the skin, by means of a brush, a coating of the following mixture:

    1 ounce borax.
    1 ounce saltpetre.
    1 ounce glauber salts (sulphate of soda).

Water sufficient to make a thin paste.

The coating should be heavier on the thicker parts of the skin; double the skin together, coated side inwards, and put it away in a cool place. At the end of twenty-four hours, apply, in the same manner as before a coating of a mixture consisting of

    1 ounce sal soda.
    ½ ounce borax.
    2 ounces hard white soap.

Melt these together slowly by heat, without allowing the mixture to boil. After coating the skin with the above, fold it together again as before, and put it in a warm place for another twenty-four hours. At the expiration of this time, take

    4 ounces alum.
    8 ounces salt.
    2 ounces saleratus.

Dissolve these in hot water sufficient in quantity to saturate the skin; when cool enough not to scald the hands, soak the skin in it for twelve hours; then wring it out, and hang it up to dry. The soaking and drying must be repeated two or three times, until the skin is sufficiently soft. Lastly, smooth the inside with fine sand-paper and pumice stone.